QUALITATIVE INQUIRY
& RESEARCH DESIGN

THIRD EDITION

3

*I dedicate this book to Uncle Jim
(James W. Marshall, M.D., 1915–1977)
who provided love, support, and inspiration.*

QUALITATIVE INQUIRY
& RESEARCH DESIGN
Choosing Among Five Approaches

THIRD EDITION

3

John W. Creswell
University of Nebraska, Lincoln

Los Angeles | London | New Delhi
Singapore | Washington DC

Los Angeles | London | New Delhi
Singapore | Washington DC

FOR INFORMATION:

SAGE Publications, Inc.

2455 Teller Road

Thousand Oaks, California 91320

E-mail: order@sagepub.com

SAGE Publications Ltd.

1 Oliver's Yard

55 City Road

London EC1Y 1SP

United Kingdom

SAGE Publications India Pvt. Ltd.

B 1/I 1 Mohan Cooperative Industrial Area

Mathura Road, New Delhi 110 044

India

SAGE Publications Asia-Pacific Pte. Ltd.

3 Church Street

#10-04 Samsung Hub

Singapore 049483

Printed in the United States of America

Library of Congress Cataloging-in-Publication Data

Creswell, John W.

Qualitative inquiry and research design : choosing among five approaches /

John W. Creswell. — 3rd ed.

p. cm.
Previous ed. cataloged as: Qualitative inquiry & research design. c2007.

Includes bibliographical references and index.

ISBN 978-1-4129-9531-3 (cloth)
ISBN 978-1-4129-9530-6 (pbk.)

1. Social sciences—Methodology. I. Creswell, John W. Qualitative inquiry & research design. II. Title.

H61.C73 2013
300.72—dc23   2011050629

Publisher: Vicki Knight

Associate Editor: Lauren Habib

Editorial Assistant: Kalie Koscielak

Production Editor: Brittany Bauhaus

Copy Editor: Melinda Masson

Typesetter: C&M Digitals (P) Ltd.

Proofreader: Sue Irwin

Indexer: Diggs Publication Services, Inc.

Cover Designer: Rose Storey

Marketing Manager: Nicole Elliott

Permissions Editor: Adele Hutchinson

SFI label applies to text stock

This book is printed on acid-free paper.

12 13 14 15 16 10 9 8 7 6 5 4 3 2 1

Brief Contents

About the Author   xiv

Acknowledgments   xv

Analytic Table of Contents by Approach   xvi

List of Tables and Figures   xx

1. Introduction   1
2. Philosophical Assumptions and Interpretive Frameworks   15
3. Designing a Qualitative Study   42
4. Five Qualitative Approaches to Inquiry   69
5. Five Different Qualitative Studies   111
6. Introducing and Focusing the Study   129
7. Data Collection   145
8. Data Analysis and Representation   179
9. Writing a Qualitative Study   213
10. Standards of Validation and Evaluation   243
11. "Turning the Story" and Conclusion   269

Appendix A. An Annotated Glossary of Terms   282

Appendix B. A Narrative Research Study— "Living in the Space Between Participant and Researcher as a Narrative Inquirer: Examining Ethnic Identity of Chinese Canadian Students as Conflicting Stories to Live By"   303
    Elaine Chan

Appendix C. A Phenomenological Study—"Cognitive Representations of AIDS"   327
Elizabeth H. Anderson and Margaret Hull Spencer

Appendix D. A Grounded Theory Study—"Developing Long-Term Physical Activity Participation: A Grounded Theory Study with African American Women"   347
Amy E. Harley, Janet Buckworth, Mira L. Katz, Sharla K. Willis, Angela Odoms-Young, and Catherine A. Heaney

Appendix E. An Ethnography—"Rethinking Subcultural Resistance: Core Values of the Straight Edge Movement"   370
Ross Haenfler

Appendix F. A Case Study—"Campus Response to a Student Gunman"   399
Kelly J. Asmussen and John W. Creswell

References   417

Author Index   435

Subject Index   442

Detailed Contents

About the Author   xiv

Acknowledgments   xv

Analytic Table of Contents by Approach   xvi

List of Tables and Figures   xx

1. Introduction   1
  Purpose and Rationale for the Book   2
  What Is New in This Edition   2
  Positioning Myself   6
  Selection of the Five Approaches   7
    Narrative Research   11
    Phenomenology   12
    Grounded Theory   12
    Ethnography   12
    Case Study   12
  Audience   12
  Organization   13

2. Philosophical Assumptions and
   Interpretive Frameworks   15
  Questions for Discussion   16
  Philosophical Assumptions   16
    A Framework for Understanding Assumptions   16
    Why Philosophy Is Important   18
    Four Philosophical Assumptions   19
    Writing Philosophical Assumptions
      Into Qualitative Studies   22
  Interpretive Frameworks   22
    Postpositivism   23
    Social Constructivism   24
    Transformative Frameworks   25
    Postmodern Perspectives   27
    Pragmatism   28

Feminist Theories   29
Critical Theory and Critical Race Theory (CRT)   30
Queer Theory   32
Disability Theories   33
The Practice of Using Social Justice Interpretive
   Frameworks in Qualitative Research   34
Linking Philosophy and Interpretive Frameworks   35
Summary   38
Additional Readings   38
Exercises   40

3. Designing a Qualitative Study   **42**
Questions for Discussion   43
The Characteristics of Qualitative Research   43
When to Use Qualitative Research   47
What a Qualitative Study Requires From Us   49
The Process of Designing a Qualitative Study   49
   Preliminary Considerations   50
   Steps in the Process   51
   Elements in All Phases of the Research   55
   Ethical Issues During All Phases of
      the Research Process   56
The General Structure of a Plan or Proposal   61
Summary   64
Additional Readings   66
Exercises   67

4. Five Qualitative Approaches to Inquiry   **69**
Questions for Discussion   70
Narrative Research   70
   Definition and Background   70
   Defining Features of Narrative Studies   71
   Types of Narratives   72
   Procedures for Conducting Narrative Research   73
   Challenges   76
Phenomenological Research   76
   Definition and Background   76
   Defining Features of Phenomenology   78
   Types of Phenomenology   79
   Procedures for Conducting
      Phenomenological Research   80
   Challenges   82

Grounded Theory Research 83
   Definition and Background 83
   Defining Features of Grounded Theory 85
   Types of Grounded Theory Studies 86
   Procedures for Conducting Grounded
     Theory Research 88
   Challenges 89
Ethnographic Research 90
   Definition and Background 90
   Defining Features of Ethnographies 91
   Types of Ethnographies 93
   Procedures for Conducting an Ethnography 94
   Challenges 96
Case Study Research 97
   Definition and Background 97
   Defining Features of Case Studies 98
   Types of Case Studies 99
   Procedures for Conducting a Case Study 100
   Challenges 101
The Five Approaches Compared 102
Summary 107
Additional Readings 107
Exercises 110

5. Five Different Qualitative Studies **111**
Questions for Discussion 112
A Narrative Study (Chan, 2010; see Appendix B) 112
A Phenomenological Study (Anderson & Spencer, 2002;
   see Appendix C) 114
A Grounded Theory Study (Harley et al., 2009;
   see Appendix D) 116
An Ethnographic Study (Haenfler, 2004;
   see Appendix E) 118
A Case Study (Asmussen & Creswell, 1995;
   see Appendix F) 119
Differences Among the Approaches 121
   Central Features of Each Approach 121
   Selecting Your Approach 123
Summary 124
Additional Readings 125
Exercises 128

6. Introducing and Focusing the Study   **129**

Questions for Discussion   130
The Research Problem Statement   130
The Purpose Statement   134
The Research Questions   138
    The Central Question   138
    Subquestions   140
Summary   142
Additional Readings   143
Exercises   143

7. Data Collection   **145**

Questions for Discussion   145
The Data Collection Circle   146
    The Site or Individual   147
    Access and Rapport   151
       Institutional Review Boards   152
       Access and Rapport Within the Five Approaches   153
    Purposeful Sampling Strategy   154
       Participants in the Sample   155
       Types of Sampling   156
       Sample Size   157
    Forms of Data   157
       Interviewing   163
       Observation   166
    Recording Procedures   168
    Field Issues   171
       Access to the Organization   171
       Observations   172
       Interviews   172
       Documents and Audiovisual Materials   174
       Ethical Issues   174
    Storing Data   175
Five Approaches Compared   176
Summary   177
Additional Readings   177
Exercises   178

8. Data Analysis and Representation   **179**

Questions for Discussion   179
Three Analysis Strategies   180
The Data Analysis Spiral   182
    Organizing the Data   182

Reading and Memoing   183
Describing, Classifying, and Interpreting Data Into
    Codes and Themes   184
Interpreting the Data   187
Representing and Visualizing the Data   187
Analysis Within Approaches to Inquiry   189
    Narrative Research Analysis and Representation   189
    Phenomenological Analysis and Representation   193
    Grounded Theory Analysis and Representation   195
    Ethnographic Analysis and Representation   197
    Case Study Analysis and Representation   199
Comparing the Five Approaches   200
Computer Use in Qualitative Data Analysis   201
    Advantages and Disadvantages   201
    A Sampling of Computer Programs   203
    Use of Computer Software Programs
        With the Five Approaches   204
    How to Choose Among the Computer Programs   209
Summary   211
Additional Readings   211
Exercises   212

9. Writing a Qualitative Study   **213**
Questions for Discussion   213
Several Writing Strategies   214
    Reflexivity and Representations in Writing   214
    Audience for Our Writings   217
    Encoding Our Writings   217
    Quotes in Our Writings   219
Overall and Embedded Writing Strategies   220
    Narrative Writing Structure   220
        Overall Structure   220
        Embedded Structure   224
    Phenomenological Writing Structure   225
        Overall Structure   226
        Embedded Structure   228
    Grounded Theory Writing Structure   229
        Overall Structure   229
        Embedded Structure   231
    Ethnographic Writing Structure   232
        Overall Structure   233
        Embedded Structure   234

Case Study Writing Structure   236
    Overall Structure   236
    Embedded Structure   238
A Comparison of Narrative Structures   239
Summary   240
Additional Readings   240
Exercises   241

10. Standards of Validation and Evaluation   **243**
Questions for Discussion   243
Validation and Reliability in Qualitative Research   244
    Perspectives on Validation   244
    Validation Strategies   250
    Reliability Perspectives   253
Evaluation Criteria   255
    Qualitative Perspectives   255
    Narrative Research   258
    Phenomenological Research   259
    Grounded Theory Research   260
    Ethnographic Research   262
    Case Study Research   264
Comparing the Evaluation Standards of
    the Five Approaches   265
Summary   265
Additional Readings   266
Exercises   268

11. "Turning the Story" and Conclusion   **269**
Turning the Story   269
A Case Study   271
A Narrative Study   272
A Phenomenology   273
A Grounded Theory Study   273
An Ethnography   274
Conclusion   277
Exercises   280

Appendix A. An Annotated Glossary of Terms   282

Appendix B. A Narrative Research Study—
   "Living in the Space Between Participant and
   Researcher as a Narrative Inquirer:
   Examining Ethnic Identity of
   Chinese Canadian Students as
   Conflicting Stories to Live By"   303
      Elaine Chan

Appendix C. A Phenomenological Study—
   "Cognitive Representations of AIDS"   327
      Elizabeth H. Anderson and Margaret Hull Spencer

Appendix D. A Grounded Theory Study—
   "Developing Long-Term Physical Activity Participation:
   A Grounded Theory Study With
   African American Women"   347
      Amy E. Harley, Janet Buckworth, Mira L. Katz,
      Sharla K. Willis, Angela Odoms-Young, and
      Catherine A. Heaney

Appendix E. An Ethnography—"Rethinking
   Subcultural Resistance: Core Values of
   the Straight Edge Movement"   370
      Ross Haenfler

Appendix F. A Case Study—
   "Campus Response to a Student Gunman"   399
      Kelly J. Asmussen and John W. Creswell

References   417

Author Index   435

Subject Index   442

About the Author

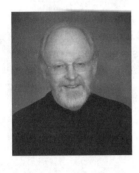 **John W. Creswell**, PhD, has been a professor of educational psychology at the University of Nebraska-Lincoln since 1978. In addition to teaching at the university, he has authored numerous articles on mixed methods research, qualitative methodology, and general research design and 12 books, many of which focus on types of research designs, comparisons of different qualitative methodologies, and the nature and use of mixed methods research. His books are translated into many languages and used around the world. For the last five years, Dr. Creswell served as a codirector at the Office of Qualitative and Mixed Methods Research at the University of Nebraska, which provided support for scholars incorporating qualitative and mixed methods research into projects for extramural funding. He served as the founding coeditor of the Sage *Journal of Mixed Methods Research*, and as an adjunct professor of family medicine at the University of Michigan where he assisted investigators in the health sciences and education with research methodology for National Institutes of Health (NIH) and National Science Foundation projects. He also served extensively as a consultant in the health services research area for the U.S. Department of Veterans Affairs. Dr. Creswell was a Senior Fulbright Scholar to South Africa and in 2008 lectured to faculty at five universities on education and the health sciences. In 2012 he served as a Senior Fulbright Scholar to Thailand. Recently he served as a co-leader of a national working group developing guidelines for mixed methods research for NIH. He lives with his wife, Karen, in Lincoln, Nebraska.

Acknowledgments

I am most thankful to the many students in my qualitative research methods classes at the University of Nebraska–Lincoln who helped to shape this book over the years. They offered suggestions, provided examples, and discussed the material in this book. Also, I benefited from capable scholars who helped to shape and form this book in the first edition: Paul Turner, Ken Robson, Dana Miller, Diane Gillespie, Gregory Schraw, Sharon Hudson, Karen Eifler, Neilida Aguilar, and Harry Wolcott. Ben Crabtree and Rich Hofmann helped form the first edition text significantly and encouraged me to proceed, and they diligently and timely responded to Sage's request to be first edition external reviewers. In addition, Keith Pezzoli, Kathy O'Byrne, Joanne Cooper, and Phyllis Langton served as first edition reviewers for Sage and added insight into content and structure that I could not see because of my closeness to the material. To the reviewers for this third edition, I appreciate your time and effort reviewing the draft of my book. As always, I am indebted to C. Deborah Laughton, who served as my acquisition editor for the first edition, to Lisa Cuevas Shaw who served as editor for the second edition, and to Vicki Knight who helped as acquisition editor for this third edition. Also for all of the editions, members of the Office of Qualitative and Mixed Methods Research (OQMMR) all provided valuable input. I especially single out Dr. Vicki Plano Clark, Dr. Ron Shope, and Yuchun Zhang who have been instrumental in refining and shaping my ideas about qualitative research through these several editions. Also, I am grateful to the Department of Educational Psychology. Finally, to members of my family—Karen, David, Kasey, Johanna, and Bonny—thanks for providing me with time to spend long hours writing and revising this book. Thank you all.

Analytic Table of Contents by Approach

NARRATIVE RESEARCH

Use of narrative approaches	11
Key books and references	11
Definition and background	70
Defining features of narrative research	71
Types of narrative studies	72
Procedures in conducting narrative research	73
Challenges in using narrative research	76
Focus of narrative research	122
Example of a narrative study, Appendix B	303
Research problem	134
Purpose statement	136
Research questions	139
Individual or site to be studied	147
Access and rapport issues	153
Sampling strategy	157
Forms of data	161
Ethical issues	174
Data analysis	189
Writing a narrative study	220
Standards of evaluation	258
Case study "turned" into a narrative study	272

PHENOMENOLOGY

Use of psychological approach	11
Key books and references	12

Definition and background 78
Defining features of phenomenology 79
Types of phenomenology 80
Procedures in conducting phenomenology 82
Challenges in using phenomenology 82
Focus of phenomenology 122
Example of a phenomenological study, Appendix C 327
Research problem 134
Purpose statement 136
Research questions 139
Participants in a phenomenological study 150
Access issues 154
Sampling strategy 157
Forms of data 161
Ethical issues 174
Data analysis 193
Writing a phenomenological study 225
Standards of evaluation 259
Case study "turned" into a phenomenology 273

GROUNDED THEORY

Use of sociological approach 11
Key books and references 12
Definition and background 83
Defining features of grounded theory 85
Types of grounded theory studies 86
Procedures in conducting grounded theory research 88
Challenges in using grounded theory research 89
Focus of grounded theory research 122
Example of a grounded theory study, Appendix D 347
Research problem 134
Purpose statement 136
Research questions 139
Participants in a grounded theory study 150
Access issues 154
Sampling strategy 157
Forms of data 162
Ethical issues 174

Data analysis   195
Writing a grounded theory study   229
Standards of evaluation   260
Case study "turned" into a grounded theory study   273

ETHNOGRAPHY

Use of anthropological, sociological, and
    interpretive approaches   11
Key books and references   12
Definition and background   90
Defining features of ethnography   91
Types of ethnographies   93
Procedures in conducting ethnography   94
Challenges in using ethnography   96
Focus of ethnography   122
Example of an ethnography, Appendix E   370
Research problem   134
Purpose statement   136
Research questions   139
Site to be studied   150
Access and rapport issues   154
Sampling strategy   157
Forms of data   162
Ethical issues   174
Data analysis   197
Writing an ethnography   232
Standards of evaluation   262
Case study "turned" into ethnography   274

CASE STUDY

Use of evaluation approach   11
Key books and references   12
Definition and background   97
Defining features of case studies   98
Types of case studies   99
Procedures for conducting a case study   100
Challenges in using a case study   101

Focus of a case study	122
Example of a case study, Appendix F	399
Research problem	134
Purpose statement	136
Research questions	140
Site to be studied	150
Access and rapport issues	154
Sampling strategy	157
Forms of data	162
Ethical issues	174
Data analysis	199
Writing a case study	236
Standards of evaluation	264
A case study revisited before "turning"	271

List of
Tables and Figures

TABLES

Table 1.1	Qualitative Approaches Mentioned by Authors and Their Disciplines/Fields	8
Table 2.1	The Research Process	17
Table 2.2	Philosophical Assumptions With Implications for Practice	21
Table 2.3	Interpretive Frameworks and Associated Philosophical Beliefs	36
Table 3.1	Characteristics of Qualitative Research	46
Table 3.2	Ethical Issues in Qualitative Research	58
Table 4.1	Contrasting Characteristics of Five Qualitative Approaches	104
Table 6.1	Words to Use in Encoding the Purpose Statement	136
Table 7.1	Data Collection Activities by Five Approaches	148
Table 7.2	Typology of Sampling Strategies in Qualitative Inquiry	158
Table 8.1	General Data Analysis Strategies Advanced by Select Authors	181
Table 8.2	Data Analysis and Representation by Research Approaches	190
Table 9.1	Overall and Embedded Writing Structures and the Five Approaches	221
Table 10.1	Perspectives and Terms Used in Qualitative Validation	244

FIGURES

Figure 5.1   Differentiating Approaches by Foci   122

Figure 6.1   Sample Research Problem Section
(Introduction) to a Study   132

Figure 7.1   Data Collection Activities   146

Figure 7.2   Sample Human Subjects Consent-to-Participate Form   152

Figure 7.3   A Compendium of Data Collection Approaches in
Qualitative Research   160

Figure 7.4   Sample Interview Protocol or Guide   165

Figure 7.5   Sample Observational Protocol   169

Figure 8.1   The Data Analysis Spiral   183

Figure 8.2   Layers of Analysis in the Gunman Case   188

Figure 8.3   Template for Coding a Narrative Study   207

Figure 8.4   Template for Coding a Phenomenological Study   207

Figure 8.5   Template for Coding a Grounded Theory Study   208

Figure 8.6   Template for Coding an Ethnography   208

Figure 8.7   Template for Coding a Case Study
(Using a Multiple or Collective Case Approach)   209

Figure 8.8   Features to Consider When Comparing
Qualitative Data Analysis Software   210

Figure 11.1 Visual Diagram of the Three Components
of Qualitative Research   270

1

Introduction

I first began work on this book during a 1994 summer qualitative seminar in Vail, Colorado, sponsored by the University of Denver under the able guidance of Edith King of the College of Education. At that seminar I facilitated a discussion about qualitative data analysis. I began on a personal note, introducing one of my recent qualitative studies—a case study of a campus response to a student gun incident (Asmussen & Creswell, 1995) (see Appendix F in this book). I knew this case might provoke some discussion and present some complex analysis issues. It involved a Midwestern university's reaction to a gunman who entered an actuarial science undergraduate class with a semiautomatic rifle and attempted to fire on students in his class. The rifle jammed and did not discharge, and the gunman fled and was captured a few miles away. Standing before the group, I chronicled the events of the case, the themes, and the lessons we learned about a university reaction to a near tragic event. Then, unplanned, Harry Wolcott of the University of Oregon, another resource person for our seminar, raised his hand and asked for the podium. He explained how *he* would approach the study as a cultural anthropologist. To my surprise, he had "turned" my case study into ethnography, framing the study in an entirely new way. After Harry had concluded, Les Goodchild, then of Denver University, discussed how he would examine the gunman case from a historical perspective. We all had, then, two different renderings of the incident, surprising "turns" of my case study using different qualitative approaches. It was this event that sparked an idea that I had long harbored—that the design of a qualitative study related to the specific *approach* taken to qualitative research. I began to write the first edition of this book, guided by a single, compelling question: How does the type or approach of qualitative inquiry shape the design or procedures of a study?

PURPOSE AND RATIONALE FOR THE BOOK

I am now into the third edition of this book, and I am still formulating an answer to this question. My primary intent in this book is to examine five different approaches to qualitative inquiry—narrative, phenomenology, grounded theory, ethnography, and case studies—and put them side-by-side so that we can see their differences. These differences can be most vividly displayed by exploring their use throughout the process of research, including the introduction to a study through its purpose and research questions; data collection; data analysis; report writing; and standards of validation and evaluation. For example, by studying qualitative articles in journals we can see that research questions framed from grounded theory look different than questions framed from a phenomenological study.

This combination of the different approaches and how their distinctiveness plays out in the process of research is what distinguishes this book from others on qualitative research that you may have read. Most qualitative researchers focus on only one approach—say ethnography or grounded theory—and try to convince their readers of the value of that approach. This makes sense in our highly specialized world of academia. However, students and beginning qualitative researchers need choices that fit their research problems and that suit their own interests in conducting research. Hopefully, this book opens up the expanse of qualitative research and invites readers to examine multiple ways of engaging in the process of research. It provides qualitative researchers with options for conducting qualitative inquiry and helps them with decisions about what approach is best to use in studying their research problems. With so many books on qualitative research in general and on the various approaches of inquiry, qualitative research students are often at a loss for understanding what options (i.e., approaches) exist and how one makes an informed choice of an option for research.

By reading this book, I hope that you will gain a better understanding of the steps in the process of research, learn five qualitative approaches to inquiry, and understand the differences and similarities among the five ***approaches to inquiry*** (see the glossary in Appendix A for definitions of terms in bold italics).

WHAT IS NEW IN THIS EDITION

Since I wrote the first and second editions of this book, the content of the book has both remained the same and changed. In this edition I introduce several new ideas:

- Based on reviewers' feedback, I reworked Chapter 2 on the philosophical assumptions and the interpretive frameworks used by qualitative researchers. I needed to better position philosophy and frameworks within the overall process of research. I also sought to clarify the relationship between philosophy and interpretive frameworks, and to discuss interpretive frameworks as they are currently being used in qualitative research (Denzin & Lincoln, 2011).

- In Chapter 3 I have added a new section on ethical issues that traces the types of qualitative ethical dilemmas likely to arise at different phases of the research process. In this way I am expanding the ethical coverage in this book.

- In discussing each of the five approaches in this book, as mentioned in Chapter 4, I have added passages on each of the five related to "defining characteristics" of the approach. Readers will have my best assessment of the key features of the approach summarized in one place. Also in Chapter 4 I have moved from relying primarily on one book for each approach in the last edition to using two books to construct a picture of the approach in this edition. I have done this because of the popularity of multiple approaches for understanding each approach, and the value of constructing an understanding of each approach from multiple authors.

- I also updated the illustrative articles that I used in the book in Chapter 5 and removed articles that were outdated. Consequently, I added two new articles: one in narrative research (Chan, 2010) and one in grounded theory (Harley et al., 2009). I decided to keep the gunman incident case study in (Asmussen & Creswell, 1995) because the issue of safety on college campuses remains a critical concern in the literature given recent campus violence.

- In the discussion about research questions, I simplified the discussion about subquestions and focused on how subquestions subdivide the central question into several parts. I also provided additional illustrations of subquestions drawn from different qualitative approaches.

- In the area of data collection, I cannot overlook the technological developments in data collection, and any treatment of qualitative methods needs to incorporate new ways of gathering qualitative data electronically. I have added online methods of qualitative data collection into the discussion in Chapter 7. I have also added information about observational techniques to expand discussions in earlier editions of this book.

- In data analysis, in Chapter 8, I added in new techniques that are being discussed for analyzing the data in each of the five approaches, and I cite recent references. I also updated the discussion about qualitative computer software analysis packages.
- In the writing of qualitative research, as presented in Chapter 9, I added more information about reflexivity, its importance, and how it might be incorporated into a qualitative study.
- At the end of each chapter you will find sample exercises to practice specific skills introduced in the chapter. Many of these exercises have been rewritten in this new edition to reflect my growing understanding of the specific skills that a qualitative researcher needs to know.
- In the final chapter, I have not only "turned" the initial qualitative gunman case study into a narrative project, a phenomenology, a grounded theory study, and an ethnography, but I have made more explicit what changes actually occurred in this reworking.
- As with all new editions, I have updated the references to include recent books on qualitative research methods as well as select journal articles that illustrate these methods.

Many areas have also remained the same as in the last edition. These include:

- The core characteristics of qualitative research have remained the same.
- An emphasis on social justice as one of the primary features of qualitative research is continued in this edition. While a social justice orientation may not be for everyone, it has again been given primacy in the latest edition of the *SAGE Handbook of Qualitative Research* (Denzin & Lincoln, 2011).
- A healthy respect exists for variations within each of the five approaches. I have come to understand that there is no single way to approach an ethnography, a grounded theory study, and so forth. I have selectively chosen what I believe to be the most popular approaches within each approach and to highlight books that emphasize them.
- On a similar note, I have continued to use the five approaches that have now stood the test of time since the first edition. This is not to say that I have not considered additional approaches. Participatory action research, for example, could certainly be a sixth approach,

but I include some discussion of it in the interpretive framework passages in Chapter 2 (Kemmis & Wilkinson, 1998). Also, discourse analysis and conversational analysis could certainly have been included as an additional approach (Cheek, 2004), but I added some thoughts about conversational approaches in narrative approaches. Mixed methods, too, is sometimes so closely associated with qualitative research that it is considered one of the genres (see Saldaña, 2011). However, I see mixed methods as a distinct methodology from qualitative inquiry, and one that bridges qualitative and quantitative research. Further, it has its own distinct literature (see Creswell & Plano Clark, 2011), and thus I wanted to limit the scope of this book to qualitative approaches. Accordingly, I have chosen to keep the five approaches that I started with and to expand within these five approaches.

● I continue to provide resources throughout the book for the qualitative researcher. I include a detailed glossary of terms (and have added terms from the last edition), an analytic table of contents that organizes the material in this book according to the five approaches, and complete journal articles that model designing and writing a study within each of the five approaches. For both inexperienced and experienced researchers, I supply recommendations at the ends of chapters for further reading that can extend the material in this book.

● The term that I used in the first edition, *traditions*, has now been replaced by *approaches*, and I continue this use of terms in the third edition. My approach signals that I not only want to respect past approaches, but I also want to encourage current practices in qualitative research. Other writers have referred to the approaches as "strategies of inquiry" (Denzin & Lincoln, 2005), "varieties" (Tesch, 1990), or "methods" (Morse & Richards, 2002). By **research design**, I refer to the entire process of research from conceptualizing a problem to writing research questions, and on to data collection, analysis, interpretation, and report writing (Bogdan & Taylor, 1975). Yin (2009) commented, "The design is the logical sequence that connects the empirical data to a study's initial research questions and, ultimately, to its conclusions" (p. 29). Hence, I include in the specific design features from the broad philosophical and theoretical perspectives to the quality and validation of a study.

POSITIONING MYSELF

You need to know some information about my background in order to understand my approach used in this book. I was trained as a quantitative researcher about 40 years ago. By the mid-1980s, I was asked to teach the first qualitative research course at my university, and I volunteered to do so. This was followed a few years later with the writing of the first edition of this book. While I have expanded my repertoire to mixed methods as well as qualitative research, I continually return to my strong interest in qualitative research. Over the years I have evolved into an applied research methodologist with a specialization in research design, qualitative research, and mixed methods research.

This background explains why I write from the standpoint of conveying an understanding of the process of qualitative research (whether you want to call it the scientific method or something else), a focus on strong methods features such as extensive qualitative data collection, rigorous data analysis through multiple steps, and the use of computer programs. Moreover, I have developed a fascination with the structure of writing, whether the writing is a qualitative study, a poem, or creative nonfiction. An enduring interest has been the *composition* of qualitative research. This compositional interest flows into how to best structure qualitative inquiry and to visualize how the structure shifts and changes given different approaches to research.

This interest in structured features has often placed me in the camp of postpositivist writers in qualitative inquiry (see Denzin & Lincoln, 2005), but, like most researchers, I defy easy categorization. In an article in *Qualitative Inquiry* about a homeless shelter (Miller, Creswell, & Olander, 1998), my ethnography assumed a realist, a confessional, and an advocacy stance. Also, I am not advocating the acceptance of qualitative research in a "quantitative" world (Ely, Anzul, Friedman, Garner, & Steinmetz, 1991). Qualitative inquiry represents a legitimate mode of social and human science exploration, without apology or comparisons to quantitative research.

I also tend to be oriented toward citing numerous ideas to document articles; to incorporate the latest writings from the ever-growing, vast literature of qualitative inquiry; and to advance an applied, practical form of conducting research. For example, it was not enough for me to convey philosophical assumptions of qualitative inquiry in Chapter 2. I also had to construct a discussion around how these philosophical ideas are applied in the design and writing of a qualitative study. I concur with Agger (1991), who says that readers and writers can understand methodology in less technical ways, thereby affording greater access to scholars and democraticizing science. Also, always before me as I write is the picture of a beginning master's or doctoral student who is learning qualitative research for the first time. Because I have this picture in my head, some may say that I oversimplify the craft of research. This picture may well blur the image for a more seasoned qualitative writer, and especially one who seeks more advanced discussions and who looks for problematizing the process of research.

SELECTION OF THE FIVE APPROACHES

Those undertaking qualitative studies have a baffling number of choices of approaches. One can gain a sense of this diversity by examining several classifications or typologies. Tesch (1990) provided a classification consisting of 28 approaches organized into four branches of a flowchart, sorting out these approaches based on the central interest of the investigator. Wolcott (1992) classified approaches in a "tree" diagram with branches of the tree designating strategies for data collection. Miller and Crabtree (1992) organized 18 types according to the "domain" of human life of primary concern to the researcher, such as a focus on the individual, the social world, or the culture. In the field of education, Jacob (1987) categorized all qualitative research into "traditions" such as ecological psychology, symbolic interactionism, and holistic ethnography. Jacob's categorization provided a key framework for me as I began to sketch out the first edition of this book. Lancy (1993) organized qualitative inquiry into discipline perspectives, such as anthropology, sociology, biology, cognitive psychology, and history. Denzin and Lincoln (2011) have organized and reorganized their types of qualitative strategies over the years.

Table 1.1 provides these and other various classifications of qualitative approaches that have surfaced over the years. This list is not meant to be exhaustive of the possibilities; it is intended to illustrate the diversity of approaches recommended by different authors and how the disciplines might emphasize some approaches over others.

Table 1.1 Qualitative Approaches Mentioned by Authors and Their Disciplines/Fields

Authors	Qualitative Approaches	Disciplines/ Fields
Jacob (1987)	Ecological Psychology Holistic Ethnography Cognitive Anthropology Ethnography of Communication Symbolic Interactionism	Education
Munhall & Oiler (1986)	Phenomenology Grounded Theory Ethnography Historical Research	Nursing
Lancy (1993)	Anthropological Perspectives Sociological Perspectives Biological Perspectives Case Studies Personal Accounts Cognitive Studies Historical Inquiries	Education
Strauss & Corbin (1990)	Grounded Theory Ethnography Phenomenology Life Histories Conversational Analysis	Sociology, Nursing
Morse (1994)	Phenomenology Ethnography Ethnoscience Grounded Theory	Nursing
Moustakas (1994)	Ethnography Grounded Theory Hermeneutics Empirical Phenomenological Research Heuristic Research Transcendental Phenomenology	Psychology

Authors	Qualitative Approaches	Disciplines/ Fields
Denzin & Lincoln (1994)	Case Studies Ethnography Phenomenology Ethnomethodology Interpretative Practices Grounded Theory Biographical Historical Clinical Research	Social Sciences
Miles & Huberman (1994)	Approaches to Qualitative Data Analysis: Interpretivism Social Anthropology Collaborative Social Research	Social Sciences
Slife & Williams (1995)	Categories of Qualitative Methods: Ethnography Phenomenology Studies of Artifacts	Psychology
Denzin & Lincoln (2005)	Performance, Critical, and Public Ethnography Interpretive Practices Case Studies Grounded Theory Life History Narrative Authority Participatory Action Research Clinical Research	Social Sciences
Marshall & Rossman (2010)	Ethnographic Approaches Phenomenological Approaches Sociolinguistic Approaches (i.e., critical genres, such as critical race theory, queer theory, etc.)	Education

(Continued)

Table 1.1 (Continued)		
Authors	*Qualitative Approaches*	*Disciplines/ Fields*
Saldaña (2011)	Ethnography Grounded Theory Phenomenology Case Study Content Analysis Mixed Methods Research Narrative Inquiry Arts-Based Research Autoethnography Evaluation Research Action Research Investigative Journalism Critical Inquiry	Arts (Theater)
Denzin & Lincoln (2011)	Research Strategies: Design Case Study Ethnography, Participant Observation, Performance Ethnography Phenomenology, Ethnomethodology Grounded Theory Life History, *Testimonio* Historical Method Action and Applied Research Clinical Research	

Looking closely at these classifications, we can discern that some approaches appear consistently over the years, such as ethnography, grounded theory, phenomenology, and case studies. Also, a number of narrative-related approaches have been discussed, such as life history, autoethnography, and biography. With so many possibilities, how did I decide on the five approaches presented in this book?

My choice of the five approaches resulted from reflecting on my own personal interests, selecting different approaches popular in the social science and health science literature, and electing to choose representative discipline orientations. I have had personal experience with each of the five, and have advised students and participated on research teams using these qualitative approaches. Beyond this personal experience, I have been reading the qualitative literature since my initial teaching assignment in the area in 1985. The five approaches discussed in this book reflect the types of qualitative research that I most frequently see in the social, behavioral, and health science literature. It is not unusual, too, for authors to state that certain approaches are most important in their fields (e.g., Morse & Field, 1995). Also, I prefer approaches with systematic procedures for inquiry. The books I have chosen to illustrate each approach tend to have procedures of rigorous data collection and analysis methods that are attractive to beginning researchers. The primary books chosen for each approach also represent different discipline perspectives in the social, behavioral, and health sciences. This is an attractive feature to broaden the audience for the book and to recognize the diverse disciplines that have embraced qualitative research. For example, narrative originates from the humanities and social sciences, phenomenology from psychology and philosophy, grounded theory from sociology, ethnography from anthropology and sociology, and case studies from the human and social sciences and applied areas such as evaluation research.

The primary ideas that I use to discuss each approach come from select books. More specifically, I will rely heavily on two books on each approach. These are the books that I highly recommend for you to get started in learning a specific approach to qualitative inquiry. These books reflect classics often cited by authors as well as new works. They also reflect diverse disciplines and perspectives.

Narrative Research

Clandinin, D. J., & Connelly, F. M. (2000). *Narrative inquiry: Experience and story in qualitative research.* San Francisco: Jossey-Bass.

Riessman, C. K. (2008). *Narrative methods for the human sciences.* Thousand Oaks, CA: Sage.

Phenomenology

Moustakas, C. (1994). *Phenomenological research methods.* Thousand Oaks, CA: Sage.

van Manen, M. (1990). *Researching lived experience: Human science for an action sensitive pedagogy.* Albany: State University of New York Press.

Grounded Theory

Charmaz, K. (2006). *Constructing grounded theory: A practical guide through qualitative analysis.* London: Sage.

Corbin, J., & Strauss, A. (2008). *Basics of qualitative research* (3rd ed.) Thousand Oaks, CA: Sage.

Ethnography

Fetterman, D. M. (2010). *Ethnography: Step-by-step.* (3rd ed.). Los Angeles: Sage.

Wolcott, H. F. (2008). *Ethnography: A way of seeing* (2nd ed.). Lanham, MD: AltaMira.

Case Study

Stake, R. (1995). *The art of case study research.* Thousand Oaks, CA: Sage.

Yin, R. K. (2009). *Case study research: Design and methods* (4th ed.). Thousand Oaks, CA: Sage.

AUDIENCE

Although multiple audiences, both known and unknown, exist for any text (Fetterman, 2010), I direct this book toward academics and scholars affiliated with the social, human, and health sciences. Examples throughout the book illustrate the diversity of disciplines and fields of study including sociology, psychology, education, nursing, family medicine, allied health, urban studies, marketing, communication and journalism, educational psychology, family science and therapy, and other social and human science areas.

My aim is to provide a useful text for those who produce scholarly qualitative research in the form of journal articles, theses, or dissertations.

I have pitched the level of discussion to be suitable for upper-division students and beyond into graduate school. For graduate students writing master's theses or doctoral dissertations, I compare and contrast the five approaches in the hope that such analysis helps in establishing a rationale for the choice of a type to use. For beginning qualitative researchers, I provide Chapter 2 on the philosophical and interpretive frameworks that shape qualitative research and Chapter 3 on the basic elements in designing a qualitative study. I feel that understanding the basics of qualitative research is essential before venturing out into the specifics of one of the qualitative approaches. I begin each chapter with an overview of the topic of the chapter and then go into how the topic might be addressed within each of the five approaches. While discussing the basic elements, I suggest several books aimed at the beginning qualitative researcher that can provide a more extensive review of the basics of qualitative research. Such basics are necessary before delving into the five approaches. A focus on comparing the five approaches throughout this book provides an introduction for experienced researchers to approaches that build on their training and research experiences.

ORGANIZATION

Following this introduction, in Chapter 2 I provide an introduction to the philosophical assumptions and interpretive frameworks that inform qualitative research. I emphasize how they might be written into a qualitative study. In Chapter 3, I review the basic elements for designing a qualitative study. These elements begin with a definition of qualitative research, the reasons for using this approach, and the phases in the process of research. In Chapter 4, I provide an introduction to each of the five approaches of inquiry: narrative research, phenomenology, grounded theory, ethnography, and case study research. The chapter includes an overview of the elements of each of the five approaches. Chapter 5 continues this discussion by presenting five published journal articles (one on each approach with the complete articles in Appendices B–F), which provide good illustrations of each of the approaches. By reading my overview in Chapter 4, and then reviewing a journal article that illustrates the approach, you can develop a working knowledge of an approach. Choosing one of the books I recommend for the approach in this chapter and beginning a mastery of it for your research study can then expand this knowledge.

These five preliminary chapters form an introduction to the five approaches and an overview of the process of research design. They set the stage for the remaining chapters, which take up in turn each step in the research process: writing introductions to studies (Chapter 6), collecting data (Chapter 7), analyzing and representing data (Chapter 8), writing qualitative studies (Chapter 9), and validating and evaluating a qualitative study (Chapter 10). Throughout these design chapters I start with the basics of qualitative research and then expand the discussion to advance and compare the five types.

As a final experience to sharpen distinctions made among the five approaches, I present Chapter 11, in which I return to the gunman case study (Asmussen & Creswell, 1995—see Appendix F), first introduced in Chapter 5, and "turn" the story from a case study into a narrative biography, a phenomenology, a grounded theory study, and an ethnography. This culminating chapter brings the reader full circle to examining the gunman case in several ways, an extension of my 1994 Vail seminar experience in looking at the same problem from diverse qualitative perspectives.

2

Philosophical Assumptions and Interpretive Frameworks

Whether we are aware of it or not, we always bring certain beliefs and philosophical assumptions to our research. Sometimes these are deeply ingrained views about the types of problems that we need to study, what research questions to ask, or how we go about gathering data. These beliefs are instilled in us during our educational training through reading journal articles and books, through advice dispensed by our advisors, and through the scholarly communities we engage at our conferences and scholarly meetings. The difficulty lies first in becoming aware of these assumptions and beliefs and second in deciding whether we will actively incorporate them into our qualitative studies. Often, at a less abstract level, these philosophical assumptions inform our choice of theories that guide our research. Theories are more apparent in our qualitative studies than philosophical assumptions and theories are made explicit for us in our scholarly training and in report research studies.

Qualitative researchers have underscored the importance of not only understanding the beliefs and theories that inform our research but also actively writing about them in our reports and studies. This chapter highlights various philosophical assumptions that have occupied the minds of qualitative researchers for some years and the various theoretical and interpretive frameworks that enact these beliefs. A close tie does exist between the philosophy that one brings to the research act and how one proceeds to use a framework to shroud his or her inquiry. This chapter details the various philosophies common to qualitative research and where both philosophy and theory fit into the large schema of the research process. Types of philosophical assumptions, and how they are often used or made explicit in qualitative studies, are advanced. Further, various interpretive frameworks are suggested that link back to philosophical assumptions. Commentary is made on how these frameworks play out in the actual practice of research.

QUESTIONS FOR DISCUSSION

- Where do philosophy and theoretical frameworks fit into the overall process of research?
- Why is it important to understand the philosophical assumptions?
- What four philosophical assumptions exist when you choose qualitative research?
- How are these philosophical assumptions used and written into a qualitative study?
- What types of interpretive frameworks are used in qualitative research?
- How are interpretive frameworks written into a qualitative study?
- How are philosophical assumptions and interpretive frameworks linked in a qualitative study?

PHILOSOPHICAL ASSUMPTIONS

An understanding of the philosophical assumptions behind qualitative research begins with assessing where it fits within the overall process of research, noting its importance as an element of research, and considering how to actively write it into a study.

A Framework for Understanding Assumptions

Philosophy means the use of abstract ideas and beliefs that inform our research. We know that philosophical assumptions are typically the first ideas in developing a study, but how they relate to the overall process of research remains a mystery. It is here that the overview of the process of research compiled by Denzin and Lincoln (2011, p. 12), as shown in Table 2.1, helps us to place philosophy and theory into perspective in the research process.

The research process begins in Phase 1 with the researchers considering what they bring to the inquiry, such as their personal history, views of

Table 2.1 The Research Process

Phase 1: The Researcher as a Multicultural Subject

History and research tradition

Conceptions of self and the other

The ethics and politics of research

Phase 2: Theoretical Paradigms and Perspectives

Positivism, postpositivism

Interpretivism, constructivism, hermeneutics

Feminism(s)

Racialized discourses

Critical theory and Marxist models

Cultural studies models

Queer theory

Postcolonialism

Phase 3: Research Strategies

Design

Case study

Ethnography, participant observation, performance ethnography

Phenomenology, ethnomethodology

Grounded theory

Life history, *testimonio*

Historical method

Action and applied research

Clinical research

Phase 4: Methods of Collection and Analysis

Interviewing

Observing

Artifacts, documents, and records

Visual methods

Autoethnography

Data management methods

Computer-assisted analysis

Textual analysis

Focus groups

Applied ethnography

(Continued)

Table 2.1 (Continued)

Phase 5: The Art, Practice, and Politics of Interpretation and Evaluation

Criteria for judging adequacy

Practices and politics of interpretation

Writing as interpretation

Policy analysis

Evaluation traditions

Applied research

Source: Denzin & Lincoln, 2011, p. 12. Used with permission, SAGE Publications.

themselves and others, and ethical and political issues. Inquirers often over-look this phase, so it is helpful to have it highlighted and positioned first in the levels of the research process. In Phase 2 the researcher brings to the inquiry certain theories, *paradigms,* and perspectives, a "basic set of beliefs that guides action" (Guba, 1990, p. 17). It is here in Phase 2 that we find the philosophical and theoretical frameworks addressed in this chapter. Following chapters in this book are devoted, then, to the Phase 3 research strategies, called "approaches" in this book, that will be enumerated as they relate to the research process. Finally, the inquirer engages in Phase 4 methods of data collection and analysis, followed by Phase 5, the interpretation and evaluation of the data. Taking Table 2.1 in its entirety, we see that research involves differing levels of abstraction from the broad assessment of individual characteristics brought by the researcher on through the researcher's philosophy and theory that lay the foundation for more specific approaches and methods of data collection, analysis, and interpretation. Also implicit in Table 2.1 is the importance of having an understanding of philosophy and theoretical orientations that informs a qualitative study.

Why Philosophy Is Important

We can begin by thinking about why it is important to understand the philo-sophical assumptions that underlie qualitative research and to be able to articu-late them in a research study or when presenting the study to an audience. Huff (2009) is helpful in articulating the importance of philosophy in research.

- It shapes how we formulate our problem and research questions to study and how we seek information to answer the questions. A cause-and-effect type of question in which certain variables are predicted to explain an outcome is different from an exploration of a single phenomenon as found in qualitative research.

● These assumptions are deeply rooted in our training and reinforced by the scholarly community in which we work. Granted, some communities are more eclectic and borrow from many disciplines (e.g., education), while others are more narrowly focused on such research components as specific research problems to study, how to go about studying these problems, and how to add to knowledge through the study. This raises the question as to whether key assumptions can change and/or whether multiple philosophical assumptions can be used in a given study. My stance is that assumptions can change over time and over a career, and they often do, especially after a scholar leaves the enclave of his or her discipline and begins to work in more of a trans- or multidisciplinary way. Whether multiple assumptions can be taken in a given study is open to debate, and again, it may be related to research experiences of the investigator, his or her openness to exploring using differing assumptions, and the acceptability of ideas taken in the larger scientific community of which he or she is a part.

● Unquestionably reviewers make philosophical assumptions about a study when they evaluate it. Knowing how reviewers stand on issues of epistemology is helpful to author-researchers. When the assumptions between the author and the reviewer (or the journal editor) diverge, the author's work may not receive a fair hearing, and conclusions may be drawn that it does not make a contribution to the literature. This unfair hearing may occur within the context of a graduate student presenting to a committee, an author submitting to a scholarly journal, or an investigator presenting a proposal to a funding agency. On the reverse side, understanding the differences used by a reviewer may enable an author-researcher to resolve points of difference before they become a focal point for critique.

Four Philosophical Assumptions

What are the philosophical assumptions made by researchers when they undertake a qualitative study? These assumptions have been articulated throughout the last 20 years in the various *SAGE Handbooks of Qualitative Research* (Denzin & Lincoln, 1994, 2000, 2005, 2011) and as the "axiomatic" issues advanced by Guba and Lincoln (1988) as the guiding philosophy behind qualitative research. These beliefs have been called paradigms (Lincoln, Lynham, & Guba, 2011; Mertens, 2010); philosophical assumptions, epistemologies, and ontologies (Crotty, 1998); broadly conceived research methodologies (Neuman, 2000); and alternative knowledge claims (Creswell, 2009). They are beliefs about ontology (the nature of reality), epistemology (what counts as knowledge and how knowledge claims are justified), axiology (the role of values in research), and methodology (the process of research). In this discussion I will first discuss each of these philosophical assumptions, detail how they might be used and written into qualitative research, and then link them to different interpretive frameworks that operate at a more specific level in the process of research (see Table 2.2).

The *ontological* issue relates to the nature of reality and its characteristics. When researchers conduct qualitative research, they are embracing the idea of multiple realities. Different researchers embrace different realities, as do the individuals being studied and the readers of a qualitative study. When studying individuals, qualitative researchers conduct a study with the intent of reporting these multiple realities. Evidence of multiple realities includes the use of multiple forms of evidence in themes using the actual words of different individuals and presenting different perspectives. For example, when writers compile a phenomenology, they report how individuals participating in the study view their experiences differently (Moustakas, 1994).

With the *epistemological* assumption, conducting a qualitative study means that researchers try to get as close as possible to the participants being studied. Therefore, subjective evidence is assembled based on individual views. This is how knowledge is known—through the subjective experiences of people. It becomes important, then, to conduct studies in the "field," where the participants live and work—these are important contexts for understanding what the participants are saying. The longer researchers stay in the "field" or get to know the participants, the more they "know what they know" from firsthand information. For example, a good ethnography requires prolonged stay at the research site (Wolcott, 2008a). In short, the researcher tries to minimize the "distance" or "objective separateness" (Guba & Lincoln, 1988, p. 94) between himself or herself and those being researched.

All researchers bring values to a study, but qualitative researchers make their values known in a study. This is the *axiological* assumption that characterizes qualitative research. How does the researcher implement this assumption in practice? In a qualitative study, the inquirers admit the value-laden nature of the study and actively report their values and biases as well as the value-laden nature of information gathered from the field. We say that they "position themselves" in a study. In an interpretive biography, for example, the researcher's presence is apparent in the text, and the author admits that the stories voiced represent an interpretation and presentation of the author as much as the subject of the study (Denzin, 1989a).

Table 2.2 Philosophical Assumptions With Implications for Practice

Assumption	Questions	Characteristics	Implications for Practice (Examples)
Ontological	What is the nature of reality?	Reality is multiple as seen through many views	Researcher reports different perspectives as themes develop in the findings
Epistemological	What counts as knowledge? How are knowledge claims justified? What is the relationship between the researcher and that being researched?	Subjective evidence from participants; researcher attempts to lessen distance between himself or herself and that being researched	Researcher relies on quotes as evidence from the participant; collaborates, spends time in field with participants, and becomes an "insider"
Axiological	What is the role of values?	Researcher acknowledges that research is value-laden and that biases are present	Researcher openly discusses values that shape the narrative and includes his or her own interpretation in conjunction with the interpretations of participants
Methodological	What is the process of research? What is the language of research?	Researcher uses inductive logic, studies the topic within its context, and uses an emerging design	Researcher works with particulars (details) before generalizations, describes in detail the context of the study, and continually revises questions from experiences in the field

The procedures of qualitative research, or its ***methodology,*** are characterized as inductive, emerging, and shaped by the researcher's experience in collecting and analyzing the data. The logic that the qualitative researcher follows is inductive, from the ground up, rather than handed down entirely from a theory or from the perspectives of the inquirer. Sometimes the research questions change in the middle of the study to reflect better the types of questions needed to understand the research problem. In response, the data collection strategy, planned before the study, needs to be modified to accompany the new questions. During the data analysis, the researcher follows a path of analyzing the data to develop an increasingly detailed knowledge of the topic being studied.

Writing Philosophical Assumptions Into Qualitative Studies

One further thought is important about philosophical assumptions. In some qualitative studies they remain hidden from view; they can be deduced, however, by the discerning reader who sees the multiple views that appear in the themes, the detailed rendering of the subjective quotes of participants, the carefully laid-out biases of the researcher, or the emerging design that evolves in ever-expanding levels of abstraction from description to themes to broad generalizations. In other studies, the philosophy is made explicit by a special section in the study—typically in the description of the characteristics of qualitative inquiry often found in the methods section. Here the inquirer talks about ontology, epistemology, and other assumptions explicitly and details how they are exemplified in the study. The form of this discussion is to convey the assumptions, to provide definitions for them, and to discuss how they are illustrated in the study. References to the literature about the philosophy of qualitative research round out the discussion. Sections of this nature are often found in doctoral dissertations, in journal articles reported in major qualitative journals, and in conference paper presentations where the audience may ask about the underlying philosophy of the study.

INTERPRETIVE FRAMEWORKS

In Table 2.1, the philosophical assumptions are embedded within interpretive frameworks that qualitative researchers use when they conduct a study. Thus, Denzin and Lincoln (2011) consider the philosophical assumptions (ontology, epistemology, axiology, and methodology) as key premises that are folded into interpretive frameworks used in qualitative research. What are these interpretive frameworks? On the one hand, they may be *social science theories* to frame their theoretical lens in studies, such as the use of these theories in ethnography (see Chapter 4). Social science theories may be theories of leadership, attribution, political influence and control, and hundreds of other possibilities that are taught in the social science disciplines. On the other hand, the theories may be *social justice theories* or advocacy/participatory theories seeking to bring about change or address social justice issues in our societies. As Denzin and Lincoln (2011) state, "We want a social science committed up front to issues of social justice, equity, nonviolence, peace, and universal human rights" (p. 11).

In Table 2.1 we saw one categorization of interpretive frameworks consisted of positivism, postpositivism; interpretivism, constructivism, hermeneutics; feminism(s); racialized discourses; critical theory and Marxist models; cultural studies models; queer theory; and postcolonialism. The frameworks seem to be ever expanding, and the list in Table 2.1 does not account for several that are popularly used in qualitative research, such as the transformative perspective, postmodernism, and disability approaches. Another approach that has been extensively discussed elsewhere is the realist perspective that combines a realist ontology (the belief that a real world exists independently of our beliefs and constructions) and a constructivist epistemology (knowledge of the world is inevitably our own construction) (see Maxwell, 2012). Consequently, any discussion (including this one) can only be a partial description of possibilities, but a review of several major interpretive frameworks can provide a sense of options. The participants in these interpretive projects often represent underrepresented or marginalized groups, whether those differences take the form of gender, race, class, religion, sexuality, or geography (Ladson-Billings & Donnor, 2005) or some intersection of these differences.

Postpositivism

Those who engage in qualitative research using a belief system grounded in postpositivism will take a scientific approach to research. They will employ a social science theoretical lens. I will use the term *postpostivism* rather than *positivism* to denote this approach because postpositivists do not believe in strict cause and effect, but rather recognize that all cause and effect is a probability that may or may not occur. *Postpositivism* has the elements of being reductionistic, logical, empirical, cause-and-effect oriented, and deterministic based on a priori theories. We can see this approach at work among individuals with prior quantitative research training, and in fields such as the health sciences in which qualitative research often plays a supportive role to quantitative research and must be couched in terms acceptable to quantitative researchers and funding agents (e.g., the a priori use of theory; see Barbour, 2000). A good overview of postpositivist approaches is available in Phillips and Burbules (2000).

In practice, postpositivist researchers view inquiry as a series of logically related steps, believe in multiple perspectives from participants rather than a single reality, and espouse rigorous methods of qualitative data collection and analysis. They use multiple levels of data analysis for rigor, employ computer programs to assist in their analysis, encourage the use of validity approaches, and write their qualitative studies in the form of scientific reports, with a structure resembling quantitative articles (e.g., problem, questions, data collection, results, conclusions). My approach to qualitative research has been identified as belonging to postpositivism (Denzin & Lincoln, 2005), as have the approaches of others (e.g., Taylor & Bogdan, 1998). I do tend to use this belief system, although I would not characterize all of my research as framed within a postpositivist qualitative orientation (e.g., see the constructivist approach in McVea, Harter, McEntarffer, & Creswell, 1999, and the social justice perspective in Miller, Creswell, & Olander, 1998). This postpositivist interpretive framework is exemplified in the systematic procedures of grounded theory found in Strauss and Corbin (1990, 1998), the analytic data analysis steps in phenomenology (Moustakas, 1994), and the data analysis strategies of case comparisons of Yin (2009).

Social Constructivism

Social constructivism (which is often described as interpretivism; see Denzin & Lincoln, 2011; Mertens, 2010) is another worldview. In *social constructivism*, individuals seek understanding of the world in which they live and work. They develop subjective meanings of their experiences—meanings directed toward certain objects or things. These meanings are varied and multiple, leading the researcher to look for the complexity of views rather than narrow the meanings into a few categories or ideas. The goal of research, then, is to rely as much as possible on the participants' views of the situation. Often these subjective meanings are negotiated socially and historically. In other words, they are not simply imprinted on individuals but are formed through interaction with others (hence social construction) and through historical and cultural norms that operate in individuals' lives. Rather than starting with a theory (as in postpositivism), inquirers generate or inductively develop a theory or pattern of meaning. Examples of recent writers who have summarized this position are Crotty (1998), Lincoln and Guba (2000), and Schwandt (2007).

In terms of practice, the questions become broad and general so that the participants can construct the meaning of a situation, a meaning typically forged in discussions or interactions with other persons. The more open-ended the questioning, the better, as the researcher listens carefully to what people say or do in their life setting. Thus, constructivist researchers often address the "processes" of interaction among individuals. They also focus on the specific contexts in which people live and work in order to understand the historical and cultural settings of the participants. Researchers recognize that their own background shapes their interpretation, and they "position themselves" in the research to acknowledge how their interpretation flows from their own personal, cultural, and historical experiences. Thus the researchers make an interpretation of what they find, an interpretation shaped by their own experiences and background. The researcher's intent, then, is to make sense of (or interpret) the meanings others have about the world. This is why qualitative research is often called "interpretive" research.

We see the constructivist worldview manifest in phenomenological studies, in which individuals describe their experiences (Moustakas, 1994), and in the grounded theory perspective of Charmaz (2006), in which she grounds her theoretical orientation in the views or perspectives of individuals.

Transformative Frameworks

Researchers might use an alternative framework, a transformative framework, because the postpositivists impose structural laws and theories that do not fit marginalized individuals or groups and the constructivists do not go far enough in advocating action to help individuals. The basic tenet of this *transformative framework* is that knowledge is not neutral and it reflects the power and social relationships within society, and thus the purpose of knowledge construction is to aid people to improve society (Mertens, 2003). These individuals include marginalized groups such as lesbians, gays, bisexuals, transgender persons, queers, and societies that need a more hopeful, positive psychology and resilience (Mertens, 2009).

Qualitative research, then, should contain an action agenda for reform that may change the lives of participants, the institutions in which they live and work, or even the researchers' lives. The issues facing these marginalized groups are of paramount importance to study, issues such as oppression, domination, suppression, alienation, and hegemony. As these issues are studied and exposed, the researchers provide a voice for these participants, raising their consciousness and improving their lives. Describing it as participatory action research, Kemmis and Wilkinson (1998) embrace features of this transformative framework:

- Participatory action is recursive or dialectical and is focused on bringing about change in practices. Thus, in participatory action research studies, inquirers advance an action agenda for change.
- It is focused on helping individuals free themselves from constraints found in the media, in language, in work procedures, and in the relationships of power in educational settings. Participatory studies often begin with an important issue or stance about the problems in society, such as the need for empowerment.
- It is emancipatory in that it helps unshackle people from the constraints of irrational and unjust structures that limit self-development and self-determination. The aim of this approach is to create a political debate and discussion so that change will occur.
- It is practical and collaborative because it is inquiry completed "with" others rather than "on" or "to" others. In this spirit, participatory authors engage the participants as active collaborators in their inquiries.

Other researchers who embrace this worldview are Fay (1987) and Heron and Reason (1997). In practice, this framework has shaped several approaches to inquiry. Specific social issues (e.g., domination, oppression, inequity) help organize the research questions. Not wanting to further marginalize the individuals participating in the research, transformative inquirers collaborate with research participants. They may ask participants to help with designing the questions, collecting the data, analyzing it, and shaping the final report of the research. In this way, the "voice" of the participants becomes heard throughout the research process. The research also contains an action agenda for reform, a specific plan for addressing the injustices of the marginalized group. These practices will be seen in the ethnographic approaches to research with a social justice agenda found in Denzin and Lincoln (2011) and in the change-oriented forms of narrative research (Daiute & Lightfoot, 2004).

Postmodern Perspectives

Thomas (1993) calls postmodernists "armchair radicals" (p. 23) who focus their critiques on changing ways of thinking rather than on calling for action based on these changes. ***Postmodernism*** might be considered a family of theories and perspectives that have something in common (Slife & Williams, 1995). The basic concept is that knowledge claims must be set within the conditions of the world today and in the multiple perspectives of class, race, gender, and other group affiliations. These conditions are well articulated by individuals such as Foucault, Derrida, Lyotard, Giroux, and Freire (Bloland, 1995). These are negative conditions, and they show themselves in the presence of hierarchies, power and control by individuals, and the multiple meanings of language. The conditions include the importance of different discourses, the importance of marginalized people and groups (the "other"), and the presence of "metanarratives" or universals that hold true regardless of the social conditions. Also included is the need to "deconstruct" texts in terms of language, their reading and their writing, and the examining and bringing to the surface of concealed hierarchies as well as dominations, oppositions, inconsistencies, and contradictions (Bloland, 1995; Clarke, 2005; Stringer, 1993). Denzin's (1989a) approach to "interpretive" biography, Clandinin and Connelly's (2000) approach to narrative research, and Clarke's (2005) perspective on grounded theory draw on postmodernism in that researchers study turning points, or problematic situations in which people find themselves during transition periods (Borgatta & Borgatta, 1992). Regarding a "postmodern-influenced ethnography," Thomas (1993) writes that such a study might "confront the centrality of media-created realities and the influence of information technologies" (p. 25). Thomas also comments that narrative texts need to be challenged (and written), according to the postmodernists, for their "subtexts" of dominant meanings.

Pragmatism

There are many forms of pragmatism. Individuals holding an interpretive framework based on *pragmatism* focus on the outcomes of the research—the actions, situations, and consequences of inquiry—rather than antecedent conditions (as in postpositivism). There is a concern with applications—"what works"—and solutions to problems (Patton, 1990). Thus, instead of a focus on methods, the important aspect of research is the problem being studied and the questions asked about this problem (see Rossman & Wilson, 1985). Cherryholmes (1992) and Murphy (1990) provide direction for the basic ideas:

- Pragmatism is not committed to any one system of philosophy and reality.
- Individual researchers have a freedom of choice. They are "free" to choose the methods, techniques, and procedures of research that best meet their needs and purposes.
- Pragmatists do not see the world as an absolute unity. In a similar way, researchers look to many approaches to collecting and analyzing data rather than subscribing to only one way (e.g., multiple qualitative approaches).
- Truth is what works at the time; it is not based in a dualism between reality independent of the mind or within the mind.
- Pragmatist researchers look to the "what" and "how" of research based on its intended consequences—where they want to go with it.
- Pragmatists agree that research always occurs in social, historical, political, and other contexts.
- Pragmatists have believed in an external world independent of the mind as well as those lodged in the mind. They believe (Cherryholmes, 1992) that we need to stop asking questions about reality and the laws of nature. "They would simply like to change the subject" (Rorty, 1983, p. xiv).
- Recent writers embracing this worldview include Rorty (1990), Murphy (1990), Patton (1990), Cherryholmes (1992), and Tashakkori and Teddlie (2003).

In practice, the individual using this worldview will use multiple methods of data collection to best answer the research question, will employ multiple sources of data collection, will focus on the practical implications of the research, and will emphasize the importance of conducting research that best addresses the research problem. In the discussion here of the five approaches to research, you will see this framework at work when ethnographers employ both quantitative (e.g., surveys) and qualitative data collection (LeCompte & Schensul, 1999) and when case study researchers use both quantitative and qualitative data (Luck, Jackson, & Usher, 2006; Yin, 2009).

Feminist Theories

Feminism draws on different theoretical and pragmatic orientations, different international contexts, and different dynamic developments (Olesen, 2011). *Feminist research approaches* center on and make problematic women's diverse situations and the institutions that frame those situations. Research topics may include a postcolonial thought related to forms of feminism depending on the context of nationalism, globalization and diverse international contexts (e.g., sex workers, domestic servants), and work by or about specific groups of women, such as standpoint theories about lesbians, women with disabilities, and women of color (Olesen, 2011). The theme of domination prevails in the feminist literature as well, but the subject matter is often gender domination within a patriarchal society. Feminist research also embraces many of the tenets of postmodern and poststructuralist critiques as a challenge to the injustices of current society. In feminist research approaches, the goals are to establish collaborative and nonexploitative relationships, to place the researcher within the study so as to avoid objectification, and to conduct research that is transformative. Recent critical trends address protecting indigenous knowledge and the intersectionality of feminist research (e.g., the intersection of race, class, gender, sexuality, able-bodied-ness, and age) (Olesen, 2011).

One of the leading scholars of this approach, Lather (1991), comments on the essential perspectives of this framework. Feminist researchers see gender as a basic organizing principle that shapes the conditions of their lives. It is "a lens that brings into focus particular questions" (Fox-Keller, 1985, p. 6). The questions feminists pose relate to the centrality of gender in the shaping of our consciousness. The aim of this ideological research is to "correct both the invisibility and distortion of female experience in ways relevant to ending women's unequal social position" (Lather, 1991, p. 71). Another writer, Stewart (1994), translates feminist critiques and methodology into procedural guides. She suggests that researchers need to look for what has been left out in social science writing, and to study women's lives and issues such as identities, sex roles, domestic violence, abortion activism, comparable worth, affirmative action, and the way in which women struggle with their social devaluation and powerlessness within their families. Also, researchers need to consciously and systematically include their own roles or positions and assess how they impact their understandings of a woman's life. In addition, Stewart views women as having agency, the ability to make choices and resist oppression, and she suggests that researchers need to inquire into how a woman understands her gender, acknowledging that gender is a social construct that differs for each individual. Stewart highlights the importance of studying power relationships and individuals' social position and how they impact women. Finally, she sees each woman as different and recommends that scholars avoid the search for a unified or coherent self or voice.

Recent discussions indicate that the approach of finding appropriate methods for feminist research has given way to the thought that any method can be made feminist (Deem, 2002; Moss, 2007). Olesen (2011) summarizes the current state of feminist research under a number of transformative developments (e.g., globalization, transnational feminism), critical trends (e.g., endarkened, decolonizing research and intersectionality), and continuing issues (e.g., bias, troubling traditional concepts), enduring concerns (e.g., participants' voices, ethics), influences on feminist work (e.g., the academy and publishing), and challenges of the future (e.g., the interplay of multiple factors in women's lives, hidden oppressions).

Critical Theory and Critical Race Theory (CRT)

Critical theory perspectives are concerned with empowering human beings to transcend the constraints placed on them by race, class, and gender (Fay, 1987). Researchers need to acknowledge their own power, engage in dialogues, and use theory to interpret or illuminate social action (Madison, 2005). Central themes that a critical researcher might explore include the scientific study of social institutions and their transformations through interpreting the meanings of social life; the historical problems of domination, alienation, and social struggles; and a critique of society and the envisioning of new possibilities (Fay, 1987; Morrow & Brown, 1994).

In research, critical theory can be defined by the particular configuration of methodological postures it embraces. The critical researcher might design, for example, an ethnographic study to include changes in how people think; encourage people to interact, form networks, become activists, and form action-oriented groups; and help individuals examine the conditions of their existence (Madison, 2005; Thomas, 1993). The end goal of the study might be social theorizing, which Morrow and Brown (1994) define as "the desire to comprehend and, in some cases, transform (through praxis) the underlying orders of social life—those social and systemic relations that constitute society" (p. 211). The investigator accomplishes this, for example, through an intensive case study or across a small number of historically comparable cases of specific actors (biographies), mediations, or systems and through "ethnographic accounts (interpretive social psychology), componential taxonomies (cognitive anthropology), and formal models (mathematical sociology)" (p. 212). In critical action research in teacher education, for example, Kincheloe (1991) recommends that the "critical teacher" exposes the assumptions of existing research orientations, critiques the knowledge base, and through these critiques reveals ideological effects on teachers, schools, and the culture's view of education. The design of research within a critical theory approach, according to sociologist Agger (1991), falls into two broad categories: *methodological,* in that it affects the ways in which people write and read, and *substantive,* in the theories and topics of the investigator (e.g., theorizing about the role of the state and culture in advanced capitalism). An often-cited classic of critical theory is the ethnography from Willis (1977) of the "lads" who participated in behavior as opposition to authority, as informal groups "having a laff" (p. 29) as a form of resistance to their school. As a study of the manifestations of resistance and state regulation, it highlights ways in which actors come to terms with and struggle against cultural forms that dominate them (Morrow & Brown, 1994). Resistance is also the theme addressed in the ethnography of a subcultural group of youths highlighted as an example of ethnography in this book (see Haenfler, 2004, in Appendix E).

Critical race theory (CRT) focuses theoretical attention on race and how racism is deeply embedded within the framework of American society (Parker & Lynn, 2002). Racism has directly shaped the U.S. legal system and the ways people think about the law, racial categories, and privilege (Harris, 1993). According to Parker and Lynn (2002), CRT has three main goals. Its first goal is to present stories about discrimination from the perspective of people of color. These may be qualitative case studies of descriptions and interviews. These cases may then be drawn together to build cases against racially biased officials or discriminatory practices. Since many stories advance White privilege through "majoritarian" master narratives, counterstories by people of color can help to shatter the complacency that may accompany such privilege and challenge the dominant discourses that serve to suppress people on the margins of society (Solorzano & Yosso, 2002). As a second goal, CRT argues for the eradication of racial subjugation while simultaneously recognizing that race is a social construct (Parker & Lynn, 2002). In this view, *race* is not a fixed term, but one that is fluid and continually shaped by political pressures and informed by individual lived experiences. Finally, the third goal of CRT addresses other areas of difference, such as gender, class, and any inequities experienced by individuals. As Parker and Lynn (2002) comment, "In the case of Black women, race does not exist outside of gender and gender does not exist outside of race" (p. 12). In research, the use of CRT methodology means that the researcher foregrounds race and racism in all aspects of the research process; challenges the traditional research paradigms, texts, and theories used to explain the experiences of people of color; and offers transformative solutions to racial, gender, and class subordination in our societal and institutional structures.

Queer Theory

Queer theory is characterized by a variety of methods and strategies relating to individual identity (Plummer, 2011a; Watson, 2005). As a body of literature continuing to evolve, it explores the myriad complexities of the construct, identity, and how identities reproduce and "perform" in social forums. Writers also use a postmodern or poststructural orientation to critique and deconstruct dominant theories related to identity (Plummer, 2011a, 2011b; Watson, 2005). They focus on how it is culturally and historically constituted, is linked to discourse, and overlaps gender and sexuality. The term itself—*queer theory,* rather than *gay, lesbian,* or *homosexual theory*—allows for keeping open to question the elements of race, class, age, and anything else (Turner, 2000), and it is a term that has changed in meaning over the years and differs across cultures and languages (Plummer, 2011b). Most queer theorists work to challenge and undercut identity as singular, fixed, or normal (Watson, 2005). They also seek to challenge categorization processes and their deconstructions, rather than focus on specific populations. The historical binary distinctions are inadequate to describe sexual identity. Plummer (2011a) provides a concise overview of the queer theory stance:

- Both the heterosexual/homosexual binary and the sex/gender split are challenged.
- There is a decentering of identity.

- All sexual categories (lesbian, gay, bisexual, transgender, heterosexual) are open, fluid, and nonfixed.
- Mainstream homosexuality is critiqued.
- Power is embodied discursively.
- All normalizing strategies are shunned.
- Academic work may become ironic, and often comic and paradoxical.
- Versions of homosexual subject positions are inscribed everywhere.
- Deviance is abandoned, and interest lies in insider and outsider perspectives and transgressions.
- Common objects of study are films, videos, novels, poetry, and visual images.
- The most frequent interests include the social worlds of the so-called radical sexual fringe (e.g., drag kings and queens, sexual playfulness) (p. 201).

Although queer theory is less a methodology and more a focus of inquiry, queer methods often find expression in a rereading of cultural texts (e.g., films, literature); ethnographies and case studies of sexual worlds that challenge assumptions; data sources that contain multiple texts; documentaries that include performances; and projects that focus on individuals (Plummer, 2011a). Queer theorists have engaged in research and/or political activities such as the AIDS Coalition to Unleash Power (ACT UP) and Queer Nation around HIV/AIDS awareness, as well as artistic and cultural representations of art and theater aimed at disrupting or rendering unnatural and strange practices that are taken for granted. These representations convey the voices and experiences of individuals who have been suppressed (Gamson, 2000). Useful readings about queer theory are found in the journal article overview provided by Watson (2005) and the chapter by Plummer (2011a, 2011b), and in key books, such as the book by Tierney (1997).

Disability Theories

Disability inquiry addresses the meaning of inclusion in schools and encompasses administrators, teachers, and parents who have children with disabilities (Mertens, 2009, 2010). Mertens (2003) recounts how disability research has moved through stages of development, from the medical model of disability (sickness and the role of the medical community in threatening it) to an environmental response to individuals with a disability. Now, researchers using a *disability interpretive lens* focus on disability as a dimension of human difference and not as a defect. As a human difference, its meaning is derived from social construction (i.e., society's response to individuals), and it is simply one dimension of human difference (Mertens, 2003). Viewing individuals with disabilities as different is reflected in the research process, such as in the types of questions asked, the labels applied to these individuals, considerations of how the data collection will benefit the community, the appropriateness of communication methods, and how the data are reported in a way that is respectful of power relationships.

THE PRACTICE OF USING SOCIAL JUSTICE INTERPRETIVE FRAMEWORKS IN QUALITATIVE RESEARCH

The practice of using social justice interpretive frameworks in a qualitative study varies, and it depends on the framework being used and the particular researcher's approach. However, some common elements can be identified:

● The problems and the research questions explored aim to allow the researcher an understanding of specific issues or topics—the conditions that serve to disadvantage and exclude individuals or cultures, such as hierarchy, hegemony, racism, sexism, unequal power relations, identity, or inequities in our society.

● The procedures of research, such as data collection, data analysis, representing the material to audiences, and standards of evaluation and ethics, emphasize an interpretive stance. During data collection, the researcher does not further marginalize the participants, but respects the participants and the sites for research. Further, researchers provide reciprocity by giving or paying back those who participate in research, and they focus on the multiple-perspective stories of individuals and who tells the stories. Researchers are also sensitive to power imbalances during all facets of the research process. They respect individual differences rather than employing the traditional aggregation of categories such as men and women, or Hispanics or African Americans.

● Ethical practices of the researchers recognize the importance of the subjectivity of their own lens, acknowledge the powerful position they have in the research, and admit that the participants or the co-construction of the account between the researchers and the participants are the true owners of the information collected.

- The research may be presented in traditional ways, such as journal articles, or in experimental approaches, such as theater or poetry. Using an interpretive lens may also lead to the call for action and transformation—the aims of social justice—in which the qualitative project ends with distinct steps of reform and an incitement to action.

LINKING PHILOSOPHY AND INTERPRETIVE FRAMEWORKS

Although the philosophical assumptions are not always stated, the interpretive frameworks do convey different philosophical assumptions, and qualitative researchers need to be aware of this connection. A thoughtful chapter by Lincoln et al. (2011) makes this connection explicit. I have taken their overview of this connection and adapted it to fit the interpretive communities discussed in this chapter. As shown in Table 2.3, the philosophical assumptions of ontology, epistemology, axiology, and methodology take different forms given the interpretive framework used by the inquirer.

The use of information from this table in a qualitative study would be to discuss the interpretive framework used in a project by weaving together the framework used by discussing its central tenets, how it informs the problem to a study, the research questions, the data collection and analysis, and the interpretation. A section of this discussion would also mention the philosophical assumptions (ontology, epistemology, axiology, methodology) associated with the interpretive framework. Thus, there would be two ways to discuss the interpretive framework: its nature and use in the study, and its philosophical assumptions. As we proceed ahead and examine the five qualitative approaches in this book, recognize that each one might use any of the interpretive frameworks. For example, if a grounded theory study were presented as a scientific paper, with a major emphasis on objectivity, with a focus on the theoretical model that results, without reporting biases of the researcher, and with a systematic rendering of data analysis, a postpositivist interpretive framework would be used. On the other hand, if the intent of the qualitative narrative study was to examine a marginalized group of disabled learners with attention to their struggles for identity about prostheses that they wear, and with

Table 2.3 Interpretive Frameworks and Associated Philosophical Beliefs

Interpretive Frameworks	Ontological Beliefs (the nature of reality)	Epistemological Beliefs (how reality is known)	Axiological Beliefs (role of values)	Methodological Beliefs (approach to inquiry)
Postpositivism	A single reality exists beyond ourselves, "out there." Researcher may not be able to understand it or get to it because of lack of absolutes.	Reality can only be approximated. But it is constructed through research and statistics. Interaction with research subjects is kept to a minimum. Validity comes from peers, not participants.	Researcher's biases need to be controlled and not expressed in a study.	Use of scientific method and writing. Object of research is to create new knowledge. Method is important. Deductive methods are important such as testing of theories, specifying important variables, making comparisons among groups.
Social constructivism	Multiple realities are constructed through our lived experiences and interactions with others.	Reality is co-constructed between the researcher and the researched and shaped by individual experiences.	Individual values are honored, and are negotiated among individuals.	More of a literary style of writing used. Use of an inductive method of emergent ideas (through consensus) obtained through methods such as interviewing, observing, and analysis of texts.
Transformative/ Postmodern	Participation between researcher and communities/ individuals being studied. Often a subjective-objective reality emerges.	Co-created findings with multiple ways of knowing.	Respect for indigenous values; values need to be problematized and interrogated.	Use of collaborative processes of research; political participation encouraged; questioning of methods highlighting issues and concerns.

Interpretive Frameworks	Ontological Beliefs (the nature of reality)	Epistemological Beliefs (how reality is known)	Axiological Beliefs (role of values)	Methodological Beliefs (approach to inquiry)
Pragmatism	Reality is what is useful, is practical, and "works."	Reality is known through using many tools of research that reflect both deductive (objective) evidence and inductive (subjective) evidence.	Values are discussed because of the way that knowledge reflects both the researchers' and the participants' views.	The research process involves both quantitative and qualitative approaches to data collection and analysis.
Critical, Race, Feminist, Queer, Disabilities	Reality is based on power and identity struggles. Privilege or oppression based on race or ethnicity, class, gender, mental abilities, sexual preference.	Reality is known through the study of social structures, freedom and oppression, power, and control. Reality can be changed through research.	Diversity of values is emphasized within the standpoint of various communities.	Start with assumptions of power and identity struggles, document them, and call for action and change.

Source: Adapted from Lincoln et al. (2011).

utmost respect for their views and values, and in the end of the study to call for changes in how the disabled group is perceived, then a strong disability interpretive framework would be in use. I could see using any of the interpretive frameworks with any of the five approaches advanced in this book.

SUMMARY

This chapter began by starting with an overview of the research process so that philosophical assumptions and interpretive frameworks could be seen as positioned at the beginning of the process and informing the procedures that follow, including the selection and use of one of the five approaches in this book. Then the philosophical assumptions of ontology, epistemology, axiology, and methodology were discussed, as were the key question being asked for each assumption, its major characteristics, and the implication for the practice of writing a qualitative study. Furthermore, the interpretive frameworks used in qualitative research were advanced. They include postpositivism, social constructivism, transformative, postmodern perspectives, pragmatism, feminist theories, critical theory, queer theory, and disability theory. How these interpretive frameworks are used in a qualitative study was suggested. Finally, a link was made between the philosophical assumptions and the interpretive frameworks, and a discussion followed about how to connect the two in a qualitative project.

ADDITIONAL READINGS

Philosophical Assumptions

Burrell, G., & Morgan, G. (1979). *Sociological paradigms and organizational analysis.* London: Heinemann.

Guba, E., & Lincoln, Y. S. (1988). Do inquiry paradigms imply inquiry methodologies? In D. M. Fetterman (Ed.), *Qualitative approaches to evaluation in education* (pp. 89–115). New York: Praeger.

Lincoln, Y. S., Lynham, S. A., & Guba, E. G. (2011). Paradigmatic controversies, contradictions, and emerging confluences. In N. K. Denzin & Y. S. Lincoln (Eds.), *The SAGE handbook of qualitative research* (4th ed., pp. 97–128). Thousand Oaks, CA: Sage.

Slife, B. D., & Williams, R. N. (1995). *What's behind the research? Discovering hidden assumptions in the behavioral sciences.* Thousand Oaks, CA: Sage.

Postmodern Thinking

Bloland, H. G. (1995). Postmodernism and higher education. *Journal of Higher Education, 66,* 521–559.

Clarke, A. E. (2005). *Situational analysis: Grounded theory after the postmodern turn.* Thousand Oaks, CA: Sage.

Rosenau, P. M. (1992). *Post-modernism and the social sciences: Insights, inroads, and intrusions.* Princeton, NJ: Princeton University Press.

Critical Theory and Critical Race Theory

Agger, B. (1991). Critical theory, poststructuralism, postmodernism: Their sociological relevance. In W. R. Scott & J. Blake (Eds.), *Annual review of sociology* (Vol. 17, pp. 105–131). Palo Alto, CA: Annual Reviews.

Carspecken, P. F., & Apple, M. (1992). Critical qualitative research: Theory, methodology, and practice. In M. L. LeCompte, W. L. Millroy, & J. Preissle (Eds.), *The handbook of qualitative research in education* (pp. 507–553). San Diego, CA: Academic Press.

Madison, D. S. (2005). *Critical ethnography: Method, ethics, and performance.* Thousand Oaks, CA: Sage.

Morrow, R. A., & Brown, D. D. (1994). *Critical theory and methodology.* Thousand Oaks, CA: Sage.

Parker, L., & Lynn, M. (2002). What race got to do with it? Critical race theory's conflicts with and connections to qualitative research methodology and epistemology. *Qualitative Inquiry, 8*(1), 7–22.

Thomas, J. (1993). *Doing critical ethnography.* Newbury Park, CA: Sage.

Feminist Research

Ferguson, M., & Wicke, J. (1994). *Feminism and postmodernism.* Durham, NC: Duke University Press.

Harding, S. (1987). *Feminism and methodology.* Bloomington: Indiana University Press.

Lather, P. (1991). *Getting smart: Feminist research and pedagogy with/in the postmodern.* New York: Routledge.

Moss, P. (2007). Emergent methods in feminist research. In S. N. Hesse-Biber (Ed.), *Handbook of feminist research methods* (pp. 371–389). Thousand Oaks, CA: Sage.

Nielsen, J. M. (Ed.). (1990). *Feminist research methods: Exemplary readings in the social sciences.* Boulder, CO: Westview Press.

Olesen, V. (2011). Feminist qualitative research in the Millennium's first decade: Developments, challenges, prospects. In N. K. Denzin & Y. S. Lincoln (Eds.), *The SAGE handbook of qualitative research* (4th ed., pp. 129–146). Thousand Oaks, CA: Sage.

Reinharz, S. (1992). *Feminist methods in social research.* New York: Oxford University Press.

Queer Theory

Plummer, K. (2011a). Critical pedagogy, and qualitative research: Moving to the bricolage. In N. K. Denzin & Y. S. Lincoln (Eds.), *The SAGE handbook of qualitative research* (4th ed., pp. 195–207). Thousand Oaks, CA: Sage.

Plummer, K. (2011b). Critical humanism and queer theory: Postscript 2011: Living with the tensions. In N. K. Denzin & Y. S. Lincoln (Eds.), *The SAGE handbook of qualitative research* (4th ed., pp. 208–211). Thousand Oaks, CA: Sage.

Tierney, W. G. (1997). *Academic outlaws: Queer theory and cultural studies in the academy.* London: Sage.

Watson, K. (2005). Queer theory. *Group Analysis, 38*(1), 67–81.

Disability Theory

Mertens, D. M. (2003). Mixed methods and the politics of human research: The transformative-emancipatory perspective. In A. Tashakkori & C. Teddlie (Eds.), *Handbook of mixed methods in social and behavioral research* (pp. 135–164). Thousand Oaks, CA: Sage.

Mertens, D. M. (2009). *Transformative research and evaluation.* New York: Guilford Press.

EXERCISES

1. Examine a qualitative journal article, such as the qualitative study by:

Brown, J., Sorrell, J. H., McClaren, J., & Creswell, J. W. (2006). Waiting for a liver transplant. *Qualitative Health Research, 16*(1), 119–136.

There are four major philosophical assumptions used in qualitative research: ontology (what is reality?), epistemology (how is reality known?), axiology (how are values of the research expressed?), and methodology (how is the research conducted?). Look closely at the Brown et al. (2006) article and identify specific ways in which these four philosophical assumptions are evident in the study. Give specific examples using Table 2.1 in this chapter as a guide.

Exercises

2. It is helpful to read qualitative articles that adopt a different interpretive lens. Examine the following articles that work from different interpretivist frameworks:

A postpostivist framework:

Churchill, S. L., Plano Clark, V. L., Prochaska-Cue, M. K., Creswell, J. W., & Onta-Grzebik, L. (2007). How rural low-income families have fun: A grounded theory study. *Journal of Leisure Research, 39*(2), 271–294.

A social constructivist framework:

Brown, J., Sorrell, J. H., McClaren, J., & Creswell, J. W. (2006). Waiting for a liver transplant. *Qualitative Health Research, 16*(1), 119–136.

A feminist framework:

Therberge, N. (1997). "It's part of the game": Physicality and the production of gender in women's hockey. *Gender & Society, 11*(1), 69–87.

Identify how these three articles differ in their interpretive frameworks.

3. Examine the Therberge (1997) feminist qualitative research article. Identify where the following elements of a feminist interpretive framework are found in the study: the feminist issue(s), the directional question, the advocacy orientation of the aim of the study, the methods of data collection, and the call for action.

3

Designing a
Qualitative Study

I think metaphorically of qualitative research as an intricate fabric composed of minute threads, many colors, different textures, and various blends of material. This fabric is not explained easily or simply. Like the loom on which fabric is woven, general assumptions and interpretive frameworks hold qualitative research together. To describe these frameworks, qualitative researchers use terms—*constructivist, interpretivist, feminist, postmodernist,* and so forth. Within these assumptions and through these frameworks are approaches to qualitative inquiry, such as narrative research, phenomenology, grounded theory, ethnography, and case studies. This field has many different individuals with different perspectives who are on their own looms creating the fabric of qualitative research. Aside from these differences, the creative artists have the common task of making a fabric. In other words, there are characteristics common to all forms of qualitative research, and the different characteristics will receive different emphases depending on the qualitative project. Not all characteristics are present in all qualitative projects, but many are.

The intent of this chapter is to provide an overview of and introduction to qualitative research so that we can see the common characteristics of qualitative research before we explore the different threads of it (through specific approaches such as narrative, phenomenology, and others). I begin with a general definition of qualitative research and highlight the essential characteristics of conducting this form of inquiry. I then discuss the types of research problems and issues best suited for a qualitative study and emphasize the requirements needed to conduct this rigorous, time-consuming research. Given that you have the essentials (the problem, the time) to engage in this inquiry, I then sketch out the overall process involved in designing and planning a study. This process entails preliminary considerations, steps in the process, and overall considerations used throughout the process. Within these aspects, qualitative researchers need to anticipate and plan for potential ethical issues. These issues arise during many phases of the research process. I end by suggesting several outlines that you might consider as the overall structure for planning or proposing a qualitative research study. The chapters to follow will then address the different types of inquiry approaches. The general design features, outlined here, will be refined for the five approaches discussed in the remainder of the book.

QUESTIONS FOR DISCUSSION

- What are the key characteristics of qualitative research?
- What types of problems are best suited for qualitative inquiry?
- What research skills are required to undertake this type of research?
- How do researchers design a qualitative study?
- What types of ethical issues need to be anticipated during the process of research?
- What is a model structure for a plan or proposal for a qualitative study?

THE CHARACTERISTICS OF QUALITATIVE RESEARCH

I typically begin talking about qualitative research by posing a definition for it. This seemingly uncomplicated approach has become more difficult in recent years. I note that some extremely useful introductory books to qualitative research these days do not contain a definition that can be easily located (Morse & Richards, 2002; Weis & Fine, 2000). Perhaps this has less to do with the authors' decision to convey the nature of this inquiry and more to do with a concern about advancing a "fixed" definition. Other authors advance a definition. The evolving definition by Denzin and Lincoln (1994, 2000, 2005, 2011) in their SAGE *Handbook of Qualitative Research* conveys the ever-changing nature of qualitative inquiry from social construction, to interpretivism, and on to social justice in the world. I include their latest definition here:

Qualitative research is a situated activity that locates the observer in the world. Qualitative research consists of a set of interpretive, material practices that make the world visible. These practices transform the world. They turn the world into a series of representations, including field notes, interviews, conversations, photographs, record-ings, and memos to the self. At this level, qualitative research involves an interpretive, naturalistic approach to the world. This means that qualitative researchers study things in their natural settings, attempt-ing to make sense of, or interpret, phenomena in terms of the mean-ings people bring to them. (Denzin & Lincoln, 2011, p. 3)

Although some of the traditional approaches to qualitative research, such as the "interpretive, naturalistic approach" and "meanings," are evi-dent in this definition, the definition also has a strong orientation toward the impact of qualitative research and its ability to transform the world.

As an applied research methodologist, my working definition of qualitative research incorporates many of the Denzin and Lincoln ele-ments, but it provides greater emphasis on the design of research and the use of distinct approaches to inquiry (e.g., ethnography, narrative). My definition is as follows:

> *Qualitative research* begins with assumptions and the use of interpretive/theoretical frameworks that inform the study of research problems addressing the meaning individuals or groups ascribe to a social or human problem. To study this problem, qualitative research-ers use an emerging qualitative approach to inquiry, the collection of data in a natural setting sensitive to the people and places under study, and data analysis that is both inductive and deductive and establishes patterns or themes. The final written report or presenta-tion includes the voices of participants, the reflexivity of the researcher, a complex description and interpretation of the problem, and its contribution to the literature or a call for change.

Notice in this definition that I place emphasis on the *process* of research as flowing from philosophical assumptions, to interpretive lens, and on to the procedures involved in studying social or human problems. Then, a framework exists for the procedures—the approach to inquiry, such as grounded theory, or case study research, or others.

It is helpful to move from a more general definition to specific char-acteristics found in qualitative research. I believe that the characteristics have evolved over time, and they certainly do not present a definitive set of elements. But a close examination of the characteristics mentioned in major books in the field shows some common threads. Examine Table 3.1 for three introductory qualitative research books and the characteristics they espouse for doing a qualitative study. As compared to a similar table I designed almost 10 years ago in the first edition of this book (drawing on other authors), qualitative research today involves closer attention to the interpretive nature of inquiry and situating the study within the political, social, and cultural context of the researchers, and the reflexivity or "presence" of the researchers in the accounts they present. By examining Table 3.1, one can arrive at several common characteristics of qualitative research. These are presented in no specific order of importance.

● Natural setting. Qualitative researchers often collect data in the field at the site where participants experience the issue or problem under study. They do not bring individuals into a lab (a contrived situation), nor do they typically send out instruments for individuals to complete, such as in survey research. Instead, qualitative researchers gather up-close information by actually talking directly to people and seeing them behave and act within their context. In the natural setting, the researchers have face-to-face interaction over time.

● Researcher as key instrument. The qualitative researchers collect data themselves through examining documents, observing behavior, and interviewing participants. They may use an instrument, but it is one designed by the researcher using open-ended questions. They do not tend to use or rely on questionnaires or instruments developed by other researchers.

● Multiple methods. Qualitative researchers typically gather multiple forms of data, such as interviews, observations, and documents, rather than rely on a single data source. Then they review all of the data and make sense of it, organizing it into categories or themes that cut across all of the data sources.

● Complex reasoning through inductive and deductive logic. Qualitative researchers build their patterns, categories, and themes from the "bottom up," by organizing the data inductively into increasingly more abstract units of information. This inductive process involves researchers working back and forth between the themes and the database until they establish a comprehensive set of themes. It may also involve collaborating with the participants interactively, so that they have a chance to shape the themes or abstractions that emerge from the process. Researchers also use deductive thinking in that they build themes that are constantly being checked against the data. The inductive-deductive logic process means that the qualitative researcher uses complex reasoning skills throughout the process of research.

Table 3.1 Characteristics of Qualitative Research

Characteristics	LeCompte & Schensul (1999)	Hatch (2002)	Marshall & Rossman (2010)
Is conducted in a natural setting (the field), a source of data for close interaction	Yes	Yes	Yes
Relies on the researcher as key instrument in data collection		Yes	
Involves using multiple methods	Yes		Yes
Involves complex reasoning going between inductive and deductive	Yes	Yes	Yes
Focuses on participants' perspectives, their meanings, their multiple subjective views	Yes	Yes	
Is situated within the context or setting of participants/sites (social/political/historical)	Yes		Yes
Involves an emergent and evolving design rather than tightly prefigured design		Yes	Yes
Is reflective and interpretive (i.e., sensitive to researcher's biographies/social identities)			Yes
Presents a holistic, complex picture		Yes	Yes

● Participants' meanings. In the entire qualitative research process, the researchers keep a focus on learning the meaning that the participants hold about the problem or issue, not the meaning that the researchers bring to the research or writers from the literature. The participant meanings further suggest multiple perspectives on a topic and diverse views. This is why a theme developed in a qualitative report should reflect multiple perspectives of the participants in the study.

● Emergent design. The research process for qualitative researchers is emergent. This means that the initial plan for research cannot be tightly prescribed, and that all phases of the process may change or shift after the researchers enter the field and begin to collect data. For example, the questions may change, the forms of data collection may be altered, and the individuals studied and the sites visited may be modified during the process of conducting the study. The key idea behind qualitative research is to learn about the problem or issue from participants and engage in the best practices to obtain that information.

● Reflexivity. Researchers "position themselves" in a qualitative research study. This means that researchers convey (i.e., in a method section, in an introduction, or in other places in a study) their background (e.g., work experiences, cultural experiences, history), how it informs their interpretation of the information in a study, and what they have to gain from the study. As Wolcott (2010) said:

> Our readers have a right to know about us. And they do not want to know whether we played in the high school band. They want to know what prompts our interest in the topics we investigate, to whom we are reporting, and what we personally stand to gain from our study. (p. 36)

● Holistic account. Qualitative researchers try to develop a complex picture of the problem or issue under study. This involves reporting multiple perspectives, identifying the many factors involved in a situation, and generally sketching the larger picture that emerges. Researchers are bound not by tight cause-and-effect relationships among factors, but rather by identifying the complex interactions of factors in any situation.

WHEN TO USE QUALITATIVE RESEARCH

When is it appropriate to use qualitative research? We conduct qualitative research because a problem or issue needs to be *explored*. This exploration is needed, in turn, because of a need to study a group or population, identify variables that cannot be easily measured, or hear silenced voices. These are all good reasons to explore a problem rather than to use predetermined information from the literature or rely on results from other research studies. We also conduct qualitative research because we need a *complex,* detailed understanding of the issue. This detail can only be established by talking directly with people, going to their homes or places of work, and allowing them to tell the stories unencumbered by what we expect to find or what we have read in the literature.

We conduct qualitative research when we want to *empower individuals* to share their stories, hear their voices, and minimize the power relationships that often exist between a researcher and the participants in a study. To further de-emphasize a power relationship, we may collaborate directly with participants by having them review our research questions, or by having them collaborate with us during the data analysis and interpretation phases of research. We conduct qualitative research when we want to write in a *literary, flexible style* that conveys stories, or theater, or poems, without the restrictions of formal academic structures of writing. We conduct qualitative research because we want to understand the *contexts* or settings in which participants in a study address a problem or issue. We cannot always separate what people say from the place where they say it—whether this context is their home, family, or work. We use qualitative research to follow up quantitative research and help *explain the mechanisms* or linkages in causal theories or models. These theories provide a general picture of trends, associations, and relationships, but they do not tell us about the processes that people experience, why they responded as they did, the context in which they responded, and their deeper thoughts and behaviors that governed their responses.

We use qualitative research to *develop theories* when partial or inadequate theories exist for certain populations and samples or existing theories do not adequately capture the complexity of the problem we are examining. We also use qualitative research because quantitative measures and the statistical analyses simply do not *fit the problem.* Interactions among people, for example, are difficult to capture with existing measures, and these measures may not be sensitive to issues such as gender differences, race, economic status, and individual differences. To level all individuals to a statistical mean overlooks the uniqueness of individuals in our studies. Qualitative approaches are simply a better fit for our research problem.

WHAT A QUALITATIVE STUDY REQUIRES FROM US

What does it take to engage in this form of research? To undertake qualitative research requires a strong commitment to study a problem and its demands of time and resources. Qualitative research keeps good company with the most rigorous quantitative approaches, and it should not be viewed as an easy substitute for a "statistical" or quantitative study. Qualitative inquiry is for the researcher who is willing to do the following:

- Commit to extensive time in the field. The investigator spends many hours in the field, collects extensive data, and labors over field issues of trying to gain access, rapport, and an "insider" perspective.
- Engage in the complex, time-consuming process of data analysis through the ambitious task of sorting through large amounts of data and reducing them to a few themes or categories. For a multi-disciplinary team of qualitative researchers, this task can be shared; for most researchers, it is a lonely, isolated time of struggling and pondering the data. The task is challenging, especially because the database consists of complex texts and images.
- Write long passages, because the evidence must substantiate claims and the writer needs to show multiple perspectives. The incorporation of quotes to provide participants' perspectives also lengthens the study.
- Participate in a form of social and human science research that does not have firm guidelines or specific procedures and is evolving and constantly changing. These guidelines complicate telling others how one plans a study and how others might judge it when the study is completed.

THE PROCESS OF DESIGNING A QUALITATIVE STUDY

There is no agreed upon structure for how to design a qualitative study. Books on qualitative research vary in their suggestions for design. You may recall from the introduction that *research design* means the plan for conducting the study. Some authors believe that by reading a study, discussing the procedures, and pointing out issues that emerge, the aspiring qualitative researcher will have a sense of how to conduct this form of inquiry (see Weis & Fine, 2000). That may be true for some individuals. For others, understanding the broader issues may suffice to help design a study (see Morse & Richards, 2002), or to seek guidance from a "how to" book (see Hatch, 2002). I am not sure whether I write exactly from a "how to" perspective; I see my approach as more in line with creating options for qualitative researchers (hence, the five approaches), weighing the options given my experiences, and then letting readers choose for themselves.

I can share, however, how I think about designing a qualitative study. It can be conveyed in three components: preliminary considerations that I think through prior to beginning a study, the steps I engage in during the conduct of the study, and the elements that flow through all phases of the process of my research.

Preliminary Considerations

There are certain design principles that I work from when I design my own qualitative research studies. I find that qualitative research generally falls within the process of the scientific method, with common phases whether one is writing qualitatively or quantitatively. The scientific method can be described as including the problem, the hypotheses (or questions), the data collection, the results, and the discussion. All researchers seem to start with an issue or problem, examine the literature in some way related to the problem, pose questions, gather data and then analyze them, and write up their reports. Qualitative research fits within this structure, and I have accordingly organized the chapters in this book to reflect this process. I like the concept of *methodological congruence* advanced by Morse and Richards (2002)—that the purposes, questions, and methods of research are all interconnected and interrelated so that the study appears as a cohesive whole rather than as fragmented, isolated parts. When engaging in the design of a qualitative study, I believe that the inquirer tends to follow these interconnected parts of the research process.

Several aspects of a qualitative project vary from study to study, and I am making preliminary decisions about what will be emphasized. For example, stances on the use of the literature vary widely, as does the emphasis on using an a priori theory. The literature may be fully reviewed and used to inform the questions actually asked, it may be reviewed late in the process of research, or it may be used solely to help document the importance of the research problem. Other options may also exist, but these possibilities point to the varied uses of literature in qualitative research. Similarly, the use of theory varies in qualitative research. For example, cultural theories form the basic building blocks of a good qualitative ethnography (LeCompte & Schensul, 1999), whereas in grounded theory, the theories are developed or generated during the process of research (Strauss & Corbin, 1990). In health science research, I find the use of a priori theories common practice, and a key element that must be included in rigorous qualitative investigations (Barbour, 2000). Another consideration in qualitative research is the writing format for the qualitative project. It varies considerably from scientific-oriented approaches, to literary storytelling, and on to performances, such as theater, plays, or poems. There is no one standard or accepted structure as one typically finds in quantitative research.

Finally, I also consider my own background and interests and what I bring to research. Researchers have a personal history that situates them as inquirers. They also have an orientation to research and a sense of personal ethics and political stances that inform their research. Denzin and Lincoln (2011) refer to the researchers as a "multicultural subject" (p. 12) and view the history, traditions, and conceptions of self, ethics, and politics as a starting point for inquiry.

Steps in the Process

With these preliminary considerations in place, I begin by acknowledging the broad *assumptions* that bring me to qualitative inquiry, and the *interpretive* lens that I will use. In addition, I bring a *topic* or a substantive area of investigation, and have reviewed the *literature* about the topic and can confidently say that a problem or issue exists that needs to be studied. This problem may be one in the "real world," or it may be a deficiency or gap in the literature or past investigations on a topic, or both. Problems in qualitative research span the topics in the social and human sciences, and a hallmark of qualitative research today is the deep involvement in issues of gender, culture, and marginalized groups. The topics about which we write are emotion laden, close to people, and practical.

To study these topics, I will ask *open-ended research questions,* wanting to listen to the participants I am studying and shape the questions after I "explore" by talking with a few individuals. I refrain from assuming the role of the expert researcher with the "best" questions. My questions will change and become more refined during the process of research to reflect an increased understanding of the problem. Furthermore, I will collect a *variety of sources of data* including information in the form of "words" or "images." I like to think in terms of four basic sources of qualitative information: interviews, observations, documents, and audio-visual materials. Certainly, new sources emerge that challenge this traditional categorization. Where do we place sounds, e-mail messages, and social networking? Unquestionably, the backbone of qualitative research is extensive collection of data, typically from multiple sources of information. Further, I collect data using these sources based on open-ended questions without much structure and by observing and collecting documents (and visual materials) without an agenda of what I hope to find. After organizing and storing my data, I *analyze* them by carefully masking the names of respondents, and I engage in the perplexing (and "lonely" if we are the sole researcher) exercise of trying to make sense of the data. I *analyze* the qualitative data working inductively from particulars to more general perspectives, whether these perspectives are called codes, categories, themes, or dimensions. I then work deductively to gather evidence to support the themes and the interpretations. One helpful way to see this process is to recognize it as working through multiple levels of abstraction, starting with the raw data and forming broader and broader categories. Recognizing the highly interrelated set of activities of data collection, analysis, and report writing, I intermingle these stages and find myself collecting data, analyzing another set of data, and beginning to write my report. I remember working on a qualitative case study (see Appendix F, Asmussen & Creswell, 1995) as interviewing, analyzing, and writing the case study—all interconnected processes, not distinct phases in the process. Also, as I write, I experiment with many *forms of narrative,* such as making metaphors and analogies, developing matrices and tables, and using visuals to convey simultaneously breaking down the data and reconfiguring them into new forms. I might layer my analysis into increasing levels of abstractions from codes, to themes, to the interrelationship of themes, to larger conceptual models. I will *(re)present* these data, partly based on participants' perspectives and partly based on my own interpretation, never clearly escaping a personal stamp on a study. In the end, I *discuss* the findings by comparing my findings with my personal views, with extant literature, and with emerging models that seem to adequately convey the essence of the findings.

At some point I ask, "Did we (I) get the story 'right'?" (Stake, 1995), knowing that there are no "right" stories, only multiple stories. Perhaps qualitative studies have no endings, only questions (Wolcott, 1994b). I also seek to have my account resonate with the participants, to be an accurate reflection of what they said. So I engage in *validation* strategies, often multiple strategies, which include confirming or triangulating data from several sources, having my study reviewed and corrected by the participants, and employing other researchers to review my procedures.

In the end, individuals such as readers, participants, graduate committees, editorial board members for journals, and reviewers of proposals for funding will apply some criteria to assess the quality of my study. Standards for assessing the quality of qualitative research are available (Howe & Eisenhardt, 1990; Lincoln, 1995; Marshall & Rossman, 2010). Here is my short list of *characteristics of a "good" qualitative study.* You will see my emphasis on rigorous methods present in this list.

● The researcher employs rigorous data collection procedures. This means that the researcher collects multiple forms of data, adequately summarizes—perhaps in tabled form—the forms of data and detail about them, and spends adequate time in the field. It is not unusual for qualitative studies to include information about the specific amount of time in the field (e.g., 25 hours observing). I especially like to see unusual forms of qualitative data collection, such as using photographs to elicit responses, sounds, visual materials, or digital text messages.

● The researcher frames the study within the assumptions and characteristics of the qualitative approach to research. This includes fundamental characteristics such as an evolving design, the presentation of multiple realities, the researcher as an instrument of data collection, and a focus on participants' views—in short, all of the characteristics mentioned in Table 3.1.

● The researcher uses an approach to qualitative inquiry such as one of the five approaches (or others) addressed in this book. Use of a recognized approach to research enhances the rigor and sophistication of the research design. It also provides some means to evaluate the qualitative study. Use of an approach means that the researcher identifies and defines the approach, cites studies that employ it, and follows the procedures outlined in the approach. Certainly, the approach taken in the study may not exhaustively cover all of the elements of the approach. However, for the beginning student of qualitative research, I would recommend staying within one approach, becoming comfortable with it, learning it, and keeping a study concise and straightforward. Later, especially in long and complex studies, features from several approaches may be useful.

● The researcher begins with a single focus or concept being explored. Although examples of qualitative research show a comparison of groups or of factors or themes, as in case study projects or in ethnographies, I like to begin a qualitative study focused on understanding a single concept or idea (e.g., What does it mean to be a professional? A teacher? A painter? A single mother? A homeless person?). As the study progresses, it can begin incorporating the comparison (e.g., How does the case of a professional teacher differ from that of a professional administrator?) or relating factors (e.g., What explains why painting evokes feelings?) All too often qualitative researchers advance to the comparison or the relationship analysis without first understanding their core concept or idea.

● The study includes detailed methods, a rigorous approach to data collection, data analysis, and report writing. Rigor is seen, for example, when extensive data collection in the field occurs, or when the researcher conducts multiple levels of data analysis, from the narrow codes or themes to broader interrelated themes to more abstract dimensions. Rigor means, too, that the researcher validates the accuracy of the account using one or more of the procedures for validation, such as member checking, triangulating sources of data, or using a peer or external auditor of the account.

● The researcher analyzes data using multiple levels of abstraction. I like to see the active work of the researcher as he or she moves from particulars to general levels of abstraction. Often, writers present their studies in stages (e.g., the multiple themes that can be combined into larger themes or perspectives) or layer their analysis from the particular to the general. The codes and themes derived from the data might show mundane, expected, and surprising ideas. Often the best qualitative studies present themes analyzed in terms of exploring the shadow side or unusual angles. I remember in one class project, the student examined how students in a distance learning class reacted to the camera focused on the class. Rather than looking at the students' reaction when the camera was on them, the researcher sought to understand what happened when the camera was *off* them. This approach led to the author taking an unusual angle, one not expected by the readers.

● The researcher writes persuasively so that the reader experiences "being there." The concept of ***verisimilitude***, a literary term, captures my thinking (Richardson, 1994, p. 521). The writing is clear, engaging, and full of unexpected ideas. The story and findings become believable and realistic, accurately reflecting all the complexities that exist in real life. The best qualitative studies engage the reader.

● The study reflects the history, culture, and personal experiences of the researcher. This is more than simply an ***autobiography***, with the writer or the researcher telling about his or her background. It focuses on how individuals' culture, gender, history, and experiences shape all aspects of the qualitative project, from their choice of a question to address, to how they collect data, to how they make an interpretation of the situation, and to what they expect to obtain from conducting the research. In some way—such as discussing their role, interweaving themselves into the text, or reflecting on the questions they have about the study—individuals position themselves in the qualitative study.

● The qualitative research in a good study is ethical. This involves more than simply the researcher seeking and obtaining the permission of institutional review committees or boards. It means that the researcher is aware of and addresses in the study all of the ethical issues mentioned earlier in this chapter that thread through all phases of the research study.

Elements in All Phases of the Research

Throughout the slow process of collecting data and analyzing them, I shape the narrative—a narrative that assumes different forms from project to project. I will tell a story that unfolds over time. I will present the study following the traditional approach to scientific research (i.e., problem, question, method, findings). Throughout these different forms, I find it important to talk about my background and experiences, and how they have shaped my interpretation of the findings. I let the voices of participants speak and carry the story through dialogue, perhaps dialogue presented in Spanish with English subtitles.

Throughout all phases of the research process I try to be sensitive to *ethical* considerations. These are especially important as I negotiate entry to the field site of the research; involve participants in the study; gather personal, emotional data that reveal the details of life; and ask participants to give considerable time to the projects. Hatch (2002) does a good job of summarizing some of the major ethical issues that researchers need to anticipate and often address in their studies. Giving back to participants for their time and efforts in our projects—*reciprocity*—is important, and we need to review how participants will gain from our studies. How to leave the scene of a research study—through slow withdrawal and conveying information about our departure—so that the participants do not feel abandoned is also important. We always need to be sensitive to the potential of our research to disturb the site and potentially (and often unintentionally) exploit the vulnerable populations we study, such as young children or underrepresented or marginalized groups. Along with this comes a need to be sensitive to any power imbalances our presence may establish at a site that could further marginalize the people under study. We do not want to place the participants at further risk as a result of our research. We need to anticipate how to address potential illegal activities that we see or hear, and, in some cases, report them to authorities. We need to honor who owns the account, and whether participants and leaders at our research sites will be concerned about this issue. As we work with individual participants, we need to respect them individually, such as by not stereotyping them, using their language and names, and following guidelines such as those found in the *Publication Manual of the American Psychological Association* (APA, 2010) for nondiscriminatory language. Most often our research is done within the context of a college or university setting where we need to provide evidence to institutional review boards or committees that we respect the privacy and right of participants to withdraw from the study and do not place them at risk.

Ethical Issues During All Phases of the Research Process

During the process of planning and designing a qualitative study, researchers need to consider what ethical issues might surface during the study and to plan how these issues need to be addressed. A common misconception is that these issues only surface during data collection. They arise, however, during several phases of the research process, and they are ever expanding in scope as inquirers become more sensitive to the needs of participants, sites, stakeholders, and publishers of research. One way to examine these issues is to consider the catalogue of possibilities such as provided by Weis and Fine (2000). They ask us to consider ethical considerations involving our roles as insiders/outsiders to the participants; assessing issues that we may be fearful of disclosing; establishing supportive, respectful relationships without stereotyping and using labels that participants do not embrace; acknowledging whose voices will be represented in our final study; and writing ourselves into the study by reflecting on who we are and the people we study. In addition, as summarized by Hatch (2002), we need to be sensitive to vulnerable populations, imbalanced power relations, and placing participants at risk.

My preferred approach in thinking about ethical issues in qualitative research is to examine them as they apply to different phases of the research process. Important recent books provide useful insight into how they array by phases, such as found in writings by Lincoln (2009), Mertens and Ginsberg (2009), and the APA (2010), as well as in my own writings (Creswell, 2012). As shown in Table 3.2, ethical issues in qualitative research can be described as occurring prior to conducting the study, at the beginning of the study, during data collection, in data analysis, in reporting the data, and in publishing a study. In this Table I also present some possible solutions to the ethical issues so that these can be actively written into a research design or plan.

Prior to conducting a study it is necessary to gather college or university approval from the institutional review board for the data collection involved in the study. Equally important is to examine standards for ethical conduct of research available from professional organizations, such as the American Historical Association, the American Sociological Association, the International Communication Association, the American Evaluation Association, the Canadian Evaluation Society, the Australasian Evaluation Society, and the American Educational Research Association (Lincoln, 2009). Local permissions to gather data from individuals and sites also need to be obtained at an early stage in the research, and interested parties and gatekeepers can assist in their endeavor. Sites should not be chosen that have a vested interest in the outcomes of the study. Also, at this early stage, authorship should be negotiated among researchers involved in the qualitative study, if more than one individual undertakes the research. The APA (2010) has useful guidelines for negotiating authorship and how it might be accomplished.

Beginning the study involves initial contact with the site and with individuals. It is important to disclose the purpose of the study to the participants. This is often stated on an informed consent form completed for college/university institutional review board purposes. This form should indicate that participating in the study is voluntary and that it would not place the participants at undue risk. Special provisions are needed (e.g., child and parent consent forms) for sensitive populations. Further, at this stage, the researcher needs to anticipate any cultural, religious, gender, or other differences in the participants and the sites that need to be respected. Recent qualitative writings have made us aware of this respect, especially for indigenous populations (LaFrance & Crazy Bull, 2009).

For example, as American Indian tribes take over the delivery of services to their members, they have reclaimed their right to determine what research will be done and how it will be reported in a sensitive way to tribal cultures and charters.

We have also become more sensitive to potential issues that may arise in collecting data, especially through interviews and observations. Researchers need to seek permission to conduct research on-site and convey to gatekeepers or individuals in authority how their research will provide the least disruption

Table 3.2 Ethical Issues in Qualitative Research

Where in the Process of Research the Ethical Issue Occurs	*Type of Ethical Issue*	*How to Address the Issue*
Prior to conducting the study	• Seek college/university approval on campus • Examine professional association standards • Gain local permission from site and participants • Select a site without a vested interest in outcome of study • Negotiate authorship for publication	• Submit for institutional review board approval • Consult types of ethical standards that are needed in professional areas • Identify and go through local approvals; find gatekeeper to help • Select site that will not raise power issues with researchers • Give credit for work done on project; decide on author order
Beginning to conduct the study	• Disclose purpose of the study • Do not pressure participants into signing consent forms • Respect norms and charters of indigenous societies • Be sensitive to needs of vulnerable populations (e.g., children)	• Contact participants and inform them of general purpose of study • Tell participants that they do not have to sign form • Find out about cultural, religious gender, and other differences that need to be respected • Obtain appropriate consent (e.g., parents, as well as children)
Collecting data	• Respect the site and disrupt as little as possible • Avoid deceiving participants • Respect potential power imbalances and exploitation of participants (e.g., interviewing, observing) • Do not "use" participants by gathering data and leaving site without giving back	• Build trust, convey extent of anticipated disruption in gaining access • Discuss purpose of the study and how data will be used • Avoid leading questions; withhold sharing personal impressions; avoid disclosing sensitive information • Provide rewards for participating

Where in the Process of Research the Ethical Issue Occurs	Type of Ethical Issue	How to Address the Issue
Analyzing data	• Avoid siding with participants (going native) • Avoid disclosing only positive results • Respect the privacy of participants	• Report multiple perspectives; report contrary findings • Assign fictitious names or aliases; develop composite profiles
Reporting data	• Falsifying authorship, evidence, data, findings, conclusions • Do not plagiarize • Avoid disclosing information that would harm participants • Communicate in clear, straightforward, appropriate language	• Report honestly • See APA (2010) guidelines for permissions needed to reprint or adapt work of others • Use composite stories so that individuals cannot be identified • Use language appropriate for audiences of the research
Publishing study	• Share data with others • Do not duplicate or piecemeal publications • Complete proof of compliance with ethical issues and lack of conflict of interest, if requested	• Provide copies of report to participants and stakeholders; share practical results; consider website distribution; consider publishing in different languages • Refrain from using the same material for more than one publication • Disclose funders for research; disclose who will profit from the research

Sources: Adapted from APA, 2010; Creswell, 2012; Lincoln, 2009; Mertens & Ginsberg, 2009.

to the activities at the site. The participants should not be deceived about the nature of the research, and, in the process of providing data (e.g., through interviews, documents, and so forth), should be appraised on the general nature of the inquiry. We are more sensitive today about the nature of the interview process, and how it creates a power imbalance through a hierarchical relationship often established between the researcher and the participant. This potential power imbalance needs to be respected, and building trust and avoiding leading questions help to remove some of this imbalance. Also, the simple act of collecting data may contribute to "using" the participants and the site for the personal gain of the researcher, and strategies such as reward might be used to create reciprocity with participants and sites.

In analyzing the data, certain ethical issues also surface. Because qualitative inquirers often spend considerable time at research sites, they may lose track of the need to present multiple perspectives and a complex picture of the central phenomenon. They may actually side with the participants on issues, and only disclose positive results that create a Pollyanna portrait of the issues. This "going native" may occur during the data collection process, and reporting multiple perspectives needs to be kept in mind for the final report. Also, the research results may unwittingly present a harmful picture of the participants or the site, and qualitative researchers need to be mindful of protecting the participants' privacy through masking names and developing composite profiles or cases.

In recent APA standards on ethics (2010), discussions report on authorship and the proper disclosure of information. For example, honesty—and how authors should not falsify authorship, the evidence provided in a report, the actual data, the findings, and the conclusions of a study—is stressed. Further, plagiarism should be avoided by knowing about the types of permissions needed to cite the works by others in a study. Reports should also not disclose information that will potentially harm participants in the present or in the future. The form of report writing should communicate in clear, appropriate language for the intended audiences of the report.

Another area of emerging interest in the APA standards on ethics (2010) resides in the publication of a study. It is important to share information from a research study with participants and stakeholders. This may include sharing practical information, posting information on websites, and publishing in languages that can be understood by a wide audience. There is also concern today about multiple publications from the same research sources and the piecemeal division of studies into parts and their separate publication. Also, publishers often ask authors to sign letters of compliance with ethical practices and to state that they do not have a conflict of interest in the results and publications of the studies.

THE GENERAL STRUCTURE
OF A PLAN OR PROPOSAL

Look at the diversity of final written products for qualitative research. No set format exists. But several writers suggest general topics to be included in a written plan or *proposal* for a qualitative study. I provide four examples of formats for plans or proposals for qualitative studies. In the first example, drawn from my own work (Creswell, 2009, pp. 74–75), I advance a constructionist/interpretivist form. This form (shown in Example 3.1) might be seen as a traditional approach to planning qualitative research, and it includes the standard introduction and procedures, including a passage in the procedures about the role of the researcher. It also incorporates anticipated ethical issues, pilot findings, and expected outcomes.

Example 3.1 A Qualitative Constructivist/Interpretivist Format (Creswell, 2009, pp. 74–75)

Introduction

  Statement of the problem (including literature about the problem)

  Purpose of the study

  The research questions

  Delimitations and limitations

Procedures

  Characteristics of qualitative research and philosophical assumptions/interpretive frameworks (optional)

  Qualitative research approach used

  Role of the researcher

  Data collection procedures

  Data analysis procedures

  Strategies for validating findings

Narrative structure

Anticipated ethical issues

Significance of the study

Preliminary pilot findings

Expected outcomes

Appendices: Interview questions, observational forms, timeline, and proposed budget

The second format provides for an transformative perspective (Creswell, 2009, pp. 75–76). This format (as shown in Example 3.2) makes explicit the advocacy, transformative approach to qualitative research by stating the advocacy issue at the beginning, by emphasizing collaboration during the data collection, and by advancing the changes advocated for the group being studied.

Example 3.2 A Qualitative Transformative Format (Creswell, 2009, pp. 75–76)

Introduction

   Statement of the problem (including literature about the problem)

   The transformative/participatory issue

   Purpose of the study

   The research questions

   Delimitations and limitations

Procedures

   Characteristics of qualitative research and philosophical assumptions (optional)

   Qualitative research approach

   Role of the researcher

   Data collection procedures (including the collaborative approaches used and sensitivity toward participants)

   Data recording procedures

   Data analysis procedures

   Strategies for validating findings

Narrative structure of study

Anticipated ethical issues

Significance of the study

Preliminary pilot findings

Expected transformative changes

Appendices: Interview questions, observational forms, timeline, and proposed budget

The third format, Example 3.3, is similar to the transformative format, but it advances the use of a theoretical lens (Marshall & Rossman, 2010). Notice that this format has a section for a theoretical lens (e.g., feminist, racial, ethnic) that informs the study in the literature review, *trustworthiness* in place of what I have been calling *validation*, a section for being reflexive through personal biography, and both the ethical and political considerations of the author.

Example 3.3 A Theoretical/Interpretive Lens Format (Marshall & Rossman, 2010, p. 58)

Introduction

Overview

Topic and purpose

Significance for knowledge, practice, policy, action

Framework and general research questions

Limitations

Literature review

Theoretical traditions and current thoughts for framing the question

Review and critique of related empirical research

Essays and opinions of experts

Design and methodology

Overall approach and rationale

Site or population selection and sampling strategies

Access, role, reciprocity, trust, rapport

Personal biography

Ethical and political considerations

Data collection methods

Data analysis procedures

Procedures to address trustworthiness and credibility

Appendices (entry letters, data collection and management details, sampling strategies, timelines, budget, notes from pilot studies)

In the fourth and final format, Example 3.4, Maxwell (2005) organizes the structure around a series of nine arguments that he feels need to cohere and be coherent when researchers design their qualitative proposals. I think that these nine arguments represent the most important points to include in a proposal, and Maxwell provides in his book a complete example of a qualitative dissertation proposal written by Martha G. Regan-Smith at the Harvard Graduate School of Education. My summary and adaptation of these arguments follow.

Example 3.4   Maxwell's Nine Arguments for a Qualitative Proposal (2005)

1. We need to better understand . . . (the topic)

2. We know little about . . . (the topic)

3. I propose to study . . . (purpose)

4. The setting and participants are appropriate for this study . . . (data collection)

5. The methods I plan to use will provide the data I need to answer the research questions . . . (data collection)

6. Analysis will generate answers to these questions . . . (analysis)

7. The findings will be validated by . . . (validation)

8. The study poses no serious ethical problems . . . (ethics)

9. Preliminary results support the practicability and value of the study . . . (pilot project)

These four examples speak only to designing a plan or proposal for a qualitative study. In addition to the topics of these proposal formats, the complete study will include additional data findings, interpretations, and a discussion of the overall results, limitations of the study, and future research needs.

SUMMARY

The definitions for qualitative research vary, but I see it as an approach to inquiry that begins with assumptions, an interpretive/theoretical lens, and the study of research problems exploring the meaning individuals or groups ascribe to a social or human problem. Researchers collect data in natural settings with a sensitivity to the people under study, and they analyze their data both inductively and deductively to establish patterns or themes. The final report provides for the voices of participants, a reflexivity of the researchers, a complex description and interpretation of the problem, and a study that adds to the literature or provides a call for action. Recent introductory textbooks underscore the characteristics embedded in this definition. Given this definition, a qualitative approach is appropriate to use to study a research problem when the problem needs to be explored; when a complex, detailed understanding is needed; when the researcher wants to write in a literary, flexible style; and when the researcher seeks to understand the context or settings of participants. Qualitative research does take time, involves ambitious data collection and analysis, results in lengthy reports, and does not have firm guidelines.

The process of designing a qualitative study emerges during inquiry, but it generally follows the pattern of scientific research. It starts with broad assumptions central to qualitative inquiry, and an interpretive/theoretical lens and a topic of inquiry. After stating a research problem or issue about this topic, the inquirer asks several open-ended research questions, gathers multiple forms of data to answer these questions, and makes sense of the data by grouping information into codes, themes or categories, and larger dimensions. The final narrative the researcher composes will have diverse formats—from a scientific type of study to narrative stories. Several aspects will make the study a good qualitative project: rigorous data collection and analysis; the use of a qualitative approach (e.g., narrative, phenomenology, grounded theory, ethnography, case study); a single focus; a persuasive account; a reflection on the researcher's own history, culture, personal experiences, and politics; and ethical practices.

Ethical issues need to be anticipated and planned for in designing a qualitative study. These issues arise in many phases of the research process. They develop prior to conducting the study when researchers seek approval for the inquiry. They arise at the beginning of the study when the researchers first contact the participants, gain consent to participate in the study, and acknowledge the customs, culture, and charters of the research site. The ethical issues especially arise during data collection with respect for the site and the participants, and gathering data in ways that will not create power imbalances and "use" the participants. They also come during the data analysis phase when researchers do not side with participants, shape findings in a particular direction, and respect the privacy of individuals as their information is reported. In the reporting phase of research, inquirers need to be honest, not plagiarize the work of others; refrain from presenting information that potentially harms participants; and communicate in a useful, clear way to stakeholders. In publishing research studies, inquirers need to openly share data with others, avoid duplicating their studies, and comply with procedures asked by publishers.

Finally, the structure of a plan or proposal for a qualitative study will vary. I include four models that differ in terms of their transformative and theoretical orientation, inclusion of personal and political considerations, and focus on the essential arguments that researchers need to address in proposals.

ADDITIONAL READINGS

American Psychological Association. (2010). *Publication manual of the American Psychological Association* (6th ed.). Washington, DC: Author.

Creswell, J. W. (2009). *Research design: Qualitative, quantitative, and mixed methods approaches* (3rd ed.). Thousand Oaks, CA: Sage.

Creswell, J. W. (2011). *Educational research: Planning, conducting, and evaluating quantitative and qualitative research* (4th ed.). Upper Saddle River, NJ: Pearson Education.

Hatch, J. A. (2002). *Doing qualitative research in education settings.* Albany: State University of New York Press.

LeCompte, M. D., & Schensul, J. J. (1999). *Designing and conducting ethnographic research* (Ethnographer's toolkit, Vol. 1). Walnut Creek, CA: AltaMira.

Lincoln, Y. S. (2009). Ethical practices in qualitative research. In D. M. Mertens & P. E. Ginsberg (Eds.), *The handbook of social research ethics* (pp. 150–169). Los Angeles: Sage.

Marshall, C., & Rossman, G. B. (2010). *Designing qualitative research* (5th ed.). Thousand Oaks, CA: Sage.

Maxwell, J. (2005). *Qualitative research design: An interactive approach* (2nd ed.). Thousand Oaks, CA: Sage.

Mertens, D. M., & Ginsberg, P. E. (2009). *The handbook of social research ethics.* Los Angeles: Sage.

Morse, J. M., & Richards, L. (2002). *README FIRST for a user's guide to qualitative methods* (2nd ed.). Thousand Oaks, CA: Sage.

Weis, L., & Fine, M. (2000). *Speed bumps: A study-friendly guide to qualitative research.* New York: Teachers College Press.

EXERCISES

1. It is important to be able to "see" how authors incorporate the characteristics of qualitative research into their published studies. Select one of the qualitative articles presented in Appendices B–F. Discuss each of the major characteristics advanced in this chapter as they have been applied in the journal article. Note which characteristics are "easy" and which are "more difficult" to identify. The characteristics mentioned earlier are the following:

- The researcher conducts the study in the field in a natural setting.
- The researcher does not use someone else's instrument but gathers data on his or her own instrument.
- The researcher collects multiple types of data.
- The researcher uses both inductive and deductive reasoning in making sense of the data.
- The researcher reports the perspectives of the participants and their multiple meanings.
- The researcher reports the setting or context in which the problem is being studied.
- The researcher allows the design or procedures of the study to emerge.
- The researcher discusses his or her background and how it shapes the interpretation of the findings.
- The researcher reports a complex picture of the phenomenon being studied.

2. Consider how to address an ethical issue. From Table 3.2, choose one of the ethical issues that arise during the process of research. Invent a dilemma that might happen in your own research and then present how you might anticipate resolving it in the design of your study.

3. Before designing your own study, it is helpful to think about the way that qualitative studies are structured. One way to begin thinking about the structure of qualitative studies is to sketch out the flow of activities that authors used in their published studies. To this end, I would like you to select one of the articles (a different one than you used to answer Exercise 1) in Appendices B–F. I would like you to draw a picture of the flow of the larger ideas using boxes or circles and arrows to indicate the sequence of the ideas. For example, one study may start with a discussion

about the "problem" and then move on to a "theoretical model" and then on to the "purpose," and so forth. By engaging in this activity, you will have a general structure for how you might organize and present the topics in your own study.

4. Overall, any project undertaken by a qualitative researcher needs to be an insightful study that someone would like to read. Here are some design elements that would make your study attractive to a reader:

- Study an unusual group of people.
- Take an angle or perspective that may not be expected. It might well be the reverse side (the shadow side) of what *is* expected.
- Study an unusual group of people or an unusual location.
- Collect data that are not typically expected in social science research (e.g., collect sounds, have participants take pictures).
- Present findings in an unusual way, such as through the creation of analogies (see Wolcott, 2010) or maps or other types of figures and tables.
- Study a timely topic that many individuals are discussing and that is in the news media.

Consider which (one or more) of these aspects fit your project and discuss how they relate to your study.

4

Five Qualitative
Approaches to Inquiry

I want to present a couple of scenarios. In the first, the qualitative researcher does not identify any specific approach to qualitative research he or she is using. Perhaps the methods discussion is short and simply limited to the collection of face-to-face interviews. The findings of the study are presented as a thematic workup of major categories of information collected during the interviews. Contrast this with a second scenario. The researcher adopts a specific approach to qualitative research, such as a narrative research approach. Now the methods section is detailed describing the meaning of such an approach, why it was used, and how it would inform the procedures of the study. The findings in this study convey the specific story of an individual, and it is told chronologically, highlighting some of the tensions in the story. It is set within a specific organization. Which approach would you find to be the most scholarly? The most inviting? The most sophisticated? I think that you would opt for the second approach.

We need to identify our approach to qualitative inquiry in order to present it as a sophisticated study, to offer it as a specific type so that reviewers can properly assess it, and, for the beginning researcher, who can profit from having a writing structure to follow, to offer some way of organizing ideas that can be grounded in the scholarly literature of qualitative research. Of course, this beginning researcher could choose several qualitative approaches, such as narrative research *and* phenomenology, but I would leave this more advanced methodological approach to more experienced researchers. I often say that the beginning researcher needs to first understand one approach thoroughly, and then venture out and try another approach, before combining different ways of conducting qualitative research.

This chapter will help you begin the mastery of one of the qualitative approaches to inquiry. I take each approach, one by one, and discuss its origin, the key defining features of it, the various types of ways to use it, steps involved in conducting a study within the approach, and challenges that you will likely incur as you proceed.

QUESTIONS FOR DISCUSSION

- What is the background for each approach (narrative study, a phenomenology, a grounded theory, an ethnography, and a case study)?
- What are the central defining features of each approach?
- What various forms can a study take within each approach?
- What are the procedures for using the approach?
- What are challenges associated with each approach?
- What are some similarities and differences among the five approaches?

NARRATIVE RESEARCH

Definition and Background

Narrative research has many forms, uses a variety of analytic practices, and is rooted in different social and humanities disciplines (Daiute & Lightfoot, 2004). "Narrative" might be the *phenomenon* being studied, such as a narrative of illness, or it might be the *method* used in a study, such as the procedures of analyzing stories told (Chase, 2005; Clandinin & Connolly, 2000; Pinnegar & Daynes, 2007). As a method, it begins with the experiences as expressed in lived and told stories of individuals. Writers have provided ways for analyzing and understanding the stories lived and told. Czarniawska (2004) defines it here as a specific type of qualitative design in which "narrative is understood as a spoken or written text giving an account of an event/action or series of events/actions, chronologically connected" (p. 17). The procedures for implementing this research consist of focusing on studying one or two individuals, gathering data through the collection of their stories, reporting individual experiences, and chronologically ordering the meaning of those experiences (or using *life course stages*).

Although narrative research originated from literature, history, anthropology, sociology, sociolinguistics, and education, different fields of study have adopted their own approaches (Chase, 2005). I find a postmodern, organizational orientation in Czarniawska (2004); a human developmental perspective in Daiute and Lightfoot (2004); a psychological approach in Lieblich, Tuval-Mashiach, and Zilber (1998); sociological approaches in Cortazzi (1993) and Riessman (1993, 2008); and quantitative (e.g., statistical stories in event history modeling) and qualitative approaches in Elliott (2005). Interdisciplinary efforts at narrative research have also been encouraged by the *Narrative Study of Lives* annual series that began in 1993 (see, e.g., Josselson & Lieblich, 1993), and the journal *Narrative Inquiry.* With many recent books on narrative research, it continues to be a popular "field in the making" (Chase, 2005, p. 651). In the discussion of narrative procedures, I rely on an accessible book written for social scientists called *Narrative Inquiry* (Clandinin & Connelly, 2000) that addresses "what narrative researchers do" (p. 48). I also bring in the data collection procedures and varied analytic strategies of Riessman (2008).

Defining Features of Narrative Studies

Reading through a number of narrative articles published in journals and reviewing major books on narrative inquiry, a specific set of features emerged that define its boundaries. Not all narrative projects contain these elements, but many do, and the list is not exhaustive of possibilities.

- Narrative researchers collect *stories* from individuals (and documents, and group conversations) about individuals' lived and told experiences. These stories may emerge from a story told to the researcher, a story that is co-constructed between the researcher and the participant, and a story intended as a performance to convey some message or point (Riessman, 2008). Thus, there may be a strong *collaborative* feature of narrative research as the story emerges through the interaction or dialogue of the researcher and the participant(s).
- Narrative stories tell of individual *experiences,* and they may shed light on the *identities* of individuals and how they see themselves.
- Narrative stories are gathered through many *different forms of data,* such as through interviews that may be the primary form of data collection, but also through observations, documents, pictures, and other sources of qualitative data.
- Narrative stories often are heard and shaped by the researchers into a *chronology* although they may not be told that way by the participant(s). There is a temporal change that is conveyed when individuals talk about their experiences and their lives. They may talk about their past, their present, or their future (Clandinin & Connelly, 2000).

- Narrative stories are *analyzed* in varied ways. An analysis can be made about what was said (thematically), the nature of the telling of the story (structural), or who the story is directed toward (dialogic/performance) (Riessman, 2008).
- Narrative stories often contain *turning points* (Denzin, 1989a) or specific tensions or interruptions that are highlighted by the researchers in the telling of the stories.
- Narrative stories occur within specific *places or situations.* The context becomes important for the researcher's telling of the story within a place.

Types of Narratives

Narrative studies can be differentiated along two different lines. One line is to consider the data analysis strategy used by the narrative researcher. Several analytic strategies are available for use. Polkinghorne (1995) discusses narrative in which the researcher extracts themes that hold across stories or taxonomies of types of stories, and a more storytelling mode in which the narrative researcher shapes the stories based on a plotline, or a literary approach to analysis. Polkinghorne (1995) goes on to emphasize the second form in his writings. More recently, Chase (2005) suggests analytic strategies based on parsing constraints on narratives, narratives that are composed interactively between researchers and participants, and the interpretations developed by various narrators. Combining both of these approaches, we see an insightful analysis of strategies for analyzing narratives in Riessman (2008). She conveys three types of approaches used to analyze narrative stories: a thematic analysis in which the researcher identifies the themes "told" by a participant; a structural analysis in which the meaning shifts to the "telling" and the story can be cast during a conversation in comic terms, tragedy, satire, romance, or other forms; and a dialogic/performance analysis in which the focus turns to how the story is produced (i.e., interactively between the researcher and the participant) and performed (i.e., meant to convey some message or point).

Another line of thinking is to consider the type of narratives. A wide variety of approaches have emerged (see, e.g., Casey, 1995/1996). Here are some popular approaches.

- A *biographical study* is a form of narrative study in which the researcher writes and records the experiences of another person's life.

- *Autoethnography* is written and recorded by the individuals who are the subject of the study (Ellis, 2004; Muncey, 2010). Muncey (2010) defines autoethnography as the idea of multiple layers of consciousness, the vulnerable self, the coherent self, critiquing the self in social contexts, the subversion of dominant discourses, and the evocative potential. They contain the personal story of the author as well as the larger cultural meaning for the individual's story. An example of autoethnography is Neyman's (2011) doctoral dissertation in which she explored her teaching experiences in the background of major problems of public schools in America and Ukraine. Her story about problems such as low academic performance, poor discipline, theft, insufficient parents' involvement, and other issues shed light on her personal and professional life.

- A *life history* portrays an individual's entire life, while a personal experience story is a narrative study of an individual's personal experience found in single or multiple episodes, private situations, or communal folklore (Denzin, 1989a).

- An *oral history* consists of gathering personal reflections of events and their causes and effects from one individual or several individuals (Plummer, 1983). Narrative studies may have a specific contextual focus, such as stories told by teachers or children in classrooms (Ollerenshaw & Creswell, 2002) or the stories told about organizations (Czarniawska, 2004). Narratives may be guided by interpretive frameworks. The framework may advocate for Latin Americans through using *testimonios* (Beverly, 2005), or report stories of women using feminist interpretations (see, e.g., Personal Narratives Group, 1989), a lens that shows how women's voices are muted, multiple, and contradictory (Chase, 2005). It may be told to disrupt the dominant discourse around teenage pregnancy (Muncey, 2010).

Procedures for Conducting Narrative Research

Using the approach taken by Clandinin and Connelly (2000) as a general procedural guide, the methods of conducting a narrative study do not follow a lockstep approach, but instead represent an informal collection of topics. Riessman (2008) adds useful information about the data collection process and the strategies for analyzing data.

- Determine if the research problem or question best fits narrative research. Narrative research is best for capturing the detailed stories or life experiences of a *single individual* or the lives of a small number of individuals.

● Select one or more individuals who have stories or life experiences to tell, and spend considerable time with them gathering their stories through multiples types of information. Clandinin and Connelly (2000) refer to the stories as "field texts." Research participants may record their stories in a journal or diary, or the researcher might observe the individuals and record field notes. Researchers may also collect letters sent by the individuals, assemble stories about the individuals from family members, gather documents such as memos or official correspondence about the individuals, or obtain photographs, memory boxes (collection of items that trigger memories), and other personal-family-social artifacts. After examining these sources, the researcher records the individuals' life experiences.

● Consider how the collection of the data and their recording can take different shapes. Riessman (2008) illustrates different ways that researchers can transcribe interviews to develop different types of stories. The transcription can highlight the researcher as a listener or a questioner, emphasize the interaction between the researcher and the participant, convey a conversation that moves through time, or include shifting meanings that may emerge through translated material.

● Collect information about the context of these stories. Narrative researchers situate individual stories within participants' personal experiences (their jobs, their homes), their culture (racial or ethnic), and their *historical contexts* (time and place).

● Analyze the participants' stories. The researcher may take an active role and "restory" the stories into a framework that makes sense. *Restorying* is the process of reorganizing the stories into some general type of framework. This framework may consist of gathering stories, analyzing them for key elements of the story (e.g., time, place, plot, and scene), and then rewriting the stories to place them within a chronological sequence (Ollerenshaw & Creswell, 2002). Often when individuals tell their stories, they do not present them in a chronological sequence. During the process of restorying, the researcher provides a causal link among ideas. Cortazzi (1993) suggests that the chronology of narrative research, with an emphasis on sequence, sets narrative apart from other genres of research. One aspect of the chronology is that the stories have a beginning, a middle, and an end. Similar to basic elements found in good novels, these aspects involve a predicament, conflict, or struggle; a protagonist, or main character; and a sequence with implied causality (i.e., a plot) during which the predicament is resolved in some fashion (Carter,

1993). A chronology further may consist of past, present, and future ideas (Clandinin & Connelly, 2000), based on the assumption that time has a unilinear direction (Polkinghorne, 1995). In a more general sense, the story might include other elements typically found in novels, such as time, place, and scene (Connelly & Clandinin, 1990). The plot, or story line, may also include Clandinin and Connelly's (2000) three-dimensional narrative inquiry space: the personal and social (the interaction); the past, present, and future (continuity); and the place (situation). This story line may include information about the setting or context of the participants' experiences. Beyond the chronology, researchers might detail themes that arise from the story to provide a more detailed discussion of the meaning of the story (Huber & Whelan, 1999). Thus, the qualitative data analysis may be a description of both the story and themes that emerge from it. A postmodern narrative writer, such as Czarniawska (2004), adds another element to the analysis: a deconstruction of the stories, an unmaking of them by such analytic strategies as exposing dichotomies, examining silences, and attending to disruptions and contradictions. Finally, the analysis process consists of the researcher looking for themes or categories; the researcher using a microlinguistic approach and probing for the meaning of words, phrases, and larger units of discourse such as is often done in conversational analysis (see Gee, 1991); or the researcher examining the stories for how they are produced interactively between the researcher and the participant or performed by the participant to convey a specific agenda or message (Riessman, 2008).

- Collaborate with participants by actively involving them in the research (Clandinin & Connelly, 2000). As researchers collect stories, they negotiate relationships, smooth transitions, and provide ways to be useful to the participants. In narrative research, a key theme has been the turn toward the relationship between the researcher and the researched in which both parties will learn and change in the encounter (Pinnegar & Daynes, 2007). In this process, the parties negotiate the meaning of the stories, adding a validation check to the analysis (Creswell & Miller, 2000). Within the participant's story may also be an interwoven story of the researcher gaining insight into her or his own life (see Huber & Whelan, 1999). Also, within the story may be epiphanies, turning points, or disruptions in which the story line changes direction dramatically. In the end, the narrative study tells the story of individuals unfolding in a chronology of their experiences, set within their personal, social, and historical context, and including the important themes in those lived experiences. "Narrative inquiry is stories lived and told," said Clandinin and Connolly (2000, p. 20).

Challenges

Given these procedures and the characteristics of narrative research, narrative research is a challenging approach to use. The researcher needs to collect extensive information about the participant, and needs to have a clear understanding of the context of the individual's life. It takes a keen eye to identify in the source material that gathers the particular stories to capture the individual's experiences. As Edel (1984) comments, it is important to uncover the "figure under the carpet" that explains the multilayered context of a life. Active collaboration with the participant is necessary, and researchers need to discuss the participant's stories as well as be reflective about their own personal and political background, which shapes how they "restory" the account. Multiple issues arise in the collecting, analyzing, and telling of individual stories. Pinnegar and Daynes (2007) raise these important questions: Who owns the story? Who can tell it? Who can change it? Whose version is convincing? What happens when narratives compete? As a community, what do stories do among us?

PHENOMENOLOGICAL RESEARCH

Definition and Background

Whereas a narrative study reports the stories of experiences of a single individual or several individuals, a *phenomenological study* describes the common meaning for several individuals of their *lived experiences* of a concept or a phenomenon. Phenomenologists focus on describing what all participants have in common as they experience a phenomenon (e.g., grief is universally experienced). The basic purpose of phenomenology is to reduce individual experiences with a phenomenon to a description of the universal essence (a "grasp of the very nature of the thing," van Manen, 1990, p. 177). To this end, qualitative researchers identify a phenomenon (an "object" of human experience; van Manen, 1990, p. 163). This human experience may be a phenomenon such as insomnia, being left out, anger, grief, or undergoing coronary artery bypass surgery (Moustakas, 1994). The inquirer then collects data from persons who have experienced the phenomenon, and develops a composite description of the essence of the experience for all of the individuals. This description consists of "what" they experienced and "how" they experienced it (Moustakas, 1994).

Beyond these procedures, phenomenology has a strong philosophical component to it. It draws heavily on the writings of the German mathematician Edmund Husserl (1859–1938) and those who expanded on his views, such as Heidegger, Sartre, and Merleau-Ponty (Spiegelberg, 1982). Phenomenology is popular in the social and health sciences, especially in sociology (Borgatta & Borgatta, 1992; Swingewood, 1991), psychology (Giorgi, 1985, 2009; Polkinghorne, 1989), nursing and the health sciences (Nieswiadomy, 1993; Oiler, 1986), and education (Tesch, 1988; van Manen, 1990). Husserl's ideas are abstract, and Merleau-Ponty (1962) raised the question, "What is phenomenology?" In fact, Husserl was known to call any project currently under way "phenomenology" (Natanson, 1973).

Writers following in the footsteps of Husserl also seem to point to different philosophical arguments for the use of phenomenology today (contrast, for example, the philosophical basis stated in Moustakas, 1994; in Stewart and Mickunas, 1990; and in van Manen, 1990). Looking across all of these perspectives, however, we see that the philosophical assumptions rest on some common grounds: the study of the lived experiences of persons, the view that these experiences are conscious ones (van Manen, 1990), and the development of descriptions of the essences of these experiences, not explanations or analyses (Moustakas, 1994). At a broader level, Stewart and Mickunas (1990) emphasize four *philosophical perspectives* in phenomenology:

- A return to the traditional tasks of philosophy. By the end of the 19th century, philosophy had become limited to exploring a world by empirical means, which was called "scientism." The return to the traditional tasks of philosophy that existed before philosophy became enamored with empirical science is a return to the Greek conception of philosophy as a search for wisdom.
- A philosophy without presuppositions. Phenomenology's approach is to suspend all judgments about what is real—the "natural attitude"—until they are founded on a more certain basis. This suspension is called "epoche" by Husserl.
- The *intentionality of consciousness*. This idea is that consciousness is always directed toward an object. Reality of an object, then, is inextricably related to one's consciousness of it. Thus, reality, according to Husserl, is divided not into subjects and objects, but into the dual Cartesian nature of both subjects and objects as they appear in consciousness.

- The refusal of the subject-object dichotomy. This theme flows naturally from the intentionality of consciousness. The reality of an object is only perceived within the meaning of the experience of an individual.
- An individual writing a phenomenology would be remiss to not include some discussion about the philosophical presuppositions of phenomenology along with the methods in this form of inquiry. Moustakas (1994) devotes over one hundred pages to the philosophical assumptions before he turns to the methods.

Defining Features of Phenomenology

There are several features that are typically included in all phenomenological studies. I rely on two books for my primary information about phenomenology: Moustakas (1994) taken from a psychological perspective and van Manen (1990) based on a human science orientation.

- An emphasis on a *phenomenon* to be explored, phrased in terms of a single concept or idea, such as the educational idea of "professional growth," the psychological concept of "grief," or the health idea of a "caring relationship."
- The exploration of this phenomenon with a *group of individuals* who have all experienced the phenomenon. Thus, a heterogeneous group is identified that may vary in size from 3 to 4 individuals to 10 to 15.
- A *philosophical discussion* about the basic ideas involved in conducting a phenomenology. This turns on the lived experiences of individuals and how they have both subjective experiences of the phenomenon and objective experiences of something in common with other people. Thus, there is a refusal of the subjective-objective perspective, and, for these reasons, phenomenology lies somewhere on a continuum between qualitative and quantitative research.
- In some forms of phenomenology, the researcher *brackets* himself or herself out of the study by discussing personal experiences with the phenomenon. This does not take the researcher completely out of the study, but it does serve to identify personal experiences with the phenomenon and to partly set them aside so that the researcher can focus on the experiences of the participants in the study. This is an ideal, but readers learn about the researcher's

experiences, and can judge for themselves whether the researcher focused solely on the participants' experiences in the description without bringing himself or herself into the picture. Giorgi (2009) sees this bracketing as a matter not of forgetting what has been experienced, but of not letting past knowledge be engaged while determining experiences. He then cites other aspects of life where this same demand holds. A juror in a criminal trial may hear a judge say that a piece of evidence is not admissible; a scientific researcher may hope that a pet hypothesis will be supported, but then note that the results do not support it.

- A *data collection* procedure that involves typically interviewing individuals who have experienced the phenomenon. This is not a universal trait, however, as some phenomenological studies involve varied sources of data, such as poems, observations, and documents.
- *Data analysis* that can follow systematic procedures that move from the narrow units of analysis (e.g., significant statements), and on to broader units (e.g., meaning units), and on to detailed descriptions that summarize two elements, "what" the individuals have experienced and "how" they have experienced it (Moustakas, 1994).
- A phenomenology ends with a descriptive passage that discusses the *essence* of the experience for individuals incorporating "what" they have experienced and "how" they experienced it. The "essence" is the culminating aspect of a phenomenological study.

Types of Phenomenology

Two approaches to phenomenology are highlighted in this discussion: hermeneutic phenomenology (van Manen, 1990) and empirical, transcendental, or psychological phenomenology (Moustakas, 1994). Van Manen (1990) is widely cited in the health literature (Morse & Field, 1995). An educator, van Manen (1990) has written an instructive book on **hermeneutical phenomenology** in which he describes research as oriented toward lived experience (phenomenology) and interpreting the "texts" of life (hermeneutics) (p. 4). Although van Manen does not approach phenomenology with a set of rules or methods, he discusses it as a dynamic interplay among six research activities. Researchers first turn to a phenomenon, an "abiding concern" (van Manen, 1990, p. 31), which seriously interests them (e.g., reading, running, driving, mothering). In the process, they reflect on essential themes, what constitutes the nature of this lived experience. They write a description of the phenomenon, maintaining a strong relation to the topic of inquiry and balancing the parts of the writing to the whole. Phenomenology is not only a description, but it is also an interpretive process in which the researcher makes an interpretation (i.e., the researcher "mediates" between different meanings; van Manen, 1990, p. 26) of the meaning of the lived experiences.

Moustakas's (1994) transcendental or psychological phenomenology is focused less on the interpretations of the researcher and more on a description of the experiences of participants. In addition, Moustakas focuses on one of Husserl's concepts, *epoche* (or bracketing), in which investigators set aside their experiences, as much as possible, to take a fresh perspective toward the phenomenon under examination. Hence, *transcendental* means "in which everything is perceived freshly, as if for the first time" (Moustakas, 1994, p. 34). Moustakas admits that this state is seldom perfectly achieved. However, I see researchers who embrace this idea when they begin a project by describing their own experiences with the phenomenon and bracketing out their views before proceeding with the experiences of others.

Besides bracketing, empirical, *transcendental phenomenology* draws on the *Duquesne Studies in Phenomenological Psychology* (e.g., Giorgi, 1985, 2009) and the data analysis procedures of Van Kaam (1966) and Colaizzi (1978). The procedures, illustrated by Moustakas (1994), consist of identifying a phenomenon to study, bracketing out one's experiences, and collecting data from several persons who have experienced the phenomenon. The researcher then analyzes the data by reducing the information to significant statements or quotes and combines the statements into themes. Following that, the researcher develops a *textural description* of the experiences of the persons (what participants experienced), a *structural description* of their experiences (how they experienced it in terms of the conditions, situations, or context), and a combination of the textural and structural descriptions to convey an overall *essence* of the experience.

Procedures for Conducting Phenomenological Research

I use the psychologist Moustakas's (1994) approach because it has systematic steps in the data analysis procedure and guidelines for assembling the textual and structural descriptions. The conduct of psychological phenomenology has been addressed in a number of writings, including Dukes (1984), Tesch (1990), Giorgi (1985, 1994, 2009), Polkinghorne (1989), and, most recently, Moustakas (1994). The major procedural steps in the process would be as follows:

- The researcher determines if the research problem is best examined using a phenomenological approach. The type of problem best suited for this form of research is one in which it is important to understand several individuals' common or shared experiences of a phenomenon. It would be important to understand these common experiences in order to develop practices or policies, or to develop a deeper understanding about the features of the phenomenon.

- A phenomenon of interest to study, such as anger, professionalism, what it means to be underweight, or what it means to be a wrestler, is identified. Moustakas (1994) provides numerous examples of phenomena that have been studied. Van Manen (1990) identifies the phenomena such as the experience of learning, riding a bike, or the beginning of fatherhood.

- The researcher recognizes and specifies the broad philosophical assumptions of phenomenology. For example, one could write about the combination of objective reality and individual experiences. These lived experiences are furthermore "conscious" and directed toward an object. To fully describe how participants view the phenomenon, researchers must bracket out, as much as possible, their own experiences.

- Data are collected from the individuals who have experienced the phenomenon. Often data collection in phenomenological studies consists of in-depth and multiple interviews with participants. Polkinghorne (1989) recommends that researchers interview from 5 to 25 individuals who have all experienced the phenomenon. Other forms of data may also be collected, such as observations, journals, poetry, music, and other forms of art. Van Manen (1990) mentions taped conversations, formally written responses, and accounts of vicarious experiences of drama, films, poetry, and novels.

- The participants are asked two broad, general questions (Moustakas, 1994): What have you experienced in terms of the phenomenon? What contexts or situations have typically influenced or affected your experiences of the phenomenon? Other open-ended questions may also be asked, but these two, especially, focus attention on gathering data that will lead to a textual and structural description of the experiences, and ultimately provide an understanding of the common experiences of the participants.

- *Phenomenological data analysis* steps are generally similar for all psychological phenomenologists who discuss the methods (Moustakas, 1994; Polkinghorne, 1989). Building on the data from the first and second research questions, data analysts go through the data (e.g., interview transcriptions) and highlight "significant statements," sentences, or quotes that provide an understanding of how the participants experienced the phenomenon. Moustakas (1994) calls this step *horizonalization*. Next, the researcher develops *clusters of meaning* from these significant statements into themes.

- These significant statements and themes are then used to write a description of what the participants experienced (*textural description*). They are also used to write a description of the context or setting that influenced how the participants experienced the phenomenon, called *imaginative variation* or *structural description*. Moustakas (1994) adds a further step: Researchers also write about their own experiences and the context and situations that have influenced their experiences. I like to shorten Moustakas's procedures, and reflect these personal statements at the beginning of the phenomenology or include them in a methods discussion of the role of the researcher (Marshall & Rossman, 2010).

- From the structural and textural descriptions, the researcher then writes a composite description that presents the "essence" of the phenomenon, called the *essential, invariant structure (or essence)*. Primarily this passage focuses on the common experiences of the participants. For example, it means that all experiences have an underlying *structure* (grief is the same whether the loved one is a puppy, a parakeet, or a child). It is a descriptive passage, a long paragraph or two, and the reader should come away from the phenomenology with the feeling, "I understand better what it is like for someone to experience that" (Polkinghorne, 1989, p. 46).

Challenges

A phenomenology provides a deep understanding of a phenomenon as experienced by several individuals. Knowing some common experiences can be valuable for groups such as therapists, teachers, health personnel, and policymakers. Phenomenology can involve a streamlined form of data collection by including only single or multiple interviews with participants. Using the Moustakas (1994) approach for analyzing the data helps provide a structured approach for novice researchers. It may be too structured for some qualitative researchers. On the other hand, phenomenology requires at least some understanding of the broader philosophical assumptions, and researchers should identify these assumptions in their studies. These philosophical ideas are abstract concepts and not easily seen in a written phenomenological study. In addition, the participants in the study need to be carefully chosen to be individuals who have all experienced the phenomenon in question, so that the researcher, in the end, can forge a common understanding. Finding individuals who have all experienced the phenomenon may be difficult given a research topic. As mentioned earlier, bracketing personal experiences may be difficult for the researcher to implement because interpretations of the data always incorporate the assumptions that the researcher brings to the topic (van Manen, 1990). Perhaps we need a new definition of *epoche* or *bracketing*, such as suspending our understandings in a reflective move that cultivates curiosity (LeVasseur, 2003). Thus, the researcher needs to decide how and in what way his or her personal understandings will be introduced into the study.

GROUNDED THEORY RESEARCH

Definition and Background

While narrative research focuses on individual stories told by participants, and phenomenology emphasizes the common experiences for a number of individuals, the intent of a **grounded theory study** is to move beyond description and to **generate or discover a theory,** a "unified theoretical explanation" (Corbin & Strauss, 2007, p. 107) for a process or an action. Participants in the study would all have experienced the process, and the development of the theory might help explain practice or provide a framework for further research. A key idea is that this theory development does not come "off the shelf," but rather is generated or "grounded" in data from participants who have experienced the process (Strauss & Corbin, 1998). Thus, grounded theory is a qualitative research design in which the inquirer generates a general explanation (a theory) of a process, an action, or an interaction shaped by the views of a large number of participants.

This qualitative design was developed in sociology in 1967 by two researchers, Barney Glaser and Anselm Strauss, who felt that theories used in research were often inappropriate and ill suited for participants under study. They elaborated on their ideas through several books (Corbin & Strauss, 2007; Glaser, 1978; Glaser & Strauss, 1967; Strauss, 1987; Strauss & Corbin, 1990, 1998). In contrast to the a priori, theoretical orientations in sociology, grounded theorists held that theories should be "grounded" in data from the field, especially in the actions, interactions, and social processes of people. Thus, grounded theory provided for the generation of a theory (complete with a diagram and hypotheses) of actions, interactions, or processes through interrelating categories of information based on data collected from individuals.

Despite the initial collaboration of Glaser and Strauss that produced such works as *Awareness of Dying* (Glaser & Strauss, 1965) and *Time for Dying* (Glaser & Strauss, 1968), the two authors ultimately disagreed about the meaning and procedures of grounded theory. Glaser has criticized Strauss's approach to grounded theory as too prescribed and structured (Glaser, 1992). More recently, Charmaz (2006) has advocated for a ***constructivist grounded theory***, thus introducing yet another perspective into the conversation about procedures. Through these different interpretations, grounded theory has gained popularity in fields such as sociology, nursing, education, and psychology, as well as in other social science fields.

Another recent grounded theory perspective is that of Clarke (2005) who, along with Charmaz, seeks to reclaim grounded theory from its "positivist underpinnings" (p. xxiii). Clarke, however, goes further than Charmaz, suggesting that social "situations" should form our unit of analysis in grounded theory and that three sociological modes can be useful in analyzing these situations—situational, social world/arenas, and positional cartographic maps for collecting and analyzing qualitative data. She further expands grounded theory "after the postmodern turn" (Clarke, 2005, p. xxiv) and relies on postmodern perspectives (i.e., the political nature of research and interpretation, reflexivity on the part of researchers, a recognition of problems of representing information, questions of legitimacy and authority, and repositioning the researcher away from the "all knowing analyst" to the "acknowledged participant") (Clarke, 2005, pp. xxvii, xxviii). Clarke frequently turns to the postmodern, poststructural writer Michael Foucault (1972) to base the grounded theory discourse. In my discussion of grounded theory, I will be relying on the books by Corbin and Strauss (2007) who provide a structured approach to grounded theory and Charmaz (2006) who offers a constructivist and interpretive perspective on grounded theory.

Defining Features of Grounded Theory

There are several major characteristics of grounded theory that might be incorporated into a research study:

- The researcher focuses on a *process* or an *action* that has distinct steps or phases that occur over time. Thus, a grounded theory study has "movement" or some action that the researcher is attempting to explain. A process might be "developing a general education program" or the process of "supporting faculty to become good researchers."
- The researcher also seeks, in the end, to develop a *theory* of this process or action. There are many definitions of a theory available in the literature, but, in general, a theory is an explanation of something or an understanding that the researcher develops. This explanation or understanding is a drawing together, in grounded theory, of theoretical categories that are arrayed to show how the theory works. For example, a theory of support for faculty may show how faculty are supported over time, by specific resources, by specific actions taken by individuals, with individual outcomes that enhance the research performance of a faculty member (Creswell & Brown, 1992).
- *Memoing* becomes part of developing the theory as the researcher writes down ideas as data are collected and analyzed. In these memos, the ideas attempt to formulate the process that is being seen by the researcher and to sketch out the flow of this process.
- The primary form of *data collection* is often interviewing in which the researcher is constantly comparing data gleaned from participants with ideas about the emerging theory. The process consists of going back and forth between the participants, gathering new interviews, and then returning to the evolving theory to fill in the gaps and to elaborate on how it works.
- *Data analysis* can be structured and follow the pattern of developing open categories, selecting one category to be the focus of the theory, and then detailing additional categories (axial coding) to form a theoretical model. The intersection of the categories becomes the theory (called selective coding). This theory can be presented as a diagram, as propositions (or hypotheses), or as a discussion (Strauss & Corbin, 1998). Data analysis can also be less structured and based on developing a theory by piecing together implicit meanings about a category (Charmaz, 2006).

Types of Grounded Theory Studies

The two popular approaches to grounded theory are the systematic procedures of Strauss and Corbin (1990, 1998) and the constructivist approach of Charmaz (2005, 2006). In the more systematic, analytic procedures of Strauss and Corbin (1990, 1998), the investigator seeks to systematically develop a theory that explains process, action, or interaction on a topic (e.g., the process of developing a curriculum, the therapeutic benefits of sharing psychological test results with clients). The researcher typically conducts 20 to 30 interviews based on several visits "to the field" to collect interview data to saturate the categories (or find information that continues to add to them until no more can be found). A *category* represents a unit of information composed of events, happenings, and instances (Strauss & Corbin, 1990). The researcher also collects and analyzes observations and documents, but these data forms are often not used. While the researcher collects data, she or he begins analysis. My image for data collection in a grounded theory study is a "zigzag" process: out to the field to gather information, into the office to analyze the data, back to the field to gather more information, into the office, and so forth. The participants interviewed are theoretically chosen (called *theoretical sampling*) to help the researcher best form the theory. How many passes one makes to the field depends on whether the categories of information become saturated and whether the theory is elaborated in all of its complexity. This process of taking information from data collection and comparing it to emerging categories is called the *constant comparative* method of data analysis.

The researcher begins with *open coding*, coding the data for its major categories of information. From this coding, axial coding emerges in which the researcher identifies one open coding category to focus on (called the "core" phenomenon), and then goes back to the data and creates categories around this core phenomenon. Strauss and Corbin (1990) prescribe the types of categories identified around the core phenomenon. They consist of *causal conditions* (what factors caused the core phenomenon), *strategies* (actions taken in response to the core phenomenon), contextual and *intervening conditions* (broad and specific situational factors that influence the strategies), and *consequences* (outcomes from using the strategies). These categories relate to and surround the core phenomenon in a visual model called the *axial coding* paradigm. The final step, then, is *selective coding*, in which the researcher takes the model and develops *propositions* (or hypotheses) that interrelate the categories in the model or assembles a story that describes the interrelationship of categories in the model. This theory, developed by the researcher, is articulated toward the end of a study and can assume several forms, such as a narrative statement (Strauss & Corbin, 1990), a visual picture (Morrow & Smith, 1995), or a series of hypotheses or propositions (Creswell & Brown, 1992).

In their discussion of grounded theory, Strauss and Corbin (1998) take the model one step further to develop a *conditional matrix*. They advance the conditional matrix as a coding device to help the researcher make connections between the macro and micro conditions influencing the phenomenon. This matrix is a set of expanding concentric circles with labels that build outward from the individual, group, and organization to the community, region, nation, and global world. In my experience, this matrix is seldom used in grounded theory research, and researchers typically end their studies with a theory developed in selective coding, a theory that might be viewed as a substantive, low-level theory rather than an abstract, grand theory (e.g., see Creswell & Brown, 1992). Although making connections between the substantive theory and its larger implications for the community, nation, and world in the conditional matrix is important (e.g., a model of work flow in a hospital, the shortage of gloves, and the national guidelines on AIDS may all be connected; see this example provided by Strauss & Corbin, 1998), grounded theorists seldom have the data, time, or resources to employ the conditional matrix.

A second variant of grounded theory is found in the constructivist writing of Charmaz (2005, 2006). Instead of embracing the study of a single process or core category as in the Strauss and Corbin (1998) approach, Charmaz advocates for a social constructivist perspective that includes emphasizing diverse local worlds, multiple realities, and the complexities of particular worlds, views, and actions. Constructivist grounded theory, according to Charmaz (2006), lies squarely within the interpretive approach to qualitative research with flexible guidelines, a focus on theory developed that depends on the researcher's view, learning about the experience within embedded, hidden networks, situations, and relationships, and making visible hierarchies of power, communication, and opportunity. Charmaz places more emphasis on the views, values, beliefs, feelings, assumptions, and ideologies of individuals than on the methods of research, although she does describe the practices of gathering rich data, coding the data, memoing, and using theoretical sampling (Charmaz, 2006). She suggests that complex terms or jargon, diagrams, conceptual maps, and systematic approaches (such as Strauss & Corbin, 1990) detract from grounded theory and represent an attempt to gain power in their use. She advocates using active codes, such as gerund-based phrases like *recasting life.* Moreover, for Charmaz, a grounded theory procedure does not minimize the role of the researcher in the process. The researcher makes decisions about the categories throughout the process, brings questions to the data, and advances personal values, experiences, and priorities. Any conclusions developed by grounded theorists are, according to Charmaz (2005), suggestive, incomplete, and inconclusive.

Procedures for Conducting Grounded Theory Research

In this discussion I include Charmaz's interpretive approach (e.g., reflexivity, being flexible in structure, as discussed in Chapter 2), and I rely on Strauss and Corbin (1990, 1998) and Corbin and Strauss (2007) to illustrate grounded theory procedures because their systematic approach is helpful to individuals learning about and applying grounded theory research.

The researcher needs to begin by determining if grounded theory is best suited to study his or her research problem. Grounded theory is a good design to use when a theory is not available to explain or understand a process. The literature may have models available, but they were developed and tested on samples and populations other than those of interest to the qualitative researcher. Also, theories may be present, but they are incomplete because they do not address potentially valuable variables or categories of interest to the researcher. On the practical side, a theory may be needed to explain how people are experiencing a phenomenon, and the grounded theory developed by the researcher will provide such a general framework.

The research questions that the inquirer asks of participants will focus on understanding how individuals experience the process and identify the steps in the process (What was the process? How did it unfold?). After initially exploring these issues, the researcher then returns to the participants and asks more detailed questions that help to shape the axial coding phase, questions such as these: What was central to the process (the core phenomenon)? What influenced or caused this phenomenon to occur (causal conditions)? What strategies were employed during the process (strategies)? What effect occurred (consequences)?

These questions are typically asked in interviews, although other forms of data may also be collected, such as observations, documents, and audiovisual materials. The point is to gather enough information to fully develop (or *saturate*) the model. This may involve 20 to 60 interviews.

The analysis of the data proceeds in stages. In open coding, the researcher forms categories of information about the phenomenon being studied by segmenting information. Within each category, the investigator finds several *properties*, or subcategories, and looks for data to dimensionalize, or show the extreme possibilities on a continuum of the property.

In axial coding, the investigator assembles the data in new ways after open coding. In this structured approach, the investigator presents a *coding paradigm or logic diagram* (i.e., a visual model) in which the researcher identifies a *central phenomenon* (i.e., a central category about the phenomenon), explores *causal conditions* (i.e., categories of conditions that influence the phenomenon), specifies strategies (i.e., the actions or interactions that result from the central phenomenon), identifies the *context* and *intervening conditions* (i.e., the narrow and broad conditions that influence the strategies), and delineates the **consequences** (i.e., the outcomes of the strategies) for this phenomenon.

In selective coding, the researcher may write a "story line" that connects the categories. Alternatively, propositions or hypotheses may be specified that state predicted relationships.

The result of this process of data collection and analysis is a theory, a *substantive-level theory*, written by a researcher close to a specific problem or population of people. The theory emerges with help from the process of *memoing*, in which the researcher writes down ideas about the evolving theory throughout the process of open, axial, and selective coding. The substantive-level theory may be tested later for its empirical verification with quantitative data to determine if it can be generalized to a sample and population (see mixed methods design procedures, Creswell & Plano Clark, 2011). Alternatively, the study may end at this point with the generation of a theory as the goal of the research.

Challenges

A grounded theory study challenges researchers for the following reasons. The investigator needs to set aside, as much as possible, theoretical ideas or notions so that the analytic, substantive theory can emerge. Despite the evolving, inductive nature of this form of qualitative inquiry, the researcher must recognize that this is a systematic approach to research with specific steps in data analysis, if approached from the Corbin and Strauss (2007) perspective. The researcher faces the difficulty of determining when categories are saturated or when the theory is sufficiently detailed. One strategy that might be used to move toward saturation is to use ***discriminant sampling***, in which the researcher gathers additional information from individuals different from those people initially interviewed to determine if the theory holds true for these additional participants. The researcher needs to recognize that the primary outcome of this study is a theory with specific components: a central phenomenon, causal conditions, strategies, conditions and context, and consequences. These are prescribed categories of information in the theory, so the Strauss and Corbin (1990, 1998) or Corbin and Strauss (2007) approach may not have the flexibility desired by some qualitative researchers. In this case, the Charmaz (2006) approach, which is less structured and more adaptable, may be used.

ETHNOGRAPHIC RESEARCH

Definition and Background

Although a grounded theory researcher develops a theory from examining many individuals who share in the same process, action, or interaction, the study participants are not likely to be located in the same place or interacting on so frequent a basis that they develop shared patterns of behavior, beliefs, and language. An ethnographer is interested in examining these shared patterns, and the unit of analysis is typically larger than the 20 or so individuals involved in a grounded theory study. An ***ethnography*** focuses on an entire culture-sharing group. Granted, sometimes this cultural group may be small (a few teachers, a few social workers), but typically it is large, involving many people who interact over time (teachers in an entire school, a community social work group). Thus, ethnography is a qualitative design in which the researcher describes and interprets the shared and learned patterns of values, ***behaviors***, beliefs, and ***language*** of a ***culture-sharing group*** (Harris, 1968). As both a process and an outcome of research (Agar, 1980), ethnography is a way of studying a culture-sharing group as well as the final, written product of that research. As a process, ethnography involves extended observations of the group, most often through ***participant observation***, in which the researcher is ***immersed*** in the day-to-day lives of the people and observes and interviews the group participants. Ethnographers study the meaning of the behavior, the language, and the interaction among members of the culture-sharing group.

Ethnography had its beginning in comparative cultural anthropology conducted by early 20th-century anthropologists, such as Boas, Malinowski, Radcliffe-Brown, and Mead. Although these researchers initially took the natural sciences as a model for research, they differed from those using traditional scientific approaches through the firsthand collection of data concerning existing "primitive" cultures (Atkinson & Hammersley, 1994). In the 1920s and 1930s, sociologists such as Park, Dewey, and Mead adapted anthropological field methods to the study of cultural groups in the United States (Bogdan & Biklen, 1992). Recently, scientific approaches to ethnography have expanded to include "schools" or subtypes of ethnography with different theoretical orientations and aims, such as structural functionalism, symbolic interactionism, cultural and cognitive anthropology, feminism, Marxism, ethnomethodology, critical theory, cultural studies, and postmodernism (Atkinson & Hammersley, 1994). This has led to a lack of orthodoxy in ethnography and has resulted in pluralistic approaches. Many excellent books are available on ethnography, including Van Maanen (1988) on the many forms of ethnography; LeCompte and Schensul (1999) on procedures of ethnography presented in a tool kit of short books; Atkinson, Coffey, and Delamont (2003) on the practices of ethnography; and Madison (2005) on critical ethnography. Major ideas about ethnography developed in this discussion will draw on Fetterman's (2010) and Wolcott's (2008a) approaches. I found Fetterman's (2010) discussion to proceed through the phases of research typically conducted by an ethnographer. His discussions about the basic features of ethnography and the use of theory, and his entire chapter on anthropological concepts, are well worth reading closely. Wolcott (2008a) takes a more topical approach to the subject of ethnography, but his chapter "Ethnography as a Way of Seeing" is unparalleled for obtaining a good understanding of the nature of ethnography, the study of groups, and the development of an understanding of culture. I also draw on Wolcott's (2010) companion "primer" on ethnographic lessons.

Defining Features of Ethnographies

From a review of published ethnographies, a brief list of defining characteristics of good ethnographies can be assembled.

- Ethnographies focus on developing a complex, complete description of the *culture* of a group, a culture-sharing group. The ethnography may be of the entire group or a subset of a group. As

Wolcott (2008a) mentioned, ethnography is not the study of a culture, but a study of the social behaviors of an identifiable group of people.

- In an ethnography, the researcher looks for patterns (also described as rituals, customary social behaviors, or regularities) of the group's mental activities, such as their *ideas and beliefs* expressed through language, or material activities, such as how they *behave* within the group as expressed through their actions observed by the researcher (Fetterman, 2010). Said in another way, the researcher looks for patterns of social organization (e.g., social networks) and ideational systems (e.g., worldview, ideas) (Wolcott, 2008a).

- This means that the culture-sharing group has been *intact* and interacting for long enough to develop discernible working patterns.

- In addition, theory plays an important role in focusing the researcher's attention when conducting an ethnography. For example, ethnographers start with a theory—a broad explanation as to what they hope to find—drawn from cognitive science to understand ideas and beliefs, or from materialist theories, such as technoenvironmentalism, Marxism, acculturation, or innovation, to observe how individuals in the culture-sharing group behave and talk (Fetterman, 2010).

- Using the theory and looking for patterns of a culture-sharing group involves engaging in extensive *fieldwork,* collecting data primarily through interviews, observations, symbols, artifacts, and many diverse sources of data (Fetterman, 2010).

- In an analysis of this data, the researcher relies on the participants' views as an insider *emic* perspective and reports them in verbatim quotes, and then synthesizes the data filtering it through the researchers' *etic* scientific perspective to develop an overall *cultural interpretation.* This cultural interpretation is a description of the group and themes related to the theoretical concepts being explored in the study. Typically, in good ethnographies, not much is known about how the group functions (e.g., how a gang operates), and the reader develops a new, and novel, understanding of the group. As Wolcott (2008a) says, we expect ethnographers to go far afield, to someplace "new and strange" (p. 45).

- This analysis results in an understanding of how the *culture-sharing group works,* the essence of how it functions, the group's way of life. Wolcott (2010) provides two helpful questions that, in the end, must be answered in an ethnography: "What do people in this setting have to know and do to make this system work?" and

"If culture, sometimes defined simply as shared knowledge, is mostly caught rather than taught, how do those being inducted into the group find their 'way in' so that an adequate level of sharing is achieved?" (p. 74).

Types of Ethnographies

There are many forms of ethnography, such as a confessional ethnography, life history, autoethnography, feminist ethnography, ethnographic novels, and the visual ethnography found in photography and video, and electronic media (Denzin, 1989a; Fetterman, 2010; LeCompte, Millroy, & Preissle, 1992; Pink, 2001; Van Maanen, 1988). Two popular forms of ethnography will be emphasized here: the realist ethnography and the critical ethnography.

The *realist ethnography* is a traditional approach used by cultural anthropologists. Characterized by Van Maanen (1988), it reflects a particular stance taken by the researcher toward the individuals being studied. Realist ethnography is an objective account of the situation, typically written in the third-person point of view and reporting objectively on the information learned from participants at a site. In this ethnographic approach, the realist ethnographer narrates the study in a third-person dispassionate voice and reports on what is observed or heard from participants. The ethnographer remains in the background as an omniscient reporter of the "facts." The realist also reports objective data in a measured style uncontaminated by personal bias, political goals, and judgment. The researcher may provide mundane details of everyday life among the people studied. The ethnographer also uses standard categories for cultural description (e.g., family life, communication networks, work life, social networks, status systems). The ethnographer produces the participants' views through closely edited quotations and has the final word on how the culture is to be interpreted and presented.

Alternatively, for many researchers, ethnography today employs a "critical" approach (Carspecken & Apple, 1992; Madison, 2005; Thomas, 1993) by including in the research an advocacy perspective. This approach is in response to current society, in which the systems of power, prestige, privilege, and authority serve to marginalize individuals who are from different classes, races, and genders. The *critical ethnography* is a type of ethnographic research in which the authors advocate for the emancipation of groups marginalized in society (Thomas, 1993). Critical researchers typically are politically minded individuals who seek, through their research, to speak out against inequality and domination (Carspecken & Apple, 1992). For example, critical ethnographers might study schools that provide privileges to certain types of students, or counseling practices that serve to overlook the needs of underrepresented groups. The major components of a critical ethnography include a value-laden orientation, empowering people by giving them more authority, challenging the status quo, and addressing concerns about power and control. A critical ethnographer will study issues of power, empowerment, inequality, inequity, dominance, repression, hegemony, and victimization.

Procedures for Conducting an Ethnography

As with all qualitative inquiry, there is no single way to conduct ethnographic research. Although current writings provide more guidance to this approach than ever (for example, see the excellent overview found in Wolcott, 2008a), the approach taken here includes elements of both realist ethnography and critical approaches. The steps I would use to conduct an ethnography are as follows:

- Determine if ethnography is the most appropriate design to use to study the research problem. Ethnography is appropriate if the needs are to describe how a cultural group works and to explore the beliefs, language, behaviors, and issues facing the group, such as power, resistance, and dominance. The literature may be deficient in actually knowing how the group works because the group is not in the mainstream, people may not be familiar with the group, or its ways are so different that readers may not identify with the group.

- Identify and locate a culture-sharing group to study. Typically, this group is one whose members have been together for an extended period of time, so that their shared language, patterns of behavior, and attitudes have merged into discernable patterns. This may also be a group that has been marginalized by society. Because ethnographers spend time talking with and observing this group, access may require finding one or more individuals in the group who will allow the researcher in—a **gatekeeper** or **key informants (or participants)**.

- Select cultural themes, issues, or theories to study about the group. These themes, issues, and theories provide an orienting framework for the study of the culture-sharing group. It also informs the *analysis of the culture-sharing group.* The themes may include such topics as enculturation, socialization, learning, cognition, domination, inequality, or child and adult development (LeCompte et al., 1992). As discussed by Hammersley and Atkinson (1995), Wolcott (1987, 1994b, 2008a), and Fetterman (2010), the ethnographer begins the study by examining people in interaction in ordinary settings and discerns pervasive patterns such as life cycles, events, and cultural themes. *Culture* is an amorphous term, not something "lying about" (Wolcott, 1987, p. 41), but something researchers attribute to a group when looking for patterns of its social world. It is inferred from the words and actions of members of the group, and it is assigned to this group by the researcher. It consists of what people do (behaviors), what they say (language), the potential tension between what they do and ought to do, and what they make and use, such as *artifacts* (Spradley, 1980). Such themes are diverse, as illustrated in Winthrop's (1991) *Dictionary of Concepts in Cultural Anthropology.* Fetterman (2010) discusses how ethnographers describe a *holistic* perspective of the group's history, religion, politics, economy, and environment. Within this description, cultural concepts such as the social structure, kinship, the political structure, and the social relations or *function* among members of the group may be described.

● To study cultural concepts, determine which type of ethnography to use. Perhaps how the group works needs to be described, or a critical ethnography can expose issues such as power, hegemony, and advocacy for certain groups. A critical ethnographer, for example, might address an inequity in society or some part of it, use the research to advocate and call for changes, and specify an issue to explore, such as inequality, dominance, oppression, or empowerment.

● Gather information in the context or setting where the group works or lives. This is called *fieldwork* (Wolcott, 2008a). Gathering the types of information typically needed in an ethnography involves going to the research site, respecting the daily lives of individuals at the site, and collecting a wide variety of materials. Field issues of respect, *reciprocity*, deciding who owns the data, and others are central to ethnography. Ethnographers bring a sensitivity to fieldwork issues (Hammersley & Atkinson, 1995), such as attending to how they gain access, give back or reciprocate with the participants, and engage in ethical research, such as presenting themselves honestly and describing the purpose of the study. LeCompte and Schensul (1999) organize types of ethnographic data into observations, tests and measures, surveys, interviews, content analysis, elicitation methods, audiovisual methods, spatial mapping, and network research.

● From the many sources collected, the ethnographer analyzes the data for a *description of the culture-sharing group,* themes that emerge from the group, and an overall interpretation (Wolcott, 1994b). The researcher begins by compiling a detailed description of the culture-sharing group, focusing on a single event, on several activities, or on the group over a prolonged period of time. The ethnographer moves into a theme analysis of patterns or topics that signifies how the cultural group works and lives, and ends with an "overall picture of how a system works" (Fetterman, 2010, p. 10).

● Forge a working set of rules or generalizations as to how the culture-sharing group works as the final product of this analysis. The final product is a holistic *cultural portrait* of the group that incorporates the views of the participants (*emic*) as well as the views of the researcher (*etic*). It might also advocate for the needs of the group or suggest changes in society. As a result, the reader learns about the culture-sharing group from both the participants and the interpretation of the researcher. Other products may be more performance based, such as theater productions, plays, or poems.

Challenges

Ethnography is challenging to use for the following reasons. The researcher needs to have an understanding of cultural anthropology, the meaning of a social-cultural system, and the concepts typically explored by those studying cultures. The time to collect data is extensive, involving prolonged time in the field. In much ethnography, the narratives are written in a literary, almost storytelling approach, an approach that may limit the audience for the work and may be challenging for authors accustomed to traditional approaches to scientific writing. There is a possibility that the researcher will "go native" and be unable to complete or be compromised in the study. This is but one issue in the complex array of fieldwork issues facing ethnographers who venture into an unfamiliar cultural group or system. Sensitivity to the needs of individuals being studied is especially important, and the researcher must access and report his or her impact in conducting the study on the people and the places being explored.

CASE STUDY RESEARCH

Definition and Background

The entire culture-sharing group in ethnography may be considered a case, but the intent in ethnography is to determine how the culture works rather than to either develop an in-depth understanding of a single case or explore an issue or problem using the case as a specific illustration. Thus, *case study* research involves the study of a case within a real-life, contemporary context or setting (Yin, 2009). Although Stake (2005) states that case study research is not a methodology but a choice of what is to be studied (i.e., a case within a *bounded system*, bounded by time and place), others present it as a strategy of inquiry, a methodology, or a comprehensive research strategy (Denzin & Lincoln, 2005; Merriam, 1998; Yin, 2009). I choose to view it as a methodology: a type of design in qualitative research that may be an object of study, as well as a product of the inquiry. Case study research is a qualitative approach in which the investigator explores a real-life, contemporary bounded system (a *case*) or multiple bounded systems (cases) over time, through detailed, in-depth data collection involving *multiple sources of information* (e.g., observations, interviews, audiovisual material, and documents and reports), and reports a *case description* and *case themes*. The unit of analysis in the case study might be multiple cases (a *multisite* study) or a single case (a *within-site* study).

The case study approach is familiar to social scientists because of its popularity in psychology (Freud), medicine (case analysis of a problem), law (case law), and political science (case reports). Case study research has a long, distinguished history across many disciplines. Hamel, Dufour, and Fortin (1993) trace the origin of modern social science case studies through anthropology and sociology. They cite anthropologist Malinowski's study of the Trobriand Islands, French sociologist LePlay's study of families, and the case studies of the University of Chicago Department of Sociology from the 1920s and '30s through the 1950s (e.g., Thomas and Znaniecki's 1958 study of Polish peasants in Europe and America) as antecedents of qualitative case study research. Today, the case study writer has a large array of texts and approaches from which to choose. Yin (2009), for example, espouses both quantitative and qualitative approaches to case study development and discusses explanatory, exploratory, and descriptive qualitative case studies. Merriam (1998) advocates a general approach to qualitative case studies in the field of education. Stake (1995) systematically establishes procedures for case study research and cites them extensively in his example of "Harper School." Stake's (2006) most recent book on multiple case study analysis presents a step-by-step approach and provides rich illustrations of multiple case studies in Ukraine, Slovakia, and Romania. In discussing the case study approach, I will rely on Stake (1995) and Yin (2009) to form the distinctive features of this approach.

Defining Features of Case Studies

A review of many qualitative case studies reported in the literature yields several defining characteristics of most of them:

- Case study research begins with the identification of a specific *case*. This case may be a concrete entity, such as an individual, a small group, an organization, or a partnership. At a less concrete level, it may be a community, a relationship, a decision process, or a specific project (see Yin, 2009). The key here is to define a case that can be bounded or described within certain parameters, such as a specific place and time. Typically, case study researchers study current, real-life cases that are in progress so that they can gather accurate information not lost by time. A single case can be selected or multiple cases identified so that they can be compared.

- The *intent* of conducting the case study is also important. A qualitative case study can be composed to illustrate a unique case, a case that has unusual interest in and of itself and needs to be described and detailed. This is called an *intrinsic case* (Stake, 1995). Alternatively, the intent of the case study may be to understand a specific issue, problem, or concern (e.g., teenage pregnancy) and a case or cases selected to best understand the problem. This is called an *instrumental case* (Stake, 1995).

- A hallmark of a good qualitative case study is that it presents an *in-depth understanding* of the case. In order to accomplish this, the researcher collects many forms of qualitative data, ranging from interviews, to observations, to documents, to audiovisual materials. Relying on one source of data is typically not enough to develop this in-depth understanding.

- The selection of how to approach the *data analysis* in a case study will differ. Some case studies involve the analysis of multiple units within the case (e.g., the school, the school district) while others report on the entire case (e.g., the school district). Also, in some studies, the researcher selects multiple cases to analyze and compare while, in other case studies, a single case is analyzed.

● A key to understanding analysis also is that good case study research involves a *description* of the case. This description applies to both intrinsic and instrumental case studies. In addition, the researcher can identify *themes* or *issues* or *specific situations* to study in each case. A complete findings section of a case study would then involve both a description of the case and themes or issues that the researcher has uncovered in studying the case.

● In addition, the themes or issues might be organized into a *chronology* by the researcher, analyzed *across cases* for similarities and differences among the cases, or presented as a *theoretical model*.

● Case studies often end with conclusions formed by the researcher about the overall meaning derived from the case(s). These are called "assertions" by Stake (1995) or building "patterns" or "explanations" by Yin (2009). I think about these as general lessons learned from studying the case(s).

Types of Case Studies

Thus, types of qualitative case studies are distinguished by the size of the bounded case, such as whether the case involves one individual, several individuals, a group, an entire program, or an activity. They may also be distinguished in terms of the intent of the case analysis. Three variations exist in terms of intent: the single instrumental case study, the collective or multiple case study, and the *intrinsic case study*. In a single *instrumental case study* (Stake, 1995), the researcher focuses on an issue or concern, and then selects one bounded case to illustrate this issue. In a *collective case study* (or multiple case study), the one issue or concern is again selected, but the inquirer selects multiple case studies to illustrate the issue. The researcher might select for study several programs from several research sites or multiple programs within a single site. Often the inquirer purposefully selects multiple cases to show different perspectives on the issue. Yin (2009) suggests that the multiple case study design uses the logic of replication, in which the inquirer replicates the procedures for each case. As a general rule, qualitative researchers are reluctant to generalize from one case to another because the contexts of cases differ. To best generalize, however, the inquirer needs to select representative cases for inclusion in the qualitative study. The final type of case study design is an intrinsic case study in which the focus is on the case itself (e.g., evaluating a program, or studying a student having difficulty—see Stake, 1995) because the case presents an unusual or unique situation. This resembles the focus of narrative research, but the case study analytic procedures of a detailed description of the case, set within its context or surroundings, still hold true.

Procedures for Conducting a Case Study

Several procedures are available for conducting case studies (see Merriam, 1998; Stake, 1995; Yin, 2009). This discussion will rely primarily on Stake's (1995) and Yin's (2009) approaches to conducting a case study.

● First, researchers determine if a case study approach is appropriate for studying the research problem. A case study is a good approach when the inquirer has clearly identifiable cases with boundaries and seeks to provide an in-depth understanding of the cases or a comparison of several cases.

● Researchers need next to identify their case or cases. These cases may involve an individual, several individuals, a program, an event, or an activity. In conducting case study research, I recommend that investigators first consider what type of case study is most promising and useful. The case can be single or collective, multisited or within-site, and focused on a case or on an issue (intrinsic, instrumental) (Stake, 1995; Yin, 2009). In choosing which case to study, an array of possibilities for *purposeful sampling* is available. I prefer to select cases that show different perspectives on the problem, process, or event I want to portray (called "purposeful maximal sampling"; see Creswell, 2012), but I also may select ordinary cases, accessible cases, or unusual cases.

● The data collection in case study research is typically extensive, drawing on multiple sources of information, such as observations, interviews, documents, and audiovisual materials. For example, Yin (2009) recommends six types of information to collect: documents, archival records, interviews, direct observations, participant observation, and physical artifacts.

● The type of analysis of these data can be a *holistic analysis* of the entire case or an *embedded analysis* of a specific aspect of the case (Yin, 2009). Through this data collection, a detailed description of the case

(Stake, 1995) emerges in which the researcher details such aspects as the history of the case, the chronology of events, or a day-by-day rendering of the activities of the case. (The gunman case study in Appendix F involved tracing the campus response to a gunman for 2 weeks immediately following the near-tragedy on campus.) After this description ("relatively uncontested data"; Stake, 1995, p. 123), the researcher might focus on a few key issues (or *analysis of themes*), not for generalizing beyond the case, but for understanding the complexity of the case. One analytic strategy would be to identify issues within each case and then look for common themes that transcend the cases (Yin, 2009). This analysis is rich in the ***context of the case*** or setting in which the case presents itself (Merriam, 1988). When multiple cases are chosen, a typical format is to provide first a detailed description of each case and themes within the case, called a ***within-case analysis,*** followed by a thematic analysis across the cases, called a ***cross-case analysis***, as well as ***assertions*** or an interpretation of the meaning of the case.

● In the final interpretive phase, the researcher reports the meaning of the case, whether that meaning comes from learning about the issue of the case (an instrumental case) or learning about an unusual situation (an intrinsic case). As Lincoln and Guba (1985) mention, this phase constitutes the lessons learned from the case.

Challenges

One of the challenges inherent in qualitative case study development is that the researcher must identify the case. The case selected may be broad in scope (e.g., the Boy Scout organization) or narrow in scope (e.g., a decision-making process at a specific college). The case study researcher must decide which bounded system to study, recognizing that several might be possible candidates for this selection and realizing that either the case itself or an issue, which a case or cases are selected to illustrate, is worthy of study. The researcher must consider whether to study a single case or multiple cases. The study of more than one case dilutes the overall analysis; the more cases an individual studies, the less the depth in any single case. When a researcher chooses multiple cases, the issue becomes, "How many cases?" There is no one answer to this question. However, researchers typically choose no more than four or five cases. What motivates the researcher to consider a large number of cases is the idea of *generalizability,* a term that holds little meaning for most qualitative researchers (Glesne & Peshkin, 1992). Selecting the case requires that the researcher establish a rationale for his or her purposeful sampling strategy for selecting the case and for gathering information about the case. Having enough information to present an in-depth picture of the case limits the value of some case studies. In planning a case study, I have individuals develop a data collection matrix in which they specify the amount of information they are likely to collect about the case. Deciding the "boundaries" of a case—how it might be constrained in terms of time, events, and processes—may be challenging. Some case studies may not have clean beginning and ending points, and the researcher will need to set boundaries that adequately surround the case.

THE FIVE APPROACHES COMPARED

All five approaches have in common the general process of research that begins with a research problem and proceeds to the questions, the data, the data analysis, and the research report. They also employ similar data collection processes, including, in varying degrees, interviews, observations, documents, and audiovisual materials. Also, a couple of potential similarities among the designs should be noted. Narrative research, ethnography, and case study research may seem similar when the unit of analysis is a single individual. True, one may approach the study of a single individual from any of these three approaches; however, the types of data one would collect and analyze would differ considerably. In *narrative research,* the inquirer focuses on the stories told from the individual and arranges these stories in chronological order; in *ethnography,* the focus is on setting the individuals' stories within the context of their culture and culture-sharing group; in *case study research,* the single case is typically selected to illustrate an issue, and the researcher compiles a detailed description of the setting for the case. My approach is to recommend, if the researcher wants to study a single individual, the narrative approach or a single case study because ethnography is a much broader picture of the culture. Then when comparing a narrative study and a single case to study a single individual, I feel that the narrative approach is seen as more appropriate because narrative studies *tend* to focus on a single individual whereas case studies often involve more than one case.

From these sketches of the five approaches, I can identify fundamental differences among these types of qualitative research. As shown in

Table 4.1, I present several dimensions for distinguishing among the five approaches. At a most fundamental level, the five differ in what they are trying to accomplish—their foci or the primary objectives of the studies. Exploring a life is different from generating a theory or describing the behavior of a cultural group. Moreover, although overlaps exist in discipline origin, some approaches have single-disciplinary traditions (e.g., grounded theory originating in sociology, ethnography founded in anthropology or sociology), and others have broad interdisciplinary backgrounds (e.g., narrative, case study). The data collection varies in terms of emphasis (e.g., more observations in ethnography, more interviews in grounded theory) and extent of data collection (e.g., only interviews in phenomenology, multiple forms in case study research to provide the in-depth case picture). At the data analysis stage, the differences are most pronounced. Not only is the distinction one of specificity of the analysis phase (e.g., grounded theory most specific, narrative research less defined), but the number of steps to be undertaken also varies (e.g., extensive steps in phenomenology, few steps in ethnography). The result of each approach, the written report, takes shape from all the processes before it. Stories about an individual's life comprise narrative research. A description of the essence of the experience of the phenomenon becomes a phenomenology. A theory, often portrayed in a visual model, emerges in grounded theory, and a holistic view of how a culture-sharing group works results in an ethnography. An in-depth study of a bounded system or a case (or several cases) becomes a case study.

Relating the dimensions of Table 4.1 to research design within the five approaches will be the focus of chapters to follow. Qualitative researchers have found it helpful to see at this point a general sketch of the overall structure of each of the five approaches.

The outlines of the general structure in writing each of the five approaches in Table 4.1 may be used in designing a journal-article-length study. However, because of the numerous steps in each, they also have applicability as chapters of a dissertation or a book-length work. I introduce them here because the reader, with an introductory knowledge of each approach, now can sketch the general "architecture" of a study. Certainly, this architecture will emerge and be shaped differently by the conclusion of the study, but it provides a framework for the design issue to follow. I recommend these outlines as general templates at this time. In Chapter 5, we will examine five published journal articles, with each study illustrating one of the five approaches, and explore the writing structure of each.

Table 4.1 Contrasting Characteristics of Five Qualitative Approaches

Characteristics	Narrative Research	Phenomenology	Grounded Theory	Ethnography	Case Study
Focus	Exploring the life of an individual	Understanding the essence of the experience	Developing a theory grounded in data from the field	Describing and interpreting a culture-sharing group	Developing an in-depth description and analysis of a case or multiple cases
Type of Problem Best Suited for Design	Needing to tell stories of individual experiences	Needing to describe the essence of a lived phenomenon	Grounding a theory in the views of participants	Describing and interpreting the shared patterns of culture of a group	Providing an in-depth understanding of a case or cases
Discipline Background	Drawing from the humanities including anthropology, literature, history, psychology, and sociology	Drawing from philosophy, psychology, and education	Drawing from sociology	Drawing from anthropology and sociology	Drawing from psychology, law, political science, and medicine
Unit of Analysis	Studying one or more individuals	Studying several individuals who have shared the experience	Studying a process, an action, or an interaction involving many individuals	Studying a group that shares the same culture	Studying an event, a program, an activity, or more than one individual

Characteristics	Narrative Research	Phenomenology	Grounded Theory	Ethnography	Case Study
Data Collection Forms	Using primarily interviews and documents	Using primarily interviews with individuals, although documents, observations, and art may also be considered	Using primarily interviews with 20–60 individuals	Using primarily observations and interviews, but perhaps collecting other sources during extended time in field	Using multiple sources, such as interviews, observations, documents, and artifacts
Data Analysis Strategies	Analyzing data for stories, "restorying" stories, and developing themes, often using a chronology	Analyzing data for significant statements, meaning units, textual and structural description, and description of the "essence"	Analyzing data through open coding, axial coding, and selective coding	Analyzing data through description of the culture-sharing group and themes about the group	Analyzing data through description of the case and themes of the case as well as cross-case themes
Written Report	Developing a narrative about the stories of an individual's life	Describing the "essence" of the experience	Generating a theory illustrated in a figure	Describing how a culture-sharing group works	Developing a detailed analysis of one or more cases

(Continued)

Table 4.1 (Continued)

Characteristics	Narrative Research	Phenomenology	Grounded Theory	Ethnography	Case Study
General Structure of Study	• Introduction (problem, questions) • Research procedures (a narrative, significance of individual, data collection, analysis outcomes) • Report of stories • Individuals theorize about their lives • Narrative segments identified • Patterns of meaning identified (events, processes, epiphanies, themes) • Summary (adapted from Denzin, 1989a, 1989b)	• Introduction (problem, questions) • Research procedures (a phenomenology and philosophical assumptions, data collection, analysis, outcomes) • Significant statements • Meanings of statements • Themes of meanings • Exhaustive description of phenomenon (adapted from Moustakas, 1994)	• Introduction (problem, questions) • Research procedures (grounded theory, data collection, analysis, outcomes) • Open coding • Axial coding • Selective coding and theoretical propositions and models • Discussion of theory and contrasts with extant literature (adapted from Strauss & Corbin, 1990)	• Introduction (problem, questions) • Research procedures (ethnography, data collection, analysis, outcomes) • Description of culture • Analysis of cultural themes • Interpretation, lessons learned, and questions raised (adapted from Wolcott, 1994b)	• Entry vignette • Introduction (problem, questions, case study, data collection, analysis, outcomes) • Description of the case/cases and its/their context • Development of issues • Detail about selected issues • Assertions • Closing vignette (adapted from Stake, 1995)

106

SUMMARY

In this chapter, I described each of the five approaches to qualitative research—narrative research, phenomenology, grounded theory, ethnography, and case study. I provided a definition, some history of the development of the approach, and the major forms it has assumed, and I detailed the major procedures for conducting a qualitative study. I also discussed some of the major challenges in conducting each approach. To highlight some of the differences among the approaches, I provided an overview table that contrasts the characteristics of focus, the type of research problem addressed, the discipline background, the unit of analysis, the forms of data collection, data analysis strategies, and the nature of the final, written report. I also presented outlines of the structure of each approach that might be useful in designing a study within each of the five types. In the next chapter, we will examine five studies that illustrate each approach and look more closely at the compositional structure of each type of approach.

ADDITIONAL READINGS

Several readings extend this brief overview of each of the five approaches of inquiry. In Chapter 1, I presented the major books that will be used to craft discussions about each approach. Here I provide a more expanded list of references that also includes the major works.

Narrative Research

Angrosino, M. V. (1989a). *Documents of interaction: Biography, autobiography, and life history in social science perspective*. Gainesville: University of Florida Press.
Clandinin, D. J. (Ed.). (2006). *Handbook of narrative inquiry: Mapping a methodology*. Thousand Oaks, CA: Sage.
Clandinin, D. J., & Connelly, F. M. (2000). *Narrative inquiry: Experience and story in qualitative research*. San Francisco: Jossey-Bass.
Czarniawska, B. (2004). *Narratives in social science research*. London: Sage.
Denzin, N. K. (1989a). *Interpretive biography*. Newbury Park, CA: Sage.
Denzin, N. K. (1989b). *Interpretive interactionism*. Newbury Park, CA: Sage.
Elliot, J. (2005). *Using narrative in social research: Qualitative and quantitative approaches*. London: Sage.
Lightfoot, C., & Daiute, C. (Eds.). (2004). *Narrative analysis: Studying the development of individuals in society*. Thousand Oaks, CA: Sage

Lightfoot-Lawrence, S., & Davis, J. H. (1997). *The art and science of portraiture.* San Francisco: Jossey-Bass.

Plummer, K. (1983). *Documents of life: An introduction to the problems and literature of a humanistic method.* London: George Allen & Unwin.

Riessman, C. K. (2008). *Narrative methods for the human sciences.* Los Angeles, CA: Sage.

Phenomenology

Colaizzi, P. F. (1978). Psychological research as the phenomenologist views it. In R. Vaile & M. King (Eds.), *Existential phenomenological alternatives for psychology* (pp. 48–71). New York: Oxford University Press.

Dukes, S. (1984). Phenomenological methodology in the human sciences. *Journal of Religion and Health, 23,* 197–203.

Giorgi, A. (Ed.). (1985). *Phenomenology and psychological research.* Pittsburgh, PA: Duquesne University Press.

Giorgi, A. (2009). *A descriptive phenomenological method in psychology: A modified Husserlian approach.* Pittsburgh, PA: Duquesne University Press.

Husserl, E. (1931). *Ideas: General introduction to pure phenomenology* (D. Carr, Trans.). Evanston, IL: Northwestern University Press.

Husserl, E. (1970). *The crisis of European sciences and transcendental phenomenology* (D. Carr, Trans.). Evanston, IL: Northwestern University Press.

LeVasseur, J. J. (2003). The problem with bracketing in phenomenology. *Qualitative Health Research, 31*(2), 408–420.

Lopez, K. A., & Willis, D. G. (2004). Descriptive versus interpretive phenomenology: Their contributions to nursing knowledge. *Qualitative Health Research, 14*(5), 726–735.

Merleau-Ponty, M. (1962). *Phenomenology of perception* (C. Smith, Trans.). London: Routledge & Kegan Paul.

Moustakas, C. (1994). *Phenomenological research methods.* Thousand Oaks, CA: Sage.

Natanson, M. (Ed.). (1973). *Phenomenology and the social sciences.* Evanston, IL: Northwestern University Press.

Oiler, C. J. (1986). Phenomenology: The method. In P. L. Munhall & C. J. Oiler (Eds.), *Nursing research: A qualitative perspective* (pp. 69–82). Norwalk, CT: Appleton-Century-Crofts.

Polkinghorne, D. E. (1989). Phenomenological research methods. In R. S. Valle & S. Halling (Eds.), *Existential-phenomenological perspectives in psychology* (pp. 41–60). New York: Plenum.

Spiegelberg, H. (1982). *The phenomenological movement* (3rd ed.). The Hague, Netherlands: Martinus Nijhoff.

Stewart, D., & Mickunas, A. (1990). *Exploring phenomenology: A guide to the field and its literature* (2nd ed.). Athens: Ohio University Press.

Tesch, R. (1990). *Qualitative research: Analysis types and software tools.* Bristol, PA: Falmer Press.

Van Kaam, A. (1966). *Existential foundations of psychology.* Pittsburgh, PA: Duquesne University Press.

van Manen, M. (1990). *Researching lived experience: Human science for an action sensitive pedagogy.* Albany: State University of New York Press.

Grounded Theory

Babchuk, W. A. (2011), Grounded theory as a "family of methods": A genealogical analysis to guide research. *US-China Education Review, 8*(2), 1548–1566.

Birks, M., & Mills, J. (2011). *Grounded theory: A practical guide.* London: Sage.

Charmaz, K. (1983). The grounded theory method: An explication and interpretation. In R. Emerson (Ed.), *Contemporary field research* (pp. 109–126). Boston: Little, Brown.

Charmaz, K. (2006). *Constructing grounded theory.* London: Sage.

Chenitz, W. C., & Swanson, J. M. (1986). *From practice to grounded theory: Qualitative research in nursing.* Menlo Park, CA: Addison-Wesley.

Clarke, A. E. (2005). *Situational analysis: Grounded theory after the postmodern turn.* Thousand Oaks, CA: Sage.

Corbin, J., & Strauss, A. (2007). *Basics of qualitative research: Techniques and procedures for developing grounded theory* (3rd ed.). Thousand Oaks, CA: Sage.

Glaser, B. G. (1978). *Theoretical sensitivity.* Mill Valley, CA: Sociology Press.

Glaser, B. G. (1992). *Basics of grounded theory analysis.* Mill Valley, CA: Sociology Press.

Glaser, B. G., & Strauss, A. (1967). *The discovery of grounded theory.* Chicago: Aldine.

Strauss, A. (1987). *Qualitative analysis for social scientists.* New York: Cambridge University Press.

Strauss, A., & Corbin, J. (1990). *Basics of qualitative research: Grounded theory procedures and techniques.* Newbury Park, CA: Sage.

Strauss, A., & Corbin, J. (1998). *Basics of qualitative research: Grounded theory procedures and techniques* (2nd ed.). Newbury Park, CA: Sage.

Ethnography

Atkinson, P., Coffey, A., & Delamont, S. (2003). *Key themes in qualitative research: Continuities and changes.* Walnut Creek, CA: AltaMira.

Fetterman, D. M. (2010). *Ethnography: Step by step* (3rd ed.). Thousand Oaks, CA: Sage.

LeCompte, M. D., & Schensul, J. J. (1999). *Designing and conducting ethnographic research* (Ethnographer's toolkit, Vol. 1). Walnut Creek, CA: AltaMira.

Madison, D. S. (2005). *Critical ethnography: Method, ethics, and performance.* Thousand Oaks, CA: Sage.

Spradley, J. P. (1979). *The ethnographic interview.* New York: Holt, Rinehart & Winston.

Spradley, J. P. (1980). *Participant observation.* New York: Holt, Rinehart & Winston.

Wolcott, H. F. (1994b). *Transforming qualitative data: Description, analysis, and interpretation.* Thousand Oaks, CA: Sage

Wolcott, H. F. (2008a). *Ethnography: A way of seeing* (2nd ed.). Walnut Creek, CA: AltaMira.

Wolcott, H. F. (2010). *Ethnography lessons: A primer.* Walnut Creek, CA: Left Coast Press.

Case Study

Lincoln, Y. S., & Guba, E. G. (1985). *Naturalistic inquiry.* Beverly Hills, CA: Sage.

Merriam, S. (1988). *Case study research in education: A qualitative approach.* San Francisco: Jossey-Bass.

Stake, R. (1995). *The art of case study research.* Thousand Oaks, CA: Sage.

Yin, R. K. (2009). *Case study research: Design and method* (4th ed.). Thousand Oaks, CA: Sage.

EXERCISES

1. Select one of the five approaches for a proposed study. Write a brief description of the approach, including a definition, the history, and the procedures associated with the approach. Include references to the literature.

2. Find a qualitative journal article that states in the article that it is a narrative study, a phenomenology, a grounded theory, an ethnography, or a case study. Using the elements of "defining features" advanced in this chapter, review the article and locate where each defining feature of the particular approach appears in the article.

3. Take a proposed qualitative study that you would like to conduct. Begin with presenting it as a narrative study, and then shape it into a phenomenology, a grounded theory, an ethnography, and finally a case study. Discuss for each type of study the focus of the study, the types of data collection and analysis, and the final written report.

5

Five Different
Qualitative Studies

I have always felt that the best way to learn how to write a qualitative study is to view a number of published qualitative journal articles and to look closely at the way they were composed. If an individual plans on undertaking, for example, a grounded theory study, I would suggest that he or she collect about 20 grounded theory published journal articles, study each one carefully, select the most complete one that advances *all* of the defining characteristics of grounded theory, and then model his or her own project after that one. This same process would hold true for an individual conducting any of the other approaches to qualitative inquiry, such as a narrative study, a phenomenology, an ethnography, or a case study. Short of this ideal, I want to get you started toward building this collection by suggesting an exemplar of each approach as discussed in this chapter.

Each of these five published studies represents one of the types of qualitative approaches being discussed in this book. They are found in Appendices B, C, D, E, and F. The best way to proceed, I believe, is to first read the entire article in the appendix, and then return to my summary of the article to compare your understanding with mine. Next read my analysis of how the article illustrates a good model of the approach to research and incorporates the defining characteristics I introduced in Chapter 4. At the conclusion of this chapter, I reflect on why one might choose one approach over another when conducting a qualitative study.

The first study, by Chan (2010), as found in Appendix B, illustrates a good narrative study of a single Chinese immigrant student, Ai Mei Zhang, as she participates in a Canadian middle school and as she interacts with her family. The second article, a phenomenological study by Anderson and Spencer (2002), located in Appendix C, is a study about individuals who have experienced AIDS and the images and ways they think about their disease. The third article is a grounded theory study by Harley et al. (2009)

as found in Appendix D. It presents a study of the behavioral process among African American women to integrate physical activity into their lifestyle. It incorporates, appropriately, a theoretical framework that explains the pathways linking these key factors in the process together. The fourth article is an ethnographic study by Haenfler (2004), as presented in Appendix E, about the core values of the straight edge (sXe) movement that emerged on the East Coast of the United States from the punk subculture of the early 1980s. The sXers adopted a "clean living" ideology of abstaining for life from alcohol, tobacco, illegal drugs, and casual sex. The final article is one of my own—a qualitative case study by Asmussen and Creswell (1995), as shown in Appendix F. It describes and suggests themes related to the reaction of people at a large Midwestern university to a student who enters a classroom in actuarial science with a machine gun and who attempts to shoot at the students. I include this article in the collection of exemplars in this book because the topic of campus violence is as relevant today as it was when we wrote the article in 1995.

QUESTIONS FOR DISCUSSION

- What is the focus in the sample narrative study?
- What experience is examined in the sample phenomenological study?
- What theory emerges in the grounded theory study?
- What culture-sharing group is studied in the sample ethnographic study?
- What is the "case" being examined in the case study?
- How do the five approaches differ?
- How does a researcher choose among the five approaches for a particular study?

A NARRATIVE STUDY
(Chan, 2010; see Appendix B)

This is the story of a Chinese immigrant student, Ai Mei Zhang, a seventh- and eighth-grade student at Bay Street School in Toronto, Canada. Ai Mei was chosen for study by the researcher because she could inform how ethnic identity is shaped by expectations from school and her teacher, her peers at school, and her home. Ai Mei told stories about specific incidents in her life, and the author based her narrative article on these stories as well as observations in her classroom. The researcher also conducted interviews with Ai Mei and other students, took extensive field notes, and sought active participation in Ai Mei's school activities (e.g., Multicultural Night), a family dinner, and classroom conversations between Ai Mei and her classmates. The author's overriding interest was in exploring the conflicting stories that emerged during this data collection. From a thematic analysis of these data, the author presented several conflicting stories: tensions in friendship because Ai Mei hid her home language at school because it was seen as a hindrance to accepted English; pressure to use the school Chinese language and to use her maternal language at home with her family; multiple conflicting influences of parental expectations for behavior and expectations from peers at school; and conflicts between family needs to help in the family business and teacher expectations to complete homework and prepare for tests and assignments. As a final element of the findings, the author reflected on her experiences in conducting the study, such as how the different events she participated in shaped her understanding, how opportunities arose to build trust, how her relationship with Ai Mei was negotiated, and how she developed a sense of advocacy for this young student. In the end, the study contributed to understanding the challenges of immigrant or minority students; the intersecting expectations of students, teachers, peers, and parents; and how the values of individuals in ethnic communities are shaped by these interactions. In a larger sense, this study informed the work of teachers and administrators working with diverse student populations, and serves as an example of a "life-based literary narrative" (Chan, 2010, p. 121).

This article presents well the defining features of a narrative study as introduced in Chapter 4:

- The researcher collected *stories* from a single individual, a Chinese immigrant student, Ai Mei Zhang.
- The researcher made explicit the *collaborative* nature of how the stories were collected and the relationship that built over time between the researcher and the participant in the study.
- The researcher chose to focus on the *experiences* of this one individual and, more specifically, on the cultural *identity* of this student and how parents, peers, and teachers helped to shape this identity.
- The researcher established an evidence base of information to explore this cultural identity through *different forms of data* such as personal observations, interviews, field notes, and attendance at events.
- The researcher collected data over time from the fall of 2001 to June 2003, so there was ample opportunity to examine the unfolding events over time. The narrative, however, was not constructed

to report a *chronology* of themes, and, in reading this account, it is difficult to determine whether one theme (e.g., hiding language in the new student orientation) occurred before or after another theme (e.g., mealtime conversation involving the school Mandarin language and the home Fujianese language).

- The researcher used a thematic *analysis* (Riessman, 2008) of reporting "what happened" to this individual student, her parents, and her school.
- The researcher highlighted specific tensions that arose in each of the themes (e.g., the tension between using Mandarin and Fujianese at home). The overall narrative, however, did not convey a specific *turning point* or epiphany in the story line.
- The researcher discussed the *place* or the context of Bay Street School where most of the incidents occurred that were reported in the narrative.

A PHENOMENOLOGICAL STUDY (Anderson & Spencer, 2002; see Appendix C)

This study discusses the images or cognitive representations that AIDS patients held about their disease. The researchers explored this topic because understanding how individuals represented AIDS and their emotional response to it influenced their therapy, reduced high-risk behaviors, and enhanced their quality of life. Thus, the purpose of this study was "to explore patients' experience and cognitive representations of AIDS within the context of phenomenology" (Anderson & Spencer, 2002, p. 1339).

The authors introduced the study by referring to the millions of individuals infected with HIV. They advanced a framework, the Self-Regulation Model of Illness Representations, which suggested that patients were active problem solvers whose behavior was a product of their cognitive and emotional responses to a health threat. Patients formed illness representations that shaped their understanding of their diseases. It was these illness representations (e.g., images) that the researchers needed to understand more thoroughly to help patients with their therapy, behaviors, and quality of life. The authors turned to the literature on patients' experiences with AIDS. They reviewed the literature on qualitative research, noting that several phenomenological studies on such topics as coping and living with HIV had already been examined. However, how patients represented AIDS in images had not been studied.

Their design involved the study of 58 men and women with a diagnosis of AIDS. To study these individuals, they used phenomenology and the procedures advanced by Colaizzi (1978) and modified by Moustakas (1994). For over 18 months, they conducted interviews with these 58 patients, and asked them: "What is your experience with AIDS? Do you have a mental image of HIV/AIDS, or how would you describe HIV/AIDS? What feeling comes to mind? What meaning does it have in your life?" (Anderson & Spencer, 2002, pp. 1341–1342). They also asked patients to draw pictures of their disease. Although only 8 of the 58 drew pictures, the authors integrated these pictures into the data analysis. Their data analysis of these interviews consisted of the following tasks:

- Reading through the written transcripts several times to obtain an overall feeling for them
- Identifying significant phrases or sentences that pertained directly to the experience
- Formulating meanings and clustering them into themes common to all of the participants' transcripts
- Integrating the results into an in-depth, exhaustive description of the phenomenon
- Validating the findings with the participants, and including participants' remarks in the final description

This analysis led to 11 major themes based on 175 significant statements. "Dreaded bodily destruction" and "devouring life" illustrated two of the themes. The results section of this study reported each of the 11 themes and provided ample quotes and perspectives to illustrate the multiple perspectives on each theme.

The study ended with a discussion in which the authors described the essence (i.e., the exhaustive description) of the patients' experiences and the coping strategies (i.e., the contexts or conditions surrounding the experience) patients used to regulate mood and disease. Finally, the authors compared their 11 themes with results reported by other authors in the literature, and they discussed the implications for nursing and questions for future research.

This study illustrated several aspects of a phenomenological study:

- A *phenomenon*—the "cognitive representations or images" of AIDS by patients—was examined in the study.
- Rigorous data collection with a *group of individuals* through 58 interviews and incorporation of patients' drawings were used.

- The authors only briefly mentioned the *philosophical* ideas behind phenomenology. They referred to bracketing their personal experiences and their need to explore lived experiences rather than to obtain theoretical explanations.
- The researchers talked about *bracketing* in the study. Specifically, they stated that the interviewer was a health care provider for and a researcher of persons with HIV/AIDS, and thus it was necessary for the interviewer to acknowledge and attempt to bracket those experiences.
- The *data collection* consisted of 58 interviews conducted over 18 months at three sites dedicated to persons with HIV/AIDS, a hospital-based clinic, a long-term care facility, and a residence.
- The use of systematic *data analysis* procedures of significant statements, meanings, themes, and an exhaustive description of the essence of the phenomenon followed the procedures recommended by Moustakas (1994).
- The inclusion of tables illustrating the significant statements, meanings, and theme clusters showed how the authors worked from the raw data to the exhaustive description of the essence of the study in the final discussion section.
- The study ended by describing the *essence* of the experience for the 58 patients and the context in which they experienced AIDS (e.g., coping mechanisms).

A GROUNDED THEORY STUDY (Harley et al., 2009; see Appendix D)

This grounded theory study sought to develop a theory of the behavioral process of African American women that explains the pathways linking key factors together in the integration of physical activity into their lifestyles. It was premised on the problem that physical activity is of concern for particular subgroups, such as African American women who remain particularly sedentary. To this end, the researchers chose grounded theory because of the lack of knowledge regarding the specific factors and relationships that comprise the process of physical activity behavioral evolution. The authors studied 15 women who met the criterion sampling of being between 25 and 45 years of age, completing at least some college or technical school beyond high school, and holding a commitment to physical activity. Participants were recruited through two local African

American sorority alumni associations, and data were collected through face-to-face in-depth interviews followed by two focus groups after preliminary findings were disseminated. These data were analyzed using the Strauss and Corbin (1998) approach to grounded theory consisting of coding, concept development, constant comparisons between the data and the emerging concepts, and the formulation of a theoretical model. The authors then presented the theoretical model as a figure, and this model consisted of three phases in the behavioral process of integrating physical activity into lifestyle: an initiation phase, a transition phase, and an integration phase. The researchers advanced categories within each of these phases, and also specified the context (i.e., African American social and cultural contexts) and the conditions influencing the physical activity integration. The authors then took one of the conditions, the planning practices for physical activity, and elaborated on these possibilities in a figure of the taxonomy of planning methods. This elaboration enabled the researchers to draw specific results for practice, such as the ideal number of physical activity sessions per week, and the maximum number of sessions per week. In conclusion, this grounded theory study advanced important lessons for future efforts at program design for physical activity for African American women.

This study met many of the defining features of a grounded theory study:

- Its central focus was to understand a behavior *process,* and the theoretical model advanced three major phases in this process.
- A theory *emerged* to suggest the framework of physical activity evolution for the African American women in the study.
- The researchers did not specifically mention *memoing* or writing down their ideas as they interviewed the women and analyzed the data.
- Their form of *data collection* was consistent with many grounded theory studies: the collection of face-to-face interview data. They also collected focus group data with the participants in the study.
- The researchers engaged in a structured approach to grounded theory *data analysis* using the Strauss and Corbin (1998) approach of coding categories and developing a theoretical model that included context and conditions. They did not follow the strict Strauss and Corbin (1998) components of open, axial, and selective coding. They did provide a detailed description of the phases of the theoretical model and compared their model with existing theoretical models in the literature.

AN ETHNOGRAPHIC STUDY
(Haenfler, 2004; see Appendix E)

This ethnography study described the core values of the straight edge (sXe) movement that emerged on the East Coast of the United States from the punk subculture of the early 1980s. The movement arose as a response to the punk subculture's nihilistic tendencies of drug and alcohol abuse and promiscuous sex. The sXers adopted a "clean living" ideology of abstaining for life from alcohol, tobacco, illegal drugs, and casual sex. Involving primarily White, middle-class males from the age of 15 to 25, the movement has been linked inseparably with the punk genre music scene, and straight edgers made a large X on each hand before they entered punk concerts. As a study that reconceptualized resistance to opposition, this ethnography examined how subculture group members expressed opposition individually as a reaction to other subcultures rather than against an ambiguous "adult" culture.

The author used ethnographic methods of data collection, including participating in the movement for 14 years and attending more than 250 music shows, interviewing 28 men and women, and gathering documents from sources such as newspaper stories, music lyrics, World Wide Web pages, and sXe magazines. From these data sources, the author first provided a detailed description of the subculture (e.g., T-shirt slogans, song lyrics, and use of the symbol X). The description also conveyed the curious blend of conservative perspectives from religious fundamentalism and progressive influences of expressing personal values. Following this description, the author identified five themes: living in a clean, positive way (e.g., committed vegetarians); reserving sex for caring relationships (e.g., sex should be part of an emotional relationship based on trust); promoting self-realization (e.g., toxins such as drugs and alcohol inhibit people from reaching their full potential); spreading the message (e.g., sXers undertook a mission to convince their peers of their values); and becoming involved in progressive causes (e.g., animal rights and environmental causes). The article concluded with the author conveying a broad understanding of the sXers' values. Participation in the youth subculture had meaning both individually and collectively. Also, the sXers' resistance was at the macro level when directed to a culture that marketed alcohol and tobacco to youths; at the meso level when aimed at other subcultures, such as "punks"; and at the micro level when the sXers embraced personal change, in part in defiance of family members' substance abuse or their own addictive tendencies. Resistance was seen as personal in everyday activities and in political resistance to youth culture. It short, resistance was found to be multilayered, contradictory, and personally and socially transforming.

Haenfler's ethnography nicely illustrates both core elements of an ethnographic study and aspects of a critical ethnography:

- This ethnography was the study of a *culture-sharing group* and its members' core values and beliefs.
- The author first described the group in terms of its members' *ideas,* then advanced five themes about the *behavior* of the group, and ended with a broad level of abstraction beyond the themes to suggest how the subculture worked. This group had been *interacting* for some time and developed ways of behaving.
- Consistent with critical ethnography, the author used a *theory* of resistance to opposition by a counterculture youth group to explain how the group worked. The group resisted dominant culture in a complex and multilayered way (e.g., macro, meso, and micro). The author also talked about the personal and social transforming qualities of participating in the culture-sharing group. Unlike other critical approaches, it did not end with a call for social transformation, but the overall study stood for reexamining subculture resistance.
- The author positioned himself by describing his involvement in the subculture and his role as a *participant observer* of the group for many years. The author also engaged in *fieldwork* by conducting unstructured in-depth interviews.
- From these *emic* data and the researcher's field notes, the *etic* data, a *cultural interpretation* was formed as to how the group worked. The members of the youth subculture constructed both individualized and collective meanings for their participation. Resistance occurred at different levels. The methods of resistance were both personal and political. We leave this study with a complex view of how the sXes worked as a group and their culture.

A CASE STUDY (Asmussen & Creswell, 1995; see Appendix F)

This qualitative case study described a campus reaction to a gunman incident in which a student attempted to fire a gun at his classmates. The case study began with a detailed description of the gunman incident, chronicled the first two weeks of events following the incident, and provided details about the city, the campus, and the building in which the incident occurred. Data were collected through the multiple sources of information, such as interviews, observations, documents, and audiovisual materials, and they were advanced in a table summarizing the forms of data. Asmussen and I did not interview the gunman or the students who were in counseling immediately following the incident, and our petition to the Institutional Review Board for Human Subjects Research had guaranteed these restrictions. From the data analysis emerged themes of denial, fear, safety, retriggering, and campus planning. Toward the end of the article we combined these narrower themes into two overarching perspectives, an organizational and a social-psychological response, and we related these to the literature, thus providing "layers" of analysis in the study and invoking broader interpretations of the meaning of the case. We suggested that campuses plan for their responses to campus violence, and we advanced key questions to be addressed in preparing these plans.

In this case study, we tried to follow Lincoln and Guba's (1985) case study structure—the problem, the context, the issues, and the "lessons learned." We also added our own personal perspective by presenting information about the extent of our data collection and the questions necessary to be addressed in planning a campus response to an incident. The epilogue at the end of the study reflexively brought our personal experiences into the discussion without disrupting the flow of the study. With our last theme on the need for the campus to design a plan for responding to another incident, we advanced practical and useful implications of the study for personnel on campuses.

Several features mark this project as a case study:

- We identified the *case* for the study, the entire campus and its response to a potentially violent crime. This "case" was a bounded system, bounded by time (six months of data collection) and place (situated on a single campus).
- Our *intent* was to report a single, *instrumental* case study. Thus, we were most interested in exploring the issue of campus violence and using the single case of one institution to illustrate the reaction of the campus to a potentially violent incident. This case study should not be seen as an intrinsic case study because campus gun violence has occurred, unfortunately, on several higher education campuses.
- We used extensive, multiple sources of information in data collection to provide the detailed *in-depth understanding* of the campus

response. The table of data collection sources was our attempt to document and to convince readers of the in-depth picture that we were building. Our two-week chronology after the event was inserted to provide detail about the incident as well as continue to build this in-depth understanding.

- In our *data analysis,* we spent considerable time *describing* the context or setting for the case, situating the case within a peaceful Midwestern city, a tranquil campus, a building, and a classroom, along with the detailed events during a two-week period following the incident. We also advanced five *themes* (e.g., denial, safety) that helped us to understand the case. These themes were not presented as a *chronology* because they all seemed important and we did not know in what order they emerged following the incident.

- We ended our case analysis by presenting *assertions* in terms of two overriding responses of the campus community to the gunman incident: organizational, and psychological or social-psychological. We further grounded our assertions in current literature that also addressed these two responses. In a sense, the literature became a larger explanation for our descriptive and thematic analyses.

DIFFERENCES AMONG THE APPROACHES

A useful perspective to begin the process of differentiating among the five approaches is to assess the central purpose or focus of each approach. As shown in Figure 5.1, the focus of a narrative is on the life of an individual, and the focus of a phenomenology is on a concept or phenomenon and the "essence" of the lived experiences of persons about that phenomenon. In grounded theory, the aim is to develop a theory, whereas in ethnography, it is to describe a culture-sharing group. In a case study, a specific case is examined, often with the intent of examining an issue with the case illustrating the complexity of the issue. Turning to the five studies, the foci of the approaches become more evident.

Central Features of Each Approach

The story of Ai Mei Zhang, the Chinese immigrant student in a Canadian middle school, is a case in point—one decides to write a narrative when a

Figure 5.1 Differentiating Approaches by Foci

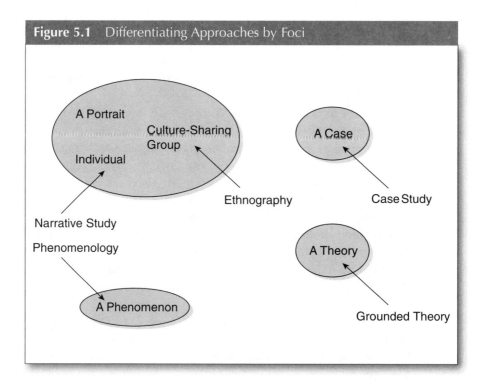

single individual needs to be studied, and that individual can illustrate with experiences the issue of being an immigrant student and the conflicting concerns that she faced. Furthermore, the researcher needs to make a case for the need to study this particular individual—someone who illustrates a problem, someone who has had a distinguished career, someone in the national spotlight, or someone who lives an ordinary life. The process of data collection involves gathering material about the person, such as from conversations or observations.

The phenomenological study, on the other hand, focuses not on the life of an individual but rather on understanding the lived experiences of individuals around a phenomenon, such as how individuals represent their illnesses (Anderson & Spencer, 2002). Furthermore, individuals are selected who have experienced the phenomenon, and they are asked to provide data, often through interviews. The researcher takes these data and, through several steps of reducing the data, ultimately develops a description of the experiences about the phenomenon that all individuals have in common—the essence of the experience.

Whereas the phenomenological project focuses on the meaning of people's experience toward a phenomenon, researchers in grounded theory have a different objective—to generate a substantive theory, such as the theory about how African American women integrate physical activity into their lifestyles (Harley et al., 2009). Thus, grounded theorists undertake research to develop theory. The data collection method involves primarily interviewing. Also, the researchers use systematic procedures for analyzing and developing this theory, procedures such as generating categories of data, relating the categories in a theoretical model, and specifying the context and conditions under which the theory operated. The overall tone of a grounded theory study is one of rigor and scientific credibility.

An ethnographic design is chosen when one wants to study the behaviors of a culture-sharing group, such as the sXers (Haenfler, 2004). In an ethnography, the researcher studies an intact culture-sharing group that has been interacting long enough to have shared or regular patterns of language and behavior. A detailed description of the culture-sharing group is essential at the beginning, and then the author may turn to identifying patterns of the group around some cultural concept such as acculturation, politics, or economy and the like. The ethnography ends with summary statements about how the group functions and works in everyday life. In this way, a reader understands a group that may be unfamiliar, such as the sXers that Haenfler studied.

Finally, a case study is chosen to study a case with clear boundaries, such as the campus in our study (Asmussen & Creswell, 1995). In this type of case study, the researcher explores an issue or problem, and a detailed understanding emerges from examining a case or several cases. It is important, too, for the researcher to have contextual material available to describe the setting for the case. Also, the researcher needs to have a wide array of information about the case to provide an in-depth picture of it. Central to writing a case study, the researcher describes the case in detail, and mentions several issues or focuses on a single issue (Stake, 1995) that emerged when examining the case. Generalizations that can be learned from studying this case or cases end a case study report.

Selecting Your Approach

Based now on a more thorough understanding of the five approaches, how do you choose one approach over the other? I recommend that you start with the outcome—what the approach is attempting to accomplish (e.g., the study of an individual, the examination of the meaning of experiences toward a phenomenon, the generation of a theory, the description and interpretation of a culture-sharing group, the in-depth study of a single case). In addition, other factors need also to be considered:

- The audience question: What approach is frequently used by gatekeepers in your field (e.g., committee members, advisors, editorial boards of journals)?
- The background question: What training do you have in the inquiry approach?
- The scholarly literature question: What is needed most as contributing to the scholarly literature in your field (e.g., a study of an individual, an exploration of the meaning of a concept, a theory, a portrait of a culture-sharing group, an in-depth case study)?
- The personal approach question: Are you more comfortable with a more structured approach to research or with a storytelling approach (e.g., narrative research, ethnography)? Or are you more comfortable with a firmer, more well-defined approach to research or with a flexible approach (e.g., grounded theory, case study, phenomenology)?

SUMMARY

This chapter examined five different short articles to illustrate good models for writing a narrative study, a phenomenology, a grounded theory study, an ethnography, and a case study. These articles show basic characteristics of each approach and should enable readers to see differences in composing and writing varieties of qualitative studies. Choose a narrative study to examine the life experiences of a single individual when material is available and accessible and the individual is willing (assuming that he or she is living) to share stories. Choose a phenomenology to examine a phenomenon and the meaning it holds for individuals. Be prepared to interview the individuals, ground the study in philosophical tenets of phenomenology, follow set procedures, and end with the "essence" of the meaning. Choose a grounded theory study to generate or develop a theory. Gather information through interviews (primarily), and use systematic procedures of data gathering and analysis built on procedures such as open, axial, and selective coding. Although the final report will be "scientific," it can still address sensitive and emotional issues. Choose an ethnography to study the behavior of a culture-sharing group (or individual). Be prepared to observe and interview, and develop a description of the group and explore themes that emerge from studying human behaviors. Choose a case study to examine a case, bounded in time or place, and look for contextual material about the setting of the case. Gather extensive material from multiple sources of information to provide an in-depth picture of the case.

These are important distinctions among the five approaches to quali tative inquiry. By studying each approach in detail, we can learn more about how to proceed and how to narrow our choice of which approach to use.

ADDITIONAL READINGS

The following are published journal articles that illustrate each of the approaches of inquiry.

Narrative Inquiry

Angrosino, M. V. (1989). Freddie: The personal narrative of a recovering alcoholic— Autobiography as case history. In M. V. Angrosino (Ed.), *Documents of interaction: Biography, autobiography, and life history in social science perspective* (pp. 29–41). Gainesville: University of Florida Press.

Chan, E. (2010). Living in the space between participant and researcher as a narrative inquirer: Examining ethnic identity of Chinese Canadian students as conflicting stories to live by. *The Journal of Educational Research, 103,* 113–122.

Ellis, C. (1993). "There are survivors": Telling a story of sudden death. *The Sociological Quarterly, 34,* 711–730.

Geiger, S. N. G. (1986). Women's life histories: Method and content. *Signs: Journal of Women in Culture and Society, 11,* 334–351.

Huber, J., & Whelan, K. (1999). A marginal story as a place of possibility: Negotiating self on the professional knowledge landscape. *Teaching and Teacher Education, 15,* 381–396.

Karen, C. S. (1990, April). *Personal development and the pursuit of higher education: An exploration of interrelationships in the growth of self-identity in returning women students—summary of research in progress.* Paper presented at the annual meeting of the American Educational Research Association, Boston.

Nelson, L. W. (1990). Code-switching in the oral life narratives of African-American women: Challenges to linguistic hegemony. *Journal of Education, 172,* 142–155.

Olson, L. N. (2004). The role of voice in the (re)construction of a battered woman's identity: An autoethnography of one woman's experiences of abuse. *Women's Studies in Communication, 27,* 1–33.

Smith, L. M. (1987). The voyage of the Beagle: Fieldwork lessons from Charles Darwin. *Educational Administration Quarterly, 23*(3), 5–30.

Phenomenology

Anderson, E. H., & Spencer, M. H. (2002). Cognitive representations of AIDS: A phenomenological study. *Qualitative Health Research, 12,* 1338–1352.

Brown, J., Sorrell, J. H., McClaren, J., & Creswell, J. W. (2006). Waiting for a liver transplant. *Qualitative Health Research, 16*(1), 119–136.

Edwards, L. V. (2006). Perceived social support and HIV/AIDS medication adherence among African American women. *Qualitative Health Research, 16,* 679–691.

Grigsby, K. A., & Megel, M. E. (1995). Caring experiences of nurse educators. *Journal of Nursing Research, 34,* 411–418.

Lauterbach, S. S. (1993). In another world: A phenomenological perspective and discovery of meaning in mothers' experience with death of a wished-for baby: Doing phenomenology. In P. L. Munhall & C. O. Boyd (Eds.), *Nursing research: A qualitative perspective* (pp. 133–179). New York: National League for Nursing Press.

Padilla, R. (2003). Clara: A phenomenology of disability. *The American Journal of Occupational Therapy, 57*(4), 413–423.

Riemen, D. J. (1986). The essential structure of a caring interaction: Doing phenomenology. In P. M. Munhall & C. J. Oiler (Eds.), *Nursing research: A qualitative perspective* (pp. 85–105). Norwalk, CT: Appleton-Century-Crofts.

Grounded Theory

Brimhall, A. C., & Engblom-Deglmann, M. L. (2011). Starting over: A tentative theory exploring the effects of past relationships on postbereavement remarried couples. *Family Process, 50*(1), 47–62.

Conrad, C. F. (1978). A grounded theory of academic change. *Sociology of Education, 51,* 101–112.

Creswell, J. W., & Brown, M. L. (1992). How chairpersons enhance faculty research: A grounded theory study. *Review of Higher Education, 16*(1), 41–62.

Harley, A. E., Buckworth, J., Katz, M. L., Willis, S. K., Odoms-Young, A., & Heaney, C. A. (2009). Developing long-term physical activity participation: A grounded theory study with African American women. *Health Education & Behavior, 36*(1), 97–112.

Kearney, M. H., Murphy, S., & Rosenbaum, M. (1994). Mothering on crack cocaine: A grounded theory analysis. *Social Science Medicine, 38*(2), 351–361.

Komives, S. R., Owen, J. E., Longerbeam, S. D., Mainella, F. C., & Osteen, L. (2005). Developing a leadership identity: A grounded theory. *Journal of College Student Development, 46*(6), 593–611.

Leipert, B. D., & Reutter, L. (2005). Developing resilience: How women maintain their health in northern geographically isolated settings. *Qualitative Health Research, 15,* 49–65.

Morrow, S. L., & Smith, M. L. (1995). Constructions of survival and coping by women who have survived childhood sexual abuse. *Journal of Counseling Psychology, 42,* 24–33.

Ethnography

Finders, M. J. (1996). Queens and teen zines: Early adolescent females reading their way toward adulthood. *Anthropology & Education Quarterly, 27,* 71–89.

Geertz, C. (1973). Deep play: Notes on the Balinese cockfight. In C. Geertz (Ed.), *The interpretation of cultures: Selected essays* (pp. 412–435). New York: Basic Books.

Haenfler, R. (2004). Rethinking subcultural resistance: Core values of the straight edge movement. *Journal of Contemporary Ethnography, 33,* 406–436.

Miller, D. L., Creswell, J. W., & Olander, L. S. (1998). Writing and retelling multiple ethnographic tales of a soup kitchen for the homeless. *Qualitative Inquiry, 4*(4), 469–491.

Rhoads, R. A. (1995). Whales tales, dog piles, and beer goggles: An ethnographic case study of fraternity life. *Anthropology and Education Quarterly, 26,* 306–323.

Trujillo, N. (1992). Interpreting (the work and the talk of) baseball. *Western Journal of Communication, 56,* 350–371.

Wolcott, H. F. (1983). Adequate schools and inadequate education: The life history of a sneaky kid. *Anthropology and Education Quarterly, 14*(1), 2–32.

Case Study

Asmussen, K. J., & Creswell, J. W. (1995). Campus response to a student gunman. *Journal of Higher Education, 66,* 575–591.

Brickhous, N., & Bodner, G. M. (1992). The beginning science teacher: Classroom narratives of convictions and constraints. *Journal of Research in Science Teaching, 29,* 471–485.

Hill, B., Vaughn, C., & Harrison, S. B. (1995, September/October). Living and working in two worlds: Case studies of five American Indian women teachers. *The Clearinghouse, 69*(1), 42–48.

Padula, M. A., & Miller, D. L. (1999). Understanding graduate women's reentry experiences: Case studies of four psychology doctoral students in a Midwestern university. *Psychology of Women Quarterly, 23,* 327–343.

Rex, L. A. (2000). Judy constructs a genuine question: A case for interactional inclusion. *Teaching and Teacher Education, 16,* 315–333.

EXERCISES

1. Begin to sketch a qualitative study using one of the approaches. Answer the questions here that apply to the approach you are considering. For a narrative study: What individual do you plan to study? And do you have access to information about this individual's life experiences? For a phenomenology: What is the phenomenon of interest that you plan to study? And do you have access to people who have experienced it? For a grounded theory: What social science concept, action, or process do you plan to explore as the basis for your theory? Can you interview individuals who have experienced the process? For an ethnography: What cultural group of people do you plan to study? Has the culture-sharing group been together long enough for patterns of behavior, language, and beliefs to form? For a case study: What is the case you plan to examine? Will the case be described because it is a unique case, or will the case be used to illustrate (and illuminate) an issue or a problem?

2. Select one of the journal articles listed in the Additional Readings section. Determine the characteristics of the approach being used by the author(s) and discuss why the author(s) may have used the approach. Go back to Chapter 4 and the "defining features" of the approach and see how many of them you can find in the journal article. Discuss specifically where the "defining features" occur.

6

Introducing and
Focusing the Study

T he beginning of a study, I have often said, is the most important
part of a research project. If the purpose of the study is unclear,
if the research questions are vague, and if the research problem
or issue is not clearly identified, then a reader has difficulty following the
remainder of the study. Consider a qualitative research journal article that
you have recently read. Did it read quickly? If so, that is usually an indica-
tion that the study is well tied together: The problem leads to certain
research questions, and the data collection naturally follows, and then the
data analysis and interpretation relate closely to the questions, which, in
turn, help the reader to understand the research problem. Often the logic
is back and forth between these components in an integrated, consistent
manner so that all parts interrelate (Morse & Richards, 2002). This integration of all parts of a good qualitative introduction begins with the identification of a clear problem that needs to be studied. It then advances the
primary intent of the study, called the purpose of the study. Of all parts of
a research project, the purpose statement is most important. It sets the
stage for the entire article and conveys what the author hopes to accomplish in the study. It is so important, I believe, that I have scripted out a
purpose statement that you might use in your qualitative project. All you
need to do is to insert several components into this statement to have a
clear, short, and concise qualitative purpose statement that will be easy for
readers to follow. Then, the qualitative research questions extend and
often narrow the purpose statement into questions that will be answered
during the course of the study. In this chapter, I will discuss how to compose a good problem statement for a qualitative study, how to compose a
clear purpose statement, and how to further specify the research through
qualitative research questions. Moreover, I will suggest how these sections

of an introduction can be adjusted to fit all five of the approaches to qualitative inquiry addressed in this book.

QUESTIONS FOR DISCUSSION

- How can the problem statement be best written to reflect one of the approaches to qualitative research?
- How can the purpose statement be best written to convey the orientation of an approach to research?
- How can a central question be written so that it encodes and foreshadows an approach to qualitative research?
- How can subquestions be presented so that they subdivide the central question into several parts?

THE RESEARCH PROBLEM STATEMENT

How does one begin a qualitative study? Have you realized that all good research begins with an issue or problem that needs to be resolved? Qualitative studies begin with an introduction advancing the research problem or issue in a study. The term *problem* may be a misnomer, and individuals unfamiliar with writing research may struggle with this writing passage. Rather than calling this passage the "problem," it might be clearer if I call it the "need for the study" or "creating a rationale for the need for the study." The intent of a ***research problem*** in qualitative research is to provide a rationale or need for studying a particular issue or "problem." This research problem discussion begins a qualitative study. But the actual research problem is framed within several other components in an opening paragraph in a good qualitative study. Here I want to analyze what these opening paragraphs might look like and to illustrate how they might be tailored to fit one of the five approaches.

Consider designing an introduction to a qualitative study. First examine in Figure 6.1 the model that I designed for a multiple case study of teen smoking in high schools. In the marginal notes on the left of this passage, you will see several topics that characterize content advanced in this introduction. My ideas for structuring a good introduction came from early study of opening passages in good research articles (see Creswell,

2009). I felt that implicit within good introductions was a model or template that authors were using. I called this model a "deficiencies model of an introduction" (Creswell, 2009, p. 100) and referred to it by this name because it centered on deficiencies in the current literature, and how studies were crafted to add to a body of literature. I know now that qualitative studies not only add to the literature, but they can give voice to underrepresented groups, probe a deep understanding of a central phenomenon, and lead to specific outcomes such as stories, the essence of a phenomenon, the generation of theory, the cultural life of a group, and an in-depth analysis of a case. You will see in Figure 6.1 the five elements of a good introduction: the topic, the research problem, the evidence from the literature about the problem, the deficiencies in the evidence, and the importance of the problem for select audiences. Added as a final sixth element in this statement would be the purpose statement, a topic to be covered shortly in this chapter.

These components of a good introduction are as follows:

1. Begin with sentences or a paragraph that creates reader interest and that advances the *topic* or general subject matter of the research study. A good first sentence—called a narrative hook in literature composition circles—would create reader interest through the use of stating timely topics, advancing a key controversy, using numbers, or citing a leading study. I would stay away from quotes for the first sentence because they not only often require the reader to focus in on the key idea of the quote, but they also need appropriate lead-in and lead-out features. Proceed beyond the first sentence to advance a general discussion about the topic being addressed in the study.

2. Discuss the *research problem* or issue that leads to a need for the study. Readers simply need to be told about the issue or concern that you plan on addressing in your qualitative project. Another way to frame the research problem is to view it as an argument as to why the topic you wish to study matters. In this way you can present to the reader the study's importance (Ravitch & Riggan, 2012). Research methods books (e.g., Creswell, 2012; Marshall & Rossman, 2010) advance several sources for locating research problems. Research problems are found in personal experience with an issue, a job-related problem, an advisor's research agenda, or the scholarly literature. I like to think about the research problem as coming from "real life" issues or from a gap in the literature, or both. "Real life" problems might be that students struggle

Figure 6.1 Sample Research Problem Section (Introduction) to a Study

The Topic	Exploring the Conceptions and Misconceptions of Teen Smoking in High Schools: A Multiple Case Analysis
The Research Problem	Tobacco use is a leading cause of cancer in American society (McGinnis & Foefe, 1993). Although smoking among adults has declined in recent years, it has actually increased for adolescents. The Center for Disease Control and Prevention reported that smoking among high school students had risen from 27.5 percent in 1991 to 34.8 percent in 1995 (USDHHS, 1996). Unless this trend is dramatically reversed, an estimated 5 million of our nations children will ultimately die a premature death (Center for Disease Control, 1996).
Evidence from Literature Justifying Problem	Previous research on adolescent tobacco use has focused on four primacy topics. Several studies have examined the question of the initiation of smoking by young people, noting that tobacco use initiation begins as early as junior high school (e.g., Heishman et al., 1997). Other studies have focused on the prevention of smoking and tobacco use in schools. This research has led to numerous school-based prevention programs and interventions (e.g., Sussman, Dent, Burton, Stacy, & Flay, 1995). Fewer studies have examined "quit attempts" or cessation of smoking behaviors among adolescents, a distinct contrast to the extensive investigations into adult cessation (Heishman et al., 1997). Of interest as well to researchers studying adolescent tobacco use has been the social context and social influence of smoking (Fearnow, Chassin, & Presson, 1998). For example, adolescent smoking may occur in work-related situations, at home where one or more parents or caretakers smoke, at teen social events, or at areas designated as "Safe" smoking places near high schools (McVea et al., in press).
Deficiencies in Evidence	Minimal research attention has been directed toward the social context of high schools as a site for examining adolescent tobacco use. During high school students form peer groups which may contribute to adolescent smoking. Often peers become a strong social influence for behavior in general, and belonging to an athletic team, a music group, or the "grunge" crowd can impact thinking about smoking (McVea et al., in press). Schools are also places where teachers and administrators need to be role models for abstaining from tobacco use and enforcing policies about tobacco use (OHara et al., 1999). Existing studies of adolescent tobacco use are primarily quantitative with a focus on outcomes and transtheoretical models (Pallonen, 1998). Qualitative investigations, however, provide detailed views of students in their own words, complex analyses of multiple perspectives, and specific school contexts of different high schools that shape student experiences with tobacco (Creswell, in press). Moreover, qualitative inquiry offers the opportunity to involve high school students as co-researchers, a data collection procedure that can enhance the validity of students' views uncontaminated by adult perspectives.
Importance of Program for Audiences	By examining these multiple school contexts, using qualitative approaches and involving students as co-researchers, we can better understand the conceptions and misconceptions adolescents hold about tobacco use in high schools. With this understanding, researchers can better isolate variables and develop models about smoking behavior. Administrators and teachers can plan interventions to prevent or change attitudes toward smoking, and school officials can assist with smoking cessation or intervention programs.

(Adapted from McVea, Harter, McEntarffer, & Creswell, 1999)

132

with their ethnic identity given the demands of friends, family, and schools, such as in Chan's (2010) study (see Appendix B). Individuals struggle to make sense of the disease of AIDS/HIV (Anderson & Spencer, 2002; see Appendix C). The need for a study also comes from certain deficiencies or gaps in the existing scholarly literature. Authors mention these gaps in "future research" sections or in "introductions" of their published studies. As suggested by Barritt (1986), the rationale is not the discovery of new elements, as in natural scientific study, but rather the heightening of awareness for experiences, which has been forgotten and overlooked. By heightening awareness and creating dialogue, it is hoped research can lead to better understanding of the way things appear to someone else and through that insight lead to improvements in practice (Barritt, 1986, p. 20). Besides dialogue and understanding, a qualitative study may lead to an in-depth understanding, fill a void in existing literature, establish a new line of thinking, lift up the voices of individuals who have been marginalized in our society, or assess an issue with an understudied group or population.

3. Briefly summarize the recent evidence, the *scholarly literature* that has addressed this research problem. Has anyone directly studied this problem? Or has anyone studied this problem in a general sense or by discussing a closely related topic? Although opinions differ about the extent of literature review needed before a study begins, qualitative texts (e.g., Creswell, 2012; Marshall & Rossman, 2010) refer to the need to review the literature so that one can provide the rationale for the problem and position one's study within the ongoing literature about the topic. I have found it helpful to visually depict where my study can be positioned into the larger literature. For example, one might develop a visual or figure—a research map (Creswell, 2009)—of existing literature and show in this figure the topics addressed in the literature and how one's proposed research fits into or extends the existing literature. I also see this section as not providing detail about any one study, such as what one finds in a complete literature review, but as a statement about the general literature—the groups of literature, if you will—that have addressed the problem. If no groups of literature have addressed the problem, then discuss the extant literature that is closest to the topic. Hopefully a good qualitative study has not already been done, and no studies directly address the topic being proposed in the present study.

4. Next, indicate in what ways the current literature or discussions are *deficient* in understanding the problem. Mention several reasons, such as

inadequate methods of data collection, a need for research, or inadequate research. It is here, in the deficiencies section of an introduction, that information can be inserted that relates to one of the five qualitative approaches. In a problem statement for a narrative study, for example, writers can mention how individual stories need to be told to gain personal experiences about the research problem. In a phenomenological study, the researcher makes the case that a need exists to know more about a particular phenomenon and the common experiences of individuals with the phenomenon. For a grounded theory study, authors state that we need a theory that explains a process because existing theories are inadequate, are nonexistent for the population under study, or need to be modified for an existing population. In an ethnographic study, the problem statement advances why it is important to describe and to interpret the cultural behavior of a certain group of people or how a group is marginalized and kept silent by others. For a case study, the researcher might discuss how the study of a case or cases can help inform the issue or concern. In all of these illustrations the researcher presents the research problem as relating to the particular approach to qualitative research taken in the study.

5. Discuss how *audiences* or *stakeholders* will profit from your study that addresses the problem. Consider different types of audiences and point out, for each one, the ways they will benefit from the study. These audiences could be other researchers, policymakers, practitioners in the field, or students.

At this point the introduction proceeds on to the purpose statement. But at this point a reader has a clear understanding of the problem leading to a need for the study, and is encouraged enough to read on to see what the overall intent of the study might be (purpose) as well as the types of questions (research questions) that will be answered in the study.

THE PURPOSE STATEMENT

This interrelationship between design and approach continues with the *purpose statement*, a statement that provides the major objective or intent, or "road map," to the study. As the most important statement in an entire qualitative study, the purpose statement needs to be carefully constructed and written in clear and concise language. Unfortunately, all too many writers leave this statement implicit, causing readers extra work in interpreting and following a study. This need not be the case, so I created a "script" of this statement (Creswell, 1994, 2009), a statement containing several sentences and blanks that an individual fills in:

The purpose of this _____ (narrative, phenomenological, grounded theory, ethnographic, case) study is (was? will be?) to _____ (understand? describe? develop? discover?) the _____ (central phenomenon of the study) for _____ (the participants) at _____ (the site). At this stage in the research, the _____ (central phenomenon) will be generally defined as _____ (a general definition of the central concept).

As I show in the script, several terms can be used to encode a passage for a specific approach to qualitative research. In the purpose statement:

- The writer identifies the specific *qualitative approach* used in the study by mentioning the type. The name of the approach comes first in the passage, thus foreshadowing the inquiry approach for data collection, analysis, and report writing.
- The writer encodes the passage with *words* that indicate the action of the researcher and the focus of the approach to research. For example, I associate certain words with qualitative research, such as *understand experiences* (useful in narrative studies), *describe* (useful in case studies, ethnographies, and phenomenologies), *meaning ascribed* (associated with phenomenologies), *develop or generate* (useful in grounded theory), and *discover* (useful in all approaches). I identify several words that a researcher would include in a purpose statement to encode the purpose statement for the approach chosen (see Table 6.1). These words indicate not only researchers' actions but also the foci and outcomes of the studies.
- The writer identifies the *central phenomenon*. The central phenomenon is the one central concept being explored or examined in the research study. I generally recommend that qualitative researchers focus on only one concept (e.g., the campus reaction to the gunman, or the values of the sXers) at the beginning of a study. Comparing groups or looking for linkages can be included in the study as one gains experiences in the field and one proceeds on with analysis after initial exploration of the central phenomenon.

- The writer foreshadows the *participants* and the *site* for the study, whether the participants are one individual (i.e., narrative or case study), several individuals (i.e., grounded theory or phenomenology), a group (i.e., ethnography), or a site (i.e., program, event, activity, or place in a case study).

I also suggest including a *general definition* for the central phenomenon. This definition is a tentative, preliminary definition that the researcher intends to use at the outset of the study. The definition may be difficult to determine with any specificity in advance. But, for example, in a narrative study, a writer might define the types of stories to be collected (e.g., life stages, childhood memories, the transition from adolescence to adulthood, attendance at an Alcoholics Anonymous meeting). In a phenomenology, the central phenomenon to be explored might be specified such as the meaning of grief, anger, or even chess playing (Aanstoos, 1985). In grounded theory, the central phenomenon might be identified as a concept central to the process being examined. In an ethnography, the writer might identify the key cultural concepts (often drawn from cultural concepts in anthropology) being examined such as roles, behaviors, acculturation, communication, myths, stories, or other concepts that the researcher plans to take into the field at the beginning of the study. Finally, in a case study such as an "intrinsic" case study (Stake, 1995), the writer might define the boundaries of the case, specifying how the case is bounded in time and place. If an "instrumental" case study is being examined, then the researcher might specify and define generally the issue being examined in the case.

Table 6.1 Words to Use in Encoding the Purpose Statement

Narrative	Phenomenology	Grounded Theory	Ethnography	Case Study
• Narrative study • Stories • Epiphanies • Lived experiences • Chronology	• Phenomenology • Describe • Experiences • Meaning • Essence	• Grounded theory • Generate • Develop • Propositions • Process • Substantive theory	• Ethnography • Culture-sharing group • Cultural behavior and language • Cultural portrait • Cultural themes	• Case study • Bounded • Single or collective case • Event, process, program, individual

Several examples of purpose statements follow that illustrate the *encoding* and foreshadowing of the five approaches to research:

Example 6.1 A Narrative Example

Notice in the following example how the purpose statement focuses on a single individual and conveys a life history of the individual.

> The author describes and analyzes the process of eliciting the life history of a man with mental retardation. (Angrosino, 1994, p. 14)

Example 6.2 A Phenomenological Example

See in the following example how the exploration is clearly of a single phenomenon—the role of these individuals as fathers:

> The present study was designed to explore the beliefs, attitudes, and needs that current and expectant adolescent fathers and young men who are fathers of children born to adolescent mothers have regarding their role as a father. (Lemay, Cashman, Elfenbein, & Felice, 2010, p. 222)

Example 6.3 A Grounded Theory Example

In the following example, the researchers are interested in studying a process around leadership identity that leads to the advancement of a theory:

> The purpose of this study was to understand the processes a person experiences in creating a leadership identity. (Komives, Owen, Longerbeam, Mainella, & Osteen, 2005, p. 594)

Example 6.4 An Ethnographic Example

From an ethnography of "ballpark" culture, the author creates a description of the employees as a culture-sharing group:

> This article examines how the work and the talk of stadium employees reinforce certain meanings of baseball in society, and it reveals how the work and the talk create and maintain ballpark culture. (Trujillo, 1992, p. 351)

Example 6.5   A Case Study Example

In this multiple case study, the focus is on understanding the issue of the integration of technology:

> The purpose of this study was to describe the ways in which three urban elementary schools, in partnership with a local, publicly funded multipurpose university, used a similar array of material and human resources to improve their integration of technology. (Staples, Pugach, & Himes, 2005, p. 287)

THE RESEARCH QUESTIONS

The intent of qualitative research questions is to narrow the purpose to several questions that will be addressed in the study. I distinguish between the purpose statement and research questions so that we can clearly see how they are conceptualized and composed; other authors may combine them or more typically state only a purpose statement in a journal article and leave out the research questions. However, in many types of qualitative studies, such as dissertations and theses, the research questions are distinct and stated separately from the purpose statement. Once again, I find that these questions provide an opportunity to encode and foreshadow an approach to inquiry.

The Central Question

Some writers offer suggestions for writing qualitative research questions (e.g., Creswell, 2012; Marshall & Rossman, 2010). Qualitative research questions are open-ended, evolving, and nondirectional. They restate the purpose of the study in more specific terms and typically start with a word such as *what* or *how* rather than *why* in order to explore a central phenomenon. They are few in number (five to seven) and posed in various forms, from the "grand tour" (Spradley, 1979, 1980) that asks, "Tell me about yourself," to more specific questions.

I recommend that a researcher reduce her or his entire study to a single, overarching *central question* and several subquestions. Drafting this central question often takes considerable work because of its breadth and the tendency of some to form specific questions based on traditional training. To reach the overarching central question, I ask qualitative researchers to state the broadest question they could possibly pose to address their research problem.

This central question can be encoded with the language of each of the five approaches to inquiry. Morse (1994) speaks directly to this issue as she reviews the types of research questions. Although she does not refer to narratives or case studies, she mentions that one finds "descriptive" questions of cultures in ethnographies, "process" questions in grounded theory studies, and "meaning" questions in phenomenological studies. For example, I searched through the five studies presented in Chapter 5 to see if I could find or imagine their central research questions. I recognized immediately that the authors of these journal articles typically did not provide central questions, but instead presented purpose statements, as is often the case in journal article reports. Still, it is helpful to consider what their central questions, if asked, might have been.

In the narrative study of the Chinese immigrant student (Chan, 2010; see Appendix B), I did not find a central question, but it might have been "What are the conflicting stories of ethnic identity that Ai Mei experienced in her school, with her peers, and with her family?" This would have been the most general question that could have been addressed in the study, and it focused on gathering Ai Mei's stories. In the phenomenological study of how persons living with AIDS represent and image their disease, Anderson and Spencer (2002; see Appendix C) also did not pose a central question, but it might have been "What meaning do 41 men and 17 women with a diagnosis of AIDS ascribe to their illness?" This central question in phenomenology implies that all of the individuals diagnosed with AIDS have something in common that provides meaning for their lives. In the grounded theory study of the process of integrating physical activity into the lifestyle of African American women (Harley et al., 2009; see Appendix D), a central question was not asked, but if it had been, it might have been "What behavioral process theory explains the integration of physical activity into the lifestyle of 15 African American women?" In this study, the authors seek to generate a theory that helps to explain the process of integrating physical activity into lifestyles. In the ethnographic study of the sXe movement by Haenfler (2004; see Appendix E), again no research question was advanced, but it might have been "What are the core values of the straight edge movement, and how do the members construct and understand their subjective experiences of being a part of the subculture?" This question asks first for a description of the core values and then for an understanding of experiences (that are presented as themes in the study). Finally, in our case study of a campus response to a gunman incident (Asmussen & Creswell, 1995; see Appendix F), we asked five central guiding questions in our introduction: "What happened? Who was involved in response to the incident? What themes of response emerged during the eight-month period that followed this incident? What theoretical constructs helped us understand the campus response, and what constructs were unique to this case?" (p. 576). This example illustrates how we were interested first in simply describing individuals' experiences and then in developing themes that represented responses of individuals on the campuses.

As these examples illustrate, authors may or may not pose a central question, although one lies implicit if not explicit in all studies. For writing journal articles, central questions may be used less than purpose statements to guide the research. However, for individuals' graduate research, such as theses or dissertations, the trend is toward writing both purpose statements and central questions.

Subquestions

An author typically presents a small number of *subquestions* that further specify the central question into some areas for inquiry. Here are some suggestions for writing these subquestions:

- State a small number of subquestions to further refine the central question. I generally recommend five to seven subquestions. New questions may arise during data collection, and, as with all qualitative research questions, they may change or evolve into new questions as the research proceeds.
- Consider the subquestions as a means of subdividing the central question into several parts. Ask yourself, "If the central question were divided into some areas that I would like to explore, what would the areas or parts be?" A good illustration comes from ethnography. Wolcott (2008a) said that the grand tour or central question such as "What is going on here?" can only be addressed when fleshed out with detail: "In terms of what?" (p. 74).

- Write the subquestions to begin with "how" or "what" words in a similar manner as the central question.
- Keep the subquestions open-ended like the central question.
- Use the subquestions to form the core questions asked during the data collection, such as in the interviews or in the observations.

You can write the subquestions focused on further analyzing the central phenomenon that relates to the type of qualitative research being used. In a narrative study, these questions may further probe the meaning of stories. In a phenomenology, it will help to establish the components of the "essence" of the study. In a grounded theory, it will help to detail the emerging theory, and in an ethnography, it will detail the aspects of the culture-sharing group you plan to study, such as members' rituals, their communication, their economic way of life, and so forth. In a case study, the subquestions will address the elements of the case or the issue that you seek to understand.

Here are some examples of subquestions used in qualitative studies:

A central question such as "What does it mean to be a college professor?" would be analyzed in subquestions on topics like "What does it mean to be a college professor in the classroom? As a researcher?"

To illustrate issue subquestions in a study, Gritz (1995, p. 4) examines "teacher professionalism" as it is understood by practicing elementary classroom teachers in her phenomenology study. She poses the following central question and subquestions:

Central question:

- What does it mean (to practitioners) to be a professional teacher?

Subquestions:

- What do professional teachers do?
- What don't professional teachers do?
- What does a person do who exemplifies the term *teacher professionalism*?
- What is difficult or easy about being a professional educator?
- How or when did you first become aware of being a professional?

For grounded theory, for example, in Mastera's (1995) dissertation proposal, she advances a study of the process of revising the general education curriculum in three private baccalaureate colleges. Her plan calls for subquestions. Her central question, "What is the theory that explains the change process in the revision of general education curricula on three college campuses?" is followed by a subquestion, "How does the chief academic officer participate in the process on each campus?"

In using good research question format for our gunman case study (Asmussen & Creswell, 1995), I would redraft the questions presented in the article. To foreshadow the case of a single campus and individuals on it, I would pose the central question—"What was the campus response to the gunman incident at the Midwestern university?"—and then I would present the subquestions guiding my study: "How did the administration respond?" "How did the counselors respond?" "How did the students who were not in the room with the gunman respond?" In this way, I could have described how each group responded and subdivided the "campus response" down into some manageable subparts for description and theme development.

SUMMARY

In this chapter, I addressed three topics related to introducing and focusing a qualitative study: the problem statement, the purpose statement, and the research questions. Although I discussed general features of designing each section in a qualitative study, I related the topics to the five approaches advanced in this book. The problem statement should indicate the topic, the research problem, the literature about the problem, the deficiencies in this literature, and the audience who will profit from learning about the problem. It is in the deficiencies section that an author can insert specific information related to his or her approach. For example, authors can advance the need for stories to be told, the need to find the "essence" of the experience, the need to develop a theory, the need to portray the life of a culture-sharing group, and the need to use a case to explore a specific issue. A script may be used to construct the purpose statement. This script should include the type of qualitative approach being used and incorporate words that signal the use of one of the five approaches. The research questions divide into one central question and about five to seven subquestions that subdivide the central questions into several parts of inquiry. The central question can be encoded to accomplish the intent of one of the approaches, such as the development of stories in narrative projects or the generation of a theory in grounded theory. Subquestions also can be used in the data collection process as the key questions asked during an interview or an observation.

ADDITIONAL READINGS

Creswell, J. W. (2009). *Research design: Qualitative, quantitative, and mixed methods approaches* (3rd ed.). Thousand Oaks, CA: Sage.

Marshall, C., & Rossman, G. B. (2010). *Designing qualitative research* (5th ed.). Thousand Oaks, CA: Sage.

Maxwell, J. (2005). *Qualitative research design: An interactive approach* (2nd ed.). Thousand Oaks, CA: Sage.

Miles, M. B., & Huberman, A. M. (1994). *Qualitative data analysis: A sourcebook of new methods* (2nd ed.). Thousand Oaks, CA: Sage.

Stake, R. (1995). *The art of case study research.* Thousand Oaks, CA: Sage.

Wolcott, H. F. (2008). *Ethnography: A way of seeing* (2nd ed.). Walnut Creek, CA: AltaMira.

EXERCISES

1. Consider how you would write about the research problem or issue in your study in an introductory passage to a study. State the issue in a couple of sentences, and then discuss the research literature that will provide evidence for a need for studying the problem. Finally, within the context of one of the five approaches to research, what rationale exists for studying the problem that reflects your approach to research?

2. Try out the script in this chapter for writing a purpose statement using one of the approaches. Now adopt a different approach and write the purpose statement using the second approach.

3. The challenge in writing a good central question is not writing it too broad or too narrow. Consider four key elements of a central question: the central phenomenon, the participants, the site, and the approach to inquiry. Write it in an open, evolving, nondirectional way, starting with the

word *how* or *what.* Keep the question short. You might first write your central phenomenon that you wish to explore. Then put the words *what is* before the central phenomenon. Examine what you have written to determine whether it will be a satisfactory central question written as the broadest question that you could ask in your study.

4. Write several subquestions. Subdivide your central question into several subtopics. Consider these subtopics the types of questions that you would ask a participant.

7

Data Collection

Atypical reaction to thinking about qualitative data collection is to focus in on the actual types of data and the procedures for gathering them. Data collection, however, involves much more. It means gaining permissions, conducting a good qualitative sampling strategy, developing means for recording information both digitally and on paper, storing the data, and anticipating ethical issues that may arise. Also, in the actual forms of data collection, researchers often opt for only conducting interviews and observations. As will be seen in this chapter, the array of qualitative sources of data are ever expanding, and I encourage researchers to use newer, innovative methods in addition to the standard interviews and observations. In addition, these new forms of data and the steps in the process of collecting qualitative data need to be sensitive to the outcomes expected for each of the five different approaches to qualitative research.

I find it useful to visualize the phases of data collection common to all approaches. A "circle" of interrelated activities best displays this process, a process of engaging in activities that include but go beyond collecting data. I begin this chapter by presenting this circle of activities, briefly introducing each activity. These activities are locating a site or an individual, gaining access and making rapport, sampling purposefully, collecting data, recording information, exploring field issues, and storing data. Then I explore how these activities differ in the five approaches to inquiry, and I end with a few summary comments about comparing the data collection activities across the five approaches.

QUESTIONS FOR DISCUSSION

- What are the steps in the overall data collection process of qualitative research?
- What are typical access and rapport issues?

- How does one select people or places to study?
- What type of information typically is collected?
- How is information recorded?
- What are common issues in collecting data?
- How is information typically stored?
- How are the five approaches both similar and different during data collection?

THE DATA COLLECTION CIRCLE

I visualize data collection as a series of interrelated activities aimed at gathering good information to answer emerging research questions. As shown in Figure 7.1, a qualitative researcher engages in a series of activities in the process of collecting data. Although I start with locating a site or an individual to study, an investigator may begin at another entry point in the circle. Most importantly, I want the researcher to consider the multiple phases in collecting data, phases that extend beyond the typical reference point of conducting interviews or making observations.

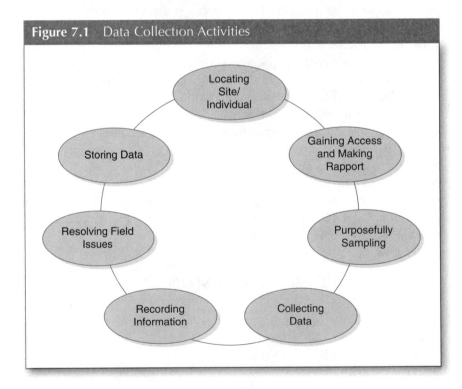

Figure 7.1 Data Collection Activities

An important step in the process is to find people or places to study and to gain access to and establish rapport with participants so that they will provide good data. A closely interrelated step in the process involves determining a strategy for the purposeful sampling of individuals or sites. This is not a probability sample that will enable a researcher to determine statistical inferences to a population; rather, it is a purposeful sample that will intentionally sample a group of people that can best inform the researcher about the research problem under examination. Thus, the researcher needs to determine which type of purposeful sampling will be best to use.

Once the inquirer selects the sites or people, decisions need to be made about the most appropriate data collection approaches. Increasingly, a qualitative researcher has more choices regarding data collection, such as e-mail messages and online data gathering, and typically the researcher will collect data from more than one source. To collect this information, the researcher develops protocols or written forms for recording the information and needs to develop some forms for recording the data, such as interview or observational protocols. Also, the researcher needs to anticipate issues of data collection, called "field issues," which may be a problem, such as having inadequate data, needing to prematurely leave the field or site, or contributing to lost information. Finally, a qualitative researcher must decide how he or she will store data so that they can easily be found and protected from damage or loss.

I now turn to each of these data collection activities, and I address each for general procedures and within each approach to inquiry. As shown in Table 7.1, these activities are both different and similar across the five approaches to inquiry.

The Site or Individual

In a narrative study, one needs to find one or more individuals to study, individuals who are accessible, willing to provide information, and distinctive for their accomplishments and ordinariness or who shed light on a specific phenomenon or issue being explored. Plummer (1983) recommends two sources of individuals to study. The pragmatic approach is where individuals are met on a chance encounter, emerge from a wider study, or are volunteers. Alternatively, one might identify a "marginal person" who lives in conflicting cultures, a "great person" who impacts the age in which he or she lives, or an "ordinary person" who provides an

Table 7.1 Data Collection Activities by Five Approaches

Data Collection Activity	Narrative	Phenomenology	Grounded Theory	Ethnography	Case Study
What is traditionally studied? (sites or individuals)	Single individual, accessible and distinctive	Multiple individuals who have experienced the phenomenon	Multiple individuals who have responded to an action or participated in a process about a central phenomenon	Members of a culture-sharing group or individuals representative of the group	A bounded system, such as a process, an activity; an event, a program, or multiple individuals
What are typical access and rapport issues? (access and rapport)	Gaining permission from individuals, obtaining access to information in archives	Finding people who have experienced the phenomenon	Locating a homogeneous sample	Gaining access through the gatekeeper, gaining the confidence of informants	Gaining access through the gatekeeper, gaining the confidence of participants
How does one select a site or individuals to study? (purposeful sampling strategies)	Several strategies, depending on the person (e.g., convenient, politically important, typical, a critical case)	Finding individuals who have experienced the phenomenon, a "criterion" sample	Finding a homogeneous sample, a "theory-based" sample, a "theoretical" sample	Finding a cultural group to which one is a "stranger," a "representative" sample	Finding a "case" or "cases," an "atypical" case, or a "maximum variation" or "extreme" case

Data Collection Activity	Narrative	Phenomenology	Grounded Theory	Ethnography	Case Study
What type of information typically is collected? (forms of data)	Documents and archival material, open-ended interviews, subject journaling, participant observation, casual chatting; typically a single individual	Interviews with 5 to 25 people (Polkinghorne, 1989)	Primarily interviews with 20 to 30 people to achieve detail in the theory	Participant observations, interviews, artifacts, and documents of a single culture-sharing group	Extensive forms, such as documents and records, interviews, observation, and physical artifacts for 1 to 4 cases
How is information recorded? (recording information)	Notes, interview protocol	Interviews, often multiple interviews with the same individuals	Interview protocol, memoing	Field notes, interview and observational protocols	Field notes, interview and observational protocols
What are common data collection issues? (field issues)	Access to materials, authenticity of account and materials	Bracketing one's experiences, logistics of interviewing	Interviewing issues (e.g., logistics, openness)	Field issues (e.g., reflexivity, reactivity, reciprocality, "going native," divulging private information, deception)	Interviewing and observing issues
How is information typically stored? (storing data)	File folders, computer files	Transcriptions, computer files	Transcriptions, computer files	Field notes, transcriptions, computer files	Field notes, transcriptions, computer files

149

example of a large population. An alternative perspective is available from Gergen (1994), who suggests that narratives "come into existence" (p. 280) not as a product of an individual, but as a facet of relationships, as a part of culture, as reflected in social roles such as gender and age. Thus, to ask which individuals will participate is not to focus on the right question. Instead, narrative researchers need to focus on the stories to emerge, recognizing that all people have stories to tell. Also instructive in considering the individual in narrative research is to consider whether first-order or second-order narratives are the focus of inquiry (Elliott, 2005). In first-order narratives, individuals tell stories about themselves and their own experiences, while in second-order narratives, researchers construct a narrative about other people's experiences (e.g., biography) or present a collective story that represents the lives of many.

In a phenomenological study, the participants may be located at a single site, although they need not be. Most importantly, they must be individuals who have all experienced the phenomenon being explored and can articulate their lived experiences. The more diverse the characteristics of the individuals, the more difficult it will be for the researcher to find common experiences, themes, and the overall essence of the experience for all participants. In a grounded theory study, the individuals may not be located at a single site; in fact, if they are dispersed, they can provide important contextual information useful in developing categories in the axial coding phase of research. They need to be individuals who have participated in the process or action the researcher is studying in the grounded theory study. For example, in Creswell and Brown (1992), we interviewed 32 department chairpersons located across the United States who had mentored faculty in their departments. In an ethnographic study, a single site, in which an intact culture-sharing group has developed shared values, beliefs, and assumptions, is often important. The researcher needs to identify a group (or an individual or individuals representative of a group) to study, preferably one to which the inquirer is a "stranger" (Agar, 1986) and can gain access. For a case study, the researcher needs to select a site or sites to study, such as programs, events, processes, activities, individuals, or several individuals. Although Stake (1995) refers to an individual as an appropriate "case," I turn to the narrative biographical approach or the life history approach in studying a single individual. However, the study of multiple individuals, each defined as a case and considered a collective case study, is acceptable practice.

A question that students often ask is whether they can study their own organization, place of work, or themselves. Such a study may raise issues of power and risk to the researcher, the participants, and the site. To study one's own workplace, for example, raises questions about whether good data can be collected when the act of data collection may introduce a power imbalance between the researcher and the individuals being studied. Although studying one's own "backyard" is often convenient and eliminates many obstacles to collecting data, researchers can jeopardize their jobs if they report unfavorable data or if participants disclose private information that might negatively influence the organization or workplace. A hallmark of all good qualitative research is the report of multiple perspectives that range over the entire spectrum of perspectives (see the section in Chapter 3 on the characteristics of qualitative research). I am not alone in sounding this cautionary note about studying one's own organization or workplace. Glesne and Peshkin (1992) question research that examines "your own *backyard*—within your own institution or agency, or among friends or colleagues" (p. 21), and they suggest that such information is "dangerous knowledge" that is political and risky for an "inside" investigator. When it becomes important to study one's own organization or workplace, I typically recommend that multiple strategies of validation (see Chapter 10) be used to ensure that the account is accurate and insightful.

Studying yourself can be a different matter. As mentioned in Chapter 4, autoethnography provides an approach or method for studying yourself. Several helpful books are available on authoethnography that discuss how personal stories are blended with larger cultural issues (see Ellis, 2004; Muncey, 2010). Ellis's (1993) story of the experiences of her brother's sudden death illustrates the power of personal emotion and the use of cultural perspectives around one's own experiences. I recommend that individuals wanting to study themselves and their own experiences turn to autoethnography or biographical memoir for scholarly procedures in how to conduct their studies.

Access and Rapport

Qualitative research involves the study of a research site(s) and gaining permission to study the site in a way that will enable the easy collection of data. This means obtaining approval from university or college institutional review boards as well as individuals at the research site. It also means finding individuals who can provide access to the research site and facilitate the collection of data.

Institutional review boards. Gaining access to sites and individuals also involves several steps. Regardless of the approach to inquiry, permissions need to be sought from a human subjects review board, a process in which campus committees review research studies for their potential harmful impact on and risk to participants. This process involves submitting to the board a proposal that details the procedures in the project. Most qualitative studies are exempt from a lengthy review (e.g., the expedited or full review), but studies involving individuals as minors (i.e., 18 years or under) or studies of high-risk, sensitive populations (e.g., HIV-positive individuals) require a thorough review, a process involving detailed, lengthy applications and an extended time for review. Because many review boards are sometimes more familiar with the quantitative approaches to social and human science research than they are with qualitative approaches, the qualitative project description may need to conform to some of the standard procedures and language of quantitative research (e.g., research questions, results) as well as provide information about the protection of human subjects. To the review board, it might be argued, qualitative interviews, if unstructured, may actually provide participants considerable control over the interview process (Corbin & Morse, 2003). It is helpful to examine a sample consent form that participants need to review and sign in a qualitative study. An example is shown in Figure 7.2.

Figure 7.2 Sample Human Subjects Consent-to-Participate Form

"Experiences in Learning Qualitative Research: A Qualitative Case Study"

Dear Participant,

The following information is provided for you to decide whether you wish to participate in the present study. You should be aware that you are free to decide not to participate or to withdraw at any time without affecting your relationship with this department, the instructor, or the University of Nebraska–Lincoln.

The purpose of this study is to understand the process of learning qualitative research in a doctoral-level college course. The procedure will be a single, holistic case study design. At this stage in the research, process will be generally defined as perceptions of the course and making sense out of qualitative research at different phases in the course.

Data will be collected at three points—at the beginning of the course, at the midpoint, and at the end of the course. Data collection will involve documents (journal entries made by students and the instructor, student evaluations of the class and the research procedure), audiovisual material (a videotape of the class), interviews (transcripts of interviews between students), and classroom observation field notes (made by students and the instructor). Individuals involved in the data collection will be the instructor and the students in the class.

Do not hesitate to ask any questions about the study either before participating or during the time that you are participating. We would be happy to share our findings with you after the research is completed. However, your name will not be associated with the research findings in any way, and only the researchers will know your identity as a participant.

There are no known risks and/or discomforts associated with this study. The expected benefits associated with your participation are the information about the experiences in learning qualitative research, the opportunity to participate in a qualitative research study, and coauthorship for those students who participate in the detailed analysis of the data. If submitted for publication, a byline will indicate the participation of all students in the class.

Please sign your consent with full knowledge of the nature and purpose of the procedures. A copy of this consent form will be given to you to keep.

Date

Signature of Participant
John W. Creswell, Ed. Psy., UNL, Principal Investigator

This consent form often requires that specific elements be included, such as

- the right of participants to voluntarily withdraw from the study at any time;
- the central purpose of the study and the procedures to be used in data collection;
- the protection of the confidentiality of the respondents;
- the known risks associated with participation in the study;
- the expected benefits to accrue to the participants in the study; and
- the signature of the participant as well as the researcher.

Access and rapport within the five approaches. The permissions and building of rapport will differ depending on the type of qualitative approach being used. For a narrative study, inquirers gain information from individuals by obtaining their permission to participate in the study. Study participants should be appraised of the motivation of the researcher for their selection, granted anonymity (if they desire it), and told by the researcher about the purpose of the study. This disclosure helps build rapport. Access to biographical documents and archives requires permission and perhaps travel to distant libraries.

In a phenomenological study in which the sample includes individuals who have experienced the phenomenon, it is also important to obtain participants' written permission to be studied. In the Anderson and Spencer (2002; see Appendix C) study of the patients' images of AIDS, 58 men and women participated in the project at three sites dedicated to persons with HIV/AIDS: a hospital clinic, a long-term care facility, and a residence. These were all individuals with a diagnosis of AIDS, 18 years of age or older, able to communicate in English, and with a Mini-Mental Status exam score above 22. In such a study, it was important to obtain permission to have access to the vulnerable individuals participating in the study.

In a grounded theory study, the participants need to provide permission to be studied, while the researcher should have established rapport with the participants so that they will disclose detailed perspectives about responding to an action or a process. The grounded theorist starts with a homogeneous sample, individuals who have commonly experienced the action or process. In an ethnography, access typically begins with a "gate-keeper," an individual who is a member of or has insider status with a cultural group. This gatekeeper is the initial contact for the researcher and leads the researcher to other participants (Hammersley & Atkinson, 1995). Approaching this gatekeeper and the cultural system slowly is wise advice for "strangers" studying the culture. For both ethnographies and case studies, gatekeepers require information about the studies that often includes answers from the researchers to the following questions, as Bogdan and Biklen (1992) suggest:

- Why was the site chosen for study?
- What will be done at the site during the research study? How much time will be spent at the site by the researchers?
- Will the researcher's presence be disruptive?
- How will the results be reported?
- What will the gatekeeper, the participants, and the site gain from the study? (reciprocity)

Purposeful Sampling Strategy

Three considerations go into the ***purposeful sampling*** approach in qualitative research, and these considerations vary depending on the specific approach. They are the decision as to whom to select as participants (or sites) for the study, the specific type of sampling strategy, and the size of the sample to be studied.

Participants in the sample. In a narrative study, the researcher reflects more on whom to sample—the individual may be convenient to study because she or he is available, a politically important individual who attracts attention or is marginalized, or a typical, ordinary person. All of the individuals need to have stories to tell about their lived experiences. Inquirers may select several options, depending on whether the person is marginal, great, or ordinary (Plummer, 1983). Vonnie Lee, who consented to participate and provided insightful information about individuals with mental retardation (Angrosino, 1994), was convenient to study but also was a critical case to illustrate the types of challenges surrounding the issues of mental retardation in our society. Ai Mei Zhang was a Chinese immigrant student in Canada who could inform an understanding of the ethnic identity through student, teacher, and parent narratives (Chan, 2010; see Appendix B).

I have found, however, a much more narrow range of sampling strategies for phenomenological studies. It is essential that all participants have experience of the phenomenon being studied. Criterion sampling works well when all individuals studied represent people who have experienced the phenomenon. In a grounded theory study, the researcher chooses participants who can contribute to the development of the theory. Strauss and Corbin (1998) refer to theoretical sampling, which is a process of sampling individuals that can contribute to building the opening and axial coding of the theory. This begins with selecting and studying a homogeneous sample of individuals (e.g., all women who have experienced childhood abuse) and then, after initially developing the theory, selecting and studying a heterogeneous sample (e.g., types of support groups other than women who have experienced childhood abuse). The rationale for studying this heterogeneous sample is to confirm or disconfirm the conditions, both contextual and intervening, under which the model holds.

In ethnography, once the investigator selects a site with a cultural group, the next decision is who and what will be studied. Thus, within-culture sampling proceeds, and several authors offer suggestions for this procedure. Fetterman (2010) recommends proceeding with the big net approach, where at first the researcher mingles with everyone. Ethnographers rely on their judgment to select members of the subculture or unit based on their research questions. They take advantage of opportunities (i.e., opportunistic sampling; Miles & Huberman, 1994) or establish criteria for studying select individuals (criterion sampling). The criteria for selecting who and what to study, according to Hammersley and Atkinson (1995), are based on gaining some perspective on chronological time in the social life of the group, people representative of the culture-sharing group in terms of demographics, and the contexts that lead to different forms of behavior.

In a case study, I prefer to select unusual cases in collective case studies and employ maximum variation as a sampling strategy to represent diverse cases and to fully describe multiple perspectives about the cases. Extreme and deviant cases may comprise my collective case study, such as the study of the unusual gunman incident on the university campus (Asmussen & Creswell, 1995; see Appendix F).

Types of sampling. The concept of purposeful sampling is used in qualitative research. This means that the inquirer selects individuals and sites for study because they can purposefully inform an understanding of the research problem and central phenomenon in the study. Decisions need to be made about who or what should be sampled, what form the sampling will take, and how many people or sites need to be sampled. Further, the researchers need to decide if the sampling will be consistent with the information within one of the five approaches to inquiry.

I will begin with some general remarks about sampling and then turn to sampling within each of the five approaches. The decision about who or what should be sampled can benefit from the conceptualization of Marshall and Rossman (2010), who provide an example of sampling four aspects: events, settings, actors, and artifacts. They also note that sampling can change during a study and that researchers need to be flexible, but despite this, researchers need to plan ahead as much as possible for their sampling strategy. I like to think as well in terms of levels of sampling in qualitative research. Researchers can sample at the site level, at the event or process level, and at the participant level. In a good plan for a qualitative study, one or more of these levels might be present, and each one needs to be identified.

On the question of what form the sampling will take, we need to note that there are several qualitative sampling strategies available (see Table 7.2 for a list of possibilities). These strategies have names and definitions, and they can be described in research reports. Also, researchers might use one or more of the strategies in a single study. Looking down the list, ***maximum variation sampling*** is listed first because it is a popular approach in qualitative studies. This approach consists of determining in advance some criteria that differentiate the sites or participants, and then selecting sites or participants that are quite different on the criteria. This approach is often selected because when a researcher maximizes differences at the beginning of the study, it increases the likelihood that the findings will reflect differences or different perspectives—an ideal in qualitative research. Other sampling strategies frequently used are critical cases, which provide specific information about a problem, and convenience cases, which represent sites or individuals from which the researcher can access and easily collect data.

Sample size. The size question is an equally important decision to sampling strategy in the data collection process. One general guideline for **sample size** in qualitative research is not only to study a few sites or individuals but also to collect extensive detail about each site or individual studied. The intent in qualitative research is not to generalize the information (except in some forms of case study research), but to elucidate the particular, the specific (Pinnegar & Daynes, 2007). Beyond these general suggestions, each of the five approaches to research raises specific sample size considerations.

In narrative research, I have found many examples with one or two individuals, unless a larger pool of participants is used to develop a collective story (Huber & Whelan, 1999). In phenomenology, I have seen the number of participants range from 1 (Dukes, 1984) up to 325 (Polkinghorne, 1989). Dukes (1984) recommends studying 3 to 10 subjects, and one phenomenology, Riemen (1986), studied 10 individuals. In grounded theory, I recommend including 20 to 30 individuals in order to develop a well-saturated theory, but this number may be much larger (Charmaz, 2006). In ethnography, I like well-defined studies of single culture-sharing groups, with numerous artifacts, interviews, and observations collected until the workings of the cultural group are clear. For case study research, I would not include more than 4 or 5 case studies in a single study. This number should provide ample opportunity to identify themes of the cases as well as conduct cross-case theme analysis. Wolcott (2008a) has recommended that any case over 1 dilutes the level of detail that a researcher can provide.

Forms of Data

New forms of qualitative data continually emerge in the literature (see Creswell, 2012), but all forms might be grouped into four basic types of

Table 7.2 Typology of Sampling Strategies in Qualitative Inquiry

Type of Sampling	Purpose
Maximum variation	Documents diverse variations of individuals or sites based on specific characteristics
Homogeneous	Focuses, reduces, simplifies, and facilitates group interviewing
Critical case	Permits logical generalization and maximum application of information to other cases
Theory based	Find examples of a theoretical construct and thereby elaborate on and examine it
Confirming and disconfirming cases	Elaborate on initial analysis, seek exceptions, looking for variation
Snowball or chain	Identifies cases of interest from people who know people who know what cases are information-rich
Extreme or deviant case	Learn from highly unusual manifestations of the phenomenon of interest
Typical case	Highlights what is normal or average
Intensity	Information-rich cases that manifest the phenomenon intensely but not extremely
Politically important	Attracts desired attention or avoids attracting undesired attention
Random purposeful	Adds credibility to sample when potential purposeful sample is too large
Stratified purposeful	Illustrates subgroups and facilitates comparisons
Criterion	All cases that meet some criterion; useful for quality assurance
Opportunistic	Follow new leads; taking advantage of the unexpected
Combination or mixed	Triangulation, flexibility; meets multiple interests and needs
Convenience	Saves time, money, and effort, but at the expense of information and credibility

Source: Miles & Huberman (1994, p. 28). Reprinted with permission from SAGE Publications.

information: observations (ranging from nonparticipant to participant), interviews (ranging from closed-ended to open-ended), documents (ranging from private to public), and audiovisual materials (including materials such as photographs, compact discs, and videotapes). Over the years, I have kept an evolving list of data types, as shown in Figure 7.3.

I organize my list into the four basic types, although some forms may not be easily placed into one category or the other. In recent years, new forms of data have emerged, such as journaling in narrative story writing, using text from e-mail messages, and observing through examining videotapes and photographs.

Krueger and Casey (2009) discuss the use of focus groups on the Internet, including chat room focus groups and bulletin board groups. They discuss how to manage the Internet groups as well as how to develop questions for the groups. In addition, Stewart and Williams (2005) discuss using online focus groups for social research. They reviewed both synchronous (real-time) and asynchronous (non-real-time) applications highlighting new developments such as virtual reality applications as well as their advantages (participants can be questioned over long periods of time, larger numbers can be managed, and more heated and open exchanges occur). Problems arise with online focus groups, such as obtaining complete informed consent, recruiting individuals to participate, and choosing times to convene given different international time zones.

Common formats of online data collection for qualitative research include virtual focus groups and web-based interviews via e-mail or text-based chat rooms, weblogs and life journals (such as open-ended diaries online), and Internet message boards (Garcia, Standlee, Bechkoff, & Cui, 2009; James & Busher, 2007; Nicholas et al., 2010). Some researchers also have conducted advanced qualitative studies online, such as ethnography research (Garcia et al., 2009). They collected data through e-mail, chat room interactions, instant messaging, videoconferencing, and the images and sound of the websites. Qualitative data collection via the Internet has the advantages of cost and time efficiency in terms of reduced costs for travel and data transcription. It also provides participants with time and space flexibility that allows them more time to consider and respond to requests for information. Thus, they can provide a deeper reflection on the discussed topics (Nicholas et al., 2010). Furthermore, online data collection helps create a nonthreatening and comfortable environment, and provides greater ease for participants discussing sensitive issues (Nicholas et al., 2010). More importantly, online data collection offers an alternative for hard-to-reach groups (due to practical constraints, disability, or

Figure 7.3 A Compendium of Data Collection Approaches in Qualitative Research

Observations

- Gather field notes by conducting an observation as a participant.
- Gather field notes by conducting an observation as an observer.
- Gather field notes by spending more time as a participant than as an observer.
- Gather field notes by spending more time as an observer than as a participant.
- Gather field notes first by observing as an "outsider" and then by moving into the setting and observing as an "insider."

Interviews

- Conduct an unstructured, open-ended interview and take interview notes.
- Conduct an unstructured, open-ended interview, audiotape the interview, and transcribe the interview.
- Conduct a semistructured interview, audiotape the interview, and transcribe the interview.
- Conduct a focus group interview, audiotape the interview, and transcribe the interview.
- Conduct different types of interviews: e-mail, face-to-face, focus group, online focus group, telephone.

Documents

- Keep a journal during the research study.
- Have a participant keep a journal or diary during the research study.
- Collect personal letters from participants.
- Analyze public documents (e.g., official memos, minutes, records, archival material).
- Examine autobiographies and biographies.
- Have participants take photographs or videotapes (i.e., photo elicitation).
- Conduct chart audits.
- Review medical records.

Audiovisual Materials

- Examine physical trace evidence (e.g., footprints in the snow).
- Videotape or film a social situation, individual, or group.
- Examine website main pages.
- Collect sounds (e.g., music, children's laughter, car horns honking).
- Collect e-mail or discussion board messages (e.g., Facebook).
- Gather phone text messages (e.g., Twitter).
- Examine favorite possessions or ritual objects.

language or communication barriers) who may be marginalized from qualitative research (James & Busher, 2007).

There are, however, increased ethical concerns with online data collection, such as participants' privacy protection, new power differentials, ownership of the data, authenticity, and trust in the data collected (James & Busher, 2007; Nicholas et al., 2010). Moreover, web-based research brings new requirements to both participants and researchers. For instance, participants are required to have some technical skills, access to the Internet, and necessary reading and writing proficiency. In using online information, researchers have to adapt to a new way of observation by watching texts on a screen, by strengthening their skills in interpreting textual data, and in improving online interview skills (Garcia et al., 2009; Nicholas et al., 2010).

Despite problems in innovative data collection such as these, I encourage individuals designing qualitative projects to include new and creative data collection methods that will encourage readers and editors to examine their studies. Researchers need to consider visual ethnography (Pink, 2001), or the possibilities of narrative research to include living stories, metaphorical visual narratives, and digital archives (see Clandinin, 2006). I like the technique of "photo elicitation" in which participants are shown pictures (their own or those taken by the researcher) and asked by the inquirer to discuss the contents of the pictures as in Photovoice (Wang & Burris, 1994). Ziller (1990), for example, handed one loaded Polaroid camera each to 40 male and 40 female fourth graders in Florida and West Germany and asked them to take pictures of images that represented war and peace.

The particular approach to research often directs a qualitative researcher's attention toward preferred approaches to data collection, although these preferred approaches cannot be seen as rigid guidelines. For a narrative study, Czarniawska (2004) mentions three ways to collect data for stories: recording spontaneous incidents of storytelling, eliciting stories through interviews, and asking for stories through such mediums as the Internet. Clandinin and Connelly (2000) suggest collecting field texts through a wide array of sources—autobiographies, journals, researcher field notes, letters, conversations, interviews, stories of families, documents, photographs, and personal-family-social artifacts. For a phenomenological study, the process of collecting information involves primarily in-depth interviews (see, e.g., the discussion about the long interview in McCracken, 1988) with as many as 10 individuals. The important point is to describe the meaning of the phenomenon for a small number of individuals who have experienced it. Often multiple interviews are conducted with the each of the research participants. Besides inter-viewing and self-reflection, Polkinghorne (1989) advocates gathering information from depictions of the experience outside the context of the research projects, such as descriptions drawn from novelists, poets, paint-ers, and choreographers. I recommend Lauterbach (1993), the study of wished-for babies from mothers, as an especially rich example of phenom-enological research using diverse forms of data collection.

Interviews play a central role in the data collection in a grounded theory study. In the study Brown and I conducted with academic chairpersons (Creswell & Brown, 1992), each of our interviews with 33 individuals lasted approximately an hour. Other data forms besides interviewing, such as par-ticipant observation, researcher reflection or journaling (memoing), partici-pant journaling, and focus groups, may be used to help develop the theory (Morrow and Smith, 1995, used these forms in their study of women's child-hood abuse). However, in my experience, these multiple data forms often play a secondary role to interviewing in grounded theory studies.

In an ethnographic study, the investigator collects descriptions of behavior through observations, interviewing, documents, and artifacts (Fetterman, 2010; Hammersley & Atkinson, 1995; Spradley, 1980), although observing and interviewing appear to be the most popular forms of eth-nographic data collection. Ethnography has the distinction among the five approaches, I believe, of advocating the use of quantitative surveys and tests and measures as part of data collection. For example, examine the wide array of forms of data in ethnography as advanced by LeCompte and Schensul (1999). They reviewed ethnographic data collection techniques of observation, tests and repeated measures, sample surveys, interviews, content analysis of secondary or visual data, elicitation methods, audio-visual information, spatial mapping, and network research. Participant observation, for example, offers possibilities for the researcher on a con-tinuum from being a complete outsider to being a complete insider (Jorgensen, 1989). The approach of changing one's role from that of an outsider to that of an insider through the course of the ethnographic study is well documented in field research (Jorgensen, 1989). Wolcott's (1994b) study of the Principal Selection Committee illustrates an outsider perspective, as he observed and recorded events in the process of select-ing a principal for a school without becoming an active participant in the committee's conversations and activities.

Like ethnography, case study data collection involves a wide array of procedures as the researcher builds an in-depth picture of the case. I am reminded of the multiple forms of data collection recommended by Yin

(2009) in his book about case studies. He referred to six forms: documents, archival records, interviews, direct observation, participant observation, and physical artifacts. Because of the extensive data collection in the gunman case study, Asmussen and I presented a matrix of information sources for the reader (Asmussen & Creswell, 1995; see Appendix F). This matrix contained four types of data (interviews, observations, documents, and audiovisual materials) in the columns and identified specific forms of information (e.g., students at large, central administration) in the rows. Our intent was to convey through this matrix the depth and multiple forms of data collection, thus inferring the complexity of our case. The use of a matrix, which is especially applicable in an information-rich case study, might serve the inquirer equally well in all approaches of inquiry.

Of all the data collection sources in Figure 7.3, interviewing and observing deserve special attention because they are frequently used in all five of the approaches to research. Entire books are available on these two topics (e.g., Kvale & Brinkmann, 2009; and Rubin & Rubin, 2012, on interviewing; Spradley, 1980, and Angrosino, 2007, on observing); thus I highlight only basic procedures that I recommend to prospective interviewers and observers.

Interviewing. One might view interviewing as a series of steps in a procedure. Several authors have advanced the steps necessary in conducting qualitative interviews, such as Kvale and Brinkmann (2009) and Rubin and Rubin (2012). The Kvale and Brinkmann (2009) seven stages of an interview inquiry report a logical sequence of stages from thematizing the inquiry, to designing the study, to interviewing, to transcribing the interview, to analyzing the data, to verifying the validity, to reliability and generalizability of the findings, and finally to reporting the study. The Rubin and Rubin (2012) seven steps, called the responsive interviewing model, are similar in scope to Kvale and Brinkmann (2009), but they view the sequence as not fixed, allowing the researcher to change questions asked, the sites chosen, and the situations to study. Both approaches to the stages of interviewing sweep across the many phases of research from deciding on a topic to the actual writing of the study. In my approach, presented here, I focus on the data collection process in some detail, recognizing that this process is embedded within a larger sequence of research. In the data collection process, I view the steps for interviewing as follows:

- Decide on the *research questions* that will be answered by interviews. These questions are open-ended, general, and focused on understanding your central phenomenon in the study.

- *Identify interviewees* who can best answer these questions based on one of the purposeful sampling procedures mentioned in the preceding discussion (see Miles & Huberman, 1994).
- Determine what *type of interview* is practical and will net the most useful information to answer research questions. Assess the types available, such as a telephone interview, a focus group interview, or a one-on-one interview. A telephone interview provides the best source of information when the researcher does not have direct access to individuals. The drawbacks of this approach are that the researcher cannot see the informal communication and must incur phone expenses. Focus groups are advantageous when the interaction among interviewees will likely yield the best information, when interviewees are similar and cooperative with each other, when time to collect information is limited, and when individuals interviewed one-on-one may be hesitant to provide information (Krueger & Casey, 2009; Morgan, 1988; Stewart & Shamdasani, 1990). With this approach, however, care must be taken to encourage all participants to talk and to monitor individuals who may dominate the conversation. For one-on-one interviewing, the researcher needs individuals who are not hesitant to speak and share ideas, and needs to determine a setting in which this is possible. The less articulate, shy interviewee may present the researcher with a challenge and less than adequate data.
- Use adequate *recording procedures* when conducting one-on-one or focus group interviews. I recommend equipment such as a lapel mic for both the interviewer and the interviewee or an adequate mic sensitive to the acoustics of the room for audiotaping the interviews.
- Design and use an *interview protocol,* or interview guide (Kvale & Brinkmann, 2009), a form about four or five pages in length (with space to write in answers), with approximately five to seven open-ended questions and ample space between the questions to write responses to the interviewee's comments (see the sample protocol in Figure 7.4 below). How are questions developed? The questions are often the subquestions in the research study, phrased in a way that interviewees can understand. These might be seen as the core of the interview protocol, bounded on the front end by questions to invite the interviewee to open up and talk and located at the end by questions about "Whom should I talk to in order to learn more?" or comments thanking the participants for their time for the interview.

Figure 7.4 Sample Interview Protocol or Guide

Interview Protocol Project: University Reaction to a Terrorist Incident

Time of interview:

Date:

Place:

Interviewer:

Interviewee:

Position of interviewee:

(Briefly describe the project)

Questions:

1. What has been your role in the incident?

2. What has happened since the event that you have been involved in?

3. What has been the impact on the university community of this incident?

4. What larger ramifications, if any, exist from the incident?

5. To whom should we talk to find out more about campus reaction to the incident?

6. (Thank the individual for participating in this interview. Assure him or her of confidentiality of responses and potential future interviews.)

- Refine the interview questions and the procedures further through *pilot testing*. Sampson (2004), in an ethnographic study of boat pilots aboard cargo vessels, recommends the use of a pilot test to refine and develop research instruments, assess the degrees of observer bias, frame questions, collect background information, and adapt research procedures. During her pilot testing, Sampson participated at the site, kept detailed field notes, and conducted detailed tape-recorded, confidential interviews. In case study research, Yin (2009) also recommends a pilot test to refine data collection plans and develop relevant lines of questions. These pilot cases are selected on the basis of convenience, access, and geographic proximity.

- Determine the *place* for conducting the interview. Find, if possible, a quiet location free from distractions. Ascertain if the physical setting lends itself to audiotaping, a necessity, I believe, in accurately recording information.

- After arriving at the interview site, obtain consent from the interviewee to participate in the study. Have the interviewee complete a *consent form* for the human relations review board. Go over the purpose of the study, the amount of time that will be needed to complete the interview, and plans for using the results from the interview (offer a copy of the report or an abstract of it to the interviewee).
- During the interview, use good *interview procedures.* Stay to the questions, complete the interview within the time specified (if possible), be respectful and courteous, and offer few questions and advice. This last point may be the most important, and it is a reminder of how a good interviewer is a good listener rather than a frequent speaker during an interview. Also, record information on the interview protocol in the event that the audio-recording does not work. Recognize that quickly inscribed notes may be incomplete and partial because of the difficulty of asking questions and writing answers at the same time.

Observation. Observation is one of the key tools for collecting data in qualitative research. It is the act of noting a phenomenon in the field setting through the five senses of the observer, often with an instrument, and recording it for scientific purposes (Angrosino, 2007). The observations are based on your research purpose and questions. You may watch physical setting, participants, activities, interactions, conversations, and your own behaviors during the observation. Use your senses, including sight, hearing, touch, smell, and taste. You should realize that writing down everything is impossible. Thus, you may start the observation broadly and then concentrate on research questions.

To one degree or another, the observer is usually involved in that which he or she is observing. Given the focus on the two forms of engagement in terms of participating and observing, we usually distinguish observations into *four types:*

- *Complete participant.* The researcher is fully engaged with the people he or she is observing. This may help him or her establish greater rapport with the people being observed (Angrosino, 2007).
- *Participant as observer.* The researcher is participating in the activity at the site. The participant role is more salient than the

researcher role. This may help the researcher gain insider views and subjective data. However, it may be distracting for the researcher to record data when he or she is integrated into the activity.

- *Nonparticipant/observer as participant.* The researcher is an outsider of the group under study, watching and taking field notes from a distance. He or she can record data without direct involvement with activity or people.
- *Complete observer.* The researcher is neither seen nor noticed by the people under study.

As a good qualitative observer, you may change your role during an observation, such as starting as a nonparticipant and then moving into the participant role, or vice versa.

Observing in a setting is a special skill that requires addressing issues such as the potential *deception* of the people being interviewed, impression management, and the potential marginality of the researcher in a strange setting (Hammersley & Atkinson, 1995). Like interviewing, I also see observing as a series of steps:

- Select a *site* to be observed. Obtain the required permissions needed to gain access to the site.
- At the site, identify who or what to observe, when, and for how long. A gatekeeper helps in this process.
- Determine, initially, a *role* to be assumed as an observer. This role can range from that of a complete participant (going native) to that of a complete observer. I especially like the procedure of being an outsider initially, followed by becoming an insider over time.
- Design an observational *protocol* as a method for recording notes in the field. Include in this protocol both descriptive and reflective notes (i.e., notes about your experiences, hunches, and learnings). Make sure this is headed by the date, place, and time of observation (Angrosino, 2007).
- *Record aspects* such as portraits of the informant, the physical setting, particular events and activities, and your own reactions (Bogdan & Biklen, 1992). Describe what happened and also reflect on these aspects, including personal reflections, insights, ideas, confusions, hunches, initial interpretations, and breakthroughs.
- During the observation, have someone *introduce you* if you are an outsider, be passive and friendly, and start with limited

objectives in the first few sessions of observation. The early observational sessions may be times in which to take few notes and simply observe.

- After observing, *slowly withdraw* from the site, thanking the participants and informing them of the use of the data and their accessibility to the study.
- *Prepare your full notes* immediately after the observation. Give thick and rich narrative description of the people and events under observation.

Recording Procedures

In discussing observation and interviewing procedures, I mention the use of a protocol, a predesigned form used to record information collected during an observation or interview. The interview protocol enables a person to take notes during the interview about the responses of the interviewee. It also helps a researcher organize thoughts on items such as headings, information about starting the interview, concluding ideas, information on ending the interview, and thanking the respondent. In Figure 7.4, I provided the interview protocol used in the gunman case study (Asmussen & Creswell, 1995; see Appendix F).

Besides the five open-ended questions in the study, this form contains several features I recommend. The instructions for using the interview protocol are as follows:

- Use a header to record essential information about the project and as a reminder to go over the purpose of the study with the interviewee. This heading might also include information about confidentiality and address aspects included in the consent form.
- Place space between the questions in the protocol form. Recognize that an individual may not always respond directly to the questions being asked. For example, a researcher may ask Question 2, but the interviewee's response may be to Question 4. Be prepared to write notes on all of the questions as the interviewee speaks.
- Memorize the questions and their order to minimize losing eye contact with the participant. Provide appropriate verbal transitions from one question to the next.
- Write out the closing comments that thank the individual for the interview and request follow-up information, if needed, from him or her.

During an observation, use an ***observational protocol*** to record information. As shown in Figure 7.5, this protocol contains notes taken by one of my students on a class visit by Harry Wolcott. I provide only one page of the protocol, but this is sufficient for one to see what it includes. It has a header giving information about the observational session, and then includes a "descriptive notes" section for recording a description of activities. The section with a box around it in the "descriptive notes" column indicates the observer's attempt to summarize, in chronological fashion, the flow of activities in the classroom. This can be useful information for developing a chronology of the ways the activities unfolded during the class session. There is also a "reflective notes" section for notes about the process, reflections on activities, and summary conclusions about activities for later theme development. A line down the center of the page divides descriptive notes from reflective notes. A visual sketch of the setting and a label for it provide additional useful information.

Figure 7.5 Sample Observational Protocol	
Length of Activity: 90 Minutes	
Descriptive Notes	*Reflective Notes*
General: What are the experiences of graduate students as they learn qualitative research in the classroom?	
See classroom layout and comments about physical setting at the bottom of this page.	*Overhead with flaps: I wonder if the back of the room was able to read it.*
Approximately 5:17 p.m., Dr. Creswell enters the filled room, introduces Dr. Wolcott. Class members seem relieved.	Overhead projector not plugged in at the beginning of the class: I wonder if this was a distraction (when it took extra time to plug it in).
Dr. Creswell gives brief background of guest, concentrating on his international experiences; features a comment about the educational ethnography "The Man in the Principal's Office."	*Lateness of the arrival of Drs. Creswell and Wolcott: Students seemed a bit anxious. Maybe it had to do with the change in starting time to 5 p.m. (some may have had 6:30 classes or appointments to get to).*

(Continued)

Figure 7.5 (Continued)

Descriptive Notes	Reflective Notes
Dr. Wolcott begins by telling the class he now writes out educational ethnography and highlights this primary occupation by mentioning two books: *Transferring Qualitative Data and The Art of Fieldwork*.	Drs. Creswell and Wolcott seem to have a good rapport between them, judging from many short exchanges that they had.
While Dr. Wolcott begins his presentation by apologizing for his weary voice (due to talking all day, apparently), Dr. Creswell leaves the classroom to retrieve the guest's overhead transparencies. Seemed to be three parts to this activity: (1) the speaker's challenge to the class of detecting pure ethnographical methodologies, (2) the speaker's presentation of the "tree" that portrays various strategies and substrategies for qualitative research in education, and (3) the relaxed "elder statesman" fielding class questions, primarily about students' potential research projects and prior studies Dr. Wolcott had written.	
The first question was "How do you look at qualitative research?" followed by "How does ethnography fit in?"	

Whether a researcher uses an observational or interview protocol, the essential process is recording information or, as Lofland and Lofland (1995) state it, "logging data" (p. 66). This process involves recording information through various forms, such as observational field notes, interview write-ups, mapping, census taking, photographing, sound recording, and documents. An informal process may occur in recording information composed of initial "jottings" (Emerson, Fretz, & Shaw, 1995), daily logs or summaries, and descriptive summaries (see Sanjek, 1990, for examples of field notes). These forms of recording information are popular in narrative research, ethnographies, and case studies.

Field Issues

Researchers engaged in studies within all five approaches face issues in the field when gathering data that need to be anticipated. During the last several years, the number of books and articles on field issues has expanded considerably as interpretive frameworks (see Chapter 2) have been widely discussed. Beginning researchers are often overwhelmed by the amount of time needed to collect qualitative data and the richness of the data encountered. As a practical recommendation, I suggest that beginners start with limited data collection and engage in a pilot project to gain some initial experiences (Sampson, 2004). This limited data collection might consist of one or two interviews or observations, so that researchers can estimate the time needed to collect data.

One way to think about and anticipate the types of issues that may arise during data collection is to view the issues as they relate to several aspects of data collection, such as entry and access, the types of information collected, and potential ethical issues.

Access to the organization. Gaining access to organizations, sites, and individuals to study has its own challenges. Convincing individuals to participate in the study, building trust and credibility at the field site, and getting people from a site to respond are all important access challenges. Factors related to considering the appropriateness of a site need to be considered as well (see Weis & Fine, 2000). For example, researchers may choose a site that is one in which they have a vested interest (e.g., employed at the site, a study of superiors or subordinates at the site) that would limit ability to develop diverse perspectives on coding data or developing themes. A researcher's own particular "stance" within the group may keep him or her from acknowledging all dimensions of the experiences. The researchers may hear or see something uncomfortable when they collect data. In addition, participants may be fearful that their issues will be exposed to people outside their community, and this may make them unwilling to accept the researcher's interpretation of the situation.

Also related to access is the issue of working with an institutional review board that may not be familiar with unstructured interviews in qualitative research and the risks associated with these interviews (Corbin & Morse, 2003). Weis and Fine (2000) raised the important question of whether the response of the institutional review board to a project influences the researcher's telling of the narrative story.

Observations. The types of challenges experienced during observations will closely relate to the role of the inquirer in observation, such as whether the researcher assumes a participant, nonparticipant, or middle-ground position. There are challenges as well with the mechanics of observing, such as remembering to take field notes, recording quotes accurately for inclusion in field notes, determining the best timing for moving from a nonparticipant to a participant (if this role change is desired), keeping from being overwhelmed at the site with information, and learning how to funnel the observations from the broad picture to a narrower one in time. Participant observation has attracted several commentaries by writers (Ezeh, 2003; Labaree, 2002). Labaree (2002), who was a participant in an academic senate on a campus, notes the advantages of this role but also discusses the dilemmas of entering the field, disclosing oneself to the participants, sharing relationships with other individuals, and attempting to disengage from the site. Ezeh (2003), a Nigerian, studied the Orring, a little-known minority ethnic group in Nigeria. Although his initial contact with the group was supportive, the more the researcher became integrated into the host community, the more he experienced human relations problems, such as being accused of spying, pressured to be more generous in his material gifts, and suspected of trysts with women. Ezeh concluded that being of the same nationality was no guarantee of a lack of challenges at the site.

Interviews. Challenges in qualitative interviewing often focus on the mechanics of conducting the interview. Roulston, deMarrais, and Lewis (2003) chronicle the challenges in interviewing by postgraduate students during a 15-day intensive course. These challenges related to unexpected participant behaviors and students' ability to create good instructions, phrase and negotiate questions, deal with sensitive issues, and develop transcriptions. Suoninen and Jokinen (2005), from the field of social work, ask whether the phrasing of our interview questions leads to subtle persuasive questions, responses, or explanations.

Undoubtedly, conducting interviews is taxing, especially for inexperienced researchers engaged in studies that require extensive interviewing, such as phenomenology, grounded theory, and case study research. Equipment issues loom large as a problem in interviewing, and both recording and transcribing equipment need to be organized in advance of the interview. The process of questioning during an interview (e.g., saying "little," handling "emotional outbursts," using "icebreakers") includes problems that an interviewer must address. Many inexperienced researchers express surprise at the difficulty of conducting interviews and the lengthy process involved in transcribing audiotapes from the interviews. In addition, in phenomenological interviews, asking appropriate questions and relying on participants to discuss the meaning of their experiences require patience and skill on the part of the researcher.

Recent discussions about qualitative interviewing highlight the importance of reflecting about the relationship that exists between the interviewer and the interviewee (Kvale & Brinkmann, 2009; Nunkoosing, 2005; Weis & Fine, 2000). Kvale and Brinkmann (2009), for example, discuss the power asymmetry in which the research interview should not be regarded as a completely open and free dialogue between egalitarian partners. Instead, the nature of an interview sets up an unequal power dynamic between the interviewer and the interviewee. In this dynamic, the interview is "ruled" by the interviewer. The interview is dialogue that is conducted one-way, provides information for the researcher, is based on the researcher's agenda, leads to the researcher's interpretations, and contains "counter control" elements by the interviewee who withholds information. To correct for this asymmetry, Kvale and Brinkmann (2009) suggest more collaborative interviewing, where the researcher and the participant approach equality in questioning, interpreting, and reporting. Nunkoosing (2005) extends the discussion by reflecting on the problems of power and resistance, distinguishing truth from authenticity, the impossibility of consent, and projection of the interviewers' own self (their status, race, culture, and gender). Weis and Fine (2000) raise additional questions for consideration: Are your interviewees able to articulate the forces that interrupt, suppress, or oppress them? Do they erase their history, approaches, and cultural identity? Do they choose not to expose their history or go on record about the difficult aspects of their lives? These questions and the points raised about the nature of the interviewer-interviewee relationship cannot be easily answered with pragmatic decisions that encompass all interview situations. They do, however, sensitize us to important challenges in qualitative interviewing that need to be anticipated.

Documents and audiovisual materials. In document research, the issues involve locating materials, often at sites far away, and obtaining permission to use the materials. For biographers, the primary form of data collection might be archival research from documents. When researchers ask participants in a study to keep journals, additional field issues emerge. Journaling is a popular data collection process in case studies and narrative research. What instructions should be given to individuals prior to writing in their journals? Are all participants equally comfortable with journaling? Is it appropriate, for example, with small children who express themselves well verbally but have limited writing skills? The researcher also may have difficulty reading the handwriting of participants who journal. Recording on videotape raises issues for the qualitative researcher such as keeping disturbing room sounds to a minimum, deciding on the best location for the camera, and determining whether to provide close-up shots or distant shots.

Ethical issues. Regardless of the approach to qualitative inquiry, a qualitative researcher faces many ethical issues that surface during data collection in the field and in analysis and dissemination of qualitative reports. In Chapter 3, we visited some of these issues, but ethical issues loom large in the data collection phase of qualitative research. Lipson (1994) groups ethical issues into informed consent procedures; deception or covert activities; confidentiality toward participants, sponsors, and colleagues; benefits of research to participants over risks; and participant requests that go beyond social norms. The criteria of the American Anthropological Association (1967) (see also Glesne & Peshkin, 1992) reflect appropriate standards. A researcher protects the anonymity of the informants, for example, by assigning numbers or aliases to individuals. A researcher develops case studies of individuals that represent a composite picture rather than an individual picture. Furthermore, to gain support from participants, a qualitative researcher conveys to participants that they are participating in a study, explains the purpose of the study, and does not engage in deception about the nature of the study. What if the study is on a sensitive topic and the participants decline to be involved if they are aware of the topic? In terms of this issue of disclosure of the researcher, widely discussed in cultural anthropology (e.g., Hammersley & Atkinson, 1995), the researcher presents general information, not specific information about the study. Another issue likely to develop is when participants share information "off the record." Although in most instances this information is deleted from analysis by the researcher, the issue becomes problematic when the information, if reported, harms individuals. I am reminded of a researcher who studied incarcerated Native Americans and learned about a potential "breakout" during one of the interviews. This researcher concluded that it would be a breach of faith with the participants if she reported the matter, and she kept quiet. Fortunately, the breakout did not occur.

A final ethical issue is whether the researcher shares personal experiences with participants in an interview setting such as in a case study, a phenomenology, or an ethnography. This sharing minimizes the "bracketing" that is essential to construct the meaning of participants in a phenomenology and reduces information shared by participants in case studies and ethnographies.

Storing Data

I am surprised at how little attention is given in books and articles to storing qualitative data. The approach to storage will reflect the type of information collected, which varies by approach to inquiry. In writing a narrative life history, the researcher needs to develop a filing system for the "wad of handwritten notes or a tape" (Plummer, 1983, p. 98). Davidson's (1996) suggestion about backing up information collected and noting changes made to the database is sound advice for all types of research studies. With extensive use of computers in qualitative research, more attention will likely be given to how qualitative data are organized and stored, whether the data are field notes, transcripts, or rough jottings. With extremely large databases being used by some qualitative researchers, this aspect assumes major importance.

Some principles about data storage and handling that are especially well suited for qualitative research include the following:

- Always develop backup copies of computer files (Davidson, 1996).
- Use high-quality tapes for audio-recording information during interviews. Also, make sure that the size of the tapes fits the transcriber's machine.
- Develop a master list of types of information gathered.
- Protect the anonymity of participants by masking their names in the data.
- Develop a data collection matrix as a visual means of locating and identifying information for a study.

FIVE APPROACHES COMPARED

Returning again to Table 7.1, there are both differences and similarities among the activities of data collection for the five approaches to inquiry. Turning to differences, certain approaches seem more directed toward specific types of data collection than others. For case and narrative studies, the researcher uses multiple forms of data to build the in-depth case or the storied experiences. For grounded theory studies and phenomenological projects, inquirers rely primarily on interviews as data. Ethnographers highlight the importance of participant observation and interviews, but, as noted earlier, they may use many different sources of information. Unquestionably, some mixing of forms occurs, but in general these patterns of collection by approach hold true. Case study writers employ multiple forms of data collection.

Second, the unit of analysis for data collection varies. Narrative researchers, phenomenologists, and ground theorists study individuals; case study researchers examine groups of individuals participating in an event or activity or an organization; and ethnographers study entire cultural systems or some subcultures of the systems.

Third, I found the amount of discussion about field issues to vary among the five approaches. Ethnographers have written extensively about field issues (e.g., Hammersley & Atkinson, 1995). This may reflect historical concerns about imbalanced power relationships, imposing objective, external standards on participants, and failures to be sensitive to marginalized groups. Narrative researchers are less specific about field issues, although their concerns are mounting about how to conduct the interview (Elliott, 2005). Across all approaches, ethical issues are widely discussed.

Fourth, the approaches vary in their intrusiveness of data collection. Conducting interviews seems less intrusive in phenomenological projects and grounded theory studies than in the high level of access needed in personal narratives, the prolonged stays in the field in ethnographies, and the immersion into programs or events in case studies.

These differences do not lessen some important similarities that need to be observed. All qualitative studies sponsored by public institutions need to be approved by a human subjects review board. Also, the use of interviews and observations is central to many of the approaches. Furthermore, the recording devices, such as observational and interview protocols, can be similar regardless of approach (although specific questions on each protocol will reflect the language of the approach). Finally, the issue of data storage of information is closely related to the form of data collection, and the basic objective of researchers, regardless of approach, is to develop some filing and storing system for organized retrieval of information.

SUMMARY

In this chapter, I addressed several components of the data collection process. The researcher attends to locating a site or person to study; gaining access to and building rapport at the site or with the individual; sampling purposefully using one or more of the many approaches to sampling in qualitative research; collecting information through many forms, such as interviews, observations, documents, and audiovisual materials and newer forms emerging in the literature; establishing approaches for recording information such as the use of interview or observational protocols; anticipating and addressing field issues ranging from access to ethical concerns; and developing a system for storing and handling the databases. The five approaches to inquiry differ in the diversity of information collected, the unit of study being examined, the extent of field issues discussed in the literature, and the intrusiveness of the data collection effort. Researchers, regardless of approach, need approval from review boards, engage in similar data collection of interviews and observations, and use recording protocols and forms for storing data.

ADDITIONAL READINGS

For a discussion about purposeful sampling strategies:

Creswell, J. W. (2012). *Educational research: Planning, conducting, and evaluating quantitative and qualitative research* (4th ed.). Upper Saddle River, NJ: Pearson Education.

Miles, M. B., & Huberman, A. M. (1994). *Qualitative data analysis: A sourcebook of new methods* (2nd ed.). Thousand Oaks, CA: Sage.

For interviewing:

Gubrium, J. F., & Holstein, J. A. (2003). *Postmodern interviewing*. Thousand Oaks, CA: Sage.

Krueger, R. A., & Casey, M. A. (2009). *Focus groups: A practical guide for applied research* (4th ed.). Thousand Oaks, CA: Sage.

Kvale, S., & Brinkmann, S. (2009). *InterViews: Learning the craft of qualitative research interviewing* (2nd ed.). Thousand Oaks, CA: Sage.

McCracken, G. (1988). *The long interview*. Newbury Park, CA: Sage.

Rubin, H. J., & Rubin, I. S. (2012). *Qualitative interviewing: The art of hearing data* (3rd ed.). Los Angeles, CA: Sage.

For discussions about making observations and taking field notes:

Angrosino, M. V. (2007). *Doing ethnographic and observational research.* Thousand Oaks, CA: Sage.

Bernard, H. R. (1994). *Research methods in anthropology: Qualitative and quantitative approaches* (2nd ed.). Thousand Oaks, CA: Sage.

Bogdewic, S. P. (1992). Participant observation. In B. F. Crabtree & W. L. Miller (Eds.), *Doing qualitative research* (pp. 45–69). Newbury Park, CA: Sage.

Emerson, R. M., Fretz, R. I., & Shaw, L. L. (1995). *Writing ethnographic fieldnotes.* Chicago: University of Chicago Press.

Hammersley, M., & Atkinson, P. (1995). *Ethnography: Principles in practice* (2nd ed.). New York: Routledge.

Jorgensen, D. L. (1989). *Participant observation: A methodology for human studies.* Newbury Park, CA: Sage.

Sanjek, R. (1990). *Fieldnotes: The makings of anthropology.* Ithaca, NY: Cornell University Press.

For information about the issues and use of documents:

Prior, L. (2003). *Using documents in social research.* London: Sage.

For a discussion of field relations and ethical issues:

Hammersley, M., & Atkinson, P. (1995). *Ethnography: Principles in practice* (2nd ed.). New York: Routledge.

Kvale, S. (2006). Dominance through interviews and dialogues. *Qualitative Inquiry, 12,* 480–500.

Lofland, J., & Lofland, L. H. (1995). *Analyzing social settings: A guide to qualitative observation and analysis* (3rd ed.). Belmont, CA: Wadsworth.

Mertens, D. M., & Ginsberg, P. E. (2009). *The handbook of social research ethics.* Los Angeles: Sage.

Nunkoosing, K. (2005). The problems with interviews. *Qualitative Health Research, 15,* 698–706.

EXERCISES

1. Gain some experience in collecting data for your project. Design an interview or an observational protocol for your study. Conduct either an interview or an observation and record the information on the protocol you have developed. After this experience, identify issues that posed challenges during this data collection.

2. It is helpful to design the data collection activities for a project. Examine Figure 7.1 for the seven activities. Develop a matrix that describes data collection for all seven activities for your project. Provide detail in this matrix for each of the seven activities.

Exercises

8

Data Analysis and Representation

nalyzing text and multiple other forms of data presents a challenging task for qualitative researchers. Deciding how to represent the data in tables, matrices, and narrative form adds to the challenge. Often qualitative researchers equate data analysis with approaches for analyzing text and image data. The process of analysis is much more. It also involves organizing the data, conducting a preliminary read-through of the database, coding and organizing themes, representing the data, and forming an interpretation of them. These steps are interconnected and form a spiral of activities all related to the analysis and representation of the data.

In this chapter I begin by summarizing three general approaches to analysis provided by leading authors so that we can see how authors follow similar processes as well as different ones. I then present a visual model—a data analysis spiral—that I find useful to conceptualize a larger picture of all steps in the data analysis process in qualitative research. I use this spiral as a conceptualization to further explore each of the five approaches to inquiry, and I examine specific data analysis procedures within each approach and compare these procedures. I end with the use of computers in qualitative analysis and introduce four software programs—MAXQDA, ATLAS.ti, NVivo, and HyperRESEARCH—and discuss the common features of using software programs in data analysis as well as templates for coding data within each of the five approaches.

QUESTIONS FOR DISCUSSION

- What are common data analysis strategies used in qualitative research?
- How might the overall data analysis process be conceptualized in qualitative research?

- What are specific data analysis procedures used within each of the approaches to inquiry, and how do they differ?
- What are the procedures available in qualitative computer analysis programs, and how would these procedures differ by approach to qualitative inquiry?

THREE ANALYSIS STRATEGIES

Data analysis in qualitative research consists of preparing and organizing the data (i.e., text data as in transcripts, or image data as in photographs) for analysis, then reducing the data into themes through a process of coding and condensing the codes, and finally representing the data in figures, tables, or a discussion. Across many books on qualitative research, this is the general process that researchers use. Undoubtedly, there will be some variations in this approach. Beyond these steps, the five approaches to inquiry have additional analysis steps. Before examining the specific analysis steps in the five approaches, it is helpful to have in mind the general analysis procedures.

Table 8.1 presents typical general analysis procedures as illustrated through the writings of three qualitative researchers. I have chosen these three authors because they represent different perspectives. Madison (2005) presents an interpretive framework taken from critical ethnography, Huberman and Miles (1994) adopt a systematic approach to analysis that has a long history of use in qualitative inquiry, and Wolcott (1994b) uses a more traditional approach to research from ethnography and case study analysis. These three sources advocate many similar processes, as well as a few different approaches to the analytic phase of qualitative research.

All of these authors comment on the central steps of coding the data (reducing the data into meaningful segments and assigning names for the segments), combining the codes into broader categories or themes, and displaying and making comparisons in the data graphs, tables, and charts. These are the core elements of qualitative data analysis.

Beyond these elements, the authors present different phases in the data analysis process. Huberman and Miles (1994), for example, provide more detailed steps in the process, such as writing marginal notes, drafting summaries of field notes, and noting relationships among the categories. Madison (2005), however, introduces the need to create a point of view—a stance that signals the interpretive framework (e.g., critical,

Table 8.1 General Data Analysis Strategies Advanced by Select Authors

Analytic Strategy	Madison (2005)	Huberman & Miles (1994)	Wolcott (1994b)
Sketching ideas		Write margin notes in field notes	Highlight certain information in description
Taking notes		Write reflective passages in notes	
Summarizing field notes		Draft a summary sheet on field notes	
Working with words		Make metaphors	
Identifying codes	Do abstract coding or concrete coding	Write codes, memos	
Reducing codes to themes	Identify salient themes or patterns	Note patterns and themes	Identify patterned regularities
Counting frequency of codes		Count frequency of codes	
Relating categories		Factor, note relations among variables, build a logical chain of evidence	
Relating categories to analytic framework in literature			Contextualize with the framework from literature
Creating a point of view	For scenes, audience, readers		
Displaying the data	Create a graph or picture of the framework	Make contrasts and comparisons	Display findings in tables, charts, diagrams, and figures; compare cases; compare with a standard case

feminist) taken in the study. This point of view is central to the analysis in critical, theoretically oriented qualitative studies. Wolcott (1994b), on the other hand, discusses the importance of forming a description from the data, as well as relating the description to the literature and cultural themes in cultural anthropology.

THE DATA ANALYSIS SPIRAL

Data analysis is not off-the-shelf; rather, it is custom-built, revised, and "choreographed" (Huberman & Miles, 1994). The processes of data collection, data analysis, and report writing are not distinct steps in the process—they are interrelated and often go on simultaneously in a research project. Qualitative researchers often "learn by doing" (Dey, 1993, p. 6) data analysis. This leads critics to claim that qualitative research is largely intuitive, soft, and relativistic or that qualitative data analysts fall back on the three "I's"—"insight, intuition, and impression" (Dey, 1995, p. 78). Undeniably, qualitative researchers preserve the unusual and serendipitous, and writers craft studies differently, using analytic procedures that often evolve while they are in the field. Despite this uniqueness, I believe that the analysis process conforms to a general contour.

The contour is best represented in a spiral image, a data analysis spiral. As shown in Figure 8.1, to analyze qualitative data, the researcher engages in the process of moving in analytic circles rather than using a fixed linear approach. One enters with data of text or images (e.g., photographs, videotapes) and exits with an account or a narrative. In between, the researcher touches on several facets of analysis and circles around and around.

Organizing the Data

Data management, the first loop in the spiral, begins the process. At an early stage in the analysis process, researchers typically organize their data into computer files. Besides organizing files, researchers convert their files to appropriate text units (e.g., a word, a sentence, an entire story) for analysis either by hand or by computer. Materials must be easily located in large databases of text (or images). As Patton (1980) says,

> The data generated by qualitative methods are voluminous. I have found no way of preparing students for the sheer massive volumes

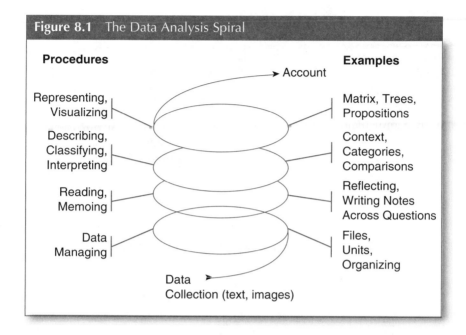

Figure 8.1 The Data Analysis Spiral

Procedures

Account

Representing, Visualizing

Describing, Classifying, Interpreting

Reading, Memoing

Data Managing

Data Collection (text, images)

Examples

Matrix, Trees, Propositions

Context, Categories, Comparisons

Reflecting, Writing Notes Across Questions

Files, Units, Organizing

of information with which they will find themselves confronted when data collection has ended. Sitting down to make sense out of pages of interviews and whole files of field notes can be overwhelming. (p. 297)

Computer programs help with this phase of analysis, and their role in this process will be addressed later in this chapter.

Reading and Memoing

Following the organization of the data, researchers continue analysis by getting a sense of the whole database. Agar (1980), for example, suggested that researchers "read the transcripts in their entirety several times. Immerse yourself in the details, trying to get a sense of the interview as a whole before breaking it into parts" (p. 103). Writing notes or memos in the margins of field notes or transcripts or under photographs helps in this initial process of exploring a database. These memos are short phrases, ideas, or key concepts that occur to the reader. We used this procedure in our gunman case study (Asmussen & Creswell, 1995; see Appendix F). We scanned all of our databases to identify major organizing ideas. Looking over our field notes from observations, interview transcriptions, physical trace evidence, and audio and visual images, we disregarded predetermined questions so we could "see" what interviewees said. We reflected on the larger thoughts presented in the data and formed initial categories. These categories were few in number (about 10), and we looked for multiple forms of evidence to support each. Moreover, we found evidence that portrayed multiple perspectives about each category (Stake, 1995).

Describing, Classifying, and Interpreting Data Into Codes and Themes

The next step consists of moving from the reading and memoing in the spiral to describing, classifying, and interpreting the data. In this loop, forming *codes* or *categories* (and these two terms will be used interchangeably) represents the heart of qualitative data analysis. Here researchers build detailed descriptions, develop themes or dimensions, and provide an interpretation in light of their own views or views of perspectives in the literature. *Detailed description* means that authors describe what they see. This detail is provided *in situ,* that is, within the context of the setting of the person, place, or event. Description becomes a good place to start in a qualitative study (after reading and managing data), and it plays a central role in ethnographic and case studies.

The process of *coding* involves aggregating the text or visual data into small categories of information, seeking evidence for the code from different databases being used in a study, and then assigning a label to the code. I think about "winnowing" the data here; not all information is used in a qualitative study, and some may be discarded (Wolcott, 1994b). Researchers develop a short list of tentative codes (e.g., 25–30 or so) that match text segments, regardless of the length of the database. Beginning researchers tend to develop elaborate lists of codes when they review their databases. I proceed differently. I begin with a short list, "lean coding" I call it—five or six categories with shorthand labels or codes—and then I expand the categories as I continue to review and re-review my database. Typically, regardless of the size of the database, I do not develop more than 25–30 categories of information, and I find myself working to reduce and combine them into the five or six themes that I will use in the end to write my narrative. Those researchers who end up with 100 or 200 categories—and it is easy to find this many in a complex database—struggle to reduce the picture to the five or six themes that they must end with for most publications.

Several issues are important to address in this coding process. The first is whether qualitative researchers should count codes. Huberman and Miles (1994), for example, suggest that investigators make preliminary counts of data codes and determine how frequently codes appear in the database. Some (but not all) qualitative researchers feel comfortable counting and reporting the number of times the codes appear in their databases. It does provide an indicator of frequency of occurrence, something typically associated with quantitative research or systematic approaches to qualitative research. In my own work, I may look at the number of passages associated with each code as an indicator of participant interest in a code, but I do not report counts in my articles (see Asmussen & Creswell, 1995). This is because counting conveys a quantitative orientation of magnitude and frequency contrary to qualitative research. In addition, a count conveys that all codes should be given equal emphasis, and it disregards that the passages coded may actually represent contradictory views.

Another issue is the use of preexisting or a priori codes that guide my coding process. Again, we have a mixed reaction to the use of this procedure. Crabtree and Miller (1992) discuss a continuum of coding strategies that range from "prefigured" categories to "emergent" categories (p. 151). Using "prefigured" codes or categories (often from a theoretical model or the literature) is popular in the health sciences (Crabtree & Miller, 1992), but use of these codes does serve to limit the analysis to the "prefigured" codes rather than opening up the codes to reflect the views of participants in a traditional qualitative way. If a "prefigured" coding scheme is used in analysis, I typically encourage the researchers to be open to additional codes emerging during the analysis.

Another issue is the question as to the origin of the code names or labels. Code labels emerge from several sources. They might be *in vivo codes*, names that are the exact words used by participants. They might also be code names drawn from the social or health sciences (e.g., coping strategies), or names the researcher composes that seem to best describe the information. In the process of data analysis, I encourage qualitative researchers to look for code segments that can be used to describe information and develop themes. These codes can represent

- information that researchers expect to find before the study;
- surprising information that researchers did not expect to find; and
- information that is conceptually interesting or unusual to researchers (and potentially participants and audiences).

Moving beyond coding, classifying pertains to taking the text or qualitative information apart, and looking for categories, themes, or dimensions of information. As a popular form of analysis, classification involves identifying five to seven general themes. *Themes* in qualitative research (also called categories) are broad units of information that consist of several codes aggregated to form a common idea. These themes, in turn, I view as a "family" of themes with children, or subthemes, and even grandchildren represented by segments of data. It is difficult, especially in a large database, to reduce the information down into five or seven "families," but my process involves winnowing the data, reducing them to a small, manageable set of themes to write into my final narrative.

A related topic is the types of information a qualitative researcher codes. The researcher might look for stories (as in narrative research); individual experiences and the context of those experiences (in phenomenology); processes, actions, or interactions (in grounded theory); cultural themes and how the culture-sharing group works that can be described or categorized (in ethnography); or a detailed description of the particular case or cases (in case study research). Another way of thinking about the types of information would be to use a deconstructive stance, a stance focused on issues of desire and power (Czarniawska, 2004). Czarniawska (2004) identifies the data analysis strategies used in deconstruction, adapted from Martin (1990, p. 355), that help focus attention on types of information to analyze from qualitative data in all approaches:

- Dismantling a dichotomy, exposing it as a false distinction (e.g., public/private, nature/culture)
- Examining silences—what is not said (e.g., noting who or what is excluded by the use of pronouns such as *we*)
- Attending to disruptions and contradictions; places where a text fails to make sense or does not continue

- Focusing on the element that is most alien or peculiar in the text—to find the limits of what is conceivable or permissible
- Interpreting metaphors as a rich source of multiple meanings
- Analyzing double entendres that may point to an unconscious subtext, often sexual in content
- Separating group-specific and more general sources of bias by "reconstructing" the text with substitution of its main elements

Interpreting the Data

Researchers engage in interpreting the data when they conduct qualitative research. Interpretation involves making sense of the data, the "lessons learned," as described by Lincoln and Guba (1985). *Interpretation* in qualitative research involves abstracting out beyond the codes and themes to the larger meaning of the data. It is a process that begins with the development of the codes, the formation of themes from the codes, and then the organization of themes into larger units of abstraction to make sense of the data. Several forms exist, such as interpretation based on hunches, insights, and intuition. Interpretation also might be within a social science construct or idea or a combination of personal views as contrasted with a social science construct or idea. Thus, the researcher would link his or her interpretation to the larger research literature developed by others. For postmodern and interpretive researchers, these interpretations are seen as tentative, inconclusive, and questioning.

Representing and Visualizing the Data

In the final phase of the spiral, researchers *represent the data*, a packaging of what was found in text, tabular, or figure form. For example, creating a visual image of the information, a researcher may present a comparison table (see Spradley, 1980) or a matrix—for example, a 2 × 2 table that compares men and women in terms of one of the themes or categories in the study (see Miles & Huberman, 1994). The cells contain text, not numbers. A hierarchical tree diagram represents another form of presentation. This shows different levels of abstraction, with the boxes in the top of the tree representing the most abstract information and those at the bottom representing the least abstract themes. Figure 8.2 illustrates

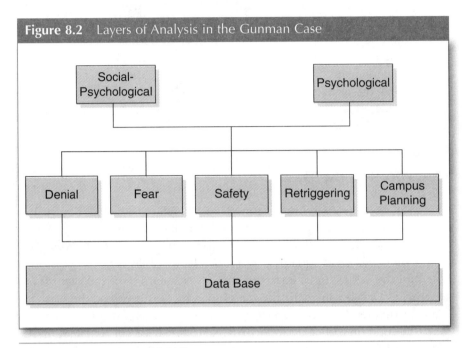

Figure 8.2 Layers of Analysis in the Gunman Case

Source: Asmussen & Creswell (1995).

the levels of abstraction that we used in the gunman case (Asmussen & Creswell, 1995; see Appendix F). Although I have presented this figure at conferences, we did not include it in the published journal article version of the study. This illustration shows inductive analysis that begins with the raw data consisting of multiple sources of information and then broadens to several specific themes (e.g., safety, denial) and on to the most general themes represented by the two perspectives of social-psychological and psychological factors.

Hypotheses or propositions that specify the relationship among categories of information also represent qualitative data. In grounded theory, for example, investigators advance propositions that interrelate the causes of a phenomenon with its context and strategies. Finally, authors present metaphors to analyze the data, literary devices in which something borrowed from one domain applies to another (Hammersley & Atkinson, 1995). Qualitative writers may compose entire studies shaped by analyses of metaphors.

At this point, the researcher might obtain feedback on the initial summaries by taking information back to informants, a procedure to be discussed in Chapter 10 as a key validation step in research.

ANALYSIS WITHIN
APPROACHES TO INQUIRY

Beyond the general spiral analysis processes, I can now relate the procedures to each of the five approaches to inquiry and highlight specific differences in analysis and representing data. My organizing framework for this discussion is found in Table 8.2. I address each approach and discuss specific analysis and representing characteristics. At the end of this discussion, I return to significant differences and similarities among the five approaches.

Narrative Research Analysis and Representation

I think that Riessman (2008) says it best when she comments that narrative analysis "refers to a family of methods for interpreting texts that have in common a storied form" (p. 11). The data collected in a narrative study need to be analyzed for the story they have to tell, a chronology of unfolding events, and turning points or epiphanies. Within this broad sketch of analysis, several options exist for the narrative researcher.

A narrative researcher can take a literary orientation to his or her analysis. For example, using a story in science education told by four fourth graders in one elementary school, Ollerenshaw and I (Ollerenshaw & Creswell, 2002) include several approaches to narrative analysis. One approach is a process advanced by Yussen and Ozcan (1997) that involves analyzing text data for five elements of plot structure (i.e., characters, setting, problem, actions, and resolution). A narrative researcher could use an approach that incorporates different elements that go into the story. The three-dimensional space approach of Clandinin and Connelly (2000) includes analyzing the data for three elements: interaction (personal and social), continuity (past, present, and future), and situation (physical places or the storyteller's places). In the Ollerenshaw and Creswell (2002) narrative we see common elements of narrative analysis: collecting stories of personal experiences in the form of field texts such as interviews or conversations, retelling the stories based on narrative elements (e.g., three-dimensional space approach and the five elements of plot), rewriting the stories into a chronological sequence, and incorporating the setting or place of the participants' experiences.

A chronological approach can also be taken in the analysis of the narratives. Denzin (1989b) suggests that a researcher begin biographical

Table 8.2 Data Analysis and Representation by Research Approaches

Data Analysis and Representation	Narrative	Phenomenology	Grounded Theory Study	Ethnography	Case Study
Data organization	• Create and organize files for data	• Create and organize files for data	• Create and organize files for data	• Create and organize files for data	• Create and organize files for data
Reading, memoing	• Read through text, make margin notes, form initial codes	• Read through text, make margin notes, form initial codes	• Read through text, make margin notes, form initial codes	• Read through text, make margin notes, form initial codes	• Read through text, make margin notes, form initial codes
Describing the data into codes and themes	• Describe the story or objective set of experiences and place it in a chronology	• Describe personal experiences through epoche • Describe the essence of the phenomenon	• Describe open coding categories	• Describe the social setting, actors, events; draw picture of setting	• Describe the case and its context
Classifying the data into codes and themes	• Identify stories • Locate epiphanies • Identify contextual materials	• Develop significant statements • Group statements into meaning units	• Select one open coding category for central phenomenon in process • Engage in axial coding—causal condition, context, intervening conditions, strategies, consequences	• Analyze data for themes and patterned regularities	• Use categorical aggregation to establish themes or patterns

Data Analysis and Representation	Narrative	Phenomenology	Grounded Theory Study	Ethnography	Case Study
Interpreting the data	• Interpret the larger meaning of the story	• Develop a textual description, "what happened" • Develop a structural description, "how" the phenomenon was experienced • Develop the "essence"	• Engage in selective coding and interrelate the categories to develop a "story" or propositions	• Interpret and make sense of the findings—how the culture "works"	• Use direct interpretation • Develop naturalistic generalizations of what was "learned"
Representing, visualizing the data	• Present narration focusing on processes, theories, and unique and general features of the life	• Present narration of the "essence" of the experience; in tables, figures, or discussion	• Present a visual model or theory • Present propositions	• Present narrative presentation augmented by tables, figures, and sketches	• Present in-depth picture of the case (or cases) using narrative, tables, and figures

191

analysis by identifying an objective set of experiences in the subject's life. Having the individual journal a sketch of his or her life may be a good beginning point for analysis. In this sketch, the researcher looks for life-course stages or experiences (e.g., childhood, marriage, employment) to develop a *chronology* of the individual's life. Stories and epiphanies will emerge from the individual's journal or from interviews. The researcher looks in the database (typically interviews or documents) for concrete, contextual biographical materials. During the interview, the researcher prompts the participant to expand on various sections of the stories and asks the interviewee to theorize about his or her life. These theories may relate to career models, processes in the life course, models of the social world, relational models of biography, and natural history models of the life course. Then, the researcher organizes larger patterns and meaning from the narrative segments and categories. Finally, the individual's biography is reconstructed, and the researcher identifies factors that have shaped the life. This leads to the writing of an analytic abstraction of the case that highlights (a) the processes in the individual's life, (b) the different theories that relate to these life experiences, and (c) the unique and general features of the life.

Another approach to narrative analysis turns on how the narrative report is composed. Riessman (2008) suggests a typology of four analytic strategies that reflect this diversity in composing the stories. Riessman calls it thematic analysis when the researcher analyzes "what" is spoken or written during data collection. She comments that this approach is the most popular form of narrative studies, and we see it in the Chan (2010) narrative project reported in Appendix B. A second form in Riessman's (2008) typology is called the structural form, and it emphasizes "how" a story is told. This brings in linguistic analysis in which the individual telling the story uses form and language to achieve a particular effect. Discourse analysis, based on Gee's (1991) method, would examine the storytellers' narrative for such elements as the sequence of utterances, the pitch of the voice, and the intonation. A third form for Riessman (2008) is the dialogic/performance analysis, in which the talk is interactively produced by the researcher and the participant or actively performed by the participant through such activities as poetry or a play. The fourth form is an emerging area of using visual analysis of images or interpreting images alongside words. It could also be a story told about the production of an image or how different audiences view an image.

In the narrative study of Ai Mei Zhang, the Chinese immigrant student presented by Chan (2010) in Appendix B, the analytic approach begins with a thematic analysis similar to Riessman's (2008) approach. After briefly mentioning a description of Ai Mei's school, Chan then discusses several themes, all of which have to do with conflict (e.g., home language conflicts with school language). That Chan saw conflict introduces the idea that she analyzed the data for this phenomenon, and rendered the theme development from a postmodern type of interpretive lens. Chan then goes on to analyze the data beyond the themes to explore her role as a narrative researcher learning about Ai Mei's experiences. Thus, while overall the analysis is based on a thematic approach, the introduction of conflict and the researcher's experiences adds a thoughtful conceptual analysis to the study.

Phenomenological Analysis and Representation

The suggestions for narrative analysis present a general template for qualitative researchers. In contrast, in phenomenology, there have been specific, structured methods of analysis advanced, especially by Moustakas (1994). Moustakas reviews several approaches in his book, but I see his modification of the Stevick-Colaizzi-Keen method as providing the most practical, useful approach. My approach, a simplified version of this method discussed by Moustakas (1994), is as follows:

- First describe personal experiences with the phenomenon under study. The researcher begins with a full description of his or her own experience of the phenomenon. This is an attempt to set aside the researcher's personal experiences (which cannot be done entirely) so that the focus can be directed to the participants in the study.
- Develop a list of significant statements. The researcher then finds statements (in the interviews or other data sources) about how individuals are experiencing the topic, lists these significant statements (horizonalization of the data) and treats each statement as having equal worth, and works to develop a list of nonrepetitive, nonoverlapping statements.
- Take the significant statements and then group them into larger units of information, called "meaning units" or themes.
- Write a description of "what" the participants in the study experienced with the phenomenon. This is called a "textural description" of the experience—what happened—and includes verbatim examples.

- Next write a description of "how" the experience happened. This is called "structural description," and the inquirer reflects on the setting and context in which the phenomenon was experienced. For example, in a phenomenological study of the smoking behavior of high school students (McVea, Harter, McEntarffer, & Creswell, 1999), my colleagues and I provide a structural description about where the phenomenon of smoking occurs, such as in the parking lot, outside the school, by student lockers, in remote locations at the school, and so forth.
- Finally, write a composite description of the phenomenon incorporating both the textural and structural descriptions. This passage is the "essence" of the experience and represents the culminating aspect of a phenomenological study. It is typically a long paragraph that tells the reader "what" the participants experienced with the phenomenon and "how" they experienced it (i.e., the context).

Moustakas (1994) is a psychologist, and the "essence" typically is of a phenomenon in psychology, such as grief or loss. Giorgi (2009), also a psychologist, provides an analytic approach similar to that of Stevick-Colaizzi-Keen. Giorgi discusses how researchers read for a sense of the whole, determine meaning units, transform the participants' expressions into psychologically sensitive expressions, and then write a description of the "essence." Most helpful in Giorgi's discussion is the example he provides of describing jealousy as analyzed by himself and another researcher.

The phenomenological study by Riemen (1986) tends to follow a structured analytic approach. In Riemen's study of caring by patients and their nurses, she presents significant statements of caring and noncaring interactions for both males and females. Furthermore, Riemen formulates meaning statements from these significant statements and presents them in tables. Finally, Riemen advances two "exhaustive" descriptions for the essence of the experience—two short paragraphs—and sets them apart by enclosing them in tables. In the phenomenological study of individuals with AIDS by Anderson and Spencer (2002; see Appendix C) reviewed in Chapter 5, the authors use Colaizzi's (1978) method of analysis, one of the approaches mentioned by Moustakas (1994). This approach follows the general guideline of analyzing the data for significant phrases, developing meanings and clustering them into themes, and presenting an exhaustive description of the phenomenon.

A less structured approach is found in van Manen (1990). He begins discussing data analysis by calling it "phenomenological reflection" (van Manen, 1990, p. 77). The basic idea of this reflection is to grasp the essential meaning of something. The wide array of data sources of expressions or forms that we would reflect on might be transcribed taped conversations, interview materials, daily accounts or stories, suppertime talk, formally written responses, diaries, other people's writings, film, drama, poetry, novels, and so forth. Van Manen (1990) placed emphasis on gaining an understanding of themes by asking, "What is this example an example of?" (p. 86). These themes should have certain qualities such as focus, a simplification of ideas, and a description of the structure of the lived experience. The process involved attending to the entire text (holistic reading approach), looking for statements or phrases (selective or highlighting approach), and examining every sentence (the detailed or line-by-line approach). Attending to four guides for reflection was also important: the space felt by individuals (e.g., the modern bank), physical or bodily presence (e.g., what does a person in love look like?), time (e.g., the dimensions of past, present, and future), and the relationships with others (e.g., expressed through a handshake). In the end, analyzing the data for themes, using different approaches to examine the information, and considering the guides for reflection should yield an explicit structure of the meaning of the lived experience.

Grounded Theory Analysis and Representation

Similar to phenomenology, grounded theory uses detailed procedures for analysis. It consists of three phases of coding—open, axial, and selective—as advanced by Strauss and Corbin (1990, 1998). Grounded theory provides a procedure for developing categories of information (open coding), interconnecting the categories (axial coding), building a "story" that connects the categories (selective coding), and ending with a discursive set of theoretical propositions (Strauss & Corbin, 1990).

In the open coding phase, the researcher examines the text (e.g., transcripts, field notes, documents) for salient categories of information supported by the text. Using the constant comparative approach, the researcher attempts to "saturate" the categories—to look for instances that represent the category and to continue looking (and interviewing) until the new information obtained does not provide further insight into the category. These categories are composed of subcategories, called "properties," that represent multiple perspectives about the categories. Properties, in turn, are *dimensionalized* and presented on a continuum. Overall, this is the process of reducing the database to a small set of themes or categories that characterize the process or action being explored in the grounded theory study.

Once an initial set of categories has been developed, the researcher identifies a single category from the open coding list as the central phenomenon of interest. The open coding category selected for this purpose is typically one that is extensively discussed by the participants or one of particular conceptual interest because it seems central to the process being studied in the grounded theory project. The inquirer selects this one open coding category (a central phenomenon), positions it as the central feature of the theory, and then returns to the database (or collects additional data) to understand the categories that relate to this central phenomenon. Specifically, the researcher engages in the coding process called axial coding in which the database is reviewed (or new data are collected) to provide insight into specific coding categories that relate to or explain the central phenomenon. These are causal conditions that influence the central phenomenon, the strategies for addressing the phenomenon, the context and intervening conditions that shape the strategies, and the consequences of undertaking the strategies. Information from this coding phase are then organized into a figure, a coding paradigm, that presents a theoretical model of the process under study. In this way, a theory is built or generated. From this theory, the inquirer generates propositions (or hypotheses) or statements that interrelate the categories in the coding paradigm. This is called selective coding. Finally, at the broadest level of analysis, the researcher can create a conditional matrix. This matrix is an analytical aid—a diagram—that helps the researcher visualize the wide range of conditions and consequences (e.g., society, world) related to the central phenomenon (Strauss & Corbin, 1990). Seldom have I found the conditional matrix actually used in studies.

A key to understanding the difference that Charmaz (2006) brings to grounded theory data analysis is to hear her say "avoid imposing a forced framework" (p. 66). Her approach emphasized an emerging process of forming the theory. Her analytic steps began with an initial phase of coding each word, line, or segment of data. At this early stage she was interested in having the initial codes treated analytically to understand a process and larger theoretical categories. This initial phase was followed by focused coding, using the initial codes to sift through large amounts of data, analyzing for syntheses and larger explanations. She did not support the Strauss and Corbin (1998) formal procedures of axial coding that organized the data into conditions, actions/interactions, consequences, and so forth. However, Charmaz (2006) did examine the categories and begins to develop links among them. She also believed in using theoretical coding, first developed by Glaser (1978). This step involved specifying possible relationships between categories based on a priori theoretical coding families (e.g., causes, context, ordering). However, Charmaz (2006) goes on to say that these theoretical codes needed to earn their way into the grounded theory that emerges. The theory that emerged for Charmaz emphasizes understanding rather than explanation. It assumes emergent, multiple realities; the link of facts and values; provisional information; and a narrative about social life as a process. It might be presented as a figure or as a narrative that pulls together experiences and shows the range of meanings.

The specific form for presenting the theory differs. In our study of department chairs, Brown and I present it as hypotheses (Creswell & Brown, 1992), and in their study of the process of the evolution of physical activity for African American women (see Appendix D), Harley et al. (2009) presented a discussion of a theoretical model as displayed in a figure with three phases. In the Harley et al. study, the analysis consisted of citing Strauss and Corbin (1998) and then creating codes, grouping these codes into concepts, and forming a theoretical framework. The specific steps of open coding were not reported; however, the results section focused on the theoretical model's phases, and the axial coding steps of context, conditions, and an elaboration on the condition most integral to the women's movement through the process, the planning methods.

Ethnographic Analysis and Representation

For ethnographic research, I recommend the three aspects of data analysis advanced by Wolcott (1994b): description, analysis, and *interpretation of the culture-sharing group*. Wolcott (1990b) believes that a good starting point for writing an ethnography is to describe the culture-sharing group and setting:

> Description is the foundation upon which qualitative research is built. . . . Here you become the storyteller, inviting the reader to see through your eyes what you have seen. . . . Start by presenting a straightforward description of the setting and events. No footnotes, no intrusive analysis—just the facts, carefully presented and interestingly related at an appropriate level of detail. (p. 28)

From an interpretive perspective, the researcher may only present one set of facts; other facts and interpretations await the reading of the ethnography by the participants and others. But this description may be analyzed by presenting information in chronological order. The writer describes through progressively focusing the description or chronicling a "day in the life" of the group or individual. Finally, other techniques involve focusing on a critical or key event, developing a "story" complete with a plot and characters, writing it as a "mystery," examining groups in interaction, following an analytical framework, or showing different perspectives through the views of participants.

Analysis for Wolcott (1994b) is a sorting procedure—"the quantitative side of qualitative research" (p. 26). This involves highlighting specific material introduced in the descriptive phase or displaying findings through tables, charts, diagrams, and figures. The researcher also analyzes through using systematic procedures such as those advanced by Spradley (1979, 1980), who called for building taxonomies, generating comparison tables, and developing semantic tables. Perhaps the most popular analysis procedure, also mentioned by Wolcott (1994b), is the search for patterned regularities in the data. Other forms of analysis consist of comparing the cultural group to others, evaluating the group in terms of standards, and drawing connections between the culture-sharing group and larger theoretical frameworks. Other analysis steps include critiquing the research process and proposing a redesign for the study.

Making an ethnographic interpretation of the culture-sharing group is a data transformation step as well. Here the researcher goes beyond the database and probes "what is to be made of them" (Wolcott, 1994b, p. 36). The researcher speculates outrageous, comparative interpretations that raise doubts or questions for the reader. The researcher draws inferences from the data or turns to theory to provide structure for his or her interpretations. The researcher also personalizes the interpretation: "This is what I make of it" or "This is how the research experience affected me" (p. 44). Finally, the investigator forges an interpretation through expressions such as poetry, fiction, or performance.

Multiple forms of analysis represent Fetterman's (2010) approach to ethnography. He did not have a lockstep procedure, but recommended triangulating the data by testing one source of data against another, looking for patterns of thought and behavior, and focusing in on key events that the ethnography can use to analyze an entire culture (e.g., ritual observance of the Sabbath). Ethnographers also draw maps of the setting, develop charts, design matrices, and sometimes employ statistical analysis to examine frequency and magnitude. They might also crystallize their thoughts to provide "a mundane conclusion, a novel insight, or an earth-shattering epiphany" (Fetterman, 2010, p. 109).

The ethnography presented in Appendix E by Haenfler (2004) applied a critical perspective to these analytic procedures of ethnography. Haenfler provided a detailed description of the straight edge core values of resistance to other cultures and then discussed five themes related to these core values (e.g., positive, clean living). Then the conclusion to the article included broad interpretations of the group's core values, such as the individualized and collective meanings for participation in the subculture. However, Haenfler began the methods discussion with a self-disclosing, positioning statement about his background and participation in the straight edge movement. This positioning was also presented as a chronology of his experiences from 1989 to 2001.

Case Study Analysis and Representation

For a case study, as in ethnography, analysis consists of making a detailed description of the case and its setting. If the case presents a chronology of events, I then recommend analyzing the multiple sources of data to determine evidence for each step or phase in the evolution of the case. Moreover, the setting is particularly important. In our gunman case (Asmussen & Creswell, 1995; see Appendix F), we analyzed the information to determine how the incident fit into the setting—in our situation, a tranquil, peaceful Midwestern community.

In addition, Stake (1995) advocates four forms of data analysis and interpretation in case study research. In categorical aggregation, the researcher seeks a collection of instances from the data, hoping that issue-relevant meanings will emerge. In *direct interpretation*, on the other hand, the case study researcher looks at a single instance and draws meaning from it without looking for multiple instances. It is a process of pulling the data apart and putting them back together in more meaningful ways. Also, the researcher establishes *patterns* and looks for a correspondence between two or more categories. This correspondence might take the form of a table, possibly a 2 × 2 table, showing the relationship between two categories. Yin (2009) advances a cross-case synthesis as an analytic technique when the researcher studies two or more cases. He suggests that a word table can be created to display the data from individual cases according to some uniform framework. The implication of this is that the researcher can then look for similarities and differences among the cases. Finally, the researcher develops **naturalistic generalizations** from analyzing the data, generalizations that people can learn from the case either for themselves or to apply to a population of cases.

To these analysis steps I would add description of the case, a detailed view of aspects about the case—the "facts." In our gunman case study (Asmussen & Creswell, 1995; Appendix F), we described the events following the incident for two weeks, highlighting the major players, the sites, and the activities. We then aggregated the data into about 20 categories (categorical aggregation) and collapsed them into five themes. In the final section of the study, we developed generalizations about the case in terms of the themes and how they compared and contrasted with published literature on campus violence.

COMPARING THE FIVE APPROACHES

Returning to Table 8.2, data analysis and representation in the five approaches have several common and distinctive features. Across all five approaches, the researcher typically begins by creating and organizing files of information. Next, the process consists of a general reading and memoing of information to develop a sense of the data and to begin the process of making sense of them. Then, all approaches have a phase of description, with the exception of grounded theory, in which the inquirer seeks to begin building toward a theory of the action or process.

However, several important differences exist in the five approaches. Grounded theory and phenomenology have the most detailed, explicated procedure for data analysis, depending on the author chosen for guidance on analysis. Ethnography and case studies have analysis procedures that are common, and narrative research represents the least structured procedure. Also, the terms used in the phase of classifying show distinct language among these approaches (see Appendix A for a glossary of terms used in each approach); what is called open coding in grounded theory is similar to the first stage of identifying significant statements in phenomenology and to categorical aggregation in case study research. The researcher needs to become familiar with the definition of these terms of analysis and employ them correctly in the chosen approach to inquiry. Finally, the presentation of the data, in turn, reflects the data analysis steps, and it varies from a narration in narrative to tabled statements, meanings, and description in phenomenology to a visual model or theory in grounded theory.

COMPUTER USE IN QUALITATIVE DATA ANALYSIS

Qualitative computer programs have been available since the late 1980s, and they have become more refined and helpful in computerizing the process of analyzing text and image data (see Weitzman and Miles, 1995, for a review of 24 programs). Friese (2012) provides a discussion about one program, ATLAS.ti. The Corbin and Strauss (2007) book contains an extensive illustration of the use of the software program MAXQDA to discuss grounded theory.

The process used for qualitative data analysis is the same for hand coding or using a computer: the inquirer identifies a text segment or image segment, assigns a code label, searches through the database for all text segments that have the same code label, and develops a printout of these text segments for the code. In this process the researcher, not the computer program, does the coding and categorizing.

Advantages and Disadvantages

The computer program simply provides a means for storing the data and easily accessing the codes provided by the researcher. I feel that computer programs are most helpful with large databases, such as 500 or more pages of text, although they can have value for small databases as well. Although using a computer may not be of interest to all qualitative researchers, there are several advantages to using them:

- A computer program provides an organized storage file system so that the researcher can quickly and easily locate material and store it in one place. This aspect becomes especially important in locating entire cases or cases with specific characteristics.
- A computer program helps a researcher locate material easily, whether this material is an idea, a statement, a phrase, or a word. No longer do we need to "cut and paste" material onto file cards and sort and resort the cards according to themes. No longer do we need to develop an elaborate "color code" system for text

related to themes or topics. The search for text can be easily accomplished with a computer program. Once researchers identify categories in grounded theory, or themes in case studies, the names of the categories can be searched using the computer program for other instances when the names occur in the database.

- A computer program encourages a researcher to look closely at the data, even line by line, and think about the meaning of each sentence and idea. Sometimes, without a program, the researcher is likely to casually read through the text files or transcripts and not analyze each idea carefully.
- The concept-mapping feature of computer programs enables the researcher to visualize the relationship among codes and themes by drawing a visual model.
- A computer program allows the researcher to easily retrieve memos associated with codes, themes, or documents.

The disadvantages of using computer programs go beyond their cost:

- Using a computer program requires that the researcher learn how to run the program. This is sometimes a daunting task that is above and beyond learning required for understanding the procedures of qualitative research. Granted, some people learn computer programs more easily than do others, and prior experience with programs shortens the learning time.
- A computer program may, to some individuals, put a machine between the researcher and the actual data. This may cause an uncomfortable distance between the researcher and his or her information.
- Although researchers may see the categories developed during computer analysis as fixed, they can be changed in software programs (Kelle, 1995). Some individuals may find changing the categories or moving information around less desirable than others and find that the computer program slows down or inhibits this process.
- Instructions for using computer programs vary in their ease of use and accessibility. Many documents for computer programs do not provide information about how to use the program to generate a qualitative study, or one of the five approaches to research discussed in this book.
- A computer program may not have the features or capability that researchers need, so researchers can shop comparatively to find a program that meets their needs.

A Sampling of Computer Programs

There are many computer programs available for analysis; some have been developed by individuals on campuses, and some are available for commercial purchase. I highlight four commercial programs that are popular and that I have examined closely (see Creswell, 2012; Creswell & Maietta, 2002)—MAXQDA, ATLAS.ti, NVivo, and HyperRESEARCH. I have intentionally left out the version numbers and have presented a general discussion of the programs because the developers are continually upgrading the programs.

MAXQDA (http://www.maxqda.com/). MAXQDA is a computer software program that helps the researcher to systematically evaluate and interpret qualitative texts. It is also a powerful tool for developing theories and testing theoretical conclusions. The main menu has four windows: the data, the code or category system, the text being analyzed, and the results of basic and complex searches. It uses a hierarchical code system, and the researcher can attach a weight score to a text segment to indicate the relevance of the segment. Memos can be easily written and stored as different types of memos (e.g., theory memos or methodological memos). It has a visual mapping feature. Data can be exported to statistical programs, such as SPSS or Excel, and the software can import Excel or SPSS programs as well. It is easily used by multiple coders on a particular project. Images and video segments can also be stored and coded in this program. MAXQDA is distributed by VERBI Software in Germany. A demonstration program is available to learn more about the unique features of this program.

ATLAS.ti (http://www.atlasti.com). This program enables you to organize your text, graphic, audio, and visual data files, along with your coding, memos, and findings, into a project. Further, you can code, annotate, and compare segments of information. You can drag and drop codes within an interactive margin screen. You can rapidly search, retrieve, and browse all data segments and notes relevant to an idea and, importantly, build unique visual networks that allow you to connect visually selected passages, memos, and codes in a concept map. Data can be exported to programs such as SPSS, HTML, XML, and CSV. This program also allows for a group of researchers to work on the same project and make comparisons of how each researcher coded the data. A demonstration software package is available to test out this program, which is described by and available from Scientific Software Development in Germany.

QSR NVivo (http://www.qsrinternational.com/). NVivo is the latest version of software from QSR International. NVivo combines the features of the popular software program N6 (or NUD*IST 6) and NVivo 2.0. NVivo helps analyze, manage, shape, and analyze qualitative data. Its streamlined look makes it easy to use. It provides security by storing the database and files together in a single file, it enables a researcher to use multiple languages, it has a merge function for team research, and it enables the researcher to easily manipulate the data and conduct searches. Further, it can display graphically the codes and categories. A good overview of the evolution of the software from N6 to NVivo is available from Bazeley (2002). NVivo is distributed by QSR International in Australia. A demonstration copy is available to see and try out the features of this software program.

HyperRESEARCH (http://www.researchware.com/). This program is an easy-to-use qualitative software package enabling you to code and retrieve, build theories, and conduct analyses of the data. Now with advanced multimedia capabilities, HyperRESEARCH allows the researcher to work with text, graphics, audio, and video sources—making it a valuable research analysis tool. HyperRESEARCH is a solid code-and-retrieve data analysis program, with additional theory-building features provided by the Hypothesis Tester. This program also allows the researcher to draw visual diagrams, and it now has a module that can be added, called "Hyper-Transcriber," that will allow researchers to create a transfer of video and audio data. This program, developed by ResearchWare, is available in the United States.

Use of Computer Software Programs With the Five Approaches

After reviewing all of these computer programs, I see several ways that they can facilitate qualitative data analysis:

● Computer programs help store and organize qualitative data. The programs provide a convenient way to store qualitative data. Data are stored in document files (files converted from a word processing program to DOS, ASCII, or rich-text files in some programs). These document files consist of information from one discrete unit of information such as a transcript from one interview, one set of observational notes, or one article scanned from a newspaper. For all five of the approaches to qualitative inquiry, the document could be one interview, one observation, or one text document.

● Computer programs help locate text or image segments associated with a code or theme. When using a computer program, the researcher goes through the text or images one line or image at a time and asks, "What is the person saying (or doing) in this passage?" Then the researcher assigns a code label using the words of the participant, employing social or human science terms, or composing a term that seems to relate to the situation. After reviewing many pages or images, the researcher can use the search function of the program to locate all the text or image segments that fit a code label. In this way, the researcher can easily see how participants are discussing the code in a similar or different way.

● Computer programs help locate common passages or segments that relate to two or more code labels. The search process can be extended to include two or more code labels. For example, the code label "two-parent family" might be combined with "females" to yield text segments in which women are discussing a "two-parent family." Alternatively, "two-parent family" might be combined with "males" to generate text segments in which men talk about the "two-parent family." One helpful code label is "quotes," and researchers can assign interesting quotes to use in a qualitative report into this code label and easily retrieve them for a report. Computer programs also enable the user to search for specific words to see how frequently they occur in the texts; in this way, specific words might be elevated to the status of code labels or possible themes based on the frequency of their use. In another usage, a code label may be created for the "title" in the study, and the information in the label might change as the author revises the title in the process of conducting the study.

● Computer programs help make comparisons among code labels. If the researcher makes both of these requests about females and males, data then exist for making comparisons among the responses of females and males on their views about the "two-parent family." The computer program thus enables a researcher to interrogate the database about the interrelationship among codes or categories.

● Computer programs help the researcher to conceptualize different levels of abstraction in qualitative data analysis. The process of qualitative data analysis, as discussed earlier in this chapter, starts with the researcher analyzing the raw data (e.g., interviews), forming the data into codes, and then combining the codes into broader themes. These themes can be and often are "headings" used in a qualitative study. The software programs provide a means for organizing codes hierarchically so that smaller units, such as codes, can be placed under larger units, such as themes. In NVivo, the concept of children and parent codes illustrates two levels of abstraction. In this

way, the computer program helps the researcher to build levels of analysis and see the relationship between the raw data and the broader
themes.

    ● Computer programs provide a visual picture of codes and themes.
Many computer programs contain the feature of concept mapping so that
the user can generate a visual diagram of the codes and themes and their
interrelationships. These codes and themes can be continually moved
around and reorganized under new categories of information as the project progresses.

    ● Computer programs provide the capability to write memos and store
them as codes. In this way, the researcher can begin to create the qualitative
report during data analysis or simply record insights as they emerge.

    ● With computer programs, the researcher can create a template for
coding data within each of the five approaches. The researcher can establish a preset list of codes that match the data analysis procedure within the
approach of choice. Then, as data are reviewed during computer analysis,
the researcher can identify information that fits into the codes or write
memos that become codes. As shown in Figures 8.3 through 8.7, I created
templates for coding within each approach that fit the general structure in
analyzing data within the approach. I developed these codes as a hierarchical picture, but they could be drawn as circles or in a less linear fashion.
Hierarchical organization of codes is the approach often used in the
concept-mapping feature of software programs.

    In narrative research (see Figure 8.3), I created codes that relate to the
story, such as the chronology, the plot or the three-dimensional space
model, and the themes that might arise from the story. The analysis might
proceed using the plot structure approach or the three-dimensional model,
but I placed both in the figure to provide the most options for analysis. The
researcher will not know what approach to use until he or she actually starts
the data analysis process. The researcher might develop a code, or "story,"
and begin writing out the story based on the elements analyzed.

    In the template for coding a phenomenological study (see Figure 8.4),
I used the categories mentioned earlier in data analysis. I placed codes for
epoche or bracketing (if this is used), significant statements, meaning units,
and textural and structural descriptions (which both might be written as
memos). The code at the top, "essence of the phenomenon," is written as
a memo about the "essence" that will become the "essence" description in
the final written report. In the template for coding a grounded theory study

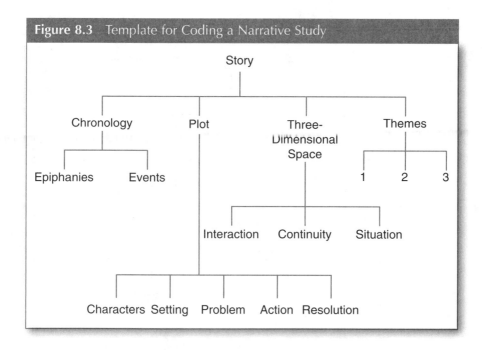

Figure 8.3 Template for Coding a Narrative Study

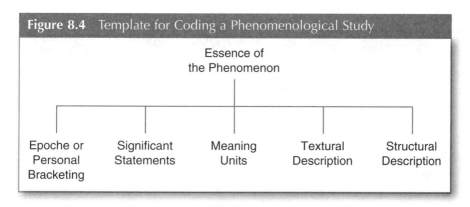

Figure 8.4 Template for Coding a Phenomenological Study

(see Figure 8.5), I included the three major coding phases: open coding, axial coding, and selective coding. I also included a code for the conditional matrix if that feature is used by the grounded theorist. The researcher can use the code at the top, "theory description or visual model," to create a visual model of the process that is linked to this code.

In the template for coding an ethnography (see Figure 8.6), I included a code that might be a memo or reference to text about the theoretical lens

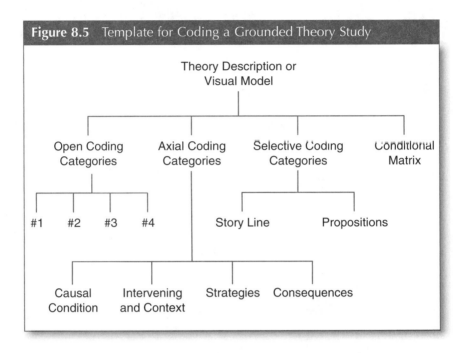

Figure 8.5 Template for Coding a Grounded Theory Study

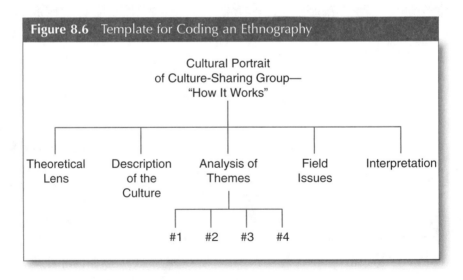

Figure 8.6 Template for Coding an Ethnography

used in the ethnography, codes on the description of the culture and an analysis of themes, a code on field issues, and a code on interpretation. The code at the top, "cultural portrait of culture-sharing group—'how it works,'" can be a code in which the ethnographer writes a memo summarizing the major cultural rules that pertain to the group. Finally, in the template for

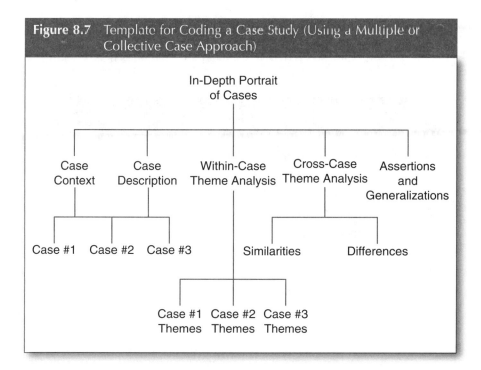

Figure 8.7 Template for Coding a Case Study (Using a Multiple or Collective Case Approach)

coding a case study (see Figure 8.7), I chose a multiple case study to illustrate the precode specification. For each case, codes exist for the context and description of the case. Also, I advanced codes for themes within each case, and for themes that are similar and different in cross-case analysis. Finally, I included codes for assertions and generalizations across all cases.

How to Choose Among the Computer Programs

With different programs available, decisions need to be made about the proper choice of a qualitative software program. Basically, all of the programs provide similar features, and some have more features than others. Many of the programs have a demonstration copy available at their websites so that you can examine and try out the program. Also, other researchers can be approached who have used the program, and you can determine their views of the software. In 2002, I wrote a chapter with Maietta (Creswell & Maietta, 2002) in which we review several computer programs using eight criteria. As shown in Figure 8.8, the criteria for selecting a program were the ease of using the program; the type of data it accepted; its capability to read and review text; its provision of memo-writing functions; its processes of categorization; its analysis features, such as concept mapping; the ability of the program to input quantitative data; and its support for multiple researchers and merging different databases. These criteria can be used to identify a computer program that will meet a researcher's needs.

Figure 8.8   Features to Consider When Comparing Qualitative Data Analysis Software

Ease of Integration in Using the Program

- Is it easy to use in getting started?
- Can you easily work through a document?

Type of Data the Program Will Accept

- Will it handle text data?
- Will it handle multimedia (image) data?

Reading and Reviewing Text

- Can it highlight and connect quotations?
- Can it search for specific text passages?

Memo Writing

- Does it have the capability for you to add notes or memos?
- Can you easily access the memos you write?

Categorization

- Can you develop codes?
- Can you easily apply codes to text or images?
- Can you easily display codes?
- Can you easily review and make changes in the codes?

Analysis Inventory and Assessment

- Can you sort for specific codes?
- Can you combine codes in a search?
- Can you develop a concept map with the codes?
- Can you make demographic comparisons with the codes?

Quantitative Data

- Can you import a quantitative database (e.g., SPSS)?
- Can you export a word or image qualitative database to a quantitative program?

Merging Project

- Can two or more researchers analyze the data, and can these analyses be merged?

Source: Adapted from Creswell & Maietta (2002), Qualitative research. In D. C. Miller & N. J. Salkind (Eds.), *Handbook of social research* (pp. 143–184). Thousand Oaks, CA: Sage. Used with permission.

SUMMARY

This chapter presented data analysis and representation. I began with a review of data analysis procedures advanced by three authors and noted the common features of coding, developing themes, and providing a visual diagram of the data. I also noted some of the differences among their approaches. I then advanced a spiral of analysis that captured the general process. This spiral contained aspects of data management; reading and memoing; describing, classifying, and interpreting; and representing and visualizing data. I next introduced each of the five approaches to inquiry and discussed how they had unique data analysis steps beyond the concept of the spiral. Finally, I described how computer programs aid in the analysis and representation of data; discussed four programs, common features of using computer software, and templates for coding each of the five approaches to inquiry; and ended with information about criteria for choosing a computer software program.

ADDITIONAL READINGS

Books on qualitative data analysis:

Marshall, C., & Rossman, G. B. (2010). *Designing qualitative research* (5th ed.). Thousand Oaks, CA: Sage.

Miles, M. B., & Huberman, A. M. (1994). *Qualitative data analysis: A sourcebook of new methods* (2nd ed.). Thousand Oaks, CA: Sage.

Specific data analysis strategies for each of the five approaches to inquiry:

Clandinin, D. J., & Connelly, F. M. (2000). *Narrative inquiry: Experience and story in qualitative research.* San Francisco: Jossey-Bass.

Czarniawska, B. (2004). *Narratives in social science research.* Thousand Oaks, CA: Sage.

Denzin, N. K. (1989). *Interpretive biography.* Newbury Park, CA: Sage.

Fetterman, D. M. (2010). *Ethnography: Step by step* (3rd ed.). Thousand Oaks, CA: Sage.

Giorgi, A. (2009). *The descriptive phenomenological method in psychology: A modified Husserlian approach.* Pittsburg, PA: Duquesne University.

Moustakas, C. (1994). *Phenomenological research methods.* Thousand Oaks, CA: Sage.

Riessman, C. K. (2008). *Narrative methods for the human sciences.* Los Angeles, CA: Sage.

Stake, R. (1995). *The art of case study research.* Thousand Oaks, CA: Sage.

Strauss, A., & Corbin, J. (1990). *Basics of qualitative research: Grounded theory procedures and techniques.* Newbury Park, CA: Sage.

van Manen, M. (1990). *Researching lived experience.* New York: State University of New York Press.

Wolcott, H. F. (1994). *Transforming qualitative data: Description, analysis, and interpretation.* Thousand Oaks, CA: Sage.

Yin, R. K. (2009). *Case study research: Design and method* (4th ed.). Thousand Oaks, CA: Sage.

For a review of computer data analysis programs in qualitative research:

Creswell, J. W., & Maietta, R. C. (2002). Qualitative research. In D. C. Miller & N. J. Salkind (Eds.), *Handbook of social research* (pp. 143–184). Thousand Oaks, CA: Sage.

Friese, S. (2012). *Qualitative data analysis with ATLAS.ti.* Thousand Oaks, CA: Sage.

Kelle, E. (Ed.). (1995). *Computer aided qualitative data analysis.* Thousand Oaks, CA: Sage.

Weitzman, E. A., & Miles, M. B. (1995). *Computer programs for qualitative data analysis.* Thousand Oaks, CA: Sage.

EXERCISES

1. It is good to practice coding text data in a general sense before coding to develop an analysis within one of the five approaches. To conduct this practice, obtain a short text file, which may be a transcript of an interview, field notes typed from an observation, or an optically scanned text file of a document, such as a newspaper article. Next code the text by bracketing large text segments and asking yourself, "What is the content being discussed in the text?" Assign code labels to the text segments. Using information in this chapter, assign labels that match (a) what you would expect to find in the database, (b) surprising information that you did not expect to find, and (c) information that is conceptually interesting or unusual to participants and audiences. In this way, you will derive code labels that might be useful in forming themes in your study, and these procedures will direct you away from weak codes such as "positives" and "negatives."

2. Obtain some pictures from students or participants who are in one of your projects (or, alternatively, select some pictures from magazine articles). Practice coding these visual data. Begin by asking yourself, "What is occurring in the picture?" Assign code labels to these pictures looking again for (a) what you would expect to find in the database, (b) surprising information that you did not expect to find, and (c) information that is conceptually interesting or unusual to participants and audiences.

3. Gain some experience using a computer software program. Select one of the computer programs mentioned in this chapter, go to its website, and find the demonstration program. Try out the program. Often these demos will enable you to input a small database so that you can actually try out the features of the program. You might experiment with demos from different software programs.

9

Writing a
Qualitative Study

Writing and composing the narrative report brings the entire study together. Borrowing a term from Strauss and Corbin (1990), I am fascinated by the *architecture* of a study, how it is composed and organized by writers. I also like Strauss and Corbin's (1990) suggestion that writers use a "spatial metaphor" (p. 231) to visualize their full reports or studies. To consider a study "spatially," they ask the following questions: Is coming away with an idea like walking slowly around a statue, studying it from a variety of interrelated views? Like walking downhill step by step? Like walking through the rooms of a house?

In this chapter, I assess the general architecture of a qualitative study, and then I invite the reader to enter specific rooms of the study to see how they are composed. In this process, I begin with four writing issues in the rendering of a study regardless of approach: reflexivity and representation, audience, encoding, and quotes. Then I take each of the five approaches to inquiry and assess two writing structures: the overall structure (i.e., overall organization of the report or study) and the embedded structure (i.e., specific narrative devices and techniques that the writer uses in the report). I return once again to the five examples of studies in Chapter 5 to illustrate overall and embedded structures. Finally, I compare the narrative structures for the five approaches in terms of four dimensions. In this chapter I will not address the use of grammar and syntax and will refer readers to books that provide a detailed treatment of these subjects (e.g., Creswell, 2009).

QUESTIONS FOR DISCUSSION

- What are several broad writing strategies associated with crafting a qualitative study?
- What are the larger writing structures used within each of the five approaches of inquiry?

- What are the embedded writing structures within each of the five approaches of inquiry?
- How do the narrative structures for the five approaches differ?

SEVERAL WRITING STRATEGIES

Unquestionably, the narrative forms are extensive in qualitative research. In reviewing the forms, Glesne and Peshkin (1992) note that narratives in "storytelling" modes blur the lines between fiction, journalism, and scholarly studies. Other qualitative forms engage the reader through a chronological approach as events unfold slowly over time, whether the subject is a study of a culture-sharing group, the narrative story of the life of an individual, or the evolution of a program or an organization. Another form is to narrow and expand the focus, evoking the metaphor of a camera lens that pans out, zooms in, and then zooms out again. Some reports rely heavily on description of events, whereas others advance a small number of "themes" or perspectives. A narrative might capture a "typical day in the life" of an individual or a group. Some reports are heavily oriented toward theory, whereas others, such as Stake's (1995) "Harper School," employ little literature and theory. In addition, since the publication of Clifford and Marcus's (1986) edited volume *Writing Culture* in ethnography, qualitative writing has been shaped by a need for researchers to be self-disclosing about their role in the writing, the impact of it on participants, and how information conveyed is read by audiences. Researcher reflexivity and representations is the first issue to which we turn.

Reflexivity and Representations in Writing

Qualitative researchers today are much more self-disclosing about their qualitative writings than they were a few years ago. No longer is it acceptable to be the omniscient, distanced qualitative writer. As Laurel Richardson wrote, researchers "do not have to try to play God, writing as disembodied omniscient narrators claiming universal and atemporal general knowledge" (Richardson & St. Pierre, 2005, p. 961). Through these omniscient narrators, postmodern thinkers "deconstruct" the narrative, challenging text as contested terrain that cannot be understood without references to ideas being concealed by the author and contexts within the author's life (Agger, 1991). This theme is espoused by Denzin (1989a) in his "interpretive" approach to biographical writing. As a response, qualitative researchers today acknowledge that the writing of a qualitative text cannot be separated from the author, how it is received by readers, and how it impacts the participants and sites under study.

How we write is a reflection of our own interpretation based on the cultural, social, gender, class, and personal politics that we bring to research. All writing is "positioned" and within a stance. All researchers shape the writing that emerges, and qualitative researchers need to accept this interpretation and be open about it in their writings. According to Richardson (1994), the best writing acknowledges its own "undecidability" forthrightly, that all writing has "subtexts" that "situate" or "position" the material within a particular historical and local specific time and place. In this perspective, no writing has "privileged status" (Richardson, 1994, p. 518) or superiority over other writings. Indeed, writings are co-constructions, representations of interactive processes between researchers and the researched (Gilgun, 2005).

Also, there is increased concern about the impact of the writing on the participants. How will they see the write-up? Will they be marginalized because of it? Will they be offended? Will they hide their true feelings and perspectives? Have the participants reviewed the material, and interpreted, challenged, and dissented from the interpretation (Weis & Fine, 2000)? Perhaps researchers' writing objectively, in a scientific way, has the impact of silencing the participants, and silencing the researchers as well (Czarniawska, 2004). Gilgun (2005) makes the point that this silence is contradictory to qualitative research that seeks to hear all voices and perspectives.

Also, the writing has an impact on the reader, who also makes an interpretation of the account and may form an entirely different interpretation than the author or the participants. Should the researcher be afraid that certain people will see the final report? Can the researcher give any kind of definitive account when it is the reader who makes the ultimate interpretation of the events? Indeed, the writing may be a performance, and the standard writing of qualitative research into text has expanded to include split-page writings, theater, poetry, photography, music, collage, drawing, sculpture, quilting, stained glass, and dance (Gilgun, 2005). Language may "kill" whatever it touches, and qualitative researchers understand that it is impossible to truly "say" something (van Manen, 2006).

Weis and Fine (2000) discuss a "set of self-reflective points of critical consciousness around the questions of how to represent responsibility" in qualitative writings (p. 33). There are questions that can be formed from their major points and should be considered by all qualitative researchers about their writings:

- Should I write about what people say or recognize that sometimes they cannot remember or choose not to remember?
- What are my political reflexivities that need to come into my report?
- Has my writing connected the voices and stories of individuals back to the set of historic, structural, and economic relations in which they are situated?
- How far should I go in theorizing the words of participants?
- Have I considered how my words could be used for progressive, conservative, and repressive social policies?
- Have I backed into the passive voice and decoupled my responsibility from my interpretation?
- To what extent has my analysis (and writing) offered an alternative to common sense or the dominant discourse?

Qualitative researchers need to "position" themselves in their writings. This is the concept of **_reflexivity_** in which the writer is conscious of the biases, values, and experiences that he or she brings to a qualitative research study. One characteristic of good qualitative research is that the inquirer makes his or her "position" explicit (Hammersley & Atkinson, 1995). I think about reflexivity as having two parts. The researcher first talks about his or her experiences with the phenomenon being explored. This involves relaying past experiences through work, schooling, family dynamics, and so forth. The second part is to discuss how these past experiences shape the researcher's interpretation of the phenomenon. This is a second important ingredient that is often overlooked or left out. It is actually the heart of being reflexive in a study, because it is important that the researcher not only detail his or her experiences with the phenomenon, but also be self-conscious about how these experiences may potentially have shaped the findings, the conclusions, and the interpretations drawn in a study. The placement of reflexive comments in a study also needs some consideration.

They may be placed in the opening passage of the study (as is sometimes the case in phenomenology), they may reside in a methods discussion in which the writer talks about his or her role in the study (see the Anderson & Spencer, 2002, phenomenological study in Appendix C), they may be threaded throughout the study (e.g., the researcher talks about his or her "position" in the introduction, the methods, and the findings or themes), or they may be at the end of the study in an epilogue as is found in the Asmussen and Creswell (1995) case study in Appendix F. A personal vignette is another option available for a reflexive statement at the beginning or at the end of case studies (see Stake, 1995).

Audience for Our Writings

A basic axiom holds that all writers write for an audience. As Clandinin and Connelly (2000) say, "A sense of an audience peering over the writer's shoulder needs to pervade the writing and the written text" (p. 149). Thus, writers consciously think about their audience or multiple audiences for their studies (Richardson, 1990, 1994). Tierney (1995), for example, identifies four potential audiences: colleagues, those involved in the interviews and observations, policymakers, and the general public. In short, how the findings are presented depends on the audience with whom one is communicating (Giorgi, 1985). For example, because Fischer and Wertz (1979) disseminated information about their phenomenological study at public forums, they produced several expressions of their findings, all responding to different audiences. One form was a general structure, four paragraphs in length, an approach that they admitted lost its richness and concreteness. Another form consisted of case synopses, each reporting the experiences of one individual and each two and a half pages in length.

Encoding Our Writings

A closely related topic is recognizing the importance of language in shaping our qualitative texts. The words we use encode our report, revealing how we perceive the needs of our audiences. Earlier, in Chapter 6, I presented encoding the problem, purpose, and research questions; now I consider encoding the entire narrative report. Richardson's (1990) study of women in affairs with married men illustrates how a writer can shape a work differently for a trade audience, an academic audience, or a moral/political audience. For a trade audience, she encoded her work with literary devices such as

> jazzy titles, attractive covers, lack of specialized jargon, marginalization of methodology, common-world metaphors and images, and book blurbs and prefatory material about the "lay" interest in the material. (Richardson, 1990, p. 32)

For the moral/political audience, she encoded through devices such as

> in-group words in the title, for example, woman/women/feminist in feminist writing; the moral or activist "credentials" of the author, for example, the author's role in particular social movements; references to moral and activist authorities; empowerment metaphors, and book blurbs and prefatory material about how this work relates to real people's lives. (Richardson, 1990, pp. 32–33)

Finally, for the academic audience (e.g., journals, conference papers, academic books), she marked it by a

> prominent display of academic credentials of author, references, footnotes, methodology sections, use of familiar academic metaphors and images (such as "exchange theory," "roles," and "stratification"), and book blurbs and prefatory material about the science or scholarship involved. (Richardson, 1990, p. 32)

Although I emphasize academic writing here, researchers encode qualitative studies for audiences other than academics. For example, in the social and human sciences, policymakers may be a primary audience, and this necessitates writing with minimal methods, more parsimony, and a focus on practice and results.

Richardson's (1990) ideas triggered my own thoughts about how one might encode a qualitative narrative. Such encoding might include the following:

- An overall structure that does not conform to the standard quantitative introduction, methods, results, and discussion format. Instead, the methods might be called "procedures," and the results might be called "findings." In fact, the researcher might phrase the headings for themes in the words of participants in the study as they discuss "denial," "retriggering," and so forth, as we did in the gunman case (Asmussen & Creswell, 1995; see Appendix F).
- A writing style that is personal, familiar, perhaps "up-close," highly readable, friendly, and applied for a broad audience. Our qualitative writings should strive for a "persuasive" effect (Czarniawska, 2004, p. 124). Readers should find the material interesting and memorable, the "grab" in writing (Gilgun, 2005).
- A level of detail that makes the work come alive—**verisimilitude** comes to mind (Richardson, 1994, p. 521). This word indicates the

presentation of a good literary study in which the writing becomes "real" and "alive," writing that transports the reader directly into the world of the study, whether this world is the cultural setting of youths' resistance to both the counterculture and the dominant culture (Haenfler, 2004; see Appendix E) or an immigrant student in a school classroom (Chan, 2010; see Appendix B). Still, we must recognize that the writing is only a representation of what we see or understand.

Quotes in Our Writings

In addition to encoding text with the language of qualitative research, authors bring in the voice of participants in the study. Writers use ample quotes, and I find Richardson's (1990) discussion about three types of quotes most useful. The first consists of short eye-catching quotations. These are easy to read, take up little space, and stand out from the narrator's text and are indented to signify different perspectives. For example, in the phenomenological study of how persons live with AIDS, Anderson and Spencer (2002; see Appendix C) used paragraph-long quotes from men and women in the study to convey the "magic of not thinking" theme:

It's a sickness, but in my mind I don't think that I got it. Because if you think about having HIV, it comes down more on you. It's more like a mind game. To try and stay alive is that you don't even think about it. It's not in the mind. (p. 1347)

The second approach consists of embedded quotes, briefly quoted phrases within the analyst's narrative. These quotes, according to Richardson (1990), prepare a reader for a shift in emphasis or display a point and allow the writer (and reader) to move on. Asmussen and I used short, embedded quotes extensively in our gunman study (Asmussen & Creswell, 1995; see Appendix F) because they consume little space and provide specific concrete evidence, in the participants' words, to support a theme.

A third type of quote is the longer quotation used to convey more complex understandings. These are difficult to use because of space limitations in publications and because longer quotes may contain many ideas, and so the reader needs to be guided both "into" the quote and "out of" the quote to focus his or her attention on the controlling idea that the writer would like the reader to see.

OVERALL AND EMBEDDED WRITING STRATEGIES

In addition to these writing approaches, the qualitative researcher needs to address how he or she is going to compose the overall narrative structure of the report and use embedded structures within the report to provide a narrative within the approach of choice. I offer Table 9.1 as a guide to the discussion to follow, in which I list many overall and embedded structural approaches as they apply to the five approaches of inquiry.

Narrative Writing Structure

As I read about the writing of studies in narrative research, I find authors unwilling to prescribe a tightly structured writing strategy (Clandinin & Connelly, 2000; Czarniawska, 2004; Riessman, 2008). Instead, I find the authors suggesting maximum flexibility in structure (see Ely, 2007), but emphasizing core elements that might go into the narrative study.

Overall structure. Narrative researchers encourage individuals to write narrative studies that experiment with form (Clandinin & Connelly, 2000). Researchers can come to their narrative form by first looking to their own preferences in reading (e.g., memoirs, novels), reading other narrative dissertations and books, and viewing the narrative study as back-and-forth writing, as a process (Clandinin & Connelly, 2000). Within these general guidelines, Clandinin and Connelly (2000) review two doctoral dissertations that employ narrative research. The two have different narrative structures: One provides narratives of a chronology of the lives of three women; the other adopts a more classical approach to a dissertation including an introduction, a literature review, and a methodology. For this second example, the remaining chapters then go into a discussion that tells the stories of the author's experiences with the participants. Reading through these two examples, I am struck by how they both reflect the three-dimensional inquiry space that Clandinin and Connelly (2000) discuss. This space, as mentioned earlier, is a text that looks backward and forward, looks inward and outward, and situates the experiences within place. For example, the dissertation of He, cited by Clandinin, is a study

Table 9.1 Overall and Embedded Writing Structures and the Five Approaches

	Overall Writing Structures	Embedded Writing Structures
Narrative	• Flexible and evolving processes (Clandinin & Connelly, 2000) • Three-dimensional space inquiry model (Clandinin & Connelly, 2000) • Story chronologies (Clandinin & Connelly, 2000) • Temporal or episodic ordering of information (Riessman, 2008) • Reporting what participants said (themes), how they said it (order of their story), or how they interacted with others (dialogue and performance) (Riessman, 2008)	• Epiphanies (Denzin, 1989b) • Themes, key events, or plots (Czarniawska, 2004; Smith, 1994) • Metaphors and transitions (Clandinin & Connelly, 2000; Lomask, 1986) • Progressive-regressive methods or zooming in and out (Czarniawska, 2004; Denzin, 1989b) • Themes or categories (Riessman, 2008) • Dialogues or conversations (Riessman, 2008)
Phenomenology	• Structure of a "research manuscript" (Moustakas, 1994) • The "research report" format (Polkinghorne, 1989) • Themes, analytic analysis, start with the essence, engage with other authors, use time, space, and other dimensions (van Manen, 1990)	• Figures or tables reporting essences (Grigsby & Megel, 1995) • Philosophical discussions (Harper, 1981) • Creative closings (Moustakas, 1994)

(Continued)

Table 9.1 (Continued)

Grounded theory	• Grounded theory study components (May, 1986) • Results of open, axial, and selective coding (Strauss & Corbin, 1990, 1998) • Focus on theory and arguments that support it (Charmaz, 2006)	• Extent of analysis (Chenitz & Swanson, 1986) • Propositions (Strauss & Corbin, 1990) • Visual diagrams (Harley et al., 2009) • Emotions, simple language, rhythm and timing, unexpected definitions and assertions, rhetorical questions, tone, pacing, stories, evocative writings (Charmaz, 2006)
Ethnography	• Types of tales (Van Maanen, 1988) • Description, analysis, and interpretation (Wolcott, 1994b) • "Thematic narrative" (Emerson, Fretz, & Shaw, 1995)	• Tropes (Hammersley & Atkinson, 1995) • "Thick" description (Denzin, 1989b; Fetterman, 2010) • Dialogue (Nelson, 1990); verbatim quotations (Fetterman, 2010) • Scenes (Emerson, Fretz, & Shaw, 1995) • Literary devices, such as voices of different speakers, expanding and contracting the narrative pace, metaphors, irony, similes (Fetterman, 2010; Richardson, 1990)
Case study	• Format with vignettes (Stake, 1995) • Substantive case report format (Lincoln & Guba, 1985) • Types of cases (Yin, 2009) • Alternative structures based on linear and nonlinear approaches (Yin, 2009)	• Funnel approach (Asmussen & Creswell, 1995) • Description (Merriam, 1988)

about the lives of two participants and the author in their past life in China and in their present situation in Canada. The story

> looks backward to the past for her and her two participants and forward to the puzzle of who they are and who they are becoming in their new land. She looks inward to her personal reasons for doing this study and outward to the social significance of the work. She paints landscapes of China and Canada and the in-between places where she imagines herself to reside. (Clandinin & Connelly, 2000, p. 156)

Later in Clandinin and Connelly (2000), there is a story about Clandinin's advice for students about the narrative form of their studies. This form again relates to the three-dimensional space model:

> When they came to Jean for conversations about their emerging texts, she found herself responding not so much with comments about preestablished and accepted forms but with response that raised questions situated within the three-dimensional narrative inquiry space. (Clandinin & Connelly, 2000, p. 165)

Notice in this passage how Clandinin "raised questions" rather than told the student how to proceed, and how she returned to the larger *rhetorical* structure of the three-dimensional inquiry space model as a framework for thinking about the writing of a narrative study. This framework also suggests a chronology to the narrative report, and this ordering within the chronology might further be organized by time or by specific episodes (Riessman, 2008).

In narrative research, as in all forms of qualitative inquiry, there is a close relationship between the data collection procedures, the analysis, and the form and structure of the writing report. For example, the larger writing structure in a thematic analysis would be the presentation of several themes (Riessman, 2008). In a more structured approach—analyzing how the individual tells a story—the elements presented in the report might follow six elements, what Riessman (2008) calls a "fully formed narrative" (p. 84). These would be the elements of

- a summary and/or the point of the story;
- orientation (the time, place, characters, and situations);
- complicating action (the event sequence, or plot usually with a crisis or turning point);

- evaluation (where the narrator comments on meaning or emotions);
- resolution (the outcome of the plot); and
- coda (ending the story and bringing it back to the present).

In a narrative study focused on the interrogation between speakers (such as the interviewer and the interviewee), the larger writing structure would focus on direct speech and dialogue. Further, the dialogue might contain features of a performance, such as direct speeches, asides to the audience, repetition, expressive sounds, and switches in verb tense. The entire report may be a poem, a play, or another dramatic rendering.

Embedded structure. Assuming that the larger writing structure proceeds with experimentation and flexibility, the writing structure at the more micro level relates to several elements of writing strategies that authors might use in composing a narrative study. These are drawn from Clandinin and Connelly (2000), Czarniawska (2004), and Riessman (2008).

The writing of a narrative needs to not silence some of the voices, and it ultimately gives more space to certain voices than others (Czarniawska, 2004).

There can be a spatial element to the writing, such as in the *progressive-regressive method* (Denzin, 1989b) whereby the biographer begins with a key event in the participant's life and then works forward and backward from that event, such as in Denzin's (1989b) study of alcoholics. Alternatively, there can be a "zooming in" and "zooming out," such as describing a large context to a concrete field of study (e.g., a site) and then telescoping out again (Czarniawska, 2004).

The writing may emphasize the "key event" or the *epiphany,* defined as interactional moments and experiences that mark people's lives (Denzin, 1989b). Denzin (1989b) distinguishes four types: the major event that touches the fabric of the individual's life; the cumulative or representative events, experiences that continue for some time; the minor epiphany, which represents a moment in an individual's life; and episodes or relived epiphanies, which involve reliving the experience. Czarniawska (2004) introduces the key element of the plot or the emplotment, a means of introducing structure that allows for making sense of the events reported.

Themes can be reported in narrative writing. Smith (1994) recommends finding a theme to guide the development of the life to be written. This theme emerges from preliminary knowledge or a review of the entire life, although researchers often experience difficulty in distinguishing the major theme from lesser or minor themes. Clandinin and Connelly (2000) refer to writing research texts at the reductionistic boundary, an approach consisting of a "reduction downward" (p. 143) to themes in which the researcher looks for common threads or elements across participants.

Specific narrative writing strategies also include the use of dialogue, such as that between the researcher and the participants (Riessman, 2008). Sometimes in this approach the specific language of the narrator is interrogated and is not taken at face value. The dialogue unfolds in the study, and often it is presented in different languages, including the language of the narrator and an English translation.

Other narrative rhetorical devices include the use of transitions. Lomask (1986) refers to these as built into the narratives in natural chronological linkages. Writers insert them through words or phrases, questions (which Lomask calls being "lazy"), and time-and-place shifts moving the action forward or backward. In addition to transitions, narrative researchers employ *foreshadowing*, the frequent use of narrative hints of things to come or of events or themes to be developed later. Narrative researchers also use metaphors, and Clandinin and Connelly (2000) suggest the metaphor of a soup (i.e., with description of people, places, and things; arguments for understandings; and richly textured narratives of people situated in place, time, scene, and plot) within containers (i.e., dissertation, journal article) to describe their narrative texts.

Chan's (2010) narrative research study (see Appendix B) illustrated several of these narrative elements. She told the story of one Chinese immigrant student and the affiliation this student had with other students, her teacher, and her family. The larger narrative structure fit within Riessman's (2008) thematic approach, and throughout the findings the reader was presented with themes related to the conflicts the student had with the school, with her family at home, with peers at school, and with her parents. A specific embedded narrative technique used by Chan was to provide evidence for each theme using dialogue between the researcher and the student. Each dialogue segment was titled to shape the meaning of the conversation, such as "Susan doesn't speak Fujianese" (Chan, 2010, p. 117).

Phenomenological Writing Structure

Those who write about phenomenology (e.g., Moustakas, 1994) provide more extensive attention to overall writing structures than to embedded ones. However, as in all forms of qualitative research, one can learn much from a careful study of research reports in journal article, monograph, or book form.

Overall structure. The highly structured approach to analysis by Moustakas (1994) presents a detailed form for composing a phenomenological study. The analysis steps—identifying significant statements, creating meaning units, clustering themes, advancing textural and structural descriptions, and ending with a composite description of textural and structural descriptions with an exhaustive description of the essential invariant structure (or essence) of the experience—provide a clearly articulated procedure for organizing a report (Moustakas, 1994). In my experience, individuals are quite surprised to find highly structured approaches to phenomenological studies on sensitive topics (e.g., "being left out," "insomnia," "being criminally victimized," "life's meaning," "voluntarily changing one's career during midlife," "longing," "adults being abused as children"; Moustakas, 1994, p. 153). But the data analysis procedure, I think, guides a researcher in that direction and presents an overall structure for analysis and ultimately the organization of the report.

Consider the overall organization of a report as suggested by Moustakas (1994). He recommends specific chapters in "creating a research manuscript":

Chapter 1: Introduction and statement of topic and outline. Topics include an autobiographical statement about experiences of the author leading to the topic, incidents that lead to a puzzlement or curiosity about the topic, the social implications and relevance of the topic, new knowledge and contribution to the profession to emerge from studying the topic, knowledge to be gained by the researcher, the research question, and the terms of the study.

Chapter 2: Review of the relevant literature. Topics include a review of databases searched, an introduction to the literature, a procedure for selecting studies, the conduct of these studies and themes that emerged in them, and a summary of core findings and statements as to how the present research differs from prior research (in question, model, methodology, and data collected).

Chapter 3: Conceptual framework of the model. Topics include the theory to be used as well as the concepts and processes related to the research design (Chapters 3 and 4 might be combined).

Chapter 4: Methodology. Topics include the methods and procedures in preparing to conduct the study, in collecting data, and in organizing, analyzing, and synthesizing the data.

Chapter 5: Presentation of data. Topics include verbatim examples of data collection, data analysis, a synthesis of data, horizonalization, meaning units, clustered themes, textural and structural descriptions, and a synthesis of meanings and essences of the experience.

Chapter 6: Summary, implications, and outcomes. Sections include a summary of the study, statements about how the findings differ from those in the literature review, recommendations for future studies, the identification of limitations, a discussion about implications, and the inclusion of a creative closure that speaks to the essence of the study and its inspiration for the researcher.

A second model, not as specific, is found in Polkinghorne (1989) where he discusses the "research report." In this model, the researcher describes the procedures to collect data and the steps to move from the raw data to a more general description of the experience. Also, the investigator includes a review of previous research, the theory pertaining to the topic, and implications for psychological theory and application. I especially like Polkinghorne's comment about the impact of such a report:

Produce a research report that gives an accurate, clear, and articulate description of an experience. The reader of the report should come away with the feeling that "I understand better what it is like for someone to experience that" (Polkinghorne, 1989, p. 46).

A third model of the overall writing structure of a phenomenological study comes from van Manen (1990). He begins his discussion of "working the text" (van Manen, 1990, p. 167) with the thought that studies that present and organize transcripts for the final report fall short of being a good phenomenological study. Instead, he recommends several options for writing the study. The study might be organized thematically examining essential aspects of the phenomenon under study. It might also be presented analytically by reworking the text data into larger ideas (e.g., contrasting ideas), or focused narrowly on the description of a particular life situation. It might begin with the essence description, and then present varying examples of how the essence is manifested. Other approaches include engaging one's writing in a dialogue with other phenomenological authors and weaving the description against time, space, the lived body, and relationships to others. In the end, van Manen suggests that authors may invest new ways of reporting their data or combine approaches.

Embedded structure. Turning to embedded rhetorical structures, the literature provides the best evidence. A writer presents the "essence" of the experience for participants in a study through sketching a short paragraph about it in the narrative or by enclosing this paragraph in a figure. This latter approach is used effectively in a study of the caring experiences of nurses who teach (Grigsby & Megel, 1995). Another structural device is to "educate" the reader through a discussion about phenomenology and its philosophical assumptions. Harper (1981) uses this approach and describes several of Husserl's major tenets as well as the advantages of studying the meaning of "leisure" in a phenomenology.

Finally, I personally like Moustakas's (1994) suggestion: "Write a brief creative close that speaks to the essence of the study and its inspiration to you in terms of the value of the knowledge and future directions of your professional-personal life" (p. 184). Despite the phenomenologist's inclination to bracket himself or herself out of the narrative, Moustakas introduces the reflexivity that psychological phenomenologists can bring to a study, such as casting their initial problem statement within an autobiographical context.

Anderson and Spencer's (2002) phenomenology of how persons living with AIDS image their disease represented many of these overall and embedded writing structures (see Appendix C). The overall article has a structured organization, with an introduction, a review of the literature, methods, and results. It followed Colaizzi's (1978) phenomenological methods by reporting a table of significant statements and a table of meaning themes. Anderson and Spencer ended with an in-depth, exhaustive description of the phenomenon. They described this exhaustive description:

> Results were integrated into an essential scheme of AIDS. The lived experience of AIDS was initially frightening, with a dread of body wasting and personal loss. Cognitive representations of AIDS included inescapable death, bodily destruction, fighting a battle, and having a chronic disease. Coping methods included searching for the "right drug," caring for oneself, accepting the diagnosis, wiping AIDS out of their thoughts, turning to God, and using vigilance. With time, most people adjusted to living with AIDS. Feelings ranged from "devastating," "sad," and "angry" to being at "peace" and "not worrying." (Anderson and Spencer, 2002, p. 1349)

Anderson and Spencer began the phenomenology with a quote from a 53-year-old man with AIDS, but did not mention themselves in a reflexive way. They also did not discuss the philosophical tenets behind phenomenology.

Grounded Theory Writing Structure

From reviewing grounded theory studies in journal article form, qualitative researchers can deduce a general form (and variations) for composing the narrative. The problem with journal articles is that the authors present truncated versions of the studies to fit within the parameters of the journals. Thus, a reader emerges from a review of a particular study without a full sense of the entire project.

Overall structure. Most importantly, authors need to present the theory in any grounded theory narrative. As May (1986) comments, "In strict terms, the findings are the theory itself, i.e., a set of concepts and propositions which link them" (p. 148). May continues to describe the research procedures in grounded theory:

- The research questions are broad, and they will change several times during data collection and analysis.
- The literature review "neither provides key concepts nor suggests hypotheses" (May, 1986, p. 149). Instead, the literature review in grounded theory shows gaps or bias in existing knowledge, thus providing a rationale for this type of qualitative study.
- The methodology evolves during the course of the study, so writing it early in a study poses difficulties. However, the researcher begins somewhere, and she or he describes preliminary ideas about the sample, the setting, and the data collection procedures.
- The findings section presents the theoretical scheme. The writer includes references from the literature to show outside support for the theoretical model. Also, segments of actual data in the form of vignettes and quotes provide useful explanatory material. This material helps the reader form a judgment about how well the theory is grounded in the data.
- The final discussion section discusses the relationship of the theory to other existing knowledge and the implications of the theory for future research and practice.

Strauss and Corbin (1990) also provide broad writing parameters for their grounded theory studies. They suggest the following:

- Develop a clear analytic story. This is to be provided in the selective coding phase of the study.
- Write on a conceptual level, with description kept secondary to concepts and the analytic story. This means that one finds little description of the phenomenon being studied and more analytic theory at an abstract level.
- Specify the relationship among categories. This is the theorizing part of grounded theory found in axial coding when the researcher tells the story and advances propositions.
- Specify the variations and the relevant conditions, consequences, and so forth for the relationships among categories. In a good theory, one finds variation and different conditions under which the theory holds. This means that the multiple perspectives or variations in each component of axial coding are developed fully. For example, the consequences in the theory are multiple and detailed.

More specifically, in a structured approach to grounded theory as advanced by Strauss and Corbin (1990, 1998), specific aspects of the final written report contain a section on open coding that identifies the various open codes that the researcher discovered in the data, and the axial coding, which includes a diagram of the theory and a discussion about each component in the diagram (i.e., causal conditions, the central phenomenon, the intervening conditions, the context, the strategies, and the consequences). Also, the report contains a section on the theory in which the researcher advances theoretical propositions tying together the elements of the categories in the diagram, or discusses the theory interrelating the categories.

For Charmaz (2006), a less structured approach flows into her suggestions for writing the draft of the grounded theory study. She emphasizes the importance of allowing the ideas to emerge as the theory develops, revising early drafts, asking yourself questions about the theory (e.g., have you raised major categories to concepts in the theory?), constructing an argument about the importance of the theory, and closely examining the categories in the theory. Thus, Charmaz does not have a template for writing a grounded theory study, but focuses our attention on the importance of the argument in the theory and the nature of the theory.

Embedded structure. In grounded theory studies, the researcher varies the narrative report based on the extent of data analysis. Chenitz and Swanson (1986), for example, present six grounded theory studies that vary in the types of analysis reported in the narrative. In a preface to these examples, they mention that the analysis (and narrative) might address one or more of the following: description; the generation of categories through open coding; linking categories around a core category in axial coding, thus developing a substantive, low-level theory; and/or a substantive theory linked to a formal theory.

I have seen grounded theory studies that include one or more of these analyses. For example, in a study of gays and their "coming out" process, Kus (1986) uses only open coding in the analysis and identifies four stages in the process of coming out: identification, in which a gay person undergoes a radical identity transformation; cognitive changes, in which the individual changes negative views about gays into positive ideas; acceptance, a stage in which the individual accepts being gay as a positive life force; and action, the process of the individual's engaging in behavior that results from accepting being gay, such as self-disclosure, expanding the circle of friends to include gays, becoming politically involved in gay causes, and volunteering for gay groups. Set in contrast to this focus on the process, Brown and I (Creswell & Brown, 1992) follow the coding steps in Strauss and Corbin (1990). We examine the faculty development practices of chairpersons who enhance the research productivity of their faculties. We begin with open coding, move to axial coding complete with a logic diagram, and state a series of explicit propositions in directional (as opposed to the null) form.

Another embedded narrative feature is to examine the form for stating propositions or theoretical relationships in grounded theory studies. Sometimes, these are presented in "discursive" form, or describing the theory in narrative form. Strauss and Corbin (1990) present such a model in their theory of "protective governing" (p. 134) in the health care setting. Another example is seen in Conrad's (1978) formal propositions about academic change in the academy.

Another embedded structure is the presentation of the "logic diagram," the "mini-framework," or the "integrative" diagram, where the researcher presents the actual theory in the form of a visual model. The researcher identifies elements of this structure in the axial coding phase, and then tells the "story" in axial coding as a narrative version of it. How is this visual model presented? A good example of this diagram is found in the Morrow and Smith (1995) study of women who have survived childhood sexual abuse. Their diagram shows a theoretical model that contains the axial coding categories of causal conditions, the central phenomenon, the context, intervening conditions, strategies, and consequences. It is presented with directional arrows indicating the flow of causality from left to right, from causal conditions to consequences. Arrows also show that the context and intervening conditions directly impact the strategies. Presented near the end of the study, this visual form represents the culminating theory for the study.

Charmaz (2006) provides an array of embedded writing strategies useful in grounded theory reports. Examples of grounded theory studies illustrate imparting mood or emotions into a theoretical discussion, straightforward language, and ways that writing can be accessible to readers such as the use of rhythm and time [e.g., "Days slip by" (Charmaz, 2006, p. 173)]. Charmaz also invites the use of unexpected definitions and assertions by the grounded theory author. Rhetorical questions are also useful, and the writing includes pacing and a tone that leads a reader into the topic. Stories can be told in grounded theory studies, and overall the writing brings evocative language to persuade the reader of the theory.

The Harley et al. (2009) grounded theory study shown in Appendix D illustrated the more formal structure of scientific grounded theory research. It began with the problem and the literature, and then moved on toward the method, results, and discussion and practical implications. The larger rhetorical structure focused on advancing a theoretical model about the evolution of physical activity. In the results section, the specific codes and categories were not presented. Instead the discussion moved quickly into the theoretical model and a detailed discussion of the phases of the model. One aspect of the model—planning methods—was highlighted for detailed discussion. In terms of embedded writing strategies, it did advance a visual of the theory, and mentioned that the researchers employed the basic principles of grounded theory data analysis (codes grouped into concepts, concepts compared with each other, concepts integrated into a theoretical framework). In this sense, the detailed writing approach and the larger presentation of grounded theory in this study reflect more of the process of writing a grounded theory study with a focus on the theory and the arguments of the theory as discussed by Charmaz (2006). It places the "analytic frameworks on center stage" (Charmaz, 2006, p. 151).

Ethnographic Writing Structure

Ethnographers write extensively about narrative construction, from how the nature of the text shapes the subject matter to the "literary" conventions and devices used by authors (Atkinson & Hammersley, 1994). The general shapes of ethnographies and embedded structures are well detailed in the literature.

Overall structure. The overall writing structure of ethnographies varies. For example, Van Maanen (1988) provides the alternative forms of ethnography. Some ethnographies are written as realist tales, reports that provide direct, matter-of-fact portraits of studied cultures without much information about how the ethnographers produced the portraits. In this type of tale, a writer uses an impersonal point of view, conveying a "scientific" and "objective" perspective. A confessional tale takes the opposite approach, and the researcher focuses more on his or her fieldwork experiences than on the culture. The final type, the impressionistic tale, is a personalized account of "fieldwork case in dramatic form" (Van Maanen, 1988, p. 7). It has elements of both realist and confessional writing and, in my opinion, presents a compelling and persuasive story. In both confessional and impressionistic tales, the first-person point of view is used, conveying a personal style of writing. Van Maanen states that other, less frequently written tales also exist—critical tales focusing on large social, political, symbolic, or economic issues; formalist tales that build, test, generalize, and exhibit theory; literary tales in which the ethnographers write like journalists, borrowing fiction-writing techniques from novelists; and jointly told tales in which the production of the studies is jointly authored by the fieldworkers and the informants, opening up shared and discursive narratives.

On a slightly different note, but yet related to the larger rhetorical structure, Wolcott (1994b) provides three components of a good qualitative inquiry that are a centerpiece of good ethnographic writing as well as steps in data analysis. First, an ethnographer writes a "description" of the culture that answers the question "What is going on here?" (Wolcott, 1994b, p. 12). Wolcott offers useful techniques for writing this description: chronological order, the researcher or narrator order, a progressive focusing, a critical or key event, plots and characters, groups in interaction, an analytical framework, and a story told through several perspectives. Second, after describing the culture using one of these approaches, the researcher "analyzes" the data. Analysis includes highlighting findings, displaying findings, reporting fieldwork procedures, identifying patterned regularities in the data, comparing the case with a known case, evaluating the information, contextualizing the information within a broader analytic framework, critiquing the research process, and proposing a redesign of the study. Of all these analytic techniques, the identification of "patterns" or themes is central to ethnographic writing. Third, interpretation is involved in the rhetorical structure. This means that the researcher can extend the analysis, make inferences from the information, do as directed or as suggested by gatekeepers, turn to theory, refocus the interpretation itself, connect with personal experience, analyze or interpret the interpretive process, or explore alternative formats. Of these interpretive strategies, I personally like the approach of interpreting the findings both within the context of the researcher's experiences and within the larger body of scholarly research on the topic.

A more detailed, structured outline for ethnography was found in Emerson, Fretz, and Shaw (1995). They discuss developing an ethnographic study as a "thematic narrative," a story "analytically thematized, but often in relatively loose ways . . . constructed out of a series of thematically organized units of fieldnote excerpts and analytic commentary" (p. 170). This thematic narrative builds inductively from a main idea or thesis that incorporates several specific analytic themes and is elaborated throughout the study. It is structured as follows:

- First is an introduction that engages the reader's attention and focuses the study, and then the researcher proceeds to link his or her interpretation to wider issues of scholarly interest in the discipline.
- After this, the researcher introduces the setting and the methods for learning about it. In this section, too, the ethnographer relates details about entry into and participation in the setting as well as advantages and constraints of the ethnographer's research role.
- The researcher presents analytic claims next, and Emerson and colleagues (1995) indicate the utility of "excerpt commentary" units, whereby an author incorporates an analytic point, provides orientation information about the point, presents the excerpt or direct quote, and then advances analytic commentary about the quote as it relates to the analytic point.
- In the conclusion, the researcher reflects and elaborates on the thesis advanced at the beginning. This interpretation may extend or modify the thesis in light of the materials examined, relate the thesis to general theory or a current issue, or offer a metacommentary on the thesis, methods, or assumptions of the study.

Embedded structure. Ethnographers use embedded rhetorical devices such as figures of speech or "tropes" (Fetterman, 2010; Hammersley & Atkinson, 1995). Metaphors, for example, provide visual and spatial images or dramaturgical characterizations of social actions as theater. Another trope is the synecdoche, in which ethnographers present examples, illustrations, cases, and/or vignettes that form a part but stand for the whole. Ethnographers present storytelling tropes examining cause and sequence that follow grand narratives to smaller parables. A final trope is irony, in which researchers bring to light contrasts of competing frames of reference and rationality.

More specific rhetorical devices depict scenes in ethnography (Emerson et al., 1995). Writers can incorporate details or "write lushly" (Goffman, 1989, p. 131) or "thickly," description that creates verisimilitude and produces for readers the feeling that they experience, or perhaps could experience, the events described (Denzin, 1989b; Fetterman, 2010). Denzin (1989b) talks about the importance of using "thick description" in writing qualitative research. By this, he means that the narrative "presents detail, context, emotion, and the webs of social relationships . . . [and] evokes emotionality and self-feelings. . . . The voices, feelings, actions, and meanings of interacting individuals are heard" (Denzin, 1989b, p. 83). As an example, Denzin (1989b) first refers to an illustration of "thick" description from Sudnow (1978), and then provides his own version as if it were "thin" description.

Thick description: "Sitting at the piano and moving into the production of a chord, the chord as a whole was prepared for as the hand moved toward the keyboard, and the terrain was seen as a field relative to the task. . . . There was chord A and chord B, separated from one another. . . . A's production entailed a tightly compressed hand, and B's . . . an open and extended spread. . . . The beginner gets from A to B disjointly." (Sudnow, 1978, pp. 9–10)

Thin description: "I had trouble learning the piano keyboard." (Denzin, 1989b, p. 85)

Also, ethnographers present dialogue, and the dialogue becomes especially vivid when written in the dialect and natural language of the culture (see, e.g., the articles on Black English vernacular or "code switching" in Nelson, 1990). Writers also rely on characterization in which human beings are shown talking, acting, and relating to others. Longer scenes take the form of sketches, a "slice of life" (Emerson et al., 1995, p. 85), or larger episodes and tales.

Ethnographic writers tell "a good story" (Richardson, 1990). Thus, one of the forms of "evocative" experimental qualitative writing for

Richardson (1990) is the fictional representation form in which writers draw on the literary devices such as flashback, flash-forward, alternative points of view, deep characterization, tone shifts, synecdoche, dialogue, interior monologue, and sometimes the omniscient narrator.

Haenfler's (2004) ethnographic study of the core values of the straight edge movement illustrated many of these writing conventions (see Appendix E). It fell somewhere between a realist tale, with its review of the literature and extensive method discussion, and a critical tale, with its orientation toward examining closely subculture resistance and the reflexivity of the author as he discussed his involvement as a participant observer. It followed Wolcott's (1994b) orientation of description with a detailed discussion about the core values of the sXe group, then analyzed through themes, and ended with a conclusion that discussed an analytic framework for understanding the group. It told a good, persuasive story, with colorful elements (e.g., T-shirt slogans), "thick" description, and extensive quotes. It did not include some of the literary tropes, such as dialogue and interior monologue, and the tone was one of an omniscient narrator as typically found in the realist tales of Van Maanen (1988).

Case Study Writing Structure

Turning to case studies, I am reminded by Merriam (1988) that "there is no standard format for reporting case study research" (p. 193). Unquestionably, some case studies generate theory, some are simply descriptions of cases, and others are more analytical in nature and display cross-case or intersite comparisons. The overall intent of the case study undoubtedly shapes the larger structure of the written narrative. Still, I find it useful to conceptualize a general form, and I turn to key texts on case studies to receive guidance.

Overall structure. One can open and close the case study narrative with vignettes to draw the reader into the case. This approach is suggested by Stake (1995), who provides an outline of topics that might be included in a qualitative case study. I feel that this is a helpful way to stage the topics in a good case study:

- The writer opens with a vignette so that the reader can develop a vicarious experience to get a feel for the time and place of the study.

- Next, the researcher identifies the issue, the purpose, and the method of the study so that the reader learns about how the study came to be, the background of the writer, and the issues surrounding the case.
- This is followed by an extensive description of the case and its context—a body of relatively uncontested data—a description the reader might make if he or she had been there.
- Issues are presented next, a few key issues, so that the reader can understand the complexity of the case. This complexity builds through references to other research or the writer's understanding of other cases.
- Next, several of the issues are probed further. At this point, too, the writer brings in both confirming and disconfirming evidence.
- Assertions are presented, a summary of what the writer understands about the case and whether the initial naturalistic generalizations, conclusions arrived at through personal experience or offered as vicarious experiences for the reader, have been changed conceptually or challenged.
- Finally, the writer ends with a closing vignette, an experiential note, reminding the reader that this report is one person's encounter with a complex case.

I like this general outline because it provides description of the case; presents themes, assertions, or interpretations of the researcher; and begins and ends with realistic scenarios.

A similar model is found in Lincoln and Guba's (1985) substantive case report. They describe a need for the explication of the problem, a thorough description of the context or setting, a description of the transactions or processes observed in that context, saliences at the site (elements studied in depth), and outcomes of the inquiry ("lessons learned").

At a more general level yet, I find Yin's (2009) 2 × 2 table of types of case studies helpful. Case studies can be either single-case or multiple-case designs and either holistic (single unit of analysis) or embedded (multiple units of analysis). Yin comments further that a single case is best when a need exists to study a critical case, an extreme or unique case, or a revelatory case. Whether the case is single or multiple, the researcher decides to study the entire case, a holistic design, or multiple subunits within the case (the embedded design). Although the holistic design may be more abstract, it captures the entire case better than the embedded design does. However, the embedded design starts with an examination of subunits and allows for the detailed perspective should the questions begin to shift and change during fieldwork.

Yin (2009) also presents several possible structures for composing a case study report. In a linear-analytic approach, a standard approach according to Yin, the researcher discusses the problem, the methods, the findings, and the conclusions. An alternative structure repeats the same case study several times and compares alternative descriptions or explanations of the same case. A chronological structure presents the case study in a sequence, such as sections or chapters that address the early, middle, and late phase of a case history. Theories are also used as a framework, and the case studies can debate various hypotheses or propositions. In a suspense structure, the "answer" or outcome of a case study and its significance is presented in an initial chapter or section. The remaining sections are then devoted to the development of an explanation for this outcome. In a final structure, the unsequenced structure, the author describes a case with no particular order to the sections or chapter.

Embedded structure. What specific narrative devices, embedded structures, do case study writers use to "mark" their studies? One might approach the description of the context and setting for the case from a broader picture to a narrower one. For example, in the gunman case (Asmussen & Creswell, 1995; see Appendix F), we described the actual campus incident first in terms of the city in which the situation developed, followed by the campus and, more narrow yet, the actual classroom on campus. This funneling approach narrowed the setting from a calm city environment to a potentially volatile campus classroom and seemed to launch the study into a chronology of events that occurred.

Researchers also need to be cognizant of the amount of description in their case studies versus the amount of analysis and interpretation or assertions. In comparing description and analysis, Merriam (1988) suggests that the proper balance might be 60%-40% or 70%-30% in favor of description. In the gunman case, Asmussen and I balanced the elements in equal thirds (33%-33%-33%)—a concrete description of the setting and the actual events (and those that occurred within two weeks after the incident); the five themes; and our interpretation, the lessons learned, reported in the discussion section. In our case study, the description of the case and its context did not loom as large as in other case studies. But these matters are up to writers to decide, and it is conceivable that a case study might contain mainly descriptive material, especially if the bounded system, the case, is quite large and complex.

Our gunman study (Asmussen & Creswell, 1995; see Appendix F) also represented a single-case study (Yin, 2009), with a single narrative about the case, its themes, and its interpretation. In another study, the case presentation might be that of multiple cases, with each case discussed separately, or multiple case studies with no separate discussions of each case but an overall cross-case analysis (Yin, 2009). Another Yin (2009) narrative format is to pose a series of questions and answers based on the case study database.

Within any of these formats, one might consider alternative embedded structures for building case analyses. For example, in our gunman study (Asmussen & Creswell, 1995; see Appendix F), we presented descriptively the chronology of the events during the incident and immediately after it. The chronological approach seemed to work best when events unfolded and followed a process; case studies often are bounded by time and cover events over time (Yin, 2009).

A COMPARISON OF NARRATIVE STRUCTURES

Looking back over Table 9.1, we see many diverse structures for writing the qualitative report. What major differences exist in the structures depending on one's choice of approach?

First, I am struck by the diversity of discussions about narrative structures. I found little crossover or sharing of structures among the five approaches, although, in practice, this undoubtedly occurs. The narrative tropes and the literary devices, discussed by ethnographers and narrative researchers, have applicability regardless of approach. Second, the writing structures are highly related to data analysis procedures. A phenomenological study and a grounded theory study follow closely the data analysis steps. In short, I am reminded once again that it is difficult to separate the activities of data collection, analysis, and report writing in a qualitative study. Third, the emphasis given to writing the narrative, especially the embedded narrative structures, varies among the approaches. Ethnographers lead the group in their extensive discussions about narrative and text construction. Phenomenologists and grounded theory writers spend less time discussing this topic. Fourth, the overall narrative structure is clearly specified in some approaches (e.g., a grounded theory study, a phenomenological study, and perhaps a case study), whereas it is flexible and evolving in others (e.g., a narrative, an ethnography). Perhaps this conclusion reflects the more structured approach versus the less structured approach, overall, among the five approaches of inquiry.

SUMMARY

In this chapter, I discussed writing the qualitative report. I began by discussing several rhetorical issues the writer must address. These issues include writing reflexively and with representation, the audience for the writing, the encoding for that audience, and the use of quotes. Then I turned to each of the five approaches of inquiry and presented overall rhetorical structures for organizing the entire study as well as specific embedded structures, writing devices, and techniques that the researcher incorporates into the study. A table of these structures shows the diversity of perspectives about structure that reflects different data analysis procedures and discipline affiliations. I concluded with observations about the differences in writing structures among the five approaches, differences reflected in the variability of approaches, the relationships between data analysis and report writing, the emphasis in the literature of each approach on narrative construction, and the amount of structure in the overall architecture of a study within each approach.

ADDITIONAL READINGS

Charmaz, K. (2006). *Constructing grounded theory*. London: Sage.

Clandinin, D. J., & Connelly, F. M. (2000). *Narrative inquiry: Experience and story in qualitative research*. San Francisco: Jossey-Bass.

Clifford, J., & Marcus, G. E. (Eds.). (1986). *Writing culture: The poetics and politics of ethnography*. Berkeley: University of California Press.

Czarniawka, B. (2004). *Narratives in social science research*. Thousand Oaks, CA: Sage.

Denzin, N. K. (1989). *Interpretive interactionism*. Newbury Park, CA: Sage.

Fetterman, D. M. (2010). *Ethnography: Step by step* (3rd ed.). Thousand Oaks, CA: Sage.

Gilgun, J. F. (2005). "Grab" and good science: Writing up the results of qualitative research. *Qualitative Health Research, 15,* 256–262.

Moustakas, C. (1994). *Phenomenological research methods*. Thousand Oaks, CA: Sage.

Richardson, L., & St. Pierre, E. A. (2005). Writing: A method of inquiry. In N. K. Denzin & Y. S. Lincoln (Eds.), *The Sage handbook of qualitative research* (3rd ed., pp. 959–978). Thousand Oaks, CA: Sage.

Riessman, C. K. (2008). *Narrative methods for the human sciences.* Los Angeles, CA: Sage.

Stake, R. (1995). *The art of case study research.* Thousand Oaks, CA: Sage.

Strauss, A., & Corbin, J. (1990). *Basics of qualitative research: Grounded theory procedures and techniques.* Newbury Park, CA: Sage.

Strauss, A., & Corbin, J. (1998). *Basics of qualitative research: Grounded theory procedures and techniques* (2nd ed.). Thousand Oaks, CA: Sage.

Van Maanen, J. (1988). *Tales of the field: On writing ethnography.* Chicago: University of Chicago Press.

van Manen, M. (1990). *Researching lived experience.* New York: State University of New York Press.

van Manen, M. (2006). Writing qualitatively, or the demands of writing. *Qualitative Health Research, 16,* 713–722.

Weis, L., & Fine, M. (2000). *Speed bumps: A student-friendly guide to qualitative research.* New York: Teachers College Press.

Wolcott, H. F. (1994). *Transforming qualitative data: Description, analysis, and interpretation.* Thousand Oaks, CA: Sage.

Wolcott, H. F. (2008). *Writing up qualitative research* (3rd ed.). Thousand Oaks, CA: Sage.

Yin, R. K. (2009). *Case study research: Design and method* (4th ed.). Thousand Oaks, CA: Sage.

EXERCISES

1. It is useful to see the overall flow of ideas in a qualitative journal article study within a particular approach to qualitative research. The flow of ideas can then be adapted to use in your specific project. Go back to Chapter 5 and select one of the journal articles that fits your particular approach (narrative, phenomenology, etc.). Find the article and then diagram its overall structure by drawing a picture of it using circles, boxes, and arrows. Where does the article start? With a personal vignette, a statement of the problem, a literature review? Draft this picture of the flow of ideas in the journal article to use as a model for your own work.

2. Look at the gunman case study in Appendix F. Learn about how to write a theme passage by examining one of the themes in this case study. Take, for example, the theme passage on "safety." Underline (a) the multiple perspectives that are advanced, (b) the different sources of information used, and (c) the quotes and whether they are short, medium, or long. In this type of analysis you will have a deeper understanding of the writing of a theme passage in your qualitative study.

Exercises

3. It is useful to actually see "thick" description in action when writing qualitative research. To do this I often turn to good novels in which the author provides exquisite detail about an event, a thing, or a person. For example, turn to page 14 in Paul Harding's award-winning book, *Tinkers* (2009), and read the passage about how George repaired a broken clock at a tag sale. Write about how Harding incorporates a physical description, includes a description of the steps (or movement), uses strong action verbs, draws on references or quotes, and relies on the five senses to convey detail (sight, hearing, taste, smell, touch). Use this type of detail in your qualitative descriptions or themes.

10

Standards of Validation and Evaluation

Qualitative researchers strive for "understanding," that deep structure of knowledge that comes from visiting personally with participants, spending extensive time in the field, and probing to obtain detailed meanings. During or after a study, qualitative researchers ask, "Did we get it right?" (Stake, 1995, p. 107) or "Did we publish a 'wrong' or inaccurate account?" (Thomas, 1993, p. 39). Is it possible to even have a "right" answer? To answer these questions, researchers need to look to themselves, to the participants, and to the readers. There are multi- or polyvocal discourses at work here that provide insight into the validation and evaluation of a qualitative narrative.

In this chapter, I address two interrelated questions: Is the account valid, and by whose standards? How do we evaluate the quality of qualitative research? Answers to these questions will take us into the many perspectives on validation to emerge within the qualitative community and the multiple standards for evaluation discussed by authors with procedural, interpretive, emancipatory, and postmodern perspectives.

QUESTIONS FOR DISCUSSION

- What are some qualitative perspectives on validation?
- What are some alternative procedures useful in establishing validation?
- How is reliability used in qualitative research?
- What are some alternative stances on evaluating the quality of qualitative research?
- How do these stances differ by types of approaches to qualitative inquiry?

VALIDATION AND RELIABILITY IN QUALITATIVE RESEARCH

Perspectives on Validation

Many perspectives exist regarding the importance of validation in qualitative research, the definition of it, terms to describe it, and procedures for establishing it. In Table 10.1, I illustrate several of the perspectives available on validation in the qualitative literature. These perspectives view qualitative validation in terms of quantitative equivalents, use qualitative terms that are distinct from quantitative terms, employ postmodern and interpretive perspectives, consider validation as unimportant, combine or synthesize many perspectives, and visualize it metaphorically as a crystal.

Table 10.1 Perspectives and Terms Used in Qualitative Validation

Study	Perspective	Terms
LeCompte & Goetz (1982)	Use of parallel, qualitative equivalents to their quantitative counterparts in experimental and survey research	Internal validity External validity Reliability Objectivity
Lincoln & Guba (1985)	Use of alternative terms that apply more to naturalistic axioms	Credibility Transferability Dependability Confirmability
Eisner (1991)	Use of alternative terms that provide reasonable standards for judging the credibility of qualitative research	Structural corroboration Consensual validation Referential adequacy Ironic validity
Lather (1993)	Use of reconceptualized validity in four types	Paralogic validity Rhizomatic validity Situated/embedded voluptuous validity

Wolcott (1994b)	Use of terms other than *validity,* because it neither guides nor informs qualitative research	Understanding better than validity
Angen (2000)	Use of validation within the context of interpretive inquiry	Two types: ethical and substantive
Whittemore, Chase, & Mandle (2001)	Use of synthesized perspectives of validity, organized into primary criteria and secondary criteria	Primary criteria: credibility, authenticity, criticality, and integrity Secondary criteria: explicitness, vividness, creativity, thoroughness, congruence, and sensitivity
Richardson & St. Pierre (2005) Lincoln, Lynham, & Guba (2011)	Use of a metaphorical, reconceptualized form of validity as a crystal Use of authenticity, transgression, and ethical relationships	Crystals: grow, change, alter, reflect externalities, refract within themselves Fairness representing views, raised awareness, and action; hidden assumptions and repressions, the crystal that can be turned many ways; relationships with research participants

Writers have searched for and found qualitative equivalents that parallel traditional quantitative approaches to validation. LeCompte and Goetz (1982) took this approach when they compared the issues of validation and reliability to their counterparts in experimental design and survey research. They contend that qualitative research has garnered much criticism in the scientific ranks for its failure to "adhere to canons of reliability and validation" (LeCompte & Goetz, 1982, p. 31) in the traditional sense. They apply threats to internal validation in experimental research to ethnographic research (e.g., history and maturation, observer effects, selection and regression, mortality, spurious conclusions). They further identify threats to external validation as "effects that obstruct or reduce a study's comparability or translatability" (LeCompte & Goetz, 1982, p. 51).

Some writers argue that authors who use positivist terminology facilitate the acceptance of qualitative research in a quantitative world. Ely and colleagues (Ely, Anzul, Friedman, Garner, & Steinmetz, 1991) assert that using quantitative terms tends to be a defensive measure that muddies the waters and that "the language of positivistic research is not congruent with or adequate to qualitative work" (p. 95). Lincoln and Guba (1985) use alternative terms that, they contend, adhere more to naturalistic research. To establish the "trustworthiness" of a study, Lincoln and Guba (1985) use unique terms, such as *credibility, authenticity, transferability, dependability,* and *confirmability,* as "the naturalist's equivalents" for *internal validation, external validation, reliability,* and *objectivity* (p. 300). To operationalize these new terms, they propose techniques such as prolonged engagement in the field and the triangulation of data sources, methods, and investigators to establish credibility. To make sure that the findings are transferable between the researcher and those being studied, thick description is necessary. Rather than reliability, one seeks dependability that the results will be subject to change and instability. The naturalistic researcher looks for confirmability rather than objectivity in establishing the value of the data. Both dependability and confirmability are established through an auditing of the research process. I find the Lincoln and Guba criteria still popular today in qualitative reports.

Rather than using the term *validation,* Eisner (1991) discusses the credibility of qualitative research. He constructs standards such as structural corroboration, consensual validation, and referential adequacy. In structural corroboration, the researcher uses multiple types of data to support or contradict the interpretation. As Eisner (1991) states, "We seek a confluence of evidence that breeds credibility, that allows us to feel confident about our observations, interpretations, and conclusions" (p. 110). He further illustrates this point with an analogy drawn from detective work: The researcher compiles bits and pieces of evidence to formulate a "compelling whole." At this stage, the researcher looks for recurring behaviors or actions and considers disconfirming evidence and contrary interpretations. Moreover, Eisner recommends that to demonstrate credibility, the weight of evidence should become persuasive. Consensual validation seeks the opinion of others, and Eisner (1991) refers to "an agreement among competent others that the description, interpretation, evaluation, and thematics of an educational situation are right" (p. 112). Referential adequacy suggests the importance of criticism, and Eisner describes the goal of criticism as illuminating the subject matter and bringing about more complex and sensitive human perception and understanding.

Qualitative researchers also have reconceptualized validation with a postmodern sensibility. Lather (1991) comments that current "paradigmatic uncertainty in the human sciences is leading to the re-conceptualizing of validation" and calls for "new techniques and concepts for obtaining and defining trustworthy data which avoids the pitfalls of orthodox notions of validation" (p. 66). For Lather, the character of a social science report changes from a closed narrative with a tight argument structure to a more open narrative with holes and questions and an admission of situatedness and partiality. In *Getting Smart,* Lather (1991) advances a "reconceptualization of validation." She identifies four types of validation, including triangulation (multiple data sources, methods, and theoretical schemes), construct validation (recognizing the constructs that exist rather than imposing theories/constructs on informants or the context), face validation [as "a 'click of recognition' and a 'yes, of course,' instead of 'yes, but' experience" (Kidder, 1982, p. 56)], and catalytic validation (which energizes participants toward knowing reality to transform it).

In a later article, Lather's (1993) terms became more unique and closely relate to feminist research in "four frames of validation." The first, *ironic* validation, is where the researcher presents truth as a problem. The second, *paralogic* validation, is concerned with undecidables, limits, paradoxes, and complexities, a movement away from theorizing things and toward providing direct exposure to other voices in an almost unmediated way. The third, *rhizomatic* validation, pertains to questioning proliferations, crossings, and overlaps without underlying structures or deeply rooted connections. The researcher also questions taxonomies, constructs, and interconnected networks whereby the reader jumps from one assemblage to another and consequently moves from judgment to understanding. The fourth type is situated, embodied, or *voluptuous* validation, which means that the researcher sets out to understand more than one can know and to write toward what one does not understand.

Other writers, such as Wolcott (1990a), have little use for validation. He suggests that "validation neither guides nor informs" his work (Wolcott, 1990a, p. 136). He does not dismiss validation, but rather places it in a broader perspective. Wolcott's (1990a) goal is to identify "critical elements" and write "plausible interpretations from them" (p. 146). He ultimately tries to understand rather than convince, and he voices the view that validation distracts from his work of understanding what is really going on. Wolcott claims that the term *validation* does not capture the essence of what he seeks, adding that perhaps someone would coin a term appropriate for the naturalistic paradigm. But for now, he says, the term *understanding* seems to encapsulate the idea as well as any other.

Validation has also been cast within an interpretive approach to qualitative research marked by a focus on the importance of the researcher, a lack of truth in validation, a form of validation based on negotiation and dialogue with participants, and interpretations that are temporal, located, and always open to reinterpretation (Angen, 2000). Angen (2000) suggests that within interpretative research, validation is "a judgment of the trustworthiness or goodness of a piece of research" (p. 387). She espouses an ongoing open dialogue on the topic of what makes interpretive research worthy of our trust. Considerations of validation are not definitive as the final word on the topic, nor should every study be required to address them. Further, she advances two types of validation: ethical validation and substantive validation. Ethical validation means that all research agendas must question their underlying moral assumptions, their political and ethical implications, and the equitable treatment of diverse voices. It also requires research to provide some practical answers to questions. Our research should also have a "generative promise" (Angen, 2000, p. 389) and raise new possibilities, open up new questions, and stimulate new dialogue. Our research must have transformative value leading to action and change. Our research should also provide nondogmatic answers to the questions we pose.

Substantive validation means understanding one's own topic, understandings derived from other sources, and the documentation of this process in the written study. Self-reflection contributes to the validation of the work. The researcher, as a sociohistorical interpreter, interacts with the subject matter to co-create the interpretations derived. Understandings derived from previous research give substance to the inquiry. Interpretive research also is a chain of interpretations that must be documented for others to judge the trustworthiness of the meanings arrived at in the end. Written accounts must resonate with their intended audiences, and must be compelling, powerful, and convincing.

A synthesis of validation perspectives comes from Whittemore, Chase, and Mandle (2001), who analyze 13 writings about validation, and extract from these studies key validation criteria. They organize these criteria into primary and secondary criteria. They find four primary criteria: credibility (Are the results an accurate interpretation of the participants' meaning?); authenticity (Are different voices heard?); criticality (Is there a critical appraisal of all aspects of the research?); and integrity (Are the investigators self-critical?). Secondary criteria relate to explicitness, vividness, creativity, thoroughness, congruence, and sensitivity. In summary, with these criteria, it seems like the validation standard has moved toward the interpretive lens of qualitative research, with an emphasis on researcher reflexivity and on researcher challenges that include raising questions about the ideas developed during a research study.

A recent postmodern perspective draws on the metaphorical image of a crystal. Richardson (in Richardson & St. Pierre, 2005) describes this image:

> I propose that the central imaginary for "validation" for postmodern texts is not the triangle—a rigid, fixed, two-dimensional object. Rather the central imaginary is the crystal, which combines symmetry and substance with an infinite variety of shapes, substances, transmutations, multidimensionalities, and angles of approach. Crystals grow, change, and are altered, but they are not amorphous. Crystals are prisms that reflect externalities and refract within themselves, creating different colors, patterns, and arrays casting off in different directions. What we see depends on our angle of response—not triangulation but rather crystallization. (p. 963)

A final perspective is that drawn from Lincoln, Lynham, and Guba (2011). They capture the many perspectives to develop through the years. They suggest that the question of validity criteria is not whether we should have such criteria or whose criteria the scientific community might adopt, but rather how criteria need to be developed within the projected transformations being suggested by social scientists. To this end they review their focus on establishing authenticity, but frame it within the perspectives of a balance of views, raising the level of awareness among participants and other stakeholders, and advancing the ability of inquiry to lead to action on the part of research participants and training those participants to take action. Lincoln and colleagues (2011) also see a role for validity in understanding hidden assumptions through the image (also shared by Richardson and St. Pierre, 2005) of a crystal that reflects and refracts the processes of research, such as discovery, seeing, telling, storying, and representation. Finally, for these authors validity is an ethical relationship with research participants through such standards as positioning themselves, having discourses, encouraging voices, and being self-reflective.

Given these many perspectives, I will summarize my own stance. I consider "validation" in qualitative research to be an attempt to assess the "accuracy" of the findings, as best described by the researcher and the participants. This view also suggests that any report of research is a representation by the author.

I also view validation as a distinct strength of qualitative research in that the account made through extensive time spent in the field, the detailed thick description, and the closeness of the researcher to participants in the study all add to the value or accuracy of a study.

I use the term *validation* to emphasize a process (see Angen, 2000), rather than *verification* (which has quantitative overtones) or historical words such as *trustworthiness* and *authenticity* (recognizing that many qualitative writers do return to these words, suggesting the "staying power" of Lincoln and Guba's, 1985, standards; see Whittemore et al., 2001). I acknowledge that there are many types of qualitative validation and that authors need to choose the types and terms with which they are comfortable. I recommend that writers reference their validation terms and strategies.

The subject of validation does arise in several of the approaches to qualitative research (e.g., Riessman, 2008; Stake, 1995; Strauss & Corbin, 1998), but I do not think that distinct validation approaches exist for the five approaches to qualitative research. At best, there might be less emphasis on validation in narrative research and more emphasis on it in grounded theory, case study, and ethnography, especially when the authors of these approaches want to employ systematic procedures. I would recommend using multiple validation strategies regardless of type of qualitative approach.

My framework for thinking about validation in qualitative research is to suggest that researchers employ accepted strategies to document the "accuracy" of their studies. These I call "validation strategies."

Validation Strategies

It is not enough to gain perspectives and terms; ultimately, these ideas are translated into practice as strategies or techniques. Whittemore and colleagues (2001) organize the techniques into 29 forms that apply to design consideration, data generating, analysis, and presentation. My colleague and I (Creswell & Miller, 2000) focus on eight strategies that are frequently used by qualitative researchers. These are not presented in any specific order of importance.

Prolonged engagement and persistent observation in the field include building trust with participants, learning the culture, and checking for misinformation that stems from distortions introduced by the researcher or informants (Ely et al., 1991; Erlandson, Harris, Skipper, & Allen, 1993; Glesne & Peshkin, 1992; Lincoln & Guba, 1985; Merriam, 1988). In the field, the researcher makes decisions about what is salient to study, relevant to the purpose of the study, and of interest for focus. Fetterman (2010) contends that "participant observation requires close, long-term contact with the people under study" (p. 39).

In *triangulation*, researchers make use of multiple and different sources, methods, investigators, and theories to provide corroborating evidence (Ely et al., 1991; Erlandson et al., 1993; Glesne & Peshkin, 1992; Lincoln & Guba, 1985; Merriam, 1988; Miles & Huberman, 1994; Patton, 1980, 1990). Typically, this process involves corroborating evidence from different sources to shed light on a theme or perspective. When qualitative researchers locate evidence to document a code or theme in different sources of data, they are triangulating information and providing validity to their findings.

Peer review or debriefing provides an external check of the research process (Ely et al., 1991; Erlandson et al., 1993; Glesne & Peshkin, 1992; Lincoln & Guba, 1985; Merriam, 1988), much in the same spirit as interrater reliability in quantitative research. Lincoln and Guba (1985) define the role of the peer debriefer as a "devil's advocate," an individual who keeps the researcher honest; asks hard questions about methods, meanings, and interpretations; and provides the researcher with the opportunity for catharsis by sympathetically listening to the researcher's feelings. This reviewer may be a peer, and both the peer and the researcher keep written accounts of the sessions, called "peer debriefing sessions" (Lincoln & Guba, 1985).

In *negative case analysis*, the researcher refines working hypotheses as the inquiry advances (Ely et al., 1991; Lincoln & Guba, 1985; Miles & Huberman, 1994; Patton, 1980, 1990) in light of negative or disconfirming evidence. Not all evidence will fit the pattern of a code or a theme. It is necessary then to report this negative analysis, and, in doing so, the researcher provides a realistic assessment of the phenomenon under study. In real life, not all evidence is either positive or negative; it is some of both.

Clarifying researcher bias from the outset of the study is important so that the reader understands the researcher's position and any biases or assumptions that impact the inquiry (Merriam, 1988). In this clarification, the researcher comments on past experiences, biases, prejudices, and orientations that have likely shaped the interpretation and approach to the study.

In *member checking*, the researcher solicits participants' views of the credibility of the findings and interpretations (Ely et al., 1991; Erlandson et al., 1993; Glesne & Peshkin, 1992; Lincoln & Guba, 1985; Merriam, 1988; Miles & Huberman, 1994). This technique is considered by Lincoln and Guba (1985) to be "the most critical technique for establishing credibility" (p. 314). This approach, *writ large* in most qualitative studies, involves taking data, analyses, interpretations, and conclusions back to the participants so that they can judge the accuracy and credibility of the account. According to Stake (1995), participants should "play a major role directing as well as acting in case study" research (p. 115). They should be asked to examine rough drafts of the researcher's work and to provide alternative language, "critical observations or interpretations" (Stake, 1995, p. 115). For this validation strategy, I convene a focus group composed of participants in my study and ask them to reflect on the accuracy of the account. I do not take back to participants my transcripts or the raw data, but take them my preliminary analyses consisting of description or themes. I am interested in their views of these written analyses as well as what was missing.

Rich, thick description allows readers to make decisions regarding transferability (Erlandson et al., 1993; Lincoln & Guba, 1985; Merriam, 1988) because the writer describes in detail the participants or setting under study. With such detailed description, the researcher enables readers to transfer information to other settings and to determine whether the findings can be transferred "because of shared characteristics" (Erlandson et al., 1993, p. 32). Thick description means that the researcher provides details when describing a case or when writing about a theme. According to Stake (2010), "A description is rich if it provides abundant, interconnected details . . ." (p. 49). Detail can emerge through physical description, movement description, and activity description. It can also involve describing from the general ideas to the narrow (as in the Asmussen & Creswell, 1995, case study; see Appendix F), interconnecting the details, using strong action verbs, and quotes.

External audits (Erlandson et al., 1993; Lincoln & Guba, 1985; Merriam, 1988; Miles & Huberman, 1994) allow an external consultant, the auditor, to examine both the process and the product of the account, assessing their accuracy. This auditor should have no connection to the study. In assessing the product, the auditor examines whether or not the findings, interpretations, and conclusions are supported by the data. Lincoln and Guba (1985) compare this, metaphorically, with a fiscal audit, and the procedure provides a sense of interrater reliability to a study.

Examining these eight procedures as a whole, I recommend that qualitative researchers engage in at least two of them in any given study. Unquestionably, procedures such as triangulating among different data sources (assuming that the investigator collects more than one), writing with detailed and thick description, and taking the entire written narrative back to participants in member checking all are reasonably easy procedures to conduct. They also are the most popular and cost-effective procedures. Other procedures, such as peer audits and external audits, are more time consuming in their application and may also involve substantial costs to the researcher.

Reliability Perspectives

Reliability can be addressed in qualitative research in several ways (Silverman, 2005). Reliability can be enhanced if the researcher obtains detailed field notes by employing a good-quality tape for recording and by transcribing the tape. Also, the tape needs to be transcribed to indicate the trivial, but often crucial, pauses and overlaps. Further coding can be done "blind" with the coding staff and the analysts conducting their research without knowledge of the expectations and questions of the project directors, and by use of computer programs to assist in recording and analyzing the data. Silverman also supports intercoder agreement.

Our focus on reliability here will be on ***intercoder agreement*** based on the use of multiple coders to analyze transcript data. In qualitative research, *reliability* often refers to the stability of responses to multiple coders of data sets. I find this practice especially used in qualitative health science research and within the form of qualitative research in which inquirers want an external check on the highly interpretive coding process. What seems to be largely missing in the literature (with the exception of Miles and Huberman, 1994, and Armstrong, Gosling, Weinman, & Marteau, 1997) is a discussion about the procedures of actually conducting intercoder agreement checks. One of the key issues is determining what exactly the codings are agreeing on, whether they seek agreement on code names, the coded passages, or the same passages coded the same way. We also need to decide on whether to seek agreement based on codes, themes, or both codes and themes (see Armstrong et al., 1997).

Undoubtedly, there is flexibility in the process, and researchers need to fashion an approach consistent with the resources and time to engage in coding. At the Veterans Affairs Healthcare System in Ann Arbor, Michigan, I had an opportunity to help design an intercoder agreement process using data related to the Health Insurance Portability and Accountability Act (HIPAA; L. J. Damschroder, personal communication, March 2006). In a project at the VA Healthcare System, we used the following steps in our intercoder agreement process:

We sought to develop a codebook of codes that would be stable and represent the coding analysis of four independent coders. We all used NVivo as a software program to help in this coding. To achieve this goal, we read through several transcripts independently and coded each manuscript.

After coding, say, three to four transcripts, we then met and examined the codes, their names, and the text segments that we coded. We began to develop a preliminary qualitative codebook of the major codes. This codebook contained a definition of each code and the text segments that we assigned to each code. In this initial codebook, we had "parent" codes and "children" codes. In our initial codebook, we were more interested in the major codes we were finding in the database than in an exhaustive list. We felt that we could add to the codes as the analyses proceeded.

Each of us then independently coded three additional transcripts, say, Transcripts 5, 6, and 7. Now we were ready to actually compare our codes. We felt that it was more important to have agreement on the text segments we were assigning to codes than to have the same, exact passages coded. Intercoder agreement to us meant that we agreed that when we assigned a code word to a passage, we all assigned this same code word to the passage. It did not mean that we all coded the same passages—an ideal that I believe would be hard to achieve because some people code short passages and others longer passages. Nor did it mean that we all bracketed the exact same lines for our code word, another ideal difficult to achieve.

So we took a realistic stance, and we looked at the passages that all four of us coded and asked ourselves whether we had all assigned the same code word to the passage, based on our tentative definitions in the codebook. The decision would be either a yes or a no, and we could calculate the percentage of agreement among all four of us on this passage that we all coded. We sought to establish an 80% agreement of coding on these passages (Miles and Huberman, 1994, recommend an 80% agreement). Other researchers might actually calculate a kappa reliability statistic on the agreement, but we felt that a percentage would suffice to report in our published study.

After we collapsed codes into broader themes, we could conduct the same process with themes, to see if the passages we all coded as themes were consistent in the use of the same theme.

After the process continued through several more transcripts, we then revised the codebook, and conducted anew an assessment of passages that we all coded and determined if we used the same or different codes or the same or different themes. With each phase in the intercoder agreement process, we achieved a higher percentage of agreed upon codes and themes for text segments.

EVALUATION CRITERIA

Qualitative Perspectives

In reviewing validation in the qualitative research literature, I am struck by how validation is sometimes used in discussing the quality of a study (e.g., Angen, 2000). Although validation is certainly an aspect of evaluating the quality of a study, other criteria are useful as well. In reviewing the criteria, I find that here, too, the standards vary within the qualitative community (see my contrast of three approaches to qualitative evaluation, Creswell, 2012). I will first review three general standards and then turn to specific criteria within each of our five approaches to qualitative research.

A methodological perspective comes from Howe and Eisenhardt (1990), who suggest that only broad, abstract standards are possible for qualitative (and quantitative) research. Moreover, to determine, for example, whether a study is a good ethnography cannot be answered apart from whether the study contributes to our understanding of important questions. Howe and Eisenhardt elaborate further, suggesting that five standards be applied to all research. First, they assess a study in terms of whether the research questions drive the data collection and analysis rather than the reverse being the case. Second, they examine the extent to which the data collection and analysis techniques are competently applied in a technical sense. Third, they ask whether the researcher's assumptions are made explicit, such as the researcher's own subjectivity. Fourth, they wonder whether the study has overall warrant, such as whether it is robust, uses respected theoretical explanations, and discusses disconfirmed theoretical explanations. Fifth, the study must have "value" both in informing and improving practice (the "So what?" question) and in protecting the confidentiality, privacy, and truth telling of participants (the ethical question).

A postmodern, interpretive framework forms a second perspective, from Lincoln (1995), who thinks about the quality issue in terms of emerging criteria. She tracks her own thinking (and that of her late colleague, Guba) from early approaches of developing parallel methodological criteria (Lincoln & Guba, 1985) to establishing the criteria of "fairness" (a balance of stakeholder views), sharing knowledge, and fostering social action (Guba & Lincoln, 1989) to her current stance. The new emerging approach to quality is based on three new commitments: to emergent relations with respondents, to a set of stances, and to a vision of research that enables and promotes justice. Based on these commitments, Lincoln (1995) then proceeds to identify eight standards:

- The standard set in the inquiry community, such as by guidelines for publication. These guidelines admit that within diverse approaches to research, inquiry communities have developed their own traditions of rigor, communication, and ways of working toward consensus. These guidelines, she also maintains, serve to exclude legitimate research knowledge and social science researchers.

- The standard of positionality guides interpretive or qualitative research. Drawing on those concerned about standpoint epistemology, this means that the "text" should display honesty or authenticity about its own stance and about the position of the author.

- Another standard is under the rubric of community. This standard acknowledges that all research takes place in, is addressed to, and serves the purposes of the community in which it is carried out. Such communities might be feminist thought, Black scholarship, Native American studies, or ecological studies.

- Interpretive or qualitative research must give voice to participants so that their voice is not silenced, disengaged, or marginalized. Moreover, this standard requires that alternative or multiple voices be heard in a text.

- Critical subjectivity as a standard means that the researcher needs to have heightened self-awareness in the research process and create personal and social transformation. This "high-quality awareness" enables the researcher to understand his or her psychological and emotional states before, during, and after the research experience.

- High-quality interpretive or qualitative research involves reciprocity between the researcher and those being researched. This standard requires that intense sharing, trust, and mutuality exist.
- The researcher should respect the sacredness of relationships in the research-to-action continuum. This standard means that the researcher respects the collaborative and egalitarian aspects of research and "make[s] spaces for the lifeways of others" (Lincoln, 1995, p. 284).
- Sharing of the privileges acknowledges that in good qualitative research, researchers share their rewards with persons whose lives they portray. This sharing may be in the form of royalties from books or the sharing of rights to publication.

A final perspective utilizes interpretive standards of conducting qualitative research. Richardson (in Richardson & St. Pierre, 2005) identifies four criteria she uses when she reviews papers or monographs submitted for social science publication:

- ***Substantive contribution.*** Does this piece contribute to our understanding of social life? Demonstrate a deeply grounded social scientific perspective? Seem "true"?
- ***Aesthetic merit.*** Does this piece succeed aesthetically? Does the use of creative analytical practices open up the text and invite interpretive responses? Is the text artistically shaped, satisfying, complex, and not boring?
- ***Reflexivity.*** How has the author's subjectivity been both a producer and a product of this text? Is there self-awareness and self-exposure? Does the author hold himself or herself accountable to the standards of knowing and telling of the people he or she has studied?
- ***Impact.*** Does this piece affect me emotionally or intellectually? Generate new questions or move me to write? Try new research practices or move me to action? (p. 964)

As an applied research methodologist, I prefer the methodological standards of evaluation, but I can also support the postmodern and interpretive perspectives. What seems to be missing in all of the approaches discussed thus far is their connection to the five approaches of qualitative inquiry. What standards of evaluation, beyond those already mentioned, would signal a high-quality narrative study, a phenomenology, a grounded theory study, an ethnography, and a case study?

Narrative Research

Denzin (1989a) is primarily interested in the problem of "how to locate and interpret the subject in biographical materials" (p. 26). He advances several guidelines for writing an interpretive biography:

> The lived experiences of interacting individuals are the proper subject matter of sociology. The meanings of these experiences are best given by the persons who experience them; thus, a preoccupation with method, validation, reliability, generalizability, and theoretical relevance of the biographical method must be set aside in favor of a concern for meaning and interpretation.
>
>   Students of the biographical method must learn how to use the strategies and techniques of literary interpretation and criticism (i.e., bring their method in line with the concern about reading and writing of social texts, where texts are seen as "narrative fictions." (Denzin, 1989a, p. 26).

When an individual writes a biography, he or she writes himself or herself into the life of the subject about whom the individual is writing; likewise, the reader reads through her or his perspective.

   Thus, within a humanistic, interpretive stance, Denzin (1989b) identifies "criteria of interpretation" as a standard for judging the quality of a biography. These criteria are based on respecting the researcher's perspective as well as on thick description. Denzin (1989b) advocates for the ability of the researcher to illuminate the phenomenon in a thickly contextualized manner (i.e., thick description of developed context) so as to reveal the historical, processual, and interactional features of the experience. Also, the researcher's interpretation must engulf what is learned about the phenomenon and incorporate prior understandings while always remaining incomplete and unfinished.

   This focus on interpretation and thick description is in contrast to criteria established within the more traditional approach to biographical writing. For example, Plummer (1983) asserts that three sets of questions related to sampling, the sources, and the validation of the account should guide a researcher to a good life history study:

- Is the individual representative? Edel (1984) asks a similar question: How has the biographer distinguished between reliable and unreliable witnesses?
- What are the sources of bias (about the participant, the researcher, and the participant-researcher interaction)? Or, as Edel (1984)

questions, how has the researcher avoided making himself or herself simply the voice of the subject?
● Is the account valid when subjects are asked to read it, when it is compared to official records, and when it is compared to accounts from other participant?

In a narrative study, I would look for the following aspects of a "good" study. The author:

● Focuses on a single individual (or two or three individuals)
● Collects stories about a significant issue related to this individual's life
● Develops a chronology that connects different phases or aspects of a story
● Tells a story that reports what was said (themes), how it was said (unfolding story), and how speakers interact or perform the narrative
● Reflexively brings himself or herself into the study

Phenomenological Research

What criteria should be used to judge the quality of a phenomenological study? From the many readings about phenomenology, one can infer criteria from the discussions about steps (Giorgi, 1985) or the "core facets" of transcendental phenomenology (Moustakas, 1994, p. 58). I have found direct discussions of the criteria to be missing, but perhaps Polkinghorne (1989) comes the closest in my readings when he discusses whether the findings are "valid" (p. 57). To him, validation refers to the notion that an idea is well grounded and well supported. He asks, "Does the general structural description provide an accurate portrait of the common features and structural connections that are manifest in the examples collected?" (Polkinghorne, 1989, p. 57). He then proceeds to identify five questions that researchers might ask themselves:

● Did the interviewer influence the contents of the participants' descriptions in such a way that the descriptions do not truly reflect the participants' actual experience?
● Is the transcription accurate, and does it convey the meaning of the oral presentation in the interview?

- In the analysis of the transcriptions, were there conclusions other than those offered by the researcher that could have been derived? Has the researcher identified these alternatives?
- Is it possible to go from the general structural description to the transcriptions and to account for the specific contents and connections in the original examples of the experience?
- Is the structural description situation specific, or does it hold in general for the experience in other situations? (Polkinghorne, 1989).

My own standards that I would use to assess the quality of a phenomenology would be:

- Does the author convey an understanding of the philosophical tenets of phenomenology?
- Does the author have a clear "phenomenon" to study that is articulated in a concise way?
- Does the author use procedures of data analysis in phenomenology, such as the procedures recommended by Moustakas (1994) or van Manen (1990)?
- Does the author convey the overall essence of the experience of the participants? Does this essence include a description of the experience and the context in which it occurred?
- Is the author reflexive throughout the study?

Grounded Theory Research

Strauss and Corbin (1990) identify the criteria by which one judges the quality of a grounded theory study. They advance seven criteria related to the general research process:

Criterion #1: How was the original sample selected? What grounds?

Criterion #2: What major categories emerged?

Criterion #3: What were some of the events, incidents, actions, and so on (as indicators) that pointed to some of these major categories?

Criterion #4: On the basis of what categories did theoretical sampling proceed? Guide data collection? Was it representative of the categories?

Criterion #5: What were some of the hypotheses pertaining to conceptual relations (that is, among categories), and on what grounds were they formulated and tested?

Criterion #6: Were there instances when hypotheses did not hold up against what was actually seen? How were these discrepancies accounted for? How did they affect the hypotheses?

Criterion #7: How and why was the core category selected (sudden, gradual, difficult, easy)? On what grounds? (Strauss & Corbin, 1990, p. 253)

They also advance six criteria related to the empirical grounding of a study:

Criterion #1: Are concepts generated?

Criterion #2: Are the concepts systematically related?

Criterion #3: Are there many conceptual linkages, and are the categories well developed? With density?

Criterion #4: Is much variation built into the theory?

Criterion #5: Are the broader conditions built into its explanation?

Criterion #6: Has process (change or movement) been taken into account? (Strauss & Corbin, 1990, pp. 254–256)

Charmaz (2006) reflects on the quality of the theory developed in a grounded theory study. She suggests that grounded theorists look at their theory and ask themselves the following evaluative questions:

- Are the definitions of major categories complete?
- Have I raised major categories to concepts in my theory?
- How have I increased the scope and depth of the analysis in this draft?
- Have I established strong theoretical links between categories and between categories and their properties, in addition to the data?
- How have I increased understanding of the studied phenomenon?
- What are the implications of this analysis for moving theoretical edges? For its theoretical reach and breadth? For methods? For substantive knowledge? For actions or interventions?

- With which theoretical, substantive, or practical problems is this analysis most closely aligned? Which audiences might be most interested in it? Where shall I go with it?
- How does my theory make a fresh contribution? (Charmaz, 2006, pp. 155, 156)

These criteria, related to the process of research and the grounding of the study in the data, represent benchmarks for assessing the quality of a study that the author can mention in his or her research. For example, in a grounded theory dissertation, Landis (1993) not only presented the Strauss and Corbin (1990) standards but also assessed for her readers the extent to which her study met the criteria. When I evaluate a grounded theory study, I, too, am looking for the general process and a relationship among the concepts. Specifically, I look for:

- The study of a process, an action, or an interaction as the key element in the theory
- A coding process that works from the data to a larger theoretical model
- The presentation of the theoretical model in a figure or diagram
- A story line or proposition that connects categories in the theoretical model and that presents further questions to be answered
- The use of memoing throughout the process of research
- A reflexivity or self-disclosure by the researcher about his or her stance in the study

Ethnographic Research

The ethnographers Spindler and Spindler (1987) emphasize that the most important requirement for an ethnographic approach is to explain behavior from the "native's point of view" (p. 20) and to be systematic in recording this information using note taking, tape recorders, and cameras. This requires that the ethnographer be present in the situation and engage in constant interaction between observation and interviews. These points are reinforced in Spindler and Spindler's nine criteria for a "good ethnography":

Criterion I. Observations are contextualized.

Criterion II. Hypotheses emerge *in situ* as the study goes on.

Criterion III. Observation is prolonged and repetitive.

Criterion IV. Through interviews, observations, and other eliciting procedures, the native view of reality is obtained.

Criterion V. Ethnographers elicit knowledge from informant-participants in a systematic fashion.

Criterion VI. Instruments, codes, schedules, questionnaires, agenda for interviews, and so forth are generated *in situ* as a result of inquiry.

Criterion VII. A transcultural, comparative perspective is frequently an unstated assumption.

Criterion VIII. The ethnographer makes explicit what is implicit and tacit to informants.

Criterion IX. The ethnographic interviewer must not predetermine responses by the kinds of questions asked. (Spindler & Spindler, 1987, p. 18)

This list, grounded in fieldwork, leads to a strong ethnography. Moreover, as Lofland (1974) contends, the study is located in wide conceptual frameworks; presents the novel but not necessarily new; provides evidence for the framework(s); is endowed with concrete, eventful interactional events, incidents, occurrences, episodes, anecdotes, scenes, and happenings without being "hyper-eventful"; and shows an interplay between the concrete and analytical and the empirical and theoretical.

My criteria for a good ethnography would include:

- The clear identification of a culture-sharing group
- The specification of a cultural theme that will be examined in light of this culture-sharing group
- A detailed description of the cultural group
- Themes that derive from an understanding of the cultural group
- The identification of issues that arose "in the field" that reflect on the relationship between the researcher and the participants, the interpretive nature of reporting, and sensitivity and reciprocity in the co-creating of the account
- An explanation overall of how the culture-sharing group works
- A self-disclosure and reflexivity by the researcher about her or his position in the research

Case Study Research

Stake (1995) provides a rather extensive "critique checklist" (p. 131) for a case study report and shares 20 criteria for assessing a good case study report:

1. Is the report easy to read?

2. Does it fit together, each sentence contributing to the whole?

3. Does the report have a conceptual structure (i.e., themes or issues)?

4. Are its issues developed in a serious and scholarly way?

5. Is the case adequately defined?

6. Is there a sense of story to the presentation?

7. Is the reader provided some vicarious experience?

8. Have quotations been used effectively?

9. Are headings, figures, artifacts, appendixes, and indexes used effectively?

10. Was it edited well, then again with a last-minute polish?

11. Has the writer made sound assertions, neither over- nor underinterpreting?

12. Has adequate attention been paid to various contexts?

13. Were sufficient raw data presented?

14. Were data sources well chosen and in sufficient number?

15. Do observations and interpretations appear to have been triangulated?

16. Is the role and point of view of the researcher nicely apparent?

17. Is the nature of the intended audience apparent?

18. Is empathy shown for all sides?

19. Are personal intentions examined?

20. Does it appear that individuals were put at risk? (Stake, 1995, p. 131)

My own criteria for evaluating a "good" case study would include the following:

- Is there a clear identification of the "case" or "cases" in the study?

- Is the "case" (or are the "cases") used to understand a research issue or used because the "case" has (or "cases" have) intrinsic merit?

- Is there a clear description of the "case"?

- Are themes identified for the "case"?

- Are assertions or generalizations made from the "case" analysis?

- Is the researcher reflexive or self-disclosing about his or her position in the study?

COMPARING THE EVALUATION STANDARDS OF THE FIVE APPROACHES

The standards discussed for each approach differ slightly depending on the procedures of the approaches. Certainly less is mentioned about narrative research and its standards of quality, and more is available about the other approaches. From within the major books used for each approach, I have attempted to extract the evaluation standards recommended for their approach to research. To these I have added my own standards that I use in my qualitative classes when I evaluate a project or study presented within each of the five approaches.

SUMMARY

In this chapter, I discuss validation, reliability, and standards of quality in qualitative research. Validation approaches vary considerably, such as strategies that emphasize using qualitative terms comparable to quantitative terms, the use of distinct terms, perspectives from postmodern and interpretive lenses, syntheses of different perspectives, descriptions based on metaphorical images, or some combination of these perspectives on validity. Reliability is used in qualitative research in several ways, one of the most popular being the use of intercoder agreements when multiple coders analyze and then compare their code segments to establish the reliability of the data analysis process. A detailed procedure for establishing intercoder agreement is described in this chapter. Also, diverse standards exist for establishing the quality of qualitative research, and these criteria are based on procedural perspectives, postmodern perspectives, and interpretive perspectives. Within each of the five approaches to inquiry, specific standards also exist; these were reviewed in this chapter. Finally, I advanced the criteria that I use to assess the quality of studies presented to me in classes in each of the five approaches.

ADDITIONAL READINGS

On validation:

Angen, M. J. (2000). Evaluating interpretive inquiry: Reviewing the validity debate and opening the dialogue. *Qualitative Health Research, 10,* 378–395.

Lincoln, Y. S. (1995). Emerging criteria for quality in qualitative and interpretive research. *Qualitative Inquiry, 1,* 275–289.

Lincoln, Y. S., Lynham, S. A., & Guba, E. G. (2011). Paradigmatic controversies, contradictions, and emerging confluences. In N. K. Denzin & Y. S. Lincoln (Eds.), *SAGE handbook of qualitative research* (4th ed., pp. 97–128). Thousand Oaks, CA: Sage.

Silverman, D. (1993). *Interpreting qualitative data: Methods for analyzing talk, text, and interaction.* London: Sage.

Whittemore, R., Chase, S. K., & Mandle, C. L. (2001). Validity in qualitative research. *Qualitative Health Research, 11,* 522–537.

For reliability:

Armstrong, D., Gosling, A., Weinman, J., & Marteau, T. (1997). The place of inter-rater reliability in qualitative research: An empirical study. *Sociology, 31,* 597–606.

Miles, M. B., & Huberman, A. M. (1994). *Qualitative data analysis: A sourcebook of new methods* (2nd ed.). Thousand Oaks, CA: Sage.

Silverman, D. (2005). *Doing qualitative research: A practical handbook* (2nd ed.). London: Sage.

For evaluation:

Creswell, J. W. (2012). *Educational research: Planning, conducting, and evaluating quantitative and qualitative research* (4th ed.). Upper Saddle River, NJ: Pearson Education.

Lincoln, Y. S. (1995). Emerging criteria for quality in qualitative and interpretive research. *Qualitative Inquiry, 1,* 275–289.

Richardson, L., & St. Pierre, E. A. (2005). Writing: A method of inquiry. In N. K. Denzin & Y. S. Lincoln (Eds.), *The Sage handbook of qualitative research* (3rd ed., pp. 959–978). Thousand Oaks, CA: Sage.

Also, specific standards in each of the five approaches:

In narrative research:

Clandinin, D. J., & Connelly, F. M. (2000). *Narrative inquiry: Experience and story in qualitative research.* San Francisco: Jossey-Bass.

Czarniawka, B. (2004). *Narratives in social science research.* Thousand Oaks, CA: Sage.

Denzin, N. K. (1989). *Interpretive biography.* Newbury Park, CA: Sage.

Riessman, C. K. (2008). *Narrative methods for the human sciences.* Los Angeles, CA: Sage.

In phenomenology:

Moustakas, C. (1994). *Phenomenological research methods.* Thousand Oaks, CA: Sage.

van Manen, M. (1990). *Researching lived experience: Human science for an action sensitive pedagogy.* Albany: State University of New York Press.

In grounded theory:

Charmaz, K. (2006). *Constructing grounded theory.* London: Sage.

Strauss, A., & Corbin, J. (1990). *Basics of qualitative research: Grounded theory procedures and techniques.* Newbury Park, CA: Sage.

In ethnography:

Fetterman, D. M. (2010). *Ethnography: Step by step* (3rd ed.). Thousand Oaks, CA: Sage.

LeCompte, M. D., & Schensul, J. J. (1999). *Designing and conducting ethnographic research.* Walnut Creek, CA: AltaMira.

Madison, D. S. (2005). *Critical ethnography: Methods, ethics, and performance.* Thousand Oaks, CA: Sage.

Wolcott, H. F. (1999). *Ethnography: A way of seeing.* Walnut Creek, CA: AltaMira.

In case study:

Stake, R. (1995). *The art of case study research.* Thousand Oaks, CA: Sage.

Yin, R. K. (2009). *Case study research: Design and methods* (4th ed.). Thousand Oaks, CA: Sage.

EXERCISES

1. One of the approaches for validation was to write "thick description" into the description of cases or settings and in themes. Look for a detailed description in a short story or a novel. If you do not find one, you might use the story about the "Cat 'n' Mouse" as found in Steven Millhauser's book (2008), *Dangorous Laughter.* Identify passages in which Millhauser creates detail by physical passages, movement, or activity description. Also identify how he interconnects the details.

2. Practice intercoder agreement. Have two or more coders go through a transcript and record their codes. Then look at the passages all coders have identified and see whether their codes are similar or match. Look back at the example of intercoder agreement I provide in this chapter as a guide for your procedure.

3. In this chapter I identify the key characteristics of each of the five approaches that might be used in evaluating a study. Select one of the approaches, find a journal article that uses the approach, and then see if you can find the key characteristics of evaluation of that approach in the article.

11

"Turning the Story" and Conclusion

How might the story be turned if it was a case study, a narrative project, a phenomenology, a grounded theory, or an ethnography? In this book, I suggest that researchers be cognizant of the procedures of qualitative research and of the differences in approaches of qualitative inquiry. This is not to suggest a preoccupation with method or methodology; indeed, I see two parallel tracks in a study: the substantive content of the study and the methodology. With increased interest in qualitative research, it is important that studies being conducted go forward with rigor and attention to the procedures developed within approaches of inquiry.

The approaches are many, and their procedures for research are well documented within books and articles. A few writers classify the approaches, and some authors mention their favorites. Unquestionably, qualitative research cannot be characterized as of one type, attested to by the multivocal discourse surrounding qualitative research today. Adding to this discourse are perspectives about philosophical, theoretical, and ideological stances. To capture the essence of a good qualitative study, I visualize such a study as comprising three interconnected circles. As shown in Figure 11.1, these circles include the approach of inquiry, research design procedures, and philosophical and theoretical frameworks and assumptions. The interplay of these three factors contributes to a complex, rigorous study.

TURNING THE STORY

In this chapter, I again sharpen the distinctions among the approaches of inquiry, but I depart from my side-by-side approach used in prior

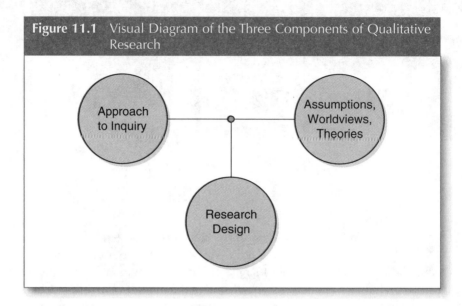

Figure 11.1 Visual Diagram of the Three Components of Qualitative Research

chapters. I focus the lens in a new direction and "turn the story" of the gunman case (Asmussen & Creswell, 1995) into a narrative study, a phenomenology, a grounded theory, and an ethnography. Before continuing on with this chapter, the reader is advised to reexamine the gunman case study as presented in Appendix F and reviewed in Chapter 5.

Turning the story through different approaches of inquiry raises the issue of whether one should match a particular problem to an approach to inquiry. Much emphasis is placed on this relationship in social and human science research. I agree this needs to be done. But for the purposes of this book, my way around this issue is to pose a *general* problem—"How did the campus react?"—and then construct scenarios for specific problems. For instance, the specific problem of studying a single individual's reaction to the gun incident is different from the specific problem of how several students as a culture-sharing group reacted, but both scenarios are reactions to the general issue of a campus response to the incident. The general problem that I address is that we know little about how campuses respond to violence and even less about how different constituent groups on campus respond to a potentially violent incident. Knowing this information would help us devise better plans for reacting to this type of problem as well as add to the literature on violence in educational settings. This was the central problem in the gunman case study (Asmussen & Creswell, 1995), and I briefly review the major dimensions of this study.

A CASE STUDY

This qualitative case study (Asmussen & Creswell, 1995) presented a campus reaction to a gunman incident in which a student attempted to fire a gun at his classmates. Asmussen and I titled this study "Campus Response to a Student Gunman," and we composed this case study with the "substantive case report" format of Lincoln and Guba (1985) and Stake (1995) in mind. These formats called for an explication of the problem, a thorough description of the context or setting and the processes observed, a discussion of important themes, and, finally, "lessons to be learned" (Lincoln & Guba, 1985, p. 362). After introducing the case study with the problem of violence on college campuses, we provided a detailed description of the setting and a chronology of events immediately following the incident and events during the following two weeks. Then we turned to important themes to emerge in this analysis—themes of denial, fear, safety, retriggering, and campus planning. In a process of layering of themes, we combined these more specific themes into two overarching themes: an organizational theme and a psychological or social-psychological theme. We gathered data through interviews with participants, observations, documents, and audiovisual materials. From the case emerges a proposed plan for campuses, and the case ends with an implied lesson for the specific Midwestern campus and a specific set of questions this campus or other campuses might use to design a plan for handling future campus terrorist incidents.

Turning to specific research questions in this case, we asked the following: What happened? Who was involved in response to the incident? What themes of response emerged during an eight-month period? What theoretical constructs helped us understand the campus response, and what constructs developed that were unique to this case? We entered the field two days after the incident and did not use any a priori theoretical lens to guide our questions or the results. The narrative first described the incident, analyzed it through levels of abstraction, and provided some interpretation by relating the context to larger theoretical frameworks. We validated our case analysis by using multiple data sources for the themes and by checking the final account with select participants, or member checking.

A NARRATIVE STUDY

How might I have approached this same general problem as an interpretive biographical study with a narrative approach? Rather than identifying responses from multiple campus constituents, I would have *focused on one individual* such as the instructor of the class involved in the incident. I would have tentatively titled the project, "Confrontation of Brothers: An Interpretive Biography of an African American Professor." This instructor, like the gunman, was African American, and his response to such an incident might be situated within racial and cultural contexts. Hence, as an interpretive biographer, I might have asked the following research question: What are the life experiences of the African American instructor of the class, and how do these experiences form and shape his reaction to the incident? This biographical approach would have relied on studying a single individual and situating this individual within his historic background. I would have examined *life events* or "epiphanies" culled from *stories* he told me. My approach would have been to *restory the stories* into an account of his experiences of the gunman that followed a chronology of events. I might have relied on the Clandinin and Connelly (2000) three-dimensional space model to organize the story into the personal, social, and interactional components. Alternatively, the story might have had a *plot* to tie it together, such as the theoretical perspective. This plot might have spoken to the issues of race, discrimination, and marginality and how these issues played out both within the African American culture and between Black culture and other cultures. These perspectives may have shaped how the instructor viewed the student gunman in the class. I also might have composed this report by discussing *my own situated beliefs* followed by those of the instructor and the changes he brought about as a result of his experiences. For instance, did he continue teaching? Did he talk with the class about his feelings? Did he see the situation as a confrontation within his racial group? For validation, my narrative story about this instructor would have contained a detailed description of the context to reveal the historical and interactional features of the experience

(Denzin, 1989b). I also would have acknowledged that any interpretation of the instructor's reaction would be incomplete, unfinished, and a rendering from my own perspective as a non-African American.

A PHENOMENOLOGY

Rather than study a single individual as in a biography, I would have studied *several individual students* and examined a psychological concept in the tradition of psychological phenomenology (Moustakas, 1994). My working title might have been "The Meaning of Fear for Students Caught in a Near Tragedy on Campus." My assumption would have been that students expressed this concept of fear during the incident, immediately after it, and several weeks later. I might have posed the following questions: What fear did the students experience, and how did they experience it? What meanings did they ascribe to this experience? As a phenomenologist, I assume that human experience makes sense to those who live it and that human experience can be consciously expressed (Dukes, 1984). Thus, I would bring to the study *a phenomenon* to explore (fear) and a *philosophical orientation* to use (I want to study the meaning of the students' experiences). I would have engaged in *extensive interviews* with up to 10 students, and I would have analyzed the interviews using the *steps* described by Moustakas (1994). I would have begun with a description of my own fears and experiences (*epoche*) with it as a means to position myself, recognizing that I could not completely remove myself from the situation. Then, after reading through all of the students' statements, I would have located *significant statements* or quotes about their meanings of fear. These significant statements would then be clustered into broader *themes*. My final step would have been to write a long paragraph providing a narrative description of what they experienced (*textural description*) and how they experienced it (*structural description*) and combine these two descriptions into a longer description that conveys the *essence* of their experiences. This would be the endpoint for the discussion.

A GROUNDED THEORY STUDY

If a theory needed to be developed (or modified) to explain the campus reaction to this incident, I would have used a grounded theory approach.

For example, I might have developed a *theory* around a process—the "surreal" experiences of several students immediately following the incident, experiences resulting in actions and reactions by students. The draft title of my study might have been "A Grounded Theory Explanation of the Surreal Experiences for Students in a Campus Gunman Incident." I might have introduced the study with a specific quote about the surreal experiences:

> In the debriefing by counselors, one female student commented, "I thought the gunman would shoot out a little flag that would say 'bang.'" For her, the event was like a dream.

My research questions might have been: What theory explains the phenomenon of the "surreal" experiences of the students immediately following the incident? What were these experiences? What caused them? What strategies did the students use to cope with them? What were the consequences of their strategies? What specific interaction issues and larger conditions influenced their strategies? Consistent with grounded theory, I would not bring into the data collection and analysis a specific theoretical orientation other than to see how the students interact and respond to the incident. Instead, my intent would be to *develop or generate a theory.* In the results section of this study I would have first identified the *open coding categories* that I found. Then, I would have described how I narrowed the study to a central category (e.g., the dream element of the process), and made that category the major feature of a theory of the process. This theory would have been presented as a *visual model,* and in the model I would have included *causal conditions* that influenced the central category, *intervening and context factors* surrounding it, and specific *strategies* and *consequences* (axial coding) as a result of it occurring. I would have advanced *theoretical propositions* or hypotheses that explained the dream element of the surreal experiences of the students (selective coding). I would have validated my account by judging the thoroughness of the research process and whether the findings are empirically grounded, two factors mentioned by Corbin and Strauss (1990).

AN ETHNOGRAPHY

In grounded theory, my focus was on generating a theory grounded in the data. In ethnography, I would turn the focus away from theory development to a description and understanding of the workings of the campus community as a *culture-sharing group*. To keep the study manageable, I might have begun by looking at how the incident, although unpredictable, triggered quite predictable responses among members of the campus community. These community members might have responded according to their roles, and thus I could have looked at some recognized campus microcultures. Students constituted one such microculture, and they, in turn, comprised a number of further microcultures or subcultures. Because the students in this class were together for 16 weeks during the semester, they had enough time to develop some *shared patterns of behavior* and could have been seen as a culture-sharing group. Alternatively, I might have studied the entire campus community composed of a constellation of groups each reacting differently.

Assuming that the entire campus comprised the culture-sharing group, the title of the study might have been "Getting Back to Normal: An Ethnography of a Campus Response to a Gunman Incident." Notice how this title immediately invites a contrary perspective into the study. I would have asked the following questions: How did this incident produce predictable role performance within affected groups? Using the entire campus as a cultural system or culture-sharing group, in what roles did the individuals and groups participate? One possibility would be that they wanted to get the campus back to normal after the incident by engaging in predictable patterns of behavior. Although no one anticipated the exact moment or nature of the incident itself, its occurrence set in motion rather predictable role performances throughout the campus community. Administrators did not close the campus and start warning, "The sky is falling." Campus police did not offer counseling sessions, although the Counseling Center did. However, the Counseling Center served the student population, not others (who were marginalized), such as the police or groundskeepers, who also felt unsafe on the campus. In short, predictable performances by campus constituencies followed in the wake of this incident.

Indeed, campus administrators routinely held a news conference following the incident. Also, predictably, police carried out their investigation, and students ultimately and reluctantly contacted their parents. The campus slowly returned to normal—an attempt to return to day-to-day business, to a steady state, or to homeostasis, as the systems thinkers say. In these predictable role behaviors, one saw culture at work.

As I entered the field, I would seek to build *rapport* with the community participants, to not further marginalize them or disturb the environment more than necessary through my presence. It was a sensitive time on campus with people who had nerves on edge. I would have explored the cultural themes of the "organization of diversity" and "maintenance" activities of individuals and groups within the culture-sharing campus. Wallace (1970) defines the "organization of diversity" as "the actual diversity of habits, of motives, of personalities, of customs that do, in fact, coexist within the boundaries of any culturally organized society" (p. 23). My data collection would have consisted of observations over time of predictable activities, behaviors, and roles in which people engaged that helped the campus return to normal. This data collection would depend heavily on *interviews and observations* of the classroom where the incident occurred and newspaper accounts. My ultimate narrative of the culture-sharing campus would be consistent with Wolcott's (1994b) three parts: a detailed description of the campus, an analysis of the cultural themes of "organizational diversity" and maintenance (possibly with taxonomies or comparisons; Spradley, 1979, 1980), and interpretation. My interpretation would be couched not in terms of a dispassionate, objective report of the facts, but rather within my own experiences of not feeling safe in a soup kitchen for the homeless (Miller, Creswell & Olander, 1998) and my own personal life experiences of having grown up in a "safe" small Midwestern city in Illinois. For an ending to the study, I might have used the "canoe into the sunset" approach (H. F. Wolcott, personal communication, November 15, 1996) or the more methodologically oriented ending of checking my account with participants. Here is the "canoe into the sunset" approach:

> The newsworthiness of the event will be long past before the ethnographic study is ready, but the event itself is of rather little consequence if the ethnographer's focus is on campus culture. Still, without such an event, the ethnographer working in his or her own society (and perhaps on his or her own campus as well) might have a difficult time "seeing" people performing in predictable everyday ways simply because that is the way in which we expect them to act. The ethnographer working "at home" has to find ways in which to

make the familiar seem strange. An upsetting event can make ordinary role behavior easier to discern as people respond in predictable ways to unpredictable circumstances. Those predictable patterns are the stuff of culture.

Here is the more methodological ending:

Some of my "facts" or hypotheses may need (and be amenable to) checking or testing if I have carried my analysis in that direction. If I have tried to be more interpretive, then perhaps I can "try out" the account on some of the people described, and the cautions and exceptions they express can be included in my final account to suggest that things are even more complex than the way I have presented them.

CONCLUSION

How have I answered my "compelling" question raised at the outset: How does the approach to inquiry shape the design of a study? First, one of the most pronounced ways is in the focus of the study. As discussed in Chapter 4, a theory differs from the exploration of a phenomenon or concept, from an in-depth case, and from the creation of an individual or group portrait. Please examine again Table 4.1 that establishes differences among the five approaches, especially in terms of foci.

However, this is not as clear-cut as it appears. A single case study of an individual can be approached either as a biography or as a case study. A cultural system may be explored as an ethnography, whereas a smaller "bounded" system, such as an event, a program, or an activity, may be studied as a case study. Both are systems, and the problem arises when one undertakes a microethnography, which might be approached either as a case study or as an ethnography. However, when one seeks to study cultural behavior, language, or artifacts, then the study of a system might be undertaken as an ethnography.

Second, an interpretive orientation flows throughout qualitative research. We cannot step aside and be "objective" about what we see and write. Our words flow from our own personal experiences, culture, history, and backgrounds. When we go to the field to collect data, we need to approach the task with care for the participants and sites and to be reflexive about our role and how it shapes what we see, hear, and write. Ultimately, our writing is an interpretation by us of events, people, and activities, and it is only our interpretation. We must recognize that participants in the field, readers, and other individuals reading our accounts will have their own interpretations. Within this perspective, our writing can only be seen as a discourse, one with tentative conclusions, and one that will be constantly changing and evolving. Qualitative research truly has an interpretation element that flows throughout the process of research.

Third, the approach to inquiry shapes the language of the research design procedures in a study, especially the terms used in the introduction to a study, the data collection, and the analysis phases of design. I incorporated these terms into Chapter 6 as I discussed the wording of purpose statements and research questions for different approaches to qualitative research. My theme continued on in Chapter 9 as I talked about encoding the text within an approach to research. The glossary in Appendix A also reinforces this theme as it presents a useful list of terms within each tradition that researchers might incorporate into the language of their studies.

Fourth, the approach to research includes the participants who are studied, as discussed in Chapter 7. A study may consist of one or two individuals (i.e., narrative study), groups of people (i.e., phenomenology, grounded theory), or an entire culture (i.e., ethnography). A case study might fit into all three of these categories as one explores a single individual, an event, or a large social setting. Also in Chapter 7, I highlighted how the approaches vary in the extent of data collection, from the use of mainly single sources of information (i.e., narrative interviews, grounded theory interviews, phenomenological interviews) to those that involve multiple sources of information (i.e., ethnographies consisting of observations, interviews, and documents; case studies incorporating interviews, observations, documents, archival material, and video). Although these forms of data collection are not fixed, I see a general pattern that differentiates the approaches.

Fifth, the distinctions among the approaches are most pronounced in the data analysis phase, as discussed in Chapter 8. Data analysis ranges from unstructured to structured approaches. Among the less structured approaches, I include ethnographies (with the exception of Spradley, 1979, 1980) and narratives (e.g., as suggested by Clandinin & Connelly, 2000, and interpretive forms advanced by

Denzin, 1989b). The more structured approaches consist of grounded theory with a systematic procedure and phenomenology (see Colaizzi's 1978 approach and those of Dukes, 1984, and Moustakas, 1994) and case studies (Stake, 1995; Yin, 2009). These procedures provide direction for the overall structure of the data analysis in the qualitative report. Also, the approach shapes the amount of relative weight given to description in the analysis of the data. In ethnographies, case studies, and biographies, researchers employ substantial description; in phenomenologies, investigators use less description; and in grounded theory, researchers seem not to use it at all, choosing to move directly into analysis of the data.

Sixth, the approach to inquiry shapes the final written product as well as the embedded rhetorical structures used in the narrative. This explains why qualitative studies look so different and are composed so differently, as discussed in Chapter 9. Take, for example, the presence of the researcher. The presence of the researcher is found little in the more "objective" accounts provided in grounded theory. Alternatively, the researcher is center stage in ethnographies and possibly in case studies where "interpretation" plays a major role.

Seventh, the criteria for assessing the quality of a study differ among the approaches, as discussed in Chapter 10. Although some overlap exists in the procedures for validation, the criteria for assessing the worth of a study are available for each tradition.

In summary, when designing a qualitative study, I recommend that the author design the study within one of the approaches of qualitative inquiry. This means that components of the design process (e.g., interpretive framework, research purpose and questions, data collection, data analysis, report writing, validation) will reflect the procedures of the selected approach and they will be composed with the encoding and features of that approach. This is not to rigidly suggest that one cannot mix approaches and employ, for example, a grounded theory analysis procedure within a case study design. "Purity" is not my aim. But in this book, I suggest that the reader sort out the approaches first before combining them and see each one as a rigorous procedure in its own right.

I find distinctions as well as overlap among the five approaches, but designing a study attuned to procedures found within one of the approaches suggested in this book will enhance the sophistication of the project and convey a level of methodological expertise for readers of qualitative research.

EXERCISES

1. Take a qualitative study that you have written and turn the story into one of the other approaches of qualitative inquiry.

2. In this chapter, I presented the study of campus response to a gunman incident in five ways. Take each scenario and define and describe each part that is labeled in italics. Look at the glossary in Appendix A for help in providing a definition.

Appendices

Appendix A. An Annotated Glossary of Terms   282

Appendix B. A Narrative Research Study—"Living in
the Space Between Participant and Researcher as
a Narrative Inquirer: Examining Ethnic Identity of
Chinese Canadian Students as Conflicting Stories
to Live By"   303

Appendix C. A Phenomenological Study—"Cognitive
Representations of AIDS"   327

Appendix D. A Grounded Theory Study—"Developing
Long-Term Physical Activity Participation: A Grounded
Theory Study With African American Women"   347

Appendix E. An Ethnography—"Rethinking Subcultural
Resistance: Core Values of the Straight Edge Movement"   370

Appendix F. A Case Study—"Campus
Response to a Student Gunman"   399

Appendix A

An Annotated Glossary of Terms

The definitions in this glossary represent key terms as they are used and defined in this book. Many definitions exist for these terms, but the most workable definitions for me (and I hope for the reader) are those that reflect the content and references presented in this book. I group the terms by approach to inquiry (narrative research, phenomenology, grounded theory, ethnography, case study) and alphabetize them within the approach, and at the end of the glossary I define additional terms that cross all of the five different approaches.

Narrative Research

autobiography This form of biographical writing is the narrative account of a person's life that he or she has personally written or otherwise recorded (Angrosino, 1989a).

autoethnography This form of narrative is written and recorded by the individuals who are the subject of the study (Ellis, 2004; Muncey, 2010). Muncey (2010) defines autoethnography as the idea of multiple layers of consciousness, the vulnerable self, the coherent self, critiquing the self in social contexts, the subversion of dominant discourses, and the evocative potential.

biographical study This is the study of a single individual and his or her experiences as told to the researcher or as found in documents and archival materials (Denzin, 1989a). I use the term to connotate the broad genre of narrative writings that includes individual biographies, autobiographies, life histories, and oral histories.

chronology This is a common approach for undertaking a narrative form of writing in which the author presents the life in stages or steps according to the age of the individual (Clandinin & Connelly, 2000; Denzin, 1989a).

epiphanies These are special events in an individual's life that represent turning points. They vary in their impact from minor to major epiphanies, and they may be positive or negative (Denzin, 1989a).

historical context This is the context in which the researcher presents the life of the participant. The context may be the participant's family, society, or the historical, social, or political trends of the participant's times (Denzin, 1989a).

life course stages These are stages in an individual's life or key events that become the focus for the biographer (Denzin, 1989a).

life history This is a form of biographical writing in which the researcher reports an extensive record of a person's life as told to the researcher (see Geiger, 1986). Thus, the individual being studied is alive and life as lived in the present is influenced by personal, institutional, and social histories. The investigator may use different disciplinary perspectives (Smith, 1994), such as the exploration of an individual's life as representative of a culture, as in an anthropological life history.

narrative research This is an approach to qualitative research that is both a product and a method. It is a study of stories or narrative or descriptions of a series of events that accounts for human experiences (Pinnegar & Daynes, 2007).

oral history In this biographical approach, the researcher gathers personal recollections of events and their causes and effects from an individual or several individuals. This information may be collected through tape recordings or through written works of individuals who have died or are still living. It often is limited to the distinctly "modern" sphere and to accessible people (Plummer, 1983).

progressive-regressive method This is an approach to writing a narrative in which the researcher begins with a key event in the participant's life and then works forward and backward from that event (Denzin, 1989a).

restorying This is an approach in narrative data analysis in which the researchers retell the stories of individual experiences, and the new story typically has a beginning, a middle, and an ending (Ollerenshaw & Creswell, 2002).

single individual This is the person studied in a narrative research. This person may be an individual with great distinction or an ordinary person.

This person's life may be a lesser life, a great life, a thwarted life, a life cut short, or a life miraculous in its unapplauded achievement (Heilbrun, 1988).

stories These are aspects that surface during an interview in which the participant describes a situation, usually with a beginning, a middle, and an end, so that the researcher can capture a complete idea and integrate it, intact, into the qualitative narrative (Clandinin & Connelly, 2000; Czarniawska, 2004; Denzin, 1989a; Riessman, 2008).

Phenomenology

clusters of meanings This is the third step in phenomenological data analysis, in which the researcher clusters the statements into themes or meaning units, removing overlapping and repetitive statements (Moustakas, 1994).

epoche or bracketing This is the first step in "phenomenological reduction," the process of data analysis in which the researcher sets aside, as far as is humanly possible, all preconceived experiences to best understand the experiences of participants in the study (Moustakas, 1994).

essential, invariant structure (or essence) This is the goal of the phenomenologist, to reduce the textural (*what*) and structural (*how*) meanings of experiences to a brief description that typifies the experiences of all of the participants in a study. All individuals experience it; hence, it is invariant, and it is a reduction to the "essentials" of the experiences (Moustakas, 1994).

hermeneutical phenomenology A form of phenomenology in which research is oriented toward interpreting the "texts" of life (hermeneutical) and lived experiences (phenomenology) (van Manen, 1990).

horizonalization This is the second step in the phenomenological data analysis, in which the researcher lists every significant statement relevant to the topic and gives it equal value (Moustakas, 1994).

imaginative variation or structural description Following the textural description, the researcher writes a "structural" description of an experience, addressing *how* the phenomenon was experienced. It involves seeking all possible meanings, looking for divergent perspectives, and varying the frames of reference about the phenomenon or using imaginative variation (Moustakas, 1994).

intentionality of consciousness Being conscious of objects always is intentional. Thus, when perceiving a tree, "my intentional experience is a combination of the outward appearance of the tree and the tree as contained in my consciousness based on memory, image, and meaning" (Moustakas, 1994, p. 55).

lived experiences This term is used in phenomenological studies to emphasize the importance of individual experiences of people as conscious human beings (Moustakas, 1994).

phenomenological data analysis Several approaches to analyzing phenomenological data are represented in the literature. Moustakas (1994) reviews these approaches and then advances his own. I rely on the Moustakas modification that includes the researcher bringing personal experiences into the study, the recording of significant statements and meaning units, and the development of descriptions to arrive at the essence of the experiences.

phenomenological study This type of study describes the common meaning of experiences of a phenomenon (or topic or concept) for several individuals. In this type of qualitative study, the researcher reduces the experiences to a central meaning or the "essence" of the experience (Moustakas, 1994).

phenomenon This is the central concept being examined by the phenomenologist. It is the concept being experienced by subjects in a study, which may include psychological concepts such as grief, anger, or love.

philosophical perspectives Specific philosophical perspectives provide the foundation for phenomenological studies. They originated in the 1930s writings of Husserl. These perspectives include the investigator's conducting research with a broader perspective than that of traditional empirical, quantitative science; suspending his or her own preconceptions of experiences; experiencing an object through his or her own senses (i.e., being conscious of an object) as well as seeing it "out there" as real; and reporting the meaning individuals ascribe to an experience in a few statements that capture the "essence" (Stewart & Mickunas, 1990).

psychological approach This is the approach taken by psychologists who discuss the inquiry procedures of phenomenology (e.g., Giorgi, 1994, 2009; Moustakas, 1994; Polkinghorne, 1989). In their writings, they examine psychological themes for meaning, and they may incorporate their own selves into the studies.

structural description From the first three steps in phenomenological data analysis, the researcher writes a description of "how" the phenomenon was experienced by individuals in the study (Moustakas, 1994).

textural description From the first three steps in phenomenological data analysis, the researcher writes about *what* was experienced, a description of the meaning individuals have experienced (Moustakas, 1994).

transcendental phenomenology According to Moustakas (1994), Husserl espoused transcendental phenomenology, and it later became a guiding concept for Moustakas as well. In this approach, the researcher sets aside prejudgments regarding the phenomenon being investigated. Also, the researcher relies on intuition, imagination, and universal structures to obtain a picture of the experience, and the inquirer uses systematic methods of analysis as advanced by Moustakas (1994).

Grounded Theory

axial coding This step in the coding process follows open coding. The researcher takes the categories of open coding, identifies one as a central phenomenon, and then returns to the database to identify (a) what caused this phenomenon to occur, (b) what strategies or actions actors employed in response to it, (c) what context (specific context) and intervening conditions (broad context) influenced the strategies, and (d) what consequences resulted from these strategies. The overall process is one of relating categories of information to the central phenomenon category (Strauss & Corbin, 1990, 1998).

category This is a unit of information analyzed in grounded theory research. It is composed of events, happenings, and instances of phenomenon (Strauss & Corbin, 1990) and given a short label. When researchers analyze grounded theory data, their analysis leads, initially, to the formation of a number of categories during the process called "open coding." Then, in "axial coding," the analyst interrelates the categories and forms a visual model.

causal conditions In axial coding, these are the categories of conditions I identify in my database that cause or influence the central phenomenon to occur.

central phenomenon This is an aspect of axial coding and the formation of the visual theory, model, or paradigm. In open coding, the researcher chooses a central category around which to develop the theory by examining his or her open coding categories and selecting one that holds the most conceptual interest, is most frequently discussed by participants in the study, and is most "saturated" with information. The researcher then places it at the center of his or her grounded theory model and labels it "central phenomenon."

coding paradigm or logic diagram In axial coding, the central phenomenon, causal conditions, context, intervening conditions, strategies, and consequences are portrayed in a visual diagram. This diagram is drawn with boxes and arrows indicating the process or flow of activities. It is helpful to view this diagram as more than axial coding; it is the theoretical model developed in a grounded theory study (see Harley et al., 2009)

conditional matrix This is a diagram, typically drawn late in a grounded theory study, that presents the conditions and consequences related to the phenomenon under study. It enables the researcher to both distinguish and link levels of conditions and consequences specified in the axial coding model (Strauss & Corbin, 1990). It is a step seldom seen in data analysis in grounded theory studies.

consequences In axial coding, these are the outcomes of strategies taken by participants in the study. These outcomes may be positive, negative, or neutral (Strauss & Corbin, 1990).

constant comparative This was an early term (Conrad, 1978) in grounded theory research that referred to the researcher identifying incidents, events, and activities and constantly comparing them to an emerging category to develop and saturate the category.

constructivist grounded theory This is a form of grounded theory squarely in the interpretive tradition of qualitative research. As such, it is less structured than traditional approaches to grounded theory. The constructivist approach incorporates the researcher's views; uncovers experiences with embedded, hidden networks, situations, and relationships; and makes visible hierarchies of power, communication, and opportunity (Charmaz, 2006).

context In axial coding, this is the particular set of conditions within which the strategies occur (Strauss & Corbin, 1990). These are specific in nature and close to the actions and interactions.

dimensionalized This is the smallest unit of information analyzed in grounded theory research. The researcher takes the properties and places them on a continuum or dimensionalizes them to see the extreme possibilities for the property. The dimensionalized information appears in the "open coding" analysis (Strauss & Corbin, 1990).

discriminant sampling This is a form of sampling that occurs late in a grounded theory project after the researcher has developed a model. The question becomes, at this point: How would the model hold if I gathered more information from people similar to those I initially interviewed? Thus, to verify the model, the researcher chooses sites, persons, and/or documents that "will maximize opportunities for verifying the story line, relationships between categories, and for filling in poorly developed categories" (Strauss & Corbin, 1990, p. 187).

generate or discover a theory Grounded theory research is the process of developing a theory, not testing a theory. Researchers might begin with a tentative theory they want to modify or no theory at all with the intent of "grounding" the study in views of participants. In either case, an inductive model of theory development is at work here, and the process is one of generating or discovering a theory grounded in views from participants in the field.

grounded theory study In this type of study, the researcher generates an abstract analytical schema of a phenomenon, a theory that explains some action, interaction, or process. This is accomplished primarily through collecting interview data, making multiple visits to the field (theoretical sampling), attempting to develop and interrelate categories (constant comparison) of information, and writing a substantive or context-specific theory (Strauss & Corbin, 1990).

in vivo codes In grounded theory research, the investigator uses the exact words of the interviewee to form the names for these codes or categories. The names are "catchy" and immediately draw the attention of the reader (Strauss & Corbin, 1990, p. 69).

intervening conditions In axial coding, these are the broader conditions—broader than the context—within which the strategies occur. They might be social, economic, and political forces that influence the strategies in response to the central phenomenon (Strauss & Corbin, 1990).

Appendix A

memoing This is the process in grounded theory research of the researcher writing down ideas about the evolving theory. The writing could be in the form of preliminary propositions (hypotheses), ideas about emerging categories, or some aspects of the connection of categories as in axial coding. In general, these are written records of analysis that help with the formulation of theory (Strauss & Corbin, 1990).

open coding This is the first step in the data analysis process for a grounded theorist. It involves taking data (e.g., interview transcriptions) and segmenting them into categories of information (Strauss & Corbin, 1990). I recommend that researchers try to develop a small number of categories, slowly reducing the number to approximately 30 codes that are then combined into major themes in the study.

properties These are other units of information analyzed in grounded theory research. Each category in grounded theory research can be subdivided into properties that provide the broad dimensions for the category. Strauss and Corbin (1990) refer to them as "attributes or characteristics pertaining to a category" (p. 61). They appear in "open coding" analysis.

propositions These are hypotheses, typically written in a directional form, that relate categories in a study. They are written from the axial coding model or paradigm and might, for example, suggest why a certain cause influences the central phenomenon that, in turn, influences the use of a specific strategy.

saturate, saturated, or saturation In the development of categories and data analysis phase of grounded theory research, researchers seek to find as many incidents, events, or activities as possible to provide support for the categories. In this process, they come to a point at which the categories are "saturated" and the inquirer no longer finds new information that adds to an understanding of the category.

selective coding This is the final phase of coding the information. The researcher takes the central phenomenon and systematically relates it to other categories, validating the relationships and filling in categories that need further refinement and development (Strauss & Corbin, 1990). I like to develop a "story" that narrates these categories and shows their interrelationship (see Creswell & Brown, 1992).

strategies In axial coding, these are the specific actions or interactions that occur as a result of the central phenomenon (Strauss & Corbin, 1990).

substantive-level theory This is a low-level theory that is applicable to immediate situations. This theory evolves from the study of a phenomenon situated in "one particular situational context" (Strauss & Corbin, 1990, p. 174). Researchers differentiate this form of theory from theories of greater abstraction and applicability, called midlevel theories, grand theories, or formal theories.

theoretical sampling In data collection for grounded theory research, the investigator selects a sample of individuals to study based on their contribution to the development of the theory. Often, this process begins with a homogeneous sample of individuals who are similar, and, as the data collection proceeds and the categories emerge, the researcher turns to a heterogeneous sample to see under what sample conditions the categories hold true.

Ethnography

analysis of the culture-sharing group In this step in ethnography, the ethnographer develops themes—cultural themes—in the data analysis. It is a process of reviewing all of the data and segmenting them into a small set of common themes, well supported by evidence in the data (Wolcott, 1994b).

artifacts This is the focus of attention for the ethnographer as he or she determines what people make and use, such as clothes and tools (cultural artifacts) (Spradley, 1980).

behaviors These are the focus of attention for the ethnographer as he or she attempts to understand what people do (cultural behavior) (Spradley, 1980).

complete observer The researcher is neither seen nor noticed by the people under study.

complete participant The researcher is fully engaged with the people he or she is observing. This may help him or her establish greater rapport with the people being observed (Angrosino, 2007).

critical ethnography This type of ethnography examines cultural systems of power, prestige, privilege, and authority in society. Critical ethnographers study marginalized groups from different classes, races, and genders, with an aim of advocating for the needs of these participants (Madison, 2005; Thomas, 1993).

cultural portrait One key component of ethnographic research is composing a holistic view of the culture-sharing group or individual. The final product of an ethnography should be this larger portrait, or overview of the cultural scene, presented in all of its complexity (Spradley, 1979).

culture This term is an abstraction, something that one cannot study directly. From observing and participating in a culture-sharing group, an ethnographer can see "culture at work" and provide a description and interpretation of it (H. F. Wolcott, personal communication, October 10, 1996; Wolcott, 2010). It can be seen in behaviors, language, and artifacts (Spradley, 1980).

culture-sharing group This is the unit of analysis for the ethnographer as he or she attempts to understand and interpret the behavior, language, and artifacts of people. The ethnographer typically focuses on an entire group—one that shares learned, acquired behaviors—to make explicit how the group "works." Some ethnographers will focus on part of the social-cultural system for analysis and engage in a microethnography.

deception This is a field issue that has become less and less of a problem since the ethical standards were published in 1967 by the American Anthropological Association. It relates to the act of the researcher intentionally deceiving the informants to gain information. This deception may involve masking the purpose of the research, withholding important information about the purpose of the study, or gathering information secretively.

description of the culture-sharing group One of the first tasks of an ethnographer is to simply record a description of the culture-sharing group and incidents and activities that illustrate the culture (Wolcott, 1994b). For example, a factual account may be rendered, pictures of the setting may be drawn, or events may be chronicled.

emic This term refers to the type of information being reported and written into an ethnography when the researcher reports the views of the participants. When the researcher reports his or her own personal views, the term used is *etic* (Fetterman, 2010).

ethnography This is the study of an intact cultural or social group (or an individual or individuals within the group) based primarily on observations and a prolonged period of time spent by the researcher in the field. The ethnographer listens and records the voices of informants with the intent of generating a cultural portrait (Thomas, 1993; Wolcott, 1987).

etic This term refers to the type of information being reported and written into an ethnography when the researcher reports his or her own personal views. When the researcher reports the views of the participants, the term used is *emic* (Fetterman, 2010).

fieldwork In ethnographic data collection, the researcher conducts data gathering in the "field" by going to the site or sites where the culture-sharing group can be studied. Often, this involves a prolonged period of time with varying degrees of immersion in activities, events, rituals, and settings of the cultural group (Sanjek, 1990).

function This is a theme or concept about the social-cultural system or group that the ethnographer studies. Function refers to the social relations among members of the group that help regulate behavior. For example, the researcher might document patterns of behavior of fights within and among various inner-city gangs (Fetterman, 2010).

gatekeeper This is a data collection term and refers to the individual the researcher must visit before entering a group or cultural site. To gain access, the researcher must receive this individual's approval (Hammersley & Atkinson, 1995).

holistic The ethnographer assumes this outlook in research to gain a comprehensive and complete picture of a social group. It might include the group's history, religion, politics, economy, and/or environment. In this way, the researcher places information about the group into a larger perspective or "contextualizes" the study (Fetterman, 2010).

immersed The ethnographic researcher becomes immersed in the field through a prolonged stay, often as long as one year. Whether the individual loses perspective and "goes native" is a field issue much discussed in the ethnographic literature.

interpretation of the culture-sharing group The researcher makes an interpretation of the meaning of the culture-sharing group. The researcher interprets this information through the use of literature, personal experiences, or theoretical perspectives (Wolcott, 1994b).

key informants (or participants) These are individuals with whom the researcher begins in data collection because they are well informed, are accessible, and can provide leads about other information (Gilchrist, 1992).

language This is the focus of attention for the ethnographer as he or she discerns what people say (speech messages) (Spradley, 1980).

nonparticipant/observer as participant The researcher is an outsider of the group under study, watching and taking field notes from a distance. He or she can record data without direct involvement with activity or people.

participant as observer The researcher is participating in the activity at the site. The participant role is more salient than the researcher role. This may help the researcher gain insider views and subjective data. However, it may be distracting for the researcher to record data when he or she is integrated into the activity.

participant observation The ethnographer gathers information in many ways, but the primary approach is to observe the culture-sharing group and become a participant in the cultural setting (Jorgensen, 1989).

realist ethnography A traditional approach to ethnography taken by cultural anthropologists, this approach involves the researcher as an "objective" observer, recording the facts and narrating the study with a dispassionate, omniscient stance (Van Maanen, 1988).

reflexivity This means that the writer is conscious of the biases, values, and experiences that he or she brings to a qualitative research study. Typically, the writer makes this explicit in the text (Hammersley & Atkinson, 1995).

structure This is a theme or concept about the social-cultural system or group that the ethnographer attempts to learn. It refers to the social structure or configuration of the group, such as the kinship or political structure of the social-cultural group. This structure might be illustrated by an organizational chart (Fetterman, 2010).

Case Study

analysis of themes Following description, the researcher analyzes the data for specific themes, aggregating information into large clusters of ideas and providing details that support the themes. Stake (1995) calls this analysis "development of issues" (p. 123).

assertions This is the last step in the analysis, where the researcher makes sense of the data and provides an interpretation of the data couched in terms of personal views or in terms of theories or constructs in the literature.

bounded system The "case" selected for study has boundaries, often bounded by time and place. It also has interrelated parts that form a whole. Hence, the proper case to be studied is both "bounded" and a "system" (Stake, 1995).

case This is the unit of analysis in a case study. It involves the study of a specific case within a real-life, contemporary context or setting (Yin, 2009). The case might be an event, a process, a program, or several people (Stake, 1995). The case could be the focus of attention (intrinsic case study) or the issue and the case used to illustrate the case (Stake, 1995).

case description This means simply stating the "facts" about the case as recorded by the investigator. This is the first step in analysis of data in a qualitative case study, and Stake (1995) calls it "narrative description" (p. 123).

case study This type of research involves the study of a case within a real-life, contemporary context or setting (Yin, 2009).

case themes These are one aspect of the major findings in a case study. In Stake's (1995) terms, these would be called "categorical aggregations," the larger categories derived during case study data analysis and composed of multiple incidents that are aggregated.

collective case study This type of case study consists of multiple cases. It might be either intrinsic or instrumental, but its defining feature is that the researcher examines several cases (e.g., multiple case studies) (Stake, 1995).

context of the case In analyzing and describing a case, the researcher sets the case within its setting. This setting may be broadly conceptualized (e.g., large historical, social, political issues) or narrowly conceptualized (e.g., the immediate family, the physical location, the time period in which the study occurred) (Stake, 1995).

cross-case analysis This form of analysis applies to a collective case (Stake, 1995; Yin, 2009) in which the researcher examines more than one case. It involves examining themes across cases to discern themes that are common and different to all cases. It is an analysis step that typically follows within-case analysis when the researcher studies multiple cases.

Appendix A

direct interpretation This is an aspect of interpretation in case study research where the researcher looks at a single instance and draws meaning from it without looking for multiple instances of it. It is a process of pulling the data apart and putting them back together in more meaningful ways (Stake, 1995).

embedded analysis In this approach to data analysis, the researcher selects one analytic aspect of the case for presentation (Yin, 2009).

holistic analysis In this approach to data analysis, the researcher examines the entire case (Yin, 2009) and presents description, themes, and interpretations or assertions related to the whole case.

instrumental case study This is a type of case study with the focus on a specific issue rather than on the case itself. The case then becomes a vehicle to better understand the issue (Stake, 1995). I would consider the gunman case study (Asmussen & Creswell, 1995) mentioned in Chapter 5 and reprinted in Appendix F of this book to be an example of an instrumental case study.

intrinsic case study This is a type of case study with the focus of the study on the case because it holds intrinsic or unusual interest (Stake, 1995).

multisite When sites are selected for the "case," they might be at different geographical locations. This type of study is considered to be "multisite." Alternatively, the case might be at a single location and considered a "within-site" study.

multiple sources of information One aspect that characterizes good case study research is the use of many different sources of information to provide "depth" to the case. Yin (2009), for example, recommends that the researcher use as many as six different types of information in his or her case study.

naturalistic generalizations In the interpretation of a case, an investigator undertakes a case study to make the case understandable. This understanding may be what the reader learns from the case or its application to other cases (Stake, 1995).

patterns This is an aspect of data analysis in case study research where the researcher establishes patterns and looks for a correspondence between two or more categories to establish a small number of categories (Stake, 1995).

purposeful sampling This is a major issue in case study research, and the researcher needs to clearly specify the type of sampling strategy in selecting the case (or cases) and a rationale for it. It applies to both the selection of the case to study and the sampling of information used within the case. I use Miles and Huberman's (1994) list of sampling strategies and apply it in this book to case studies as well as to other approaches of inquiry.

within-case analysis This type of analysis may apply to either a single case or multiple collective case studies. In within-case analysis, the researcher analyzes each case for themes. In the study of multiple cases, the researcher may compare the within-case themes across multiple cases in cross-case analysis.

within-site When a site is selected for the "case," it might be located at a single geographical location. This is considered a "within-site" study. Alternatively, the case might be different locations and considered to be "multisite."

General Qualitative Terms

aesthetic merit A piece succeeds aesthetically when the use of creative analytical practices opens up the text and invites interpretive responses. The text is artistically shaped, satisfying, complex, and not boring.

approaches to inquiry This is an approach to qualitative research that has a distinguished history in one of the social science disciplines and that has spawned books, journals, and distinct methodologies. These approaches, as I call them, are known in other books as "strategies of inquiry" (Denzin & Lincoln, 1994) or "varieties" (Tesch, 1990). I refer to narrative research, phenomenology, grounded theory, ethnography, and case studies in this book as approaches to inquiry.

axiological This qualitative assumption holds that all research is value laden and includes the value systems of the inquirer, the theory, the paradigm used, and the social and cultural norms for either the inquirer or the respondents (Creswell, 2009; Guba & Lincoln, 1988). Accordingly, the researcher admits and discusses these values in his or her research.

central question A central question in a study is the broad, overarching question being answered in the research study. It is the most general question that could be asked to address the research problem.

coding This is the process of aggregating the text or visual data into small categories of information, seeking evidence for the code from different databases being used in a study, and then assigning a label to the code.

critical race theory (CRT) This is an interpretive lens used in qualitative research that focuses attention on race and how racism is deeply embedded within the framework of American society (Parker & Lynn, 2002).

critical theory This is an interpretive lens used in qualitative research in which a researcher examines the study of social institutions and their transformations through interpreting the meanings of social life; the historical problems of domination, alienation, and social struggles; and a critique of society and the envisioning of new possibilities (Fay, 1987; Madison, 2005; Morrow & Brown, 1994).

disability interpretive lens Disability is focused on as a dimension of human difference and not as a defect. As a human difference, its meaning is derived from social construction (i.e., society's response to individuals), and it is simply one dimension of human difference.

encoding This term means that the writer places certain features in his or her writing to help a reader know what to expect. These features not only help the reader but also aid the writer, who can then draw on the habits of thought and specialized knowledge of the reader (Richardson, 1990). Such features might be the overall organization, code words, images, and other "signposts" for the reader. As applied in this book, the features consist of terms and procedures of a tradition that become part of the language of all facets of research design (e.g., purpose statement, research subquestions, methods).

epistemological This is another philosophical assumption for the qualitative researcher. It addresses the relationship between the researcher and that being studied as interrelated, not independent. Rather than "distance," as I call it, a "closeness" follows between the researcher and that being researched. This closeness, for example, is manifest through time in the field, collaboration, and the impact that being researched has on the researcher.

feminist research approaches In feminist research methods, the goals are to establish collaborative and nonexploitative relationships, to place the researcher within the study so as to avoid objectification, and to conduct research that is transformative (Olesen, 2011; Stewart, 1994).

foreshadowing This term refers to the technique that writers use to portend the development of ideas (Hammersley & Atkinson, 1995). The wording of the problem statement, purpose statement, and research subquestions foreshadows the methods—the data collection and data analysis—used in the study.

impact A piece has an impact when it affects the reader emotionally or intellectually, generates new questions, or moves him or her to write, try new research practices, or move to action.

intercoder agreement This term means that researchers check for reliability of their coding. It involves coding agreements when multiple coders assign and check their code segments to establish the reliability of the data analysis process.

interpretation In qualitative research, this term represents a phase in qualitative data analysis involving abstracting out beyond the codes and themes to the larger meaning of the data.

interpretation In qualitative research interpretation involves abstracting out beyond the codes and themes to the larger meaning of the data.

interview protocol The interview protocol is a form in qualitative data collection in which the researcher directs the activities of an interview and records information provided by the interviewee. It consists of a header, the major substantive question (typically five to seven research subquestions phrased in a way that interviewees can answer), and closing instructions.

maximum variation sampling This is a popular form of qualitative sampling. This sampling approach consists of determining in advance some criteria that differentiate the sites or participants, and then selecting sites or participants that are quite different on the criteria.

methodology This assumption holds that a qualitative researcher conceptualizes the research process in a certain way. For example, a qualitative inquirer relies on views of participants, and discusses their views within the context in which they occur, to inductively develop ideas in a study from particulars to abstractions (Creswell, 1994, 2009).

observational protocol This is a form used in qualitative data collection for guiding and recording observational data. It typically consists of two columns representing descriptive and reflective notes. The researcher records information from the observation on this form.

ontological This is a philosophical assumption about the nature of reality. It addresses the question: When is something real? The answer provided is that something is real when it is constructed in the minds of the actors involved in the situation (Guba & Lincoln, 1988). Thus, reality is not "out there," apart from the minds of actors.

paradigm This is the philosophical stance taken by the researcher that provides a basic set of beliefs that guides action (Denzin & Lincoln, 1994). It defines, for its holder, "the nature of the world, the individual's place in it, and the range of possible relationships to that world" (Denzin & Lincoln, 1994, p. 107). Denzin and Lincoln (1994) further call this the "net that contains the researcher's epistemological, ontological, and methodological premises" (p. 13). In this discussion, I extend this "net" to also include the axiological assumptions.

postmodernism This interpretive perspective is considered a family of theories and perspectives that have something in common (Slife & Williams, 1995). Postmodernists advance a reaction or critique of the 19th-century Enlightenment and early 20th-century emphasis on technology, rationality, reason, universals, science, and the positivist, scientific method (Bloland, 1995; Stringer, 1993). Postmodernists assert that knowledge claims must be set within the conditions of the world today and in the multiple perspectives of class, race, gender, and other group affiliations.

postpositivism This interpretive perspective has the elements of being reductionistic, logical, empirical, cause-and-effect oriented, and deterministic based on a priori theories.

pragmatism This interpretive lens focuses on the outcomes of the research—the actions, situations, and consequences of inquiry—rather than antecedent conditions. There is a concern with applications—"what works"—and solutions to problems. Thus, instead of a focus on methods, the important aspect of research is the problem being studied and the questions asked about this problem.

purpose statement This is a statement typically found in an introduction to a qualitative study in which the author sets forth the major objective or intent of the study. It can be considered "a road map" to the entire study.

purposeful sampling This is the primary sampling strategy used in qualitative research. It means that the inquirer selects individuals and sites for study because they can purposefully inform an understanding of the research problem and central phenomenon in the study.

qualitative research This is an inquiry process of understanding based on a distinct methodological approach to inquiry that explores a social or human problem. The researcher builds a complex, holistic picture; analyzes words; reports detailed views of participants; and conducts the study in a natural setting.

queer theory This is an interpretive lens that may be used in qualitative research that focuses on gay, lesbian, or homosexual identity and how it is culturally and historically constituted, is linked to discourse, and overlaps gender and sexuality (Watson, 2005).

reciprocity This is an aspect of good data collection in which the author gives back to participants by providing rewards for their participation in the study. These rewards may be money or gifts or other forms of remuneration. The idea is that the researcher gives back to participants rather than taking the data from the participant and leaving without offering something in return.

reflexivity An approach in writing qualitative research in which the writer is conscious of the biases, values, and experiences that he or she brings to a qualitative research study. In writing a reflexive passage, the researcher discusses her or his experiences with the central phenomenon and then how these experiences may potentially shape the interpretation that the researcher provides. This passage can be written into a qualitative project in different places in the final report (e.g., methods, vignette, threaded throughout, at the end).

represent the data This is a step in the data analysis process of packaging findings (codes, themes) into text, tabular, or figure form.

research design I use this term to refer to the entire process of research, from conceptualizing a problem to writing the narrative, not simply the methods such as data collection, analysis, and report writing (Bogdan & Taylor, 1975).

research problem A research problem typically introduces a qualitative study, and in this opening passage, the author advances the issue or concern that leads to a need to conduct the study. I discuss this problem as framed from a "real-life" perspective or a deficiency in the literature perspective.

rhetorical This assumption means that the qualitative investigator uses terms and a narrative unique to the qualitative approach. The narrative is personal and literary (Creswell, 1994, 2009). For example, the researcher might use the first-person pronoun *I* instead of the impersonal third-person voice.

sample size Sample size in qualitative research generally follows the guidelines to study a few individuals or sites, but to collect extensive detail about the individuals or sites studied.

social constructivism In this interpretive framework, qualitative researchers seek understanding of the world in which they live and work. They develop subjective meanings of their experiences—meanings directed toward certain objects or things. These meanings are varied and multiple, leading the researcher to look for the complexity of views rather than narrow the meanings into a few categories or ideas. The goal of research, then, is to rely as much as possible on the participants' views of the situation. Often these subjective meanings are negotiated socially and historically.

social justice theories These advocacy/participatory theories seek to bring about change or address social justice issues in our societies.

social science theories These are the theoretical explanations that social scientists use to explain the world (Slife & Williams, 1995). They are based on empirical evidence that has accumulated in social science fields such as sociology, psychology, education, economics, urban studies, and communication. As a set of interrelated concepts, variables, and propositions, they serve to explain, predict, and provide generalizations about phenomena in the world (Kerlinger, 1979). They may have broad applicability (as in grand theories) or narrow applications (as in minor working hypotheses) (Flinders & Mills, 1993).

subquestions Subquestions are a form of research questions in a qualitative study in which the researcher subdivides the central question into parts and examines these parts. These subquestions are often used in interview and observational protocols as the major topics.

substantive contribution A piece makes a substantive contribution when it contributes to our understanding of social life, demonstrates a deeply grounded social scientific perspective, and seems "true."

themes In qualitative research, themes (also called categories) are broad units of information that consist of several codes aggregated to form a common idea.

triangulation Researchers make use of multiple and different sources, methods, investigators, and theories to provide corroborating evidence for validating the accuracy of their study.

transformative framework Researchers who use this interpretive framework advocate that knowledge is not neutral and it reflects the power and social relationships within society, and thus the purpose of knowledge construction is to aid people to improve society (Mertens, 2003). These individuals include marginalized groups such as lesbians, gays, bisexuals, transgenders, queers, and societies that need a more hopeful, positive psychology and resilience (Mertens, 2009).

verisimilitude This is a criterion for a good literary study, in which the writing seems "real" and "alive," transporting the reader directly into the world of the study (Richardson, 1994).

Appendix B

A Narrative Research Study—"Living in the Space Between Participant and Researcher as a Narrative Inquirer: Examining Ethnic Identity of Chinese Canadian Students as Conflicting Stories to Live By"

Elaine Chan

ABSTRACT. Schooling experiences of lst-generation Canadians interact with cultural experiences in their immigrant households to shape a sense of ethnic identity both as Canadians and as members of an ethnic community. This long-term, school-based narrative inquiry is an examination of ways in which expectations for academic performance and behavior by teachers and peers at school and immigrant parents at home contributed to shaping the ethnic identity of an immigrant Chinese student as conflicting stories to live by. A narrative approach revealed challenges of supporting immigrant students in North American schools, and contributed to understanding of the nuances of multicultural education.

Keywords: narrative inquiry, ethnic identity, curriculum, multicultural education, student experiences

Author's Note: Address correspondence to Elaine Chan, Department of Teaching. Learning, and Teacher Education, College of Education and Human Sciences, University of Nebraska-Lincoln, 24 Henzlik Hall, Lincoln, NE 68588-0355. (E-mail: echan2@unl.edu)

For children, school has enormous implications for their sense of identity as members of society, of their families, and of their ethnic communities. Each individual brings to their school context experiences shaped by their participation in schools, whether in Canada or in their home country, whether positive or negative, enriching or demoralizing. For a child of immigrant parents, tensions between home and school, the interaction of parent and teacher experiences of schooling, and their own experiences of schooling may be felt especially strongly, to the point of being experienced as conflicting stories to live by (Connelly & Clandinin, 1999). These students have their own ideas of how they should be in their school context, shaped by interaction with peers, exposure to popular culture and media, and prior experiences of schooling, schools, and teachers. At the same time, they are evaluated by teachers and supported by parents whose experiences of schooling may be vastly different, by nature of social and political influences as well as personal circumstances of the societies of which their own childhood schools were a part.

In the present study, I examined the experiences of one Chinese immigrant student, Ai Mei Zhang. I explore her participation in her Canadian middle school curriculum as the interaction of student, teacher, and parent narratives, a story of interwoven lives (Clandinin et al., 2006). I examined ways in which her sense of ethnic identity may be shaped by expectations for her academic performance and her behavior in her school and her home. I focus in particular on ways in which participation in her urban, multicultural school setting may contribute to shaping her sense of affiliation to family members and members of her ethnic and school communities, and contribute to her maternal-language development and maintenance. I also examined ways in which she experienced well-intended school practices and curriculum activities designed to support her academic performance in ways not anticipated by policymakers and educators. I explored these influences as conflicting stories to live by (Connelly & Clandinin, 1999).

I examined experientially the intersection of school and home influences from the perspective of one middle school student as a long-term, school-based narrative inquirer. I explored features of narrative inquiry, such as the critical role of researcher–participant relationships, and the role of temporal and spatial factors (Clandinin & Connelly, 2000) of the research context in contributing to a nuanced understanding of multicultural education in this diverse school context. The present study is holistic, in that I examined the impact of multiple influences in a connected way as they intersected in the life of one student rather than as examples of ways in which an issue or theme may be experienced by different members of the same ethnic group.

Given the increasing diversity of the North American population (Statistics Canada, 2008; U.S. Census Bureau, 2002) that is in turn reflected in North American schools (Chan & Ross, 2002; He, Phillion, Chan, & Xu, 2007), addressing the curricular needs of students of minority background and supporting the professional development of teachers who work with them is essential. The present study contributes to existing research in the area of multicultural education and, in particular, curriculum development for diverse student populations, and student experiences of multicultural education.

To date, research addressing the interaction of culture and curriculum is often presented as an argument for the inclusion of culture in the school curriculum or as documentation for ways in which the inclusion of culture in the curriculum was successful (Ada, 1988; Cummins et al., 2005). There is an abundance of research highlighting the importance of culturally relevant and responsive pedagogy (Gay, 2000; Ladson-Billings, 1995, 2001; Villegas, 1991) and a culturally sensitive curriculum that builds on the experiences and knowledge of immigrant and minority students (Ada; Cummins, 2001; Igoa, 1995; Nieto & Bode, 2008).

Acknowledging the cultural knowledge of minority students in the classroom has been found to have important implications for their well-being outside of school. For example, Banks (1995) highlighted the inclusion of culture in the curriculum as a means of helping students to develop positive racial attitudes. Rodriguez (1982), Wong-Fillmore (1991), and Kouritzin (1999) presented compelling accounts of ways in which the failure to support the maintenance and development of maternal-language proficiency for students of minority background had dire consequences for their sense of ethnic identity and their sense of belonging in their families and ethnic communities. McCaleb (1994), Cummins (2001), and Wong-Fillmore elaborated on some of the dangers, such as increased dropout rates among immigrant and minority youth as well as increased likelihood of gang involvement, or failing to recognize the cultural communities from which students come.

Existing research has been invaluable in highlighting the importance of acknowledging the cultural knowledge that immigrant and minority students bring to a school context, and the work of educators as they develop curricula and teach an increasingly diverse student population (Banks, 1995; Cummins, 2001; Moodley, 1995). Research has also accentuated the need to develop ways of learning about the ethnic, linguistic, and religious backgrounds of students to inform curriculum development and policymaking for students of diverse backgrounds. Cochran-Smith (1995),

Ladson-Billings (1995, 2001), and Conle (2000) explored the practice of drawing on the cultural knowledge of preservice teachers as a resource for preparing them to teach in culturally diverse classrooms. It is interesting to note that although there is research that has acknowledged the potential difficulties of moving from home to school for students of a minority back-ground, and the difficulties of moving from school back home when minor-ity students have assimilated to the school and societal expectations that differ from those of their home cultures, the day-to-day transition as minor-ity and immigrant students move from home to school and back home again seems to have been overlooked. In the present study, I examine the nuances that one student lives as she makes this transition on a daily basis.

This work addresses the need for experiential research, focusing spe-cifically on exploring the intersection of home and school influences from the perspective of the students themselves. Presently, there is a surprising lack of research examining ways in which students, in general (Cook-Sather, 2002), and immigrant and minority students, in particular, person-ally experience their school curriculum and school contexts (He et al., 2007). Bullough's (2007) examination of a Muslim student's response to curriculum and peer interactions in his U.S. school is among the few pieces examining school-curriculum activities from the perspective of a student of ethnic-minority background. Feuerverger's (2001) ethno-graphic work exploring tensions that Israeli and Palestinian youth experi-ence in their Israeli-Palestinian school is among few studies documenting and exploring student perspectives of their schooling experiences. Sarroub (2005) and Zine's (2001) accounts of Muslim students in American and Canadian schools, respectively, illustrate the complexities of negotiat-ing a sense of identity among peers in a school context when values in the home differ significantly.

Within the relatively limited body of existing research addressing stu-dent experiences of schooling and curriculum presented, I present exam-ples of student experiences thematically to address specific issues, topics, or arguments rather than ways that acknowledge multiple facets and ten-sions interacting at once to shape the experiences of an individual stu-dent. Smith-Hefner (1993), in her ethnographic study of female high school Khmer students, presented examples of Puerto Rican female stu-dents whose limited academic success was shaped by cultural and socio-historical influences in their ethnic communities. Rolon-Dow (2004) examined tensions Puerto Rican students and their teachers experience when values supported in their home and in their ethnic communities seem to conflict with those encouraged in school. Lee's (1994, 1996) eth-nographic study focused on ways in which Asian high school students' sense of identity and academic achievement was influenced by self-identified labels and membership in specific peer groups. There does not exist a large body of research examining the experiences of one student in the context of their North American school in a way that presents the stories to illustrate ways in which the interaction of multiple influences and issues of relevance may impact on an immigrant or minority student.

This narrative inquiry is intended to provide a glimpse of the intersection of complex influences shaping the life of an immigrant student. I drew on existing narrative and ethnographic accounts of immigrant and minority students attending North American schools to inform this work. Valdes's (1996) work documenting the experiences of a small number of Latino and Mexican American families in their school and community and Li's (2002) ethnographic study with Chinese families as they supported their children's literacy development provide a glimpse of ways in which transitions between home and school may be challenging, and even overwhelming, due to differences in expectations about the school curriculum and the work of teachers. Carger's (1996) long-term narrative account of a Mexican American family's experiences provides an organizational structure for the present study, in that it is an in-depth account of one family's experiences of supporting their child in school, taking into consideration the intersection of multiple influences shaping the child's education. Ross & Chan's (2008) narrative account of an immigrant student, Raj, and his family's academic, financial, and familial difficulties highlighted the many challenges the family encountered in the process of supporting their children's adaptation to their Canadian school and community. This examination of Ai Mei's experiences contributes to the growing but still limited body of research addressing Chinese students in North American schools (Chan, 2004; Kao, 1995; Kim & Chun, 1994; Lee, 1994, 1996, 2001; Li, 2002, 2005).

Theoretical Framework

Given the focus on experience in contributing to Ai Mei's sense of ethnic identity, I used Dewey's (1938) philosophy of the interconnectedness between experience and education as the theoretical foundation for this study. I examined, in particular, ways in which the many influences in her home, school, and neighborhood life with family members, peers, teachers, administrators, and school curriculum events intersected to contribute to her overall experience or learning of a sense of ethnic identity as an immigrant student in a Canadian school context. Ai Mei's stories are set into the framework of a three-dimensional narrative inquiry space (Clandinin & Connelly, 2000), with Bay Street School as the spatial dimension, the years 2001–2003 as the temporal dimension, and my interactions with Ai Mei, her classmates, her teachers, her parents, and other members of the Bay Street School community as the sociopersonal dimension. The stories are a means of exploring the interaction of influences contributing to Ai Mei's sense of identity; they highlight the extent to which this intersection of narratives may be interpreted as conflicting stories to live by (Connelly & Clandinin, 1999).

Method

I first met Ai Mei when I began observations in her seventh-grade class as a classroom-based participant observer for a research project exploring the ethnic identity of first-generation Canadian students. The focus on examining the intersection of culture and curriculum as experienced by Chinese Canadian students over the course of their 2 years in middle school was deliberate from the beginning. As I learned about the details of the students' experiences, the complex interaction of factors contributing to Ai Mei's sense of ethnic identity became apparent and merited further analysis.

Ai Mei's homeroom teacher, William, told me about how she had arrived at Bay Street School from an urban area of Fuchien province in China as a 7-year-old. Although she did not initially speak English at all, she was relatively proficient by the time I met her 4 1/2 years after her arrival. Her English was distinct from that of her native-English-speaking peers by the unusual turns of phrases and unconventional uses of some words, but the animated way in which she spoke about her experiences caught my attention from the beginning. I later appreciated this quality even more as I began to work more closely with her as a research participant. Her dark eyes, partially hidden behind wisps of hair, seemed to flicker and dance as she elaborated on details of interactions with peers and family members, especially when she recounted amusing or troublesome events pertaining to difficulties she had experienced in communicating with others. She also seemed to enjoy telling me about incidents that had occurred at home, at school, or in the community. As I learned about Ai Mei's stories of immigration and settlement, the conflicting influences and expectations of her family members, peers and teachers at school, and members of her ethnic community became more apparent, thus further contributing to my decision to focus on her stories in this study.

As a narrative inquirer, I learned about Ai Mei's stories of experience (Connelly & Clandinin, 1988) using a variety of narrative approaches, including long-term, school-based participant observations, document collection set into the context of ongoing conversational interviews with key participants, and the writing of extensive field notes following each school visit, interview, and interaction with participants (Clandinin & Connelly, 1994, 2000; Clandinin et al., 2006) to explore the interwoven quality of Ai Mei, her teacher, her classmates, and her family members' lives. I observed and interacted with her in the context of regular classroom lessons as I assisted her and her classmates with assignments, accompanied them on field trips, attended their band concerts and performances, and took part in school activities such as Multicultural Night, Curriculum and Hot Dog Night, school assemblies, and festivals. School visits began during the fall of 2001 as Ai Mei and her classmates began seventh grade and continued until June 2003 when they graduated from eighth grade at Bay Street School.

I conducted interviews as well as ongoing informal conversations with Ai Mei over the course of the 2 years I spent in her homeroom classroom. I also collected documents such as school notices, announcements of community and school events, notices from bulletin boards and classroom walls in the school, agendas and minutes from School Council meetings, and samples of student work. Descriptive field notes, interview transcripts, researcher journals, and theoretical memos written following school visits were computerized and filed into an existing research project archival system. I examined field notes pertaining to Ai Mei's experiences numerous times to identify recurring themes. Her stories were set into the context of field notes written about her classroom teacher, her peers, and her school community since I began research at the school in 2000.

Results

Ai Mei's Stories of Home and School: Conflicting Stories to Live By

I subsequently present some of Ai Mei's stories of experience to explore challenges and complexities, harmonies and tensions (Clandinin & Connelly, 2002) she lived as she attempted to balance affiliation to her peers while at the same time accommodating for expectations placed on her by her teachers and parents. I explore ways in which parent, teacher, and peer expectations may contribute to shaping her sense of identity, and examine the contribution of narrative methodology in revealing nuances of the intersection of multiple influences in her life.

Appendix B

Bay Street School Context

Ai Mei's stories were set in the context of Bay Street School, a school known to consist of a diverse student community from the time of its establishment (Cochrane, 1950; Connelly, He, Phillion, Chan, & Xu, 2004), located in an urban Toronto neighborhood where the ethnic composition of residents is known to reflect Canadian immigration and settlement patterns (Connelly, Phillion, & He, 2003). Accordingly, the student population at the school reflects this diversity. An Every Student Survey administered to students during the 2001–2002 school year (Chan & Ross, 2002) confirmed the ethnic and linguistic diversity of the students. More specifically, 39 countries and 31 languages were represented in the school. This was the context in which Ai Mei's stories played out.

Home Language Conflicting with School Language

I subsequently present the story, "I was trying to hide my identity," as a starting point for examining Ai Mei's experiences of her academic program at Bay Street School.

"I was trying to hide my identity"

Ai Mei: When I first came to Bay Street School, I stayed with the IL (International Language)[1] teacher, Mrs. Lim . . . I stayed with her for the whole week, and she taught me things in English.

Elaine: What did she teach you?

Ai Mei: You know, easy things, like the alphabet, and how to say "Hello." Then I went to Ms. Jenkins' class. I sat with a strange boy.

Elaine: A strange boy?

Ai Mei: Well, he wasn't that strange. My desk was facing his desk, and he did this to me (Ai Mei demonstrates what the boy did), he stuck his tongue out at me. I didn't know what it meant. He had messy orange hair.

Elaine: Did you make any friends?

Ai Mei: No, not for a long time. Some people tried to talk to me but I didn't understand them. Then Chao tried to talk with me in Fujianese and I pretended I didn't understand her. She tried a few times, then gave up. Then one day, my sister said something to me in Fujianese and Chao heard. She looked at me—she was really surprised because she tried to talk with me and I pretended I couldn't understand her. She didn't like me at all.

Elaine: Why did you do that? Why did you pretend you couldn't understand her?

Ai Mei: I don't know. I was trying to hide my identity.

Ai Mei: (calling over to Chao): Chao, remember how I didn't talk with you, how I pretended I didn't understand you?

Chao: Yeah, I remember. (Chao scowls at Ai Mei.) I didn't like you for a long time.

Ai Mei: Yeah, a long time.

(Fieldnotes, April, 2003)

When Ai Mei arrived at Bay Street School, new students coming into the school spent a week or two with the respective International Language (IL) teacher prior to placement into a classroom. The new student orientation provided teachers the opportunity to assess the English and maternal-language proficiency of new students, identify potential learning difficulties, and learn about their previous schooling experiences. The orientation also provided students an opportunity to learn about school routines in their home language while being gradually introduced into their age-appropriate classroom.

Ai Mei's response to the new student orientation, however, was surprising for a number of reasons. From her teachers' perspective, Chao would have seemed like an ideal friend for Ai Mei—both girls were from the same rural province of southern China, grew up speaking Fujianese at home and Mandarin in school, and Chao could help Ai Mei to adapt to Bay Street School because she had arrived two years earlier. However, Ai Mei did not seem to welcome the opportunity to speak with Chao in Fujianese. Her teachers were also likely puzzled that she would try to "hide [her] identity," because, from their perspective, they worked hard to create programs that would acknowledge students' home cultures in a positive way.

In this context, it is possible that Ai Mei, similar to many students featured in research on immigrant and minority students (Cummins, 2001; Kouritzin, 1999), perceived her affiliation to her family's home language as a hindrance to acceptance by English-speaking peers. She seemed to appreciate learning English from her IL teacher and perhaps felt that her inability to speak in English was an obstacle to forming friendships with English-speaking peers. One day, as we were walking back to her home-room classroom after art class, she has told me about an incident when she felt embarrassed when she attempted to order drinks at a shopping mall and the vendor could not understand her because "[her] English accent was so bad!" Ai Mei may have been attempting to distance herself from those she perceived as non-English-speaking when she said she "tried to hide [her] identity." Wong-Fillmore (1991) elaborated on how a language minority child might abandon the home language when she or he realizes the low status of this language in relation to the English that is used by peers in school. At the same time, in choosing not to respond to her Fujianese-speaking classmate who attempted to befriend her, Ai Mei was giving up the opportunity to make a friend at a time when she did not have the English proficiency to build friendships easily with English-speaking peers.

School Language Conflicting with Home Language

In addition to pressure to achieve a higher level of English proficiency, Ai Mei seemed to be under pressure from her IL Mandarin teacher, Mrs. Lim, to maintain and to develop her Mandarin proficiency. She was in a high level of language within her grade-level Mandarin program,[2] and she was doing well in the class, judging from the grades I saw when she showed me her Mandarin language textbook and workbooks. Her teacher has said that she did well in her assignments and tests, and that she was a strong student in Mandarin. She stated that it was important for Ai Mei to work hard to maintain the advantage she had over her Canadian-born Chinese peers. Mrs. Lim believed that Ai Mei has an easier time learning the characters that many Canadian-born Chinese students have difficulty with, due to her early years of schooling in China before arriving in Canada. She also felt that Ai Mei had an advantage over her Chinese-born peers, in that her schooling prior to leaving China was regular and uninterrupted in a way some of her Chinese-born peers had not experienced.

Maintenance of her Mandarin language proficiency is an achievement her parents support. At the same time, they would like her to maintain fluency in her family's home dialect of Fujianese. For Ai Mei and her parents, maternal language maintenance has important implications for communication within the family. Ai Mei told me about the following meal-time conversation involving her mother and her younger sister, Susan.

"Susan doesn't speak Fujianese"

Ai Mei: We were eating supper and my mother said to my sister, "(phrase in Fujianese)." My sister asked me, "What did she say?" so I told her, "She wants to know if you want more vegetables."

Elaine: Your sister doesn't understand Fujianese?

Ai Mei: She does but not everything.

Elaine: What did your mother say? Is she worried that your sister doesn't understand her?

Ai Mei: She looked at her like this—(Ai Mei showed me how her mother gave her sister a dirty look).

(Fieldnotes, April, 2003)

From the fieldnote, it seems that Ai Mei's parents were beginning to feel the effects of maternal language loss within the family. Fujianese is not easy to develop and maintain because its use in Canada is not widely supported outside the home, with the exception of exposure to the dialect through other recent immigrants from Fuchien Province. Susan's inability to understand basic vocabulary in her home language likely worried her and Ai Mei's parents, but given the limited resources to support it and limited time to encourage her themselves, they might wonder what can be done. Ai Mei spoke about how her parents reminded her often to speak with her sister in Fujianese. Meanwhile, the sisters had long grown into the habit of speaking to one another in English; communication in their home language of Fujianese would have been stifled at that point due to the lack of ease both felt in using it as well as Susan's limited vocabulary. It might be the case that their parents, as they began to realize the extent of their daughter's maternal language loss, might already be too late to stop it. This pressure to develop and to maintain language proficiency interacted with other factors contributing to Ai Mei's sense of identity and affiliation in her school and in her home and ethnic communities.

Parent Values Conflicting with Peer Values

In addition to pressure to succeed academically, Ai Mei was also under pressure to behave according to the expectations of her peers, teachers, and parents. Through interaction with Ai Mei at Bay Street School over the course of two full academic years, it became apparent that being included within her peer group was very important to her. Like her peers, Ai Mei was becoming more firmly entrenched into popular movies, music, and fashion trends as she moved into adolescence. These influences were coupled with increasing pressure from peers to scoff at school success and downplay the importance of academic work. During the fall of 2001, there were a number of days when I arrived at Ai Mei's classroom to find her friends trying to console her after a popular and outspoken male classmate, Felix, had made unflattering comments about her appearance. Her homeroom teacher also told me about incidents when she had left school in tears after being excluded from an after school activity that had been planned by classmates. Another day, I overheard Felix mimicking one of the stories from Ai Mei's Mandarin IL text; although he spoke in English, the tone and storyline were along the lines of what might be found in the text. Ai Mei laughed at Felix's attempts and seemed to appreciate that he knew a little about what she did in IL class but I also wondered whether she was embarrassed or annoyed with him.

In addition to concerns about being excluded by her peers and feeling the pull of multiple influences in school to behave in certain ways, Ai Mei also seemed to live the tensions of parental expectations and standards for her behavior and comportment that, at times, conflicted with those of her peers, and ways in which she saw herself. I wrote the following fieldnote after a conversation with Ai Mei in which she complained about her mother's comments about her in relation to her mother's friend during a family outing.

"Dim Sum with her mother's friend"

Ai Mei told me today about going out to dim sum with her mother's friend and her family. She said she was very annoyed at being compared to her mother's friend's daughter who is close in age to Ai Mei but who seems like a perfect daughter in her mother's eyes. Ai Mei told me, "My mother said, 'Look at Ming Ming, so pretty and tall. And so quiet! She helps her mother do the cooking and the cleaning at home.' She said to Ming Ming's mother, 'Look at Ai Mei, 13 years old and so short. And she doesn't help me at home, and she doesn't cook!' She kept comparing us, saying how nice Ming Ming is and how terrible I am." Ai Mei rolled her eyes.

(Fieldnotes, April, 2003)

The interaction between Ai Mei and her mother highlighted the potential for tensions to develop when expressing differences in perspective about the value of certain kinds of behaviors over others. It sounded as if Ai Mei resented that her mother did not think she was quiet or helpful or tall enough when compared with her friend's daughter. Although a generational gap might account for some of the tension about what constituted appropriate behavior and goals for Ai Mei with respect to what she did to contribute to the family, some of this tension might also have been shaped by the very different contexts in which Ai Mei and her mother have spent their childhood. Ai Mei has spent a good portion of her childhood living in different homes in an urban, commercial district of Toronto. Her perception of appropriate behavior and practices has likely been shaped by influences different from what her mother experienced in rural Fuchien province of China where she spent her own childhood.

Teacher Expectations Conflicting with Parent Expectations

Moreover, although Ai Mei's parents and her teachers had in common the goal of academic success for her, tensions surfaced about the time commitment needed to fulfill these school and family responsibilities. Ai Mei seemed to be caught between pressures to help in the family business and teacher expectations for completed homework and thorough preparation for tests and assignments.

Ai Mei's family acquired a dumpling restaurant during the fall of her eighth-grade year, and since then, the whole family had devoted much time and energy toward building a successful business. I knew that Ai Mei's family owned a dumpling restaurant because she had told me about what she did to help.

Ai Mei: There's a door that no one can close but me.

Elaine: What's wrong with it?

Ai Mei: It's stuck, so I have to kick it shut. (She demonstrates as she says this, kicking to one side as she leans over.) Then, we go home, me, my mom, and my dad.

Elaine: How about your sister?

Ai Mei: She goes home a little earlier, with my grandmother and grandfather.

(Fieldnotes, October, 2002)

Each day after school, Ai Mei and her sister, Susan, after spending some time with their friends in the classroom or in the school yard, headed to the dumpling restaurant to spend the evening there helping their parents. Ai Mei's sister, Susan, has told me about how she helped their father by standing outside the restaurant where the family sells vegetables and fruits to watch for people who attempted to take food without paying for it. When I asked her whether this often happened, she nodded gravely.

The importance of Ai Mei and Susan's participation in the family business could be denied, but Ai Mei's teachers had questioned the time commitment involved. Late in the fall after the family acquired the dumpling restaurant, Ai Mei's teacher, William, noticed that she had begun to come to school looking very tired, and without her homework done. One day while he was meeting with her to discuss the report card that would soon be sent home to her parents, he told her that she could have done better had she submitted all of her homework and done a better job on recent tests. Ai Mei surprised him by bursting into tears. Little by little, William learned that Ai Mei had little opportunity to do her homework or to study because she was helping out at the restaurant during evenings and weekends. By the time the family had closed up the restaurant, traveled home, and eaten supper, it was past 11:00 pm or 12:00 am, beyond what William thought was appropriate for a 12-year-old. With a sense of professional responsibility to report potentially negligent situations to officials and the support of school board policies guiding his actions, William spoke with his principal about the situation. Both decided it was a borderline case, and with the principal's knowledge, William contacted the Children's Aid Society (CAS) about Ai Mei's family. I wrote the following field note the day William told me about his call to the CAS.

"I called the CAS"

I was helping William straighten up the textbooks, sort student assignments into piles, and organize pens, pencils, and chalk into appropriate places in the classroom. We have gotten into the habit of talking about events of the day as we tidy up the classroom after the students have left for French class toward the end of the day. Today, William said to me, "I called the CAS about Ai Mei. She doesn't do her homework or have time to study because she's up late working in the family restaurant. She's exhausted." (Fieldnotes, December, 2002)

The dumpling restaurant was tied to Ai Mei's family's dreams of financial success and family reunification. Ai Mei had spoken about how her parents had sponsored her maternal grandparents to come to Toronto from Fuchien province, and were in the process of trying to bring her paternal grandparents over to join the family as well. The importance of helping her family with their business could not be denied from her parents' perspective and, from what Ai Mei has said about the ways in which she helped the family, it could be assumed that she also recognized the importance of her role as well.

At the same time, it was beginning to become apparent that assisting her parents in the family business might have diverted her attention away from fulfilling her parents' desire for her to do well in school, in that time spent in the restaurant helping her family was time that she could have otherwise devoted to her school work. Ai Mei was caught between her parents' dreams of financial and business success, her sense of responsibility, as the oldest daughter in the family, to help them achieve this success, her parents' desire for her to perform well academically to secure her own future economic success, and her teacher's professional responsibility to report potentially negligent situations to officials. She lived the tensions of deciding how best to use her time to assist her parents in the family business as well as to perform well academically.

This situation also needed to be examined in terms of her teacher's professional tensions and ways in which these tensions might have contributed to Ai Mei's sense of identity. Her teacher, William, was aware that the cultural and social narratives guiding his professional practices might have differed from those guiding the practices of the parents of his students, and had expressed a commitment to acknowledging the diversity of his students. The potential for conflict between teacher, student, and parent perspectives pertaining to Ai Mei's use of time in the evenings and on weekends became apparent when William contacted child-protection officials to report that Ai Mei's time in the family's restaurant in the evenings was contributing to her late arrival at school in the mornings, without her assigned homework completed. He did so with the belief in the importance of protecting Ai Mei's time to ensure that she had adequate time and necessary conditions in her home to complete her school work.

William's call to the CAS, however well intentioned, had the potential to cause difficulties in Ai Mei's family as well as a rift in his own relationship with Ai Mei. In fact, he later told me about how Ai Mei, on realizing that he had reported her parents to the CAS, neither came around after school to spend time in his classroom nor did she tell him about what was happening in her life as she was accustomed to doing up until that time. He felt he had lost her trust and believed that his call to the CAS had been the cause. This example highlights some of the tension William felt as he attempted to balance his professional obligation to report potentially negligent situations to child protection officials and his ideal of the role of teacher as an advocate who supported students in ways they would appreciate.

Learning About Ai Mei's Experiences as a Narrative Inquirer

These stories highlight some of the complexities of the interaction of multiple influences in contributing to Ai Mei's sense of identity. Underlying these accounts of Ai Mei's experiences with her peers, teachers, and parents in the context of school and community-based events are accounts of my interactions with Ai Mei as a narrative inquirer. The narrative inquiry approach used in this study facilitated the identification of the many nuances of living as an immigrant student in a North American school context, and provided a framework in which to ponder these complexities. To begin, the stories of experience documenting Ai Mei's experiences as an immigrant student at Bay Street School were gathered over a long period of time as I spent 2 full school years in her homeroom classroom with her, her teachers, and her peers as a participant observer. During this time, I became a member of the classroom, joining the class for activities such as field trips, special school events, band concerts, and school assemblies. More importantly, however, I was a part of their class during the uneventful days of lessons and regular school activities. It was during these times that I was able to build a relationship with Ai Mei and her peers and teachers. They grew to see me as an additional teacher in the classroom who was able to help them with assignments, act as an adult supervisor during in-school activities or field trips, and as a listening ear when they had disagreements with friends or with teachers.

I learned about the details of Ai Mei's life as she told me about her classmates, her parents, her family's dumpling restaurant, her sister, and family outings. I heard about her perceptions of how she fit into her peer group, her ethnic community, and her family as she told me about specific interactions, such as the family dinner when her sister did not understand what her mother had said in Fujianese, her mother's criticisms of her in comparison with her mother's friend's daughter, or her impressions of the new student orientation that was in place to ease her transition into the school as a new student from China.

As the students came to realize my interest in learning about their school lives, they began to update me on events I had missed between visits, and to fill me in on what they referred to as "gossip" at school. At one point partway through my second year with Ai Mei's homeroom class, I conducted interviews with the students. As I planned the questions and discussed them with William, I remember wondering whether this shift to a more formal kind of interaction with the students would change the relationship we had established. My concern about negatively impacting the relationship turned out to be unfounded. In fact, I was pleased to realize one day when Ai Mei approached me to tell me about a family dinner (see "Susan doesn't speak Fujianese") that the process had opened up further opportunities to learn about the students' lives. Realizing that I was interested in hearing about their interactions at home and in the community with members of their ethnic groups, the students began to tell me more about them. Our existing relationship had provided a foundation such that I could talk with the students about their experiences with family and members of their ethnic communities, and the interviews provided an opportunity for the students to learn, in a more explicit way, about my interest in hearing about out-of-school aspects of their lives. Our relationship was such that they knew they could trust that I would treat their stories and their perceptions of these stories with interest and respect.

I also saw Ai Mei in the neighborhood with her friends during the after school hours as they moved from house to house visiting one another in the housing project while their parents worked in nearby restaurants and shops, and on weekends as she shopped with her sister and her parents in the stores that lined the commercial area near the school. These brief interactions provided further glimpses of influences interacting in her life to contribute to shaping a sense of identity in ways that would not be possible through formal interviews or a more structured schedule of research observations. In addition, these interactions provided an opportunity for Ai Mei's friends and family to become familiar with my presence and participation in the school.

Tensions of acting as a researcher with a focus on learning about the experiences of my participants became more apparent as my role as researcher became less clear. As I got to know Ai Mei and her family, I felt the tensions she experienced as she balanced the multiple influences in her life and wanted to advocate for her. I felt a sense of responsibility to Ai Mei, to support her learning and to attempt to ease some of the tensions she experienced as she balanced affiliation to her home and school cultures. I understood a little of the betrayal she felt when her parents were reported to child protection officials, and the fear her parents might have felt. When she told me about how her parents would not be able to attend her eighth-grade graduation because they needed to work, I wanted to be sure to attend and to take photos of her with her sister so that she would have a record of the event. The nature of the researcher-participant relationship in contributing to understanding about the nuances of experiences lived by my student participant heightened my understanding of what the events might mean for her.

The role of narrative inquiry, and, more specifically, the role of long-term participation in the day to day school life of an immigrant student that was critical to this narrative inquiry, contributed to the researcher-participant relationship I was able to develop with Ai Mei, her peers, and her teachers. Careful attention to the details of life in classrooms (Jackson, 1990) and within the school, and respect for the ongoing negotiation so critical to building a research relationship from initial negotiation of entry into the school-research site to negotiation of exit towards the completion of school-based narrative inquiries—features foundational to Clandinin & Connelly's (2000) approach—further contributed to the development of a research relationship based on trust and familiarity with Ai Mei. This trust, in turn, engaged me in careful consideration of the potential implications of telling and retelling Ai Mei's stories, and what they might mean for her, as well as other immigrant and minority students who may struggle with similar challenges of balancing tensions of affiliation to home and school cultures in a North American school context. It was also through this commitment to examining these tensions narratively from multiple perspectives of others in Ai Mei's school, as well as in relation to temporal, spatial, and sociopersonal dimensions at play in her school, that enabled me to see some of the nuances and complexities of the conflicting influences in Ai Mei's life. In the process of examining Ai Mei's experiences narratively, I also became a participant, in that my experiences and interpretations of Ai Mei's stories were continually being examined and reflected on as I shared my interpretations with Ai Mei in an ongoing process to better understand the stories she told.

This relationship, in turn, was critical to my learning about the complexities of Ai Mei's experiences. In this way, this long-term, school-based narrative inquiry approach contributes not only to knowledge about the experiences of my participants as I focus on examining nuances of the research phenomenon at hand but it also raises awareness about the intricacies, and the impact, of the work of researchers in the lives of our participants.

Discussion

*Conflicting Student, Teacher, and
Parent Stories to Live By: Implications
for Practice, Research, and Theory*

This examination of the intersection of home, school, and ethnic community influences in Ai Mei's life provided a glimpse of the challenges

Appendix B

immigrant or minority students might encounter as they negotiate a sense of ethnic identity. More specifically, examining Ai Mei's stories reveals ways in which immigrant and minority students may be pulled in many directions, with some of these influences experienced as conflicting stories to live by as teacher, peer, and parent expectations intersect on a school landscape. The stories highlight the potential for conflict when immigrant students have values shaped by interaction with family and members of their ethnic community as well as values shaped by interaction with peers, teachers, and other members of their North American school communities.

As Ai Mei grows up, she needs to determine which aspects of her home and school communities she incorporates into her own set of values. The age-old tension between children and their parents as children move toward adulthood and make decisions pertaining to their education and the kind of life they see themselves leading is exacerbated by differences in perspective that are influenced by differences in culture between their new host society that the children are navigating and the landscape that their immigrant parents experienced as children in their home countries. This tension is further complicated by struggles that their parents have endured in the immigration process as they settle into new countries. Ai Mei's stories revealed the extent to which ideas for innovative curricula and the good intentions of teachers, administrators, researchers, and policymakers may unfold in unexpected ways. Learning about Ai Mei's conflicting stories to live by highlighted the importance of examining ways in which curriculum and school events may contribute to shaping the ethnic identity of immigrant and minority students in ways much more complex than anticipated by their teachers, their parents, and even the students themselves.

This knowledge, in turn, informs the work of teachers and administrators as they attempt to meet the needs of their increasingly diverse student populations. Teachers need to learn to meet the academic and social needs of their immigrant and minority students in a school context with sometimes little knowledge about the cultures and education systems from which they are coming. In this way, knowledge gained from this study has implications for teachers working in diverse school contexts, professional development for in-service and pre-service educators, and decision making pertaining to the development of curriculum policies for multicultural school contexts. Examining Ai Mei's experiences of the intersection of home and school influences informs the development and implementation of programs designed to facilitate the adaptation of immigrant students in North American schools. Ai Mei's stories of experience may be referred to as an example of a life-based literary narrative (Phillion & He, 2004), and contribute to the body of student lore introduced by Schubert and Ayers (1992) and recognized by Jackson (1992) in Pinar, Reynolds, Slattery, and Taubman's book, *Understanding Curriculum* (1995). Attention to the narratives of students and their families is a reminder not to lose sight of the diversity in student populations and highlights the need for attention to issues of social justice and equity in education. Not only does this research address the dearth of research focused specifically on students' experiences from their perspective, but it also contributes to understanding of the experiences of immigrant and minority students to provide insights into the experiences of a group about which educators and policymakers involved in developing and implementing school curriculum are desperately in need of better understanding.

Conclusion

Teachers and administrators with whom I shared this piece appreciated the acknowledgment of the challenges they encounter in their work with their students. William, as a beginning teacher, recognized the need for further attention to prepare teachers for diverse classrooms and felt that stories such as those presented in this article contributed to raising awareness of difficulties teachers may encounter; he recognized the potential of the stories as a forum to generate discussion among teachers and administrators. His administrators spoke of the challenges inherent to meeting the needs of their student population, and referred to the tensions of needing to abide by existing policies even as they lived the difficulties of implementing some of the policies with their students and teachers.

Exploring the multitude of influences shaping student participation in school curriculum using a narrative inquiry approach to examining student experiences is also a means of acknowledging the complexity of schooling and teacher preparation (Cochran Smith, 2006), and the need for guidance about how best to develop curriculum and pedagogy for students of minority background, and the challenges associated with working with diverse student populations. Given the increasingly diverse North American context, is it essential that educators and policymakers are well informed about the students for whom educational practices and policies are developed.

Appendix B

NOTES

1. Students at Bay Street School chose from IL classes in Cantonese or Mandarin Chinese, Vietnamese, Arabic, Swahili/Black History, or Spanish that were integrated into their regular school day.

2. The Mandarin texts used in the IL program were based on a multi-grade format in which each grade level was in turn divided into six levels of difficulty ranging from beginner to advanced to accommodate for differences in language proficiency among students in the same grade level.

REFERENCES

Ada, A. F. (1988). The Pajaro Valley experience: Working with Spanish-speaking parents to develop children's reading and writing skills in the home through the use of children's literature. In T. Skutnabb-Kangas & J. Cummins (Eds.), *Minority education: From shame to struggle* (pp. 223–237). Clevedon, UK: Multilingual Matters.

Banks, J. A. (1995). Multicultural education: Its effects on students' racial and gender role attitudes. In J. A. Banks & C. A. McGee Banks (Eds.), *Handbook of research on multicultural education* (pp. 617–627). Toronto, Canada: Prentice Hall International.

Bullough, R. V., Jr. (2007). Ali: Becoming a student—A life history. In D. Thiessen & A. Cook-Sather (Eds.), *International handbook of student experience in elementary and secondary school* (pp. 493–516). Dordecht, The Netherlands: Springer.

Carger, C. (1996). *Of borders and dreams: Mexican-American experience of urban education.* New York: Teachers College Press.

Chan, E. (2004). *Narratives of ethnic identity: Experiences of first generation Chinese Canadian students.* Unpublished doctoral dissertation, University of Toronto, Ontario, Canada.

Chan, E., & Ross, V. (2002). *ESL Survey Report. Sponsored by the ESL Work-group in collaboration with the OISE/UT Narrative and Diversity Research Team.* Toronto, Canada: Centre for Teacher Development, Ontario Institute for Studies in Education, University of Toronto, Ontario, Canada.

Clandinin, D. J., & Connelly, F. M. (1994). Personal experience methods. In N. K. Denzin & Y. S. Lincoln (Eds.), *Handbook of qualitative research in the social sciences* (pp. 413–427). Thousand Oaks, CA: Sage.

Clandinin, D. J., & Connelly, F. M. (2000). *Narrative inquiry: Experience and story in qualitative research.* San Francisco: Jossey-Bass.

Clandinin, D. J., & Connelly, F. M. (2002, October). Intersecting narratives: Cultural harmonies and tensions in inner-city urban Canadian schools. Proposal submitted to the Social Sciences and Humanities Research Council of Canada.

Clandinin, D. J., Huber, J., Huber, M., Murphy, M. S., Murray Orr, A., Pearce, M., et al. (2006). *Composing diverse identities: Narrative inquiries into the interwoven lives of children and teachers.* New York: Routledge.

Cochrane, M. (Ed.). (1950). *Centennial story: Board of education for the city of Toronto: 1850–1950.* Toronto, Canada: Thomas Nelson.

Cochran-Smith, M. (1995). Uncertain allies: Understanding the boundaries of race and teaching. *Harvard Educational Review, 65,* 541–570.

Cochran-Smith, M. (2006). Thirty editorials later: Signing off as editor. *Journal of Teacher Education,* 57(2), 95–101.

Conle, C. (2000). The asset of cultural pluralism: an account of cross-cultural learning in pre-service teacher education. *Teaching and Teacher Education, 16,* 365–387.

Connelly, F. M., & Clandinin, D. J. (1988). *Teachers as curriculum planners: Narratives of experience.* New York: Teachers College Press.

Connelly, F. M., & Clandinin, D. J. (1999). Stories to live by: Teacher identities on a changing professional knowledge landscape. In F. M. Connelly & D. J. Clandinin (Eds.), *Shaping a professional identity: Stories of educational practice* (pp. 114–132). London, Canada: Althouse Press.

Connelly, F. M., He, M. F., Phillion, J., Chan, E., & Xu, S. (2004). Bay Street Community School: Where you belong. *Orbit,* 34(3), 39–42.

Connelly, F. M., Phillion, J., & He, M. F. (2003). An exploration of narrative inquiry into multiculturalism in education: Reflecting on two decades of research in an inner-city Canadian community school. *Curriculum Inquiry, 33,* 363–384.

Cook-Sather, A. (2002) Authorizing students' perspectives: toward trust, dialogue, and change in education. *Educational Researcher, 31* (4), 3–14.

Cummins, J. (2001). *Negotiating identities: Education for empowerment in a diverse society* (2nd ed.). Ontario, CA: CABE (California Association for Bilingual Education).

Cummins, J., Bismilla, V., Chow, P., Cohen, S., Giampapa, F., Leoni, L., et al. (2005). Affirming identity in multilingual classrooms. *Educational Leadership,* 63(1), 38–43.

Dewey, J. (1938). *Experience and education.* New York: Simon & Schuster.

Feuerverger, G. (2001). *Oasis of dreams: Teaching and learning peace in a Jewish-Palestinian village in Israel.* New York: Routledge.

Gay, G. (2000). *Culturally responsive teaching: Theory, research, & practice.* New York: Teachers College Press.

He, M. F., Phillion, J., Chan, E., & Xu, S. (2007). Chapter 15—Immigrant students' experience of curriculum. In F. M. Connelly, M. F. He, & J. Phillion (Eds.), *Handbook of curriculum and instruction* (pp. 219–239). Thousand Oaks, CA: Sage.

Igoa, C. (1995). *The inner world of the immigrant child.* New York: St. Martin's Press.

Jackson, P. (1990). *Life in classrooms.* New York: Teachers College Press. Jackson, P. (1992). Conceptions of curriculum specialists. In P. Jackson (Ed.), *Handbook of research on curriculum* (pp. 3–40). New York: Peter Lang.

Kao, G. (1995). Asian Americans as model minorities? A look at their academic performance. *American Journal of Education, 103,* 121–159.

Kim, U., & Chun, M. J. B. (1994). The educational 'success' of Asian Americans: An indigenous perspective. *Journal of Applied Developmental Psychology,* 15, 329–339.

Kouritzin, S. G. (1999). *Face(t)s of first language* loss.Mahwah, NJ: Erlbaum.

Ladson-Billings, G. (1995). Multicultural teacher education: Research, practice, and policy. In J. A. Banks & C. A. McGee Banks (Eds.), *Handbook of research on multicultural education* (pp. 747–759). Toronto, Canada: Prentice Hall International.

Ladson-Billings, G. (2001). *Crossing over to Canaan: The journey of new teachers in diverse classrooms.* San Francisco: Jossey-Bass.

Lee, S. J. (1994). Behind the model-minority stereotype: Voices of high and low-achieving Asian American students. *Anthropology & Education Quarterly,* 25, 413–429.

Lee, S. J. (1996). *Unravelling the "modelminority" stereotype: Listening to Asian American youth.* New York: Teachers College Press.

Lee, S. J. (2001). More than "model minority" or "delinquents": A look at Hmong American high school students. *Harvard Educational Review, 71,* 505–528.

Li, G. (2002). "East is East, West is West"? Home literacy, culture, and schooling. In J. L. Kincheloe & J. A. Jipson (Eds.), *Rethinking childhood book series* (Vol. 28). New York: Peter Lang.

Li, G. (2005). *Culturally contested pedagogy: Battles of literacy and schooling between mainstream teachers and Asian immigrant parents.* Albany, NY: SUNY Press.

McCaleb, S. P. (1994). *Building communities of learners: A collaboration among teachers, students, families and community.* New York: St. Martin's Press.

Moodley, K. A. (1995). Multicultural education in Canada: Historical development and current status. In J. A. Banks & C. A. McGee Banks (Eds.), *Handbook of research on multicultural education* (pp. 801–820). Toronto, Canada: Prentice Hall International.

Nieto, S., & Bode, P. (2008). *Affirming diversity: The sociopolitical context of multicultural education* (5th ed.). New York: Longman.

Phillion, J., & He, M. F. (2004). Using life based literary narratives in multicultural teacher education. *Multicultural Perspectives, 6*(2), 3–9.

Pinar, W. F., Reynolds, W. M., Slattery, P., & Taubman, P. M. (1995). *Understanding curriculum: An introduction to the study of historical and contemporary curriculum discourses.* New York: Peter Lang.

Rodriguez, R. (1982). *Hunger of memory: The education of Richard Rodriguez.* Boston: David R. Godine.

Rolon-Dow, R. (2004). Seduced by images: Identity and schooling in the lives of Puerto Rican girls. *Anthropology & Education Quarterly, 35,* 8–29.

Ross, V., & Chan, E. (2008). Multicultural education: Raj's story using a curricular conceptual lens of the particular. *Teaching and Teacher Education, 24,* 1705–1716.

Sarroub, L. K. (2005). *All-American Yemeni girls: Being Muslim in a public school.* Philadelphia: University of Pennsylvania Press.

Schubert, W., & Ayers, W. (Eds.) *Teacher lore: Learning from our own experience.* New York: Longman.

Smith-Hefner, N. (1993). Education, gender, and generational conflict among Khmer refugees. *Anthropology & Education Quarterly, 24,* 135–158.

Statistics Canada. (2008). *Canada's ethnocultural mosaic, 2006* census. Retrieved July 1, 2008, from http://www12.statcan.ca/english/census06/analysis/ethnic-origin/pdf/97-562-XIE2006001.pdf

U.S. Census Bureau. (2002). *United States Census 2000.* Washington, D.C: U.S. Government Printing Office.

Valdes, G. (1996). *Con respeto: Bridging the distances between culturally diverse families and schools. An ethnographic portrait.* New York: Teachers College Press.

Villegas, A. M. (1991). *Culturally responsive pedagogy for the 1990's and beyond.* Princeton, NJ: Educational Testing Service.

Wong-Fillmore, L. (1991). When learning a second language means losing the first. *Early Childhood Research Quarterly, 6,* 323–346.

Zine, J. (2001). Muslim youth in Canadian schools: Education and the politics of religious identity. *Anthropology & Education Quarterly, 32,* 399–423.

AUTHOR NOTE

Elaine Chan is an assistant professor of Diversity and Curriculum Studies in the Department of Teaching, Learning, and Teacher Education at the College of Education and Human Sciences, the University of Nebraska-Lincoln. Her research and teaching interests are in the areas of: narrative inquiry, culture and curriculum; multicultural education; ethnic identity of first-generation North Americans; student experiences of schooling; and educational equity policies. She has taught and conducted long-term classroom-based research in Canadian, Japanese, and American schools. She is currently co-authoring a book on engaging ELL students in arts education with Margaret Macintyre Latta.

Appendix B

Appendix C

A Phenomenological Study—
"Cognitive Representations of AIDS"

Elizabeth H. Anderson

Margaret Hull Spencer

C ognitive representations of illness determine behavior. How persons living with AIDS image their disease might be key to understanding medication adherence and other health behaviors. The authors' purpose was to describe AIDS patients' cognitive representations of their illness. A purposive sample of 58 men and women with AIDS were interviewed. Using Colaizzi's (1978) phenomenological method, rigor was established through application of verification, validation, and validity. From 175 significant statements, 11 themes emerged. Cognitive representations included imaging AIDS as death, bodily destruction, and just a disease. Coping focused on wiping AIDS out of the mind, hoping for the right drug, and caring for oneself. Inquiring about a patient's image of AIDS might help nurses assess coping processes and enhance nurse-patient relationships.

A 53-year-old man with a history of intravenous drug use, prison, shelters, and methadone maintenance described AIDS as follows:

> My image of the virus was one of total destruction. It might as well
> have killed me, because it took just about everything out of my life. It

Authors' Note: This study was funded in part by a University of Connecticut Intramural Faculty Small Grants and School of Nursing Dean's Fund.

We wish to thank Cheryl Beck, D.N.Sc., and Deborah McDonald, Ph.D., for reading an earlier draft. Special thanks go to Stephanie Lennon, BSN, for her research assistance.

Address reprint requests to Elizabeth H. Anderson, Ph.D., A.P.R.N., Assistant Professor, University of Connecticut School of Nursing, 231 Glenbrook Road, U-2026, Storrs, CT 06269-2026, USA.

was just as bad as being locked up. You have everything taken away from you. The only thing to do is to wait for death. I was afraid and I was mad. Mostly I didn't care about myself anymore. I will start thinking about the disease, and I'll start wondering if these meds are really going to do it for me.

To date, 36 million people worldwide (Centers for Disease Control and Prevention [CDC], 2001b) are infected with Human Immunodeficiency Virus (HIV) that develops into end-stage Acquired Immunodeficiency Syndrome (AIDS). In the United States, 448,060 have died of AIDS-related illnesses, and more than 322,000 persons are living with AIDS, the highest number ever reported (CDC, 2001a).With HIV/AIDS, 95% adherence to antiretroviral (ART) drug regimens is necessary for complete viral suppression and prevention of mutant strains (Bartlett & Gallant, 2001). Adherence to ART regimens can slow the disease process but does not cure HIV or AIDS. Persons with AIDS experience numerous side effects associated with ART drugs, which can lead to missed doses, profound weight loss, and decreased quality of life (Douaihy & Singh, 2001). The incidence of HIV/AIDS is reduced through prevention that is dependent on life-long commitment to the reduction of high-risk drug and sexual behaviors. To achieve maximum individual and public health benefits, it might be helpful to explore patients' lived experience of AIDS within the framework of the self-regulation model of illness.

In the Self-Regulation Model of Illness Representations, patients are active problem solvers whose behavior is a product of their cognitive and emotional responses to a health threat (Leventhal, Leventhal, & Cameron, 2001). In an ongoing process, people transform internal (e.g., symptoms) or external (e.g., laboratory results) stimuli into cognitive representations of threat and/or emotional reactions that they attempt to understand and regulate. The meaning placed on a stimulus (internal or external) will influence the selection and performance of one or more coping procedures (Leventhal, Idler, & Leventhal, 1999). Emotions influence the formation of illness representations and can motivate a person to action or dissuade him or her from it. Appraisal of the consequences of coping efforts is the final step in the model and provides feedback for further information processing.

Although very individual, illness representations are the central cognitive constructs that guide coping and appraisal of outcomes. A patient's theory of illness is based on many factors, including bodily experience, previous illness, and external information. An illness representation has five sets of attributes: (a) identity (i.e., label, symptoms), (b) time line (i.e., onset, duration), (c) perceived cause (i.e., germs, stress, genetics), (d) consequences (i.e., death, disability, social loss), and (e) controllability (i.e., cured, controlled) (Leventhal, Idler, et al., 1999; Leventhal, Leventhal, et al., 2001).

Attributes have both abstract and concrete form. For example, the attribute "identity" can have an abstract disease label (e.g., AIDS) and concrete physical symptoms (e.g., nausea and vomiting). Symptoms are convenient and available cues or suggestions that can shape an illness representation and help a person correctly or incorrectly interpret the experience. Although symptoms are not medically associated with hypertension, patients who believed medications reduced their symptoms reported greater adherence and better blood pressure control (Leventhal, Leventhal, et al., 2001).

Understanding how individuals cognitively represent AIDS and their emotional responses can facilitate adherence to therapeutic regimens, reduce high-risk behaviors, and enhance quality of life. Phenomenology provides the richest and most descriptive data (Streubert & Carpenter, 1999) and thus is the ideal research process for eliciting cognitive representations. Consequently, the purpose of this study was to explore patients' experience and cognitive representations of AIDS within the context of phenomenology.

REVIEW OF THE LITERATURE

Vogl et al. (1999), in a study of 504 ambulatory patients with AIDS who were not taking protease inhibitor (PI) drugs, found the most prevalent symptoms were worry, fatigue, sadness, and pain. Both the number of symptoms and the level of symptom distress were associated with psychological distress and poorer quality of life. Persons with a history of intravenous drug use reported more symptoms and greater symptom distress. In contrast, a telephone survey and chart review of 45 men and women with HIV/AIDS suggested that PI therapy was associated with weight gain, improved CD4 counts, decreased HIV RNA viral loads, fewer opportunistic infections, and better quality of life (Echeverria, Jonnalagadda, Hopkins, & Rosenbloom, 1999).

Reporting on pain from patients' perspective, Holzemer, Henry, and Reilly (1998) noted that 249 AIDS patients reported experiencing a moderate level of pain, but only 80% had effective pain control. A higher level of pain was associated with lower quality of life. In a phenomenological study focusing on pain, persons with HIV/AIDS viewed pain as not only physical but also an experience of loss, not knowing, and social (Laschinger & Fothergill-Bourbonnais, 1999).

Turner (2000), in a hermeneutic study of HIV-infected men and women, found that AIDS-related multiple loss was an intense, repetitive process of grief. Two constitutive patterns emerged: Living with Loss and Living beyond Loss. Likewise, Brauhn (1999), in a phenomenological study of 12 men and 5 women, found that although persons with HIV/AIDS experienced their illness as a chronic disease, their illness had a profound and pervasive impact on their identity. Participants planned for their future with cautious optimism but could identify positive aspects about their illness.

McCain and Gramling (1992), in a phenomenological study on coping with HIV disease, reported three processes: Living with Dying, Fighting the Sickness, and Getting Worn Out. Koopman et al. (2000) found that among 147 HIV-positive persons, those with the greatest level of stress in their daily lives had lower incomes, disengaged behaviorally/emotionally in coping with their illness, and approached interpersonal relationships in a less secure or more anxious manner. With somewhat similar results, Farber, Schwartz, Schaper, Moonen, and McDaniel (2000) noted that adaptation to HIV/AIDS was associated with lower psychological distress, higher quality of life, and more positive personal beliefs related to the world, people, and self-worth. Fryback and Reinert (1999), in a qualitative study of women with cancer and men with HIV/AIDS, found spirituality to be an essential component to health and well-being. Respondents who found meaning in their disease reported a better quality of life than before diagnosis.

Dominguez (1996) summarized the essential structure of living with HIV/AIDS for women of Mexican heritage as struggling in despair to endure a fatal, transmittable, and socially stigmatizing illness that threatens a woman's very self and existence. Women were seen as suffering in silence while experiencing shame, blame, and concern for children. In a phenomenological study of five HIV-infected African American women, 12 themes emerged, ranging from violence, shock, and denial to uncertainty and survival (Russell & Smith, 1999). The researchers concluded that women have complex experiences that need to be better understood before effective health care interventions can be designed.

No studies reported AIDS patients' cognitive representations or images of AIDS. Consequently, this study focused on how persons with AIDS cognitively represented and imaged their disease.

METHOD

Sample

A purposive sample of 41 men and 17 women with a diagnosis of AIDS participated in this phenomenological study. Participants were predominately Black (40%), White (29%), and Hispanic (28%). Average age was 42 years (*SD* = 8.2). The majority had less than a high school education (52%) and were never married (53%), although many reported being in a relationship. Mean CD4 count was 153.4 (*SD* = 162.8) and mean viral load, 138,113 (*SD* = 270,564.9). Average time from HIV diagnosis to interview was 106.4 months (*SD* = 64.2). Inclusion criteria were (a) diagnosis of AIDS, (b) 18 years of age or older, (c) able to communicate in English, and (d) Mini-Mental Status exam score > 22.

Research Design

In phenomenology, the researcher transcends or suspends past knowledge and experience to understand a phenomenon at a deeper level (Merleau-Ponty, 1956). It is an attempt to approach a lived experience with a sense of "newness" to elicit rich and descriptive data. Bracketing is a process of setting aside one's beliefs, feelings, and perceptions to be more open or faithful to the phenomenon (Colaizzi, 1978; Streubert & Carpenter, 1999). As a health care provider for and researcher with persons with HIV/AIDS, it was necessary for the interviewer to acknowledge and attempt to bracket those experiences. No participant had been a patient of the interviewer.

Colaizzi (1978) held that the success of phenomenological research questions depends on the extent to which the questions touch lived experiences distinct from theoretical explanations. Exploring a person's image of AIDS taps into a personal experience not previously studied or shared clinically with health care providers.

PROCEDURE

After approval from the university's Institutional Review Board and a city hospital's Human Subject Review Committee, persons who met inclusion criteria were approached and asked to participate. Interviews were conducted over 18 months at three sites dedicated to persons with HIV/ AIDS: a hospital-based clinic, a long-term care facility, and a residence. All interviews were tape-recorded and transcribed verbatim. Participants were involved in multiple life situations and were unavailable for repeated interviews related to personal plans, discharge, returning to life on the street, or progression of the disease. One participant died within 4 weeks of the interview. Interviews lasted between 10 and 40 minutes and proceeded until no new themes emerged. Persons who reported not thinking about AIDS provided the shortest interviews. Consequently, to obtain greater richness of data and variation of images, we interviewed 58 participants (Morse, 2000). The first researcher conducted all 58 interviews.

After obtaining informed consent, each participant was asked to verbally respond to the following: "What is your experience with AIDS? Do you have a mental image of HIV/AIDS, or how would you describe HIV/ AIDS? What feelings come to mind? What meaning does it have in your life?" As the richness of cognitive representations emerged, it became apparent that greater depth could be achieved by asking participants to draw their image of AIDS and provide an explanation of their drawing. Eight participants drew their image of AIDS.

Background information was obtained through a paper-and-pencil questionnaire. Most recent CD4 and Viral Load laboratory values were obtained from patient charts. Based on institution policy, participants at the long-term care facility and residence received a $5.00 movie pass. Clinic participants received $20.00.

Data Analysis

Colaizzi's (1978) phenomenological method was employed in analyzing participants' transcripts. In this method, all written transcripts are read several times to obtain an overall feeling for them. From each transcript, significant phrases or sentences that pertain directly to the lived experience of AIDS are identified. Meanings are then formulated from the significant statements and phrases. The formulated meanings are clustered into themes allowing for the emergence of themes common to all of the participants' transcripts. The results are then integrated into an in-depth, exhaustive description of the phenomenon. Once descriptions and themes have been obtained, the researcher in the final step may approach some participants a second time to validate the findings. If new relevant data emerge, they are included in the final description.

Appendix C

Methodological rigor was attained through the application of verification, validation, and validity (Meadows & Morse, 2001). Verification is the first step in achieving validity of a research project. This standard was fulfilled through literature searches, adhering to the phenomenological method, bracketing past experiences, keeping field notes, using an adequate sample, identification of negative cases, and interviewing until saturation of data was achieved (Frankel, 1999; Meadows & Morse, 2001). Validation, a within-project evaluation, was accomplished by multiple methods of data collection (observations, interviews, and drawings), data analysis and coding by the more experienced researcher, member checks by participants and key informants, and audit trails. Validity is the outcome goal of research and is based on trustworthiness and external reviews. Clinical application is suggested through empathy and assessment of coping status (Kearney, 2001).

RESULTS

From 58 verbatim transcripts, 175 significant statements were extracted. Table 1 includes examples of significant statements with their formulated meanings. Arranging the formulated meanings into clusters resulted in 11 themes. Table 2 contains two examples of theme clusters that emerged from their associated meanings.

Theme 1: Inescapable death. Focusing on negative consequences of their disease was the pervading image for many persons with AIDS. Responding quickly and spontaneously, AIDS was described as "death, just death," "leprosy," "a nightmare," "a curse," a "black cloud," and "an evil force getting back at you." The sense of not being able to escape was evident in descriptions of AIDS as "The blob. It's a big Jell-O thing that comes and swallows you up" and "It's like I'm in a hole and I can't get out." Another stated, "AIDS, it's a killer and it will get you at any God-given time."

A sense of defeat was evident in a Hispanic man's explanation that with AIDS you are a "goner." He stated, "With HIV you still have a chance to fight. Once that word 'AIDS' starts coming up in your records, you bought a ticket [to death]."

A 29-year-old woman, diagnosed with HIV and AIDS 9 months before the interview, drew a picture of a grave with delicate red and yellow flowers and wrote on the tomb stone "RIP Devoted Sister and Daughter." Over

Table 1   Selected Examples of Significant Statements of Persons With AIDS and Related Formulated Meanings

Significant Statement	Formulated Meaning
In the beginning, I had a sense that I did have it, so it wasn't an unexpected thing although it did bother me. I know it was a bad thing to let it traumatize so.	AIDS is such a traumatizing reality that people have difficulty verbalizing the word "AIDS."
[AIDS] a disease that has no cure. Meaning of dread and doom and you got to fight it the best way you can. You got to fight it with everything you can to keep going.	AIDS is a dangerous disease that requires every fiber of your being to fight so you can live.
I see people go from somebody being really healthy to just nothing—to skin and bones and deteriorate. I've lost a lot of friends that way. It's nothing pretty. I used to be a diesel mechanic. I can't even carry groceries up a flight of stairs anymore.	As physical changes are experienced, an image of AIDS wasting dominates thoughts.
First image—death. Right away fear and death. That's because I didn't know any better. Now it's destruction. Pac-man eating all your immune cells up and you have nothing to fight with.	Overwhelming image of AIDS is one of death and destruction, with no hope of winning

the grave, she drew a black cloud with the sun peeking around the edge, which she described as symbolizing her family's sadness at her death.

Theme 2: Dreaded bodily destruction. In this cluster, respondents focused on physical changes associated with their illness. AIDS was envisioned as people who were skin and bones, extremely weak, in pain, losing their minds, and lying in bed waiting for the end. Descriptions were physically consistent but drawn from a variety of experiences, such as seeing a family member or friend die from AIDS, or from pictures of holocaust victims. It is an ending that is feared and a thought that causes

Table 2	Example of Two Theme Clusters With Their Associated Formulated Meanings

Dreaded bodily destruction

Physical changes include dry mouth, weight loss, mental changes

Expects tiredness, loss of vision, marks all over the body

Holocaust victims

Confined to bed with sores all over

Extreme weight loss

Horrible way to die

Changes from being really healthy to skin and bones

Bodily deterioration

Devouring life

Whole perspective on life changed

Never had a chance to have a family

Life has stopped

No longer able to work

Will never have normal relations with women

Uncertain what's going to happen from day to day

Worked hard and lost everything

deep pain. Body image became a marker for level of wellness or approach of death.

One woman described her image of AIDS as a skeleton crying. An extremely tall, thin man awaiting a laryngectomy on the eve of his 44th birthday described his image of AIDS by saying, "Look at me." Another recalled Tom Hanks in the movie *Philadelphia* (Saxon & Demme, 1993): "The guy in the hospital and how he aged and how thin he got. You start worrying about . . . you don't want to end like that. I don't like the image I see when I see AIDS." A 53-year-old man with a 10-year history of HIV/AIDS drew his image of AIDS as a devil with multiple ragged horns, bloodshot eyes, and a mouth with numerous sharp, pointed teeth. He described the mouth as "teeth with blood dripping down and sucking you dry." Another man drew AIDS as an angry purple animal with red teeth. He stated the color purple symbolized a "bruise" and the red teeth "destruction." The extensive physical and emotional devastation of AIDS was evident in the drawing by a 36-year-old Black woman, who pictured herself lying on a bed surrounded by her husband and children. She wrote, "Pain from head to toe, no hair, 75 pounds, can't move, can't eat, lonely and scared. Family loving you and you can't love them back."

Theme 3: Devouring life. Persons grieved for their past lives. A 41-year-old man described AIDS as, "It's not like I can walk around the corner or go to the park with friends because it has devoured your life." Another man noted, "My life has stopped." A 48-year-old woman stated, "I feel like I have no life. It has changed my whole perspective."

With the diagnosis of AIDS, dreams of marrying, having children, or working were no longer perceived as possible. The impact on each one's life was measured differently from loss of ability to work to loss of children, family, possessions, and sense of oneself. The thought of leaving children, family, and friends was extremely difficult but considered a reality. A woman with four children aged 8 to 12 years stated,

> It's not a disease that you would want to have because it's really bad. I know I get upset sometimes because I have it. You know you are going to die and I have kids. I really don't want to leave them. I want to see them grow up and everything. I know that's not going to happen.

Consistently, participants felt a deep rupture in life as illustrated in the following statement: "It just took my whole life and turned it upside down. I can't do a lot of the things I used to. I lost a house because of it. Everything I worked for I lost." A 44-year-old Hispanic mother of two boys reported with sadness,

> It has affected my life. I have lost my children by not being able to take care of them. It has changed my freedom and relationships. Being sick all the time and I couldn't take care of my little one, so he was taken away from me.

A Black woman described the far-reaching effect AIDS had on her life as follows:

> Everything is different about me now. The way I look, the way I talk, the way I walk, the way I feel on a daily basis. I miss my life before, I really do. I miss it a lot. I don't think about it because it makes me sad.

Theme 4: Hoping for the right drug. In this theme, people focused on pharmacological treatment/cure for AIDS. Hope was evident as participants expressed anticipation that a medication recently started would help them or a cure would be found in their lifetime. One person described it as, "You start becoming anxious and you're hoping that you get some kind of good news today about a new pill or something that's going to help you with the disease." Another, diagnosed within the last 3 years, wondered, "With all the new meds and everything, they say you can live a normal life and a long life. Time will tell, I guess."

Some participants had been told that there were no drugs available for them. A 31-year-old woman, diagnosed for 16 years, reported, "They haven't been able to find a medicine that won't keep me from being sick, so I'm not taking any HIV meds." Others spoke of waiting to see how their bodies responded to newly prescribed ART medications. A Hispanic man articulated his search:

> I try not to let it bother me because my viral load and everything is real low. The meds are not working for me. We [health care provider and patient] are still trying to find the right one. As long as I'm still living, that's what I'm happy about.

The hope of finding a cure was on the minds of many. A 53-year-old man diagnosed for 10 years noted, "I'm just happy to be here now and hope to be here when they find something." Another stated, "Just hope [for a cure] and hold on." In contrast, a 41-year-old man diagnosed for 9 years stated, "There is no cure and I don't see any coming either." A 56-year-old man, living 13 years with HIV/AIDS, expressed a similar view: "I don't think there is a cure, not right around the corner anyhow. Not in my lifetime."

Theme 5: Caring for oneself. Persons with AIDS attempted to control the progress of their disease by caring for themselves. This was evident in the following responses: "If I don't take care of myself, I know I can die from it [AIDS]" and "It's a deadly disease if you don't take care of yourself." A Hispanic man explained, "We never know how long we are going to live. I have to take care of myself if I want to live a couple of years." One woman spoke of her fears and efforts to cope:

> I'm scared—losing the weight and losing the mind and whatnot. I'm scared, but I don't let it get me down. I think about it and whatever is going to happen. I can't stop it. I try to take care of myself and go on.

How to take care of oneself was not always articulated. Eating and taking prescribed medications seemed to be a major focus. "When I get up I know that my first priority is to eat and take my medication." This singleness of purpose is further illustrated in the statement, "I can't think of anything else other than keeping myself healthy so that I can live a little longer. Take my medications. Live a little longer."

Theme 6: Just a disease. In this cluster of images, people cognitively represented the cause of AIDS as "an unseen virus," "like any infection," "a common cold," and "a little mini bug the size of a mite." Minimizing the external cause, one participant viewed AIDS as an "inconvenience" and another as having been dealt a "bad card."

Some normalized AIDS by imaging it as a chronic disease. Like people with cancer or diabetes, persons with AIDS felt the need to get on with their lives and not focus on their illness. The supposition was that if medications were taken and treatments followed they could control their illness the same as persons do with cancer or diabetes. The physical or psychological consequences that occur with other chronic diseases were not mentioned. The following two excerpts illustrate the disease image:

It's just a disease. Since I go to support groups and everything, they tell me to look at it as if it were cancer or diabetes and just do what you have to do. Take your medicine, leave the drugs alone, and you will acquire a long life.

And

[AIDS is] a controllable disease, not a curse. I'm going to control it for the rest of my life. I feel lucky. There is nothing wrong with me. I'm insisting on seeing it that way. It may not be right, but it keeps me going good.

Sometimes, the explanations for AIDS were scientifically incorrect but presented a means for coping. One man described AIDS: "It's just a disease. It's a form of cancer and that's been going on for years and they just come up with the diagnosis."

Theme 7: Holding a wildcat. In this theme, people focused on hypervigilance during battle. While under permanent siege, every fiber of their being was used to fight "a life-altering disease." A 48-year-old man diagnosed 6 months before the interview stated, "I have to pay attention to it. It's serious enough to put me out of work." Another man, diagnosed for 6 years, was firm in his resolve: "I'm a fighter and I'm never going to give up until they come up with a cure for this." These images were essentially positive as can be seen in the following description of AIDS in which a scratch by a wildcat is not "super serious."

> To me HIV is sort of like you've got a wildcat by the head staring you in the face, snapping and snarling. As long as you are attentive, you can keep it at bay. If you lose your grip or don't maintain the attentiveness, it will reach out and scratch you. Which in most cases is not a super serious thing, but it's something of a concern that it will put you in the hospital or something like that. You got to follow the rules quite regimentally and don't let go. If you let go, it will run you over.

Vigilance was used not only to control one's own disease progression but also to protect others. A woman diagnosed for 3 years noted,

> Just being conscious of it because when you got kids and when you got family that you live with, you have to be extremely cautious. You got to realize it at all times. It has to just be stuck in your mind that you have it and don't want to share it. Even attending to one of your children's cuts.

Theme 8: Magic of not thinking. Some made a strong effort to forget their disease and, at times, their need for treatment. A few reported no image of AIDS. Thinking about AIDS caused anger, anxiety, sadness, and depression. Not thinking about AIDS seemed to magically erase the reality, and it provided a means for controlling emotions and the disease. A 41-year-old man who has lived with his disease 10 years described AIDS:

> It's a sickness, but in my mind I don't think that I got it. Because if you think about having HIV, it comes down more on you. It's more like a mind game. To try and stay alive is that you don't even think about it. It's not in the mind.

The extent to which some participants tried not to think about AIDS can be seen in the following descriptions in which the word *AIDS* was not spoken and only referred to as "it." A 44-year-old Hispanic woman stated, "It's a painful thing. It's a sad thing. It's an angry thing. I don't think much of it. I try to keep it out of my mind." Another woman asserted, "It's a terrible experience. It's very bad, I can't even explain it. I never think about it. I try not to think about it. I just don't think about it. That's it, just cross it out of my mind."

Theme 9: Accepting AIDS. In this theme, cognitive representations centered on a general acceptance of the diagnosis of AIDS. Accepting the fact of having AIDS was seen as vital to coping well. People with AIDS readily assessed their coping efforts.

A Hispanic woman noted, "I'm not in denial any more." A 39-year-old Hispanic man who has had the disease for 8 years stated, "Like it or not you have to deal with this disease." Another noted, "You have to live with it and deal with it and that's what I'm trying to do." A 56-year-old man who has had the disease for 13 years summarized his coping:

> Either you adjust or you don't adjust. What are you going to do? That's life. It's up to you. I'm happy. I eat well and I take care of myself. I go out. I don't let this put me in a box. Sometimes you don't like it, but you have to accept it because you really can't change it.

Individuals diagnosed more recently struggled to accept their disease. A Black man diagnosed for 2 years vacillated in his acceptance: "I hate that word. I'm still trying to accept it, I think. Yes, I am trying to accept it." However, he stated that he avoids conversation about HIV/AIDS and is not as open with his family. Another man diagnosed 3 years prior noted,

> I still don't believe that it's happen to me and it's taken all this time to get a grip on it or to deal with it. I still haven't got a grip on it, but I'm trying. It's finally sinking in that I do have it and I'm starting to feel lousy about it.

Neither of these last participants mentioned the word "HIV" or "AIDS."

Theme 10: Turning to a higher power. In this theme, cognitive representations of AIDS were associated with "God," "prayer," "church," and "spirituality." Some saw AIDS as a motivation to change their lives and reach for God. An Hispanic man living with HIV/AIDS for 6 years stated, "If I didn't have AIDS, I'd probably still be out there drinking, drugging, and hurting people. I turned my life around. I gave myself over to the Lord and

Jesus Christ." Another noted, "It [AIDS] worries me. What I do is a lot of praying. It really makes me reach for God."

Others saw religion as a means to help them cope with AIDS. One person expressed it as "I know I can make it from the grace of God. My Jesus Christ is my Savior and that's what's keeping me going every day." One man reported how his spirituality not only helped him cope but also made him a better person:

At one point I just wanted to give up. If it wasn't for knowing the love of Jesus I couldn't have the strength to keep going. I feel today that I'm a better person spiritually. Maybe not healthwise, but more understanding of this disease.

In contrast, a man diagnosed in jail attributed AIDS to a punishment from God: "Sometimes God punishes you. It's like I told my wife. I should have cleaned up my act."

Theme 11: Recouping with time. Although the initial fear and shock was overwhelming, time became a healer such that images, feelings, and processes of coping changed. A sense of imminent doom hurled some into constant preoccupation with their illness, despondency, and increased addiction. Living with HIV/AIDS facilitated change. One woman noted, "When I first found out, I wanted to kill myself and just get it over with. But now it's different. I want to live and just live out the rest of my life." Another described her transition as, "At first I thought I was going to be all messed up, all dried up and looking weird and stuff like that, but I don't think of those things anymore. I just keep living life."

As time passed, negative behaviors were replaced with knowledge about their illness, efforts at medication adherence, and a journey of personal growth facilitated by people who believed in them. One man reported that his initial image changed from being in bed with tubes coming out of his nose and Kaposi sarcoma over his body to living a normal life except for not being able to work.

Change was evident in one man's image of AIDS as a time line. He drew a wide vertical line beginning at the top with the first phase, diagnosis, colored red because "it means things are not good, like a red light on a machine." The next phase was shaded blue and labeled "medication, education, and acceptance" to reflect the sky that he could see from his inpatient bed. The final stage was colored bright yellow and labeled "hope."

A 40-year-old Hispanic man drew a chronicle of his life with five addictive substances beginning with alcohol to the injection of heroin. He then sketched four views of himself showing the end stage of his disease: a standing skeleton without face, hair, clothes, or shoes; a sad-faced person without hair lying in a hospital bed; and a grave with flowers. The final picture drawn was of a drug-free person with a well-developed body, smiling face, hair, shoes, shirt, and shorts, symbolizing his readiness for a vacation in Florida. In contrast, a 53-year-old man reported that in 14 years he had no change in his image of AIDS as a "black cloud."

Results were integrated into an essential schema of AIDS. The lived experience of AIDS was initially frightening, with a dread of body wasting and personal loss.

Cognitive representations of AIDS included inescapable death, bodily destruction, fighting a battle, and having a chronic disease. Coping methods included searching for the "right drug," caring for oneself, accepting the diagnosis, wiping AIDS out of their thoughts, turning to God, and using vigilance. With time, most people adjusted to living with AIDS. Feelings ranged from "devastating," "sad," and "angry" to being at "peace" and "not worrying."

DISCUSSION

In this study, persons with AIDS focused on the end stage of wasting, weakness, and mental incapacity as a painful, dreaded, inevitable outcome. An initial response was to ignore the disease, but symptoms pressed in on their reality and forced a seeking of health care. Hope was manifested in waiting for a particular drug to work and holding on until a cure is found. Many participants saw a connection between caring for themselves and the length of their lives.

Some participants focused on the final outcome of death, whereas others spoke of the emotional and social consequences of AIDS in their lives. Efforts were made to regulate mood and disease by increased attentiveness, controlling thoughts, accepting their illness, and turning to spirituality. Some coped by thinking of AIDS as a chronic illness like cancer or diabetes.

As noted earlier, McCain and Gramling (1992) identified three methods of coping with HIV, namely, Living with Dying, Fighting the Sickness, and Getting Worn Out. Images of Dying and Fighting were strong in Themes 1 (Inescapable Death) and 7 (Holding a Wildcat). Participants in this study were well aware of whether they were coping. Many spoke about accepting or dealing with AIDS, whereas others could not stand the word, tried to wipe it out of their minds, or referred to AIDS as "it."

Consistent with Fryback and Reinert's study (1999), Theme 10, Turning to a Higher Power, emerged as a means of coping as participants faced their mortality. Like Turner's (2000) sample, participants in the current study experienced many changes/losses in their lives and reflected on death and dying. Similar to Turner's theme of Lessons Learned, some participants saw AIDS as a turning point in their lives.

Aligned with Brauhn's (1999) study, chronic disease emerged as an image. In contrast to Brauhn's sample, these participants used the nomenclature of chronic illness to minimize the negative aspects of AIDS. It can be posited that the lack of cautious optimism in planning their future was not present in this study because the entire sample had AIDS.

Theoretical Elements

As Diefenbach and Leventhal (1996) noted, cognitive representations were highly individual and not always in accord with medical facts. Consistent with research in other illnesses, persons with AIDS had cognitive representations reflecting attributes of consequences, causes, disease time line, and controllability (Leventhal, Leventhal, et al., 2001). In particular, we identified three themes that centered on anticipated or experienced consequences associated with AIDS. Inescapable Death and Dreaded Bodily Destruction involved negative physical consequences that are understandable at end stage in a disease with no known cure. The theme Devouring Life focused on the far-reaching emotional, social, and economic consequences experienced by participants. The Just a Disease theme reflected cognitive representations of the cause of AIDS and Recouping with Time had elements of a disease time line from diagnosis to burial.

Six themes (Hoping for the Right Drug, Caring for Oneself, Holding a Wildcat, Magic of Not Thinking, Accepting AIDS, and Turning to a Higher Power) were similar to the controllability attribute of illness representations. Previous research centered on controlling a disease or condition through an intervention by the individual or an expert, such as taking a medication or having surgery (Leventhal, Leventhal, et al., 2001). This finding was substantiated in the themes Hoping for the Right Drug and Caring for Oneself. Unique to this study, persons with AIDS attempted to control not only their emotions but also their disease through vigilance, avoidance, acceptance, and spirituality coping methods. This is particularly evident in the statement that "To try and stay alive is that you don't even think about it." This study extends previous research on illness representations to persons with AIDS and contributes to the theory of Self-Regulation by suggesting that in AIDS coping methods function like the attribute controllability. Of note is that eight participants drew and described their dominant image of AIDS. These drawings provide a unique revelation of participants' concerns, fears, and beliefs. Having participants draw images of AIDS provides a new method of assessing a person's dominant illness representation.

Implications for Nursing

Inquiring about a patient's image of AIDS might be an efficient, cost-effective method for nurses to assess a patient's illness representation and coping processes as well as enhance nurse-patient relationships. Patients who respond that AIDS is "death" or "they wipe it out of their minds" might need more psychological support.

Many respondents used their image of AIDS as a starting point to share their illness experiences. As persons with AIDS face their mortality, reminiscing with someone who treasures their stories can be a priceless gift. Asking patients about their image of AIDS might touch feelings not previously shared and facilitate patients' self-discovery and acceptance of their illness.

Future Research

Cognitive representations have been identified with AIDS. From this research, it can be posited that how a person images AIDS might influence medication adherence, high-risk behavior, and quality of life. If persons with AIDS believed that there is no hope for them, would they adhere to a difficult medication regimen or one with noxious side effects? Would a person who experienced emotional and social consequences of AIDS be more likely to protect others from contracting the disease? Would it be reasonable to expect that persons who focus on fighting AIDS or caring for themselves would be more likely to adhere to medication regimens? Do persons who turn to a higher power, accept their diagnosis, or minimize the disease have a better quality of life? Further research combining images of AIDS and objective measures of medication adherence, risk behaviors, and quality of life is needed to determine if there is an association between specific illness representations and adherence, risk behaviors, and/or quality of life.

REFERENCES

Bartlett, J. G., & Gallant, J. E. (2001). *Medical management of HIV infection, 2001–2002.* Baltimore: Johns Hopkins University, Division of Infectious Diseases.

Brauhn, N. E. H. (1999). *Phenomenology of having HIV/AIDS at a time when medical advances are improving prognosis.* Unpublished doctoral dissertation, University of Iowa.

Centers for Disease Control and Prevention. (2001a). HIV and AIDS—United States, 1981–2000. *MMWR 2001, 50*(21), 430–434.

Centers for Disease Control and Prevention. (2001b). The global HIV and AIDS epidemic, 2001. *MMWR 2001, 50*(21), 434–439.

Colaizzi, P. F. (1978). Psychological research as the phenomenologist views it. In R. Valle & M. King (Eds.), *Existential phenomenological alternatives in psychology* (pp. 48–71). New York: Oxford University Press.

Diefenbach, M. A., & Leventhal, H. (1996). The common-sense model of illness representation: Theoretical and practical considerations. *Journal of Social Distress and the Homeless, 5*(1), 11–38.

Dominguez, L. M. (1996). *The lived experience of women of Mexican heritage with HIV/AIDS.* Unpublished doctoral dissertation, University of Arizona.

Douaihy, A., & Singh, N. (2001). Factors affecting quality of life in patients with HIV infection. *AIDS Reader, 11*(9), 450–454, 460–461.

Echeverria, P. S., Jonnalagadda, S. S., Hopkins, B. L., & Rosenbloom, C. A. (1999). Perception of quality of life of persons with HIV/AIDS and maintenance of nutritional parameters while on protease inhibitors. *AIDS Patient Care and STDs, 13*(7), 427–433.

Farber, E. W., Schwartz, J. A., Schaper, P. E., Moonen, D. J., & McDaniel, J. S. (2000). Resilience factors associated with adaptation to HIV disease. *Psychosomatics, 41*(2), 140–146.

Frankel, R. M. (1999). Standards of qualitative research. In B. F. Crabtree & W. L. Miller (Eds.), *Doing qualitative research* (2nd ed., pp. 333–346). Thousand Oaks, CA: Sage.

Fryback, P. B., & Reinert, B. R. (1999). Spirituality and people with potentially fatal diagnoses. *Nursing Forum, 34*(1), 13–22.

Holzemer, W. L., Henry, S. B., & Reilly, C. A. (1998). Assessing and managing pain in AIDS care: The patient perspective. *Journal of the Association of Nurses in AIDS Care, 9*(1), 22–30.

Kearney, M. H. (2001). Focus on research methods: Levels and applications of qualitative research evidence. *Research in Nursing & Health, 24,* 145–153.

Koopman, C., Gore, F. C., Marouf, F., Butler, L. D., Field, N., Gill, M., Chen, X., Israelski, D., & Spiegel, D. (2000). Relationships of perceived stress to coping, attachment and social support among HIV positive persons. *AIDS Care, 12*(5), 663–672.

Laschinger, S. J., & Fothergill-Bourbonnais, F. (1999). The experience of pain in persons with HIV/AIDS. *Journal of the Association of Nurses in AIDS Care, 10*(5), 59–67.

Leventhal, H., Idler, E. L., & Leventhal, E. A. (1999). The impact of chronic illness on the self system. In R. J. Contrada & R. D. Ashmore (Eds.), *Self, social identity, and physical health* (pp. 185–208). New York: Oxford University Press.

Leventhal, H., Leventhal, E. A., & Cameron, L. (2001). Representations, procedures, and affect in illness self-regulation: A perceptual-cognitive model. In A. Baum, T. A. Revenson, & J. E. Singer (Eds.), *Handbook of health psychology* (pp. 19–47). Mahwah, NJ: Lawrence Erlbaum.

McCain, N. L., & Gramling, L. F. (1992). Living with dying: Coping with HIV disease. *Issues in Mental Health Nursing, 13*(3), 271–284.

Meadows, L. M., & Morse, J. M. (2001). Constructing evidence within the qualitative project. In J. M. Morse, J. M. Swansen, & A. Kuzel (Eds.), *Nature of qualitative evidence* (pp. 187–200). Thousand Oaks, CA: Sage.

Merleau-Ponty, M. (1956). What is phenomenology? *Cross Currents, 6,* 59–70.

Morse, J. M. (2000). Determining sample size. *Qualitative Health Research, 10*(1), 3–5.

Russell, J. M., & Smith, K. V. (1999). A holistic life view of human immunodeficiency virus-infected African American women. *Journal of Holistic Nursing, 17*(4), 331–345.

Saxon, E. (Producer), & Demme, J. (Producer/Director). (1993). *Philadelphia* [motion picture]. Burbank, CA: Columbia Tristar Home Video.

Streubert, H. J., & Carpenter, D. R. (1999). *Qualitative research in nursing: Advancing the humanistic imperative* (2nd ed.). New York: Lippincott.

Turner, J. A. (2000). *The experience of multiple AIDS-related loss in persons with HIV disease: A Heideggerian hermeneutic analysis.* Unpublished doctoral dissertation, Georgia State University.

Vogl, D., Rosenfeld, B., Breitbart, W., Thaler, H., Passik, S., McDonald, M., et al. (1999). Symptom prevalence, characteristics, and distress in AIDS outpatients. *Journal of Pain and Symptom Management, 18*(4), 253–262.

Appendix D

A Grounded Theory Study—"Developing Long-Term Physical Activity Participation: A Grounded Theory Study With African American Women"

Amy E. Harley

Janet Buckworth

Mira L. Katz

Sharla K. Willis

Angela Odoms-Young

Catherine A. Heaney

Regular physical activity is linked to a reduced risk of obesity and chronic disease. African American women bear a disproportionate burden from these conditions and many do not get the recommended amount of physical activity. Long-term success of interventions to initiate and maintain a physically active lifestyle among African American women has not been realized. By clearly elucidating the process of physical activity adoption and maintenance, effective programming could be implemented to reduce African American women's burden from chronic conditions. In-depth interviews were conducted with physically active African American women. Grounded theory, a rigorous

(Continued)

Amy E. Harley, Harvard School of Public Health, Boston. Janet Buckwork, The Ohio State University School of Physical Activity and Educational Services, Columbus. Mira L. Katz and Sharla K. Willis, The Ohio State University College of Public Health, Columbus. Angela Odoms-Young, Northern Illinois University College of Health and Human Sciences, De Kalb, Illinois. Catherine A. Heaney, Stanford University Psychology Department, California.

Address correspondence to Amy E. Harley, Harvard School of Public Health, 677 Huntington Avenue, 7th Floor, Boston, MA 02115; phone: (617) 582-8292; e-mail: amy_harley@dfci .harvard.edu.

Health Education & Behavior, Vol. 36 (1): 97–112 (February 2009)
DOI: 10.1177/1090198107306434
© 2009 by SOPHE

(Continued)

qualitative research method used to develop theoretical explanation of human behavior grounded in data collected from those exhibiting that behavior, was used to guide the data collection and analysis process. Data derived inductively from the interviews and focus groups guided the development of a behavioral framework explaining the process of physical activity evolution.

Keywords: physical activity; African American; women's health; qualitative research

The link between physical activity and health is well established. Not only does lack of participation in physical activity contribute to the rising obesity rates in the United States, but it also directly contributes to the risk for several chronic diseases and leading causes of death in the United States, such as heart disease, hypertension, Type 2 diabetes, and certain cancers (Friedenreich & Orenstein, 2002; U.S. Department of Health and Human Services [USDHHS], 1996). In addition, regular physical activity is linked to a reduction in the risk of dying prematurely in general and improvements in psychological well-being (USDHHS, 1996). Despite the Centers for Disease Control and Prevention (CDC) and American College of Sports Medicine (ACSM) recommendation to engage in at least 30 min of moderate-intensity activity on 5 or more days per week (Pate et al., 1995) and the Healthy People 2010 objective to increase participation in at least 20 min of vigorous-intensity activity on 3 or more days per week (USDHHS, 2000), only 47.2% of U.S. adults were classified as physically active by the Behavioral Risk Factor Surveillance System in 2003 (CDC, 2003). In addition, about 23% of adults get no physical activity at all (CDC, 2003).

Although lack of physical activity is of concern for the entire U.S. population, it is of particular concern for certain subgroups, including African American women, who remain particularly sedentary (CDC, 2003; National Center for Health Statistics, 2004). In a large study comparing four racial/ethnic groups of women (African American, White, Hispanic, Asian; Brownson et al., 2000), the proportion of African American women reporting recommended levels of regular physical activity was 8.4%, the lowest rate of the four groups. A larger proportion of African American women (37.2%) also reported no leisure time physical activity compared to White (31.7%) or Hispanic (32.5%) women. Other studies of racially diverse women also have shown lower participation for African American women in a wide range of activities, including household and occupational physical activity (Ainsworth, Irwin, Addy, Whitt, & Stolarcyzk, 1999; Sternfeld, Ainsworth, & Quesenberry, 1999). Paired with higher cardiovascular disease death rates than other groups of women (Malarcher et al., 2001), higher obesity rates (USDHHS, 2001), and higher rates of Type 2 diabetes (CDC, 2002), lack of physical activity among African American women is an especially important public health issue to address.

Factors influencing participation in physical activity among African American women have been increasingly studied. Important factors identified in previous studies include the social and physical environment, caregiving/family responsibility roles, hair type, time, cost, enjoyment, and embarrassment (Carter-Nolan, Adams-Campbell, & Williams, 1996; Fleury & Lee, 2006). Studies also have found that these factors vary by racial/ ethnic group (Henderson & Ainsworth, 2000; King et al., 2002). Although this body of literature provides insight into why African American women do not participate in physical activity, studies are not available that weave these factors together to portray an overall understanding of how African American women become and stay physically active.

Researchers also have drawn on the current knowledge of correlates of participation and application of behavioral theory to implement intervention programs to increase physical activity participation among African American women (Banks-Wallace & Conn, 2002; Wilbur, Miller, Chandler, & McDevitt, 2003). Many of these studies resulted in modest success through reduced body weight or blood pressure or increased physical activity level during the short term, thus indicating that physical activity behavior and/or its related health effects can be affected through intervention activities. However, they do not elucidate the pathways linking the key factors and steps in a behavioral process that result in subsequent physical activity participation.

Many studies have attempted to verify these pathways through the application of existing behavioral frameworks in the physical activity domain. Most of them have been focused on explaining variation in physical activity levels and have only been able to account for a small percentage of that change (King, Stokols, Talen, Brassington, & Killingsworth, 2002). Even those that have found support for existing behavioral theories, including investigations of the Transtheoretical Model (TTM; Prochaska & DiClemente, 1983), have not been focused on illustrating the behavioral process of physical activity adoption and maintenance that would be most effective in informing interventions to enhance physical activity participation.

To thoroughly understand this process, the important factors and their interrelationships must be clearly elucidated through continued behavioral theory refinement. In the physical activity domain, theoretical explanation of behavior has shown promise for certain constructs, such as self-efficacy and self-regulation. However, a behavioral theory or framework is not currently available explaining the full process from behavioral adoption through maintenance in this domain. The purpose of this study was to understand this behavioral process among African American women through the development of a theoretical framework explaining the pathways linking the key factors together that result in subsequent integration of physical activity into the lifestyle.

METHOD

A grounded theory approach (Strauss & Corbin, 1998) was selected because of the lack of knowledge regarding the specific factors and factor relationships that comprise the process of physical activity behavioral evolution. An iterative process of data collection and analysis was used to develop a theoretical explanation of human behavior grounded in data collected from those exhibiting that behavior. In this study, the grounded theory approach was used to develop a framework of the process by which physical activity is adopted and maintained among African American women. The study was approved by the Institutional Review Board of The Ohio State University.

Sampling

Purposeful sampling methods (Patton, 1990) were used to gather information-rich cases, primarily criterion sampling. Criterion sampling refers to picking cases that meet some prespecified criterion. Inclusion criteria for this study were African American, female, 25 to 45 years of age, completion of at least some college or technical school beyond high school, and commitment to physical activity. Based on the focus of the study, it was crucial to only include physically active women. Women had to be currently active at recommended levels (CDC, 2001) for at least 1 year. Exclusion criteria included having difficulty walking or moving around, recent diagnosis of an eating disorder, diagnosis with a terminal illness, or having participated in varsity athletics in college or on a professional athletic team. Theoretical sampling (Strauss & Corbin, 1998) also was used to ensure that the women who participated in the study had adequately experienced the phenomenon to provide rich description.

Participants were primarily recruited through two local African American sorority alumni associations. The researcher met with contacts at each sorority and identified meetings or other events where study information could be presented. At each event a sign-up sheet was circulated requesting interested women's names and phone numbers. Follow-up phone calls were made after the events using a comprehensive screening tool addressing each factor of the inclusion and exclusion criteria.

DATA COLLECTION

Data were collected by conducting face-to-face, in-depth interviews. These interviews were guided by the research questions but were unstructured enough to allow the discovery of new ideas and themes. The guide was modified as data collection proceeded to further refine questions that were not eliciting the intended information and to reflect the categories and concepts that required further development (Spradley, 1979; Strauss & Corbin, 1998).

When the interviews and the preliminary data analysis were complete, two focus groups of the study participants were held. The purpose of these groups was to disseminate the preliminary findings from the study and to gather feedback from the participants to ensure that the findings reflected their experience with physical activity. Data from the focus groups were incorporated into the analysis for further refinement of the framework.

All interviews and focus groups were tape-recorded with the permission of the participants and transcribed verbatim. Transcribed interviews and field notes were entered into the Atlas.TI qualitative data analysis program for analysis (Muhr, 1994). The lead researcher performed all data analysis tasks with regular consultation and feedback from the coinvestigators.

Sample Size

In grounded theory, the ultimate criterion for the final sample size is theoretical saturation (Strauss & Corbin, 1998). Theoretical saturation employs the general rule that when building theory, data should be gathered until each category (or theme) is saturated. A sample size of 15 women was used as a baseline (Lincoln & Guba, 1985; Strauss & Corbin, 1998) and theoretical saturation was employed to determine the final sample size.

Thirty women were screened for the study and, of those, 17 women were eligible. Fifteen of the 17 women participated in the interviews. An interview could not be scheduled with 2 women who did not return phone calls from the researcher.

Using theoretical saturation as the desired criterion, interviews were analyzed to determine the need for additional sampling. Based on the depth of the data provided by the 15 women, the scarcity of new information emerging from the last two interviews, and the importance of analyzing the rich experiences of the women in the study in great depth and detail to unearth the structure of a very specific process, sampling for the interviews was completed with 15 women. Characteristics of the participants are presented in Table 1. Nine of the women interviewed also participated in the focus groups.

Data Analysis

The basic principles of grounded theory data analysis (Strauss & Corbin, 1998) guided this study. Microanalysis was used for all of the interviews to ensure that no important ideas or constructs were overlooked. Codes were created for each new idea and themes that were found to be conceptually similar in nature or related in meaning were grouped together as concepts. These concepts were then developed through constant comparison, with the most relevant concepts being integrated to form a theoretical framework. This framework, the final product of the study, explains the central theme of the data as well as accounts for variation.

RESULTS

The Physical Activity Evolution Model

The women's rich and illustrative descriptions provided the basis for the framework explaining the process of physical activity adoption and maintenance. The framework or model, Physical Activity Evolution, presents the psychological and behavioral changes that African American women experienced throughout the process of becoming physically active (see

Table 1 Participant Characteristics

Age (years)	Body Mass Index[a]	Primary Activity	% Active[b]	Time Active	Commit Score[c]
41	29.4	Weights/treadmill	435	1 year	53
35	30.9	Group fitness	465	8 months	
45	21.0	Treadmill	230	4 months	44
31	26.0	Group fitness	590	10+ years	48
42	39.7	Weights/walking	650	2 months	
			280	1+ years	46
			350	3 months	
26	20.4	Weights/misc. cardio[d]	158	1+ years	48
26	19.4	Weights/misc. cardio	1,280	5+ years	43
33	25.8	Dance/volleyball/gym	150	1 year	40
42	23.0	Group fitness	370	15 years	41
33	24.8	Tae Bo/lifestyle	1,305	1 year	49
33	21.1	Exercise videos	165	4 years	41
31	22.1	Weights/misc. cardio	575	20+ years	55
30	27.7	Weights/misc. cardio	120	20+ years	41
45	23.4	Group fitness/running	580	3 years	45
25	21.9	Group fitness/running	280	3 years	52
			490	15+ years	48

a. Body Mass Index calculated from self-reported height and weight.

b. Percentage of minimum eligible physical activity participation criteria as calculated from the adapted Godin Leisure-Time Questionnaire (Godin & Shephard, 1985).

c. Score on the adapted Commitment to Physical Activity Scale (possible range =11 -55; Corbin, Nielsen, Bordsdorf, & Laurie, 1987).

d. Refers to use of miscellaneous cardiovascular fitness equipment, including treadmill, stair stepper, stationary bicycle, and elliptical machine.

Figure 1). The model indicates a main flow through which women progress as well as two alternative loops. Flow through the process is characterized by three phases: the Initiation Phase, Transition Phase, and Integration Phase. Alternative loops are the Modification Loop and the Cessation Loop. Each pivotal psychological or behavioral change is indicated by a step in the process. Arrows direct movement from one step to another, into and out of the loops. An important feature of the process is that it exists within the context of the women's lives, in this case African American social and cultural context. Furthermore, certain conditions emerged as important for helping women progress through the physical activity evolution process, including planning methods, physical activity companions, and types of benefits experienced.

Initiation Phase

The first phase of the process, the Initiation Phase, is characterized by the early decision-making and initiation behaviors of the women. The women entered the process by contemplating the start or restart of physical activity. Although not the only reason, many of the women cited body weight as their impetus to begin a program. In this phase, women were experimenting with physical activity and beginning to experience some of the benefits associated with physical activity participation. It was during the Initiation Phase of the process that women began to learn which activities they enjoyed, how well different activities fit into their schedules, and which ones might meet the needs that prompted physical activity participation (e.g., weight management). One woman said of starting her physical activity program,

> It evolved because baby fat does not go away. So the first baby—I retained 10 pounds . . . the 10 pounds though was the issue for me because after the first baby is when I really started working out.

Shortly after engaging in some form of physical activity, the women started experiencing benefits. Women discussed mental benefits such as feeling good, relieving stress, feeling more alert, and feeling like they were taking time for themselves or taking care of themselves. Other benefits were the discovery of activities that brought them enjoyment or enabled them to do other activities during their exercise sessions such as reading or praying. Although mental benefits dominated the discussions of early exercise experiences, some of the women did experience physical benefits

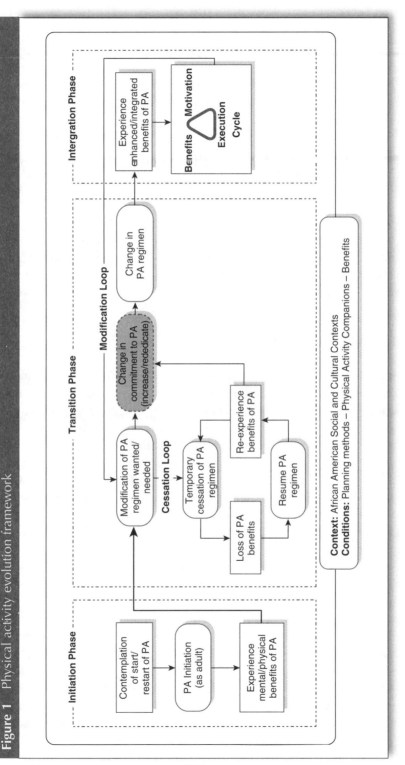

Figure 1 Physical activity evolution framework

early in their physical activity experience, such as initial weight loss, although the majority of these benefits occurred later in the process. Other important benefits experienced during the Initiation Phase included having more energy and sleeping better. One of the women said of the benefits she was experiencing,

> This is something that I need to do because it makes me feel good and it relieves stress . . . even though I'm hot and sweaty and stinky, mentally I feel more alert . . . my body feels more alert . . . I feel more energetic.

Many of the women were juggling careers and family, so time out for themselves was another important benefit of physical activity. One woman explained, "I had a little time for me. I started enjoying it. I started liking it."

Transition Phase

After experiencing the Initiation Phase, women moved into the Transition Phase. The time it took to progress to this phase varied. As women entered the Transition Phase, they became aware that a modification of their regimen was needed. This need arose from a number of situations, including having scheduling problems, not seeing expected benefits, not enjoying chosen routines, or experiencing increased fitness or skill requiring more challenging activities. Women started physical activity and experimented to build experience and knowledge during the Initiation Phase. During the Transition Phase, they then restructured their regimens to fit their lifestyle or desired benefits.

Once the women realized that their regimens needed modification, they needed to commit to their pursuit of a physically active lifestyle and make the necessary changes. For some of the women, this commitment was a reprioritization of physical activity or an increase in their dedication to a physically active lifestyle. For others, it was a reaffirmation of previous commitment. This marks a pivotal point in the process and serves as the bridge through the Transition Phase. This key step in the model is shaded to highlight its importance in the process. Without this conscious commitment to physical activity, the women would not have moved farther along in the process, becoming more experienced with, and dedicated to, a lifetime of physical activity. Some women spoke about this point using words such as "breakthrough" or "light clicking on." For example, one woman said, "So then the light clicked on that I needed to make a change. It is a lifestyle change." Highlighting that change in commitment, one woman explained, "You know you have to increase your exercise . . . you just have to make that change, increase, rededicate. It's a continual thing."

Women talked about realizing that physical activity was something that they would have to do for the rest of their lives. They finally understood that they could not exercise until they reached a short-term goal and then quit and expect to maintain that success. One of the women who had been sporadically exercising in the past for weight control purposes realized

> I have to keep remembering that all these changes are lifestyle changes so I know I am in it for the long haul . . . it is not when I get to my goal weight I am done working out. I know I have to keep working out forever and so sometimes I am a little disenchanted like I got to get up every morning for the rest of my life, but then sometimes I enjoy it. I like the time by myself on the treadmill at the gym with no kids, no husband, so sometimes it's just like freedom.

This quotation was presented during the focus groups and one woman stated, "I know that's me!" when in fact it was another participant. Clearly, the notion of physical activity as a source of personal time or freedom from other obligations was an important benefit for these busy women.

Integration Phase

The Integration Phase represents the last phase of the main flow of the process. At this point in the process, women began to see some of the enhanced results of their efforts and the results that took longer to realize. Many of these results were the physical benefits that the women started physical activity to achieve, including weight loss, weight maintenance, or muscle toning. Enhanced benefits also included health benefits, such as blood pressure or diabetes control. These benefits were more integrated into life or transcendent of the exercise experience, for example, the formation of a new social network or the opportunity to serve as a role model for other women who were trying to become physically active.

Appendix D

After realizing enhanced or integrated benefits, motivation was rein-forced for continuing physical activity. Women wanted to maintain the changes they had achieved. One woman explained,

> But once you actually learn and try to get some benefits from it and it makes you feel better . . . outside of the other health benefits that you know exercise can play. You just want to do it. Sort of like you want to go shopping—you just want to exercise after awhile.

At this point in the process, women entered the Benefits-Motivation-Execution cycle. This cycle indicates that once an appropriate (e.g., fre-quency and intensity) and successful (e.g., consistent) physical activity regimen was planned and executed, enhanced benefits were noticed and these benefits provided motivation to continue, creating a circular cycle. The reason for the cycle occurring at the end of the process is that long-term, significant benefits from physical activity took time and energy to achieve. Because it took time to achieve these benefits, it took time to experience the Benefits-Motivation-Execution cycle.

Experiencing the cycle led women to feel that physical activity had become integrated into their lives. Although they still had to work on maintaining the behavior, some of the early efforts could be relaxed because physical activity had become part of their usual routine. Women described this feeling of integration in a variety of ways, including, "I think it frustrates me not to go. Like something's missing. I'm at that point" and "It's something that's routine, like you get up in the morning and you brush your teeth."

Modification Loop

Although the Benefits-Motivation-Execution cycle appears as the final box in the process, there was an important dynamic component to even the most successful exercise regimens. The dynamic and flexible nature of women's physical activity regimens was expressed in each of the inter-views within the context of each woman's life. After experiencing the cycle and integration, women found themselves having to modify their regi-mens to fit with changes in lifestyles and goals over time as depicted by the feedback arrows at the top of the main flow labeled Modification Loop.

With experience, women learned to change their regimens as needed for reasons that included change in job or school schedule/responsibilities, dealing with a health problem or injury, or change in child care. The

Modification Loop began with the realization that a change to the regimen was wanted or needed and was defined by the decision to continue her commitment to physical activity and make the required changes. By choosing to modify her program and stick with physical activity, she set herself up to continue to see results and to successfully navigate a life change. In doing so, she furthered her experience with the Benefits-Motivation-Execution cycle. For example, one woman describes her work-related modification as follows:

> It used to be up until last week that I got to work at about 10:30 . . . but now [my colleague] is on maternity leave so I am her until the end of the year. In the mornings I used to take my daughter to the bus stop and then I would work out at the Y. But now I have to get up at 6:30, workout, take her to the bus stop, and go straight to [work] so it has been a juggle. We have a gym in our basement so I have been working out in the basement. She has to wake herself up. I set her alarm. I'm working out. By 7:45 I have to be leaving my house—so it has been working.

Alternatively, there were times when women were unwilling or unable to commit to making the necessary changes, resulting in their temporary progression through the Cessation Loop.

Cessation Loop

An important aspect of the dynamic nature of the physical activity regimen was the Cessation Loop. It became apparent in the analysis that there were times when women temporarily could not maintain their physical activity regimens. As the arrows indicate, it is possible to experience the Cessation Loop the first time through the process, after reaching the Benefits-Motivation-Execution cycle (through the Modification Loop), or both.

This loop accommodates the situation revealed in all of the women's lives where regular physical activity had to be temporarily ceased for various reasons. Furthermore, when women fell into this loop early in their experience with physical activity, it was sometimes due to having reached their goals. They thought their mission was accomplished and ceased regular participation. Key to the resumption of physical activity was the loss of benefits from the previous level of involvement. The women knew what they could achieve, so they were aware of what they were missing and wanted to get it back. Thus, even though they were not regularly active at this point in the process, they were different from when they had first adopted the behavior. They now had a frame of reference for what they could achieve through physical activity. This loss served as the motivation to resume physical activity to realize those achievements again. One woman explained,

> So that was that thing where you wake up one morning and you can't fit into your jeans— you're just too big. And that actually happened to me. . . . So I hated that so it was a really good incentive for me to get back into my routine of incorporating exercise back into life.

Successfully executing the regimen and reexperiencing benefits led women back to the main flow of the process with a renewed commitment to physical activity.

The number of times women experienced the Cessation Loop as well as the length of time in the loop varied with each woman. However, it was apparent that temporary hiatus from regular physical activity was a normal part of integrating physical activity into daily life and that navigating potential interruptions was something that needed to be learned. Indeed, the experience of overcoming such challenges improved a woman's belief that she could overcome the next challenge, perhaps without falling into the Cessation Loop.

Context and Conditions

The Physical Activity Evolution process occurred within the context and conditions of the women's lives, such as their social network, racial/cultural background, and elements of their personal experience with physical activity, including their conceptualization of planning and benefits realized. The roles of social network for physical activity and African American social and cultural contexts were significant aspects of the study and will be presented in subsequent articles as they are beyond the scope of this article, which focuses on the framework and personal experiences with physical activity.

Planning Methods

One of the conditions most integral to movement through the process model and interwoven into the women's experiences was their planning practices for physical activity. The two main themes that emerged were Scheduling Physical Activity and Planning Alternates for Missed Sessions. The concept of Planning with Flexibility transcended these themes and described the practices of every woman in the study. Regardless of how they scheduled their regimens, the overall plan for the physical activity sessions had to be flexible and remain dynamic in response to interruptions in daily life. A taxonomy of the key concepts related to planning methods is presented in Figure 2. Illustrative quotations for this condition are presented in Table 2.

One of the most compelling concepts that emerged from this condition was the technique of scheduling physical activity using the minimum acceptable-maximum possible criterion. This criterion refers to the successful practice of many of the women of planning an ideal number of sessions for the week, a maximum, but also setting a minimum number of sessions that had to be completed. The minimum acceptable-maximum possible conceptualization allowed women to shoot for their highest goal while ensuring they did not fall below a prespecified minimum. This planning method also provided a technique for dealing with missed sessions. Using this criterion, a missed session could either be made up if time permitted or simply skipped if it would not cause the total number of sessions to fall below the minimum.

Although planning methods seems like a very simple condition associated with integration of physical activity into daily life, the overall concept of planning with flexibility was vital and interwoven throughout both main themes. Furthermore, it defined the method by which women incorporated the sessions into their lives and viewed the role of physical activity within the context of their daily experience. Physical activity was a priority, but for it to remain a reality it could not be viewed as static or prescriptive. It had to be dynamic, ever-changing, and constantly adaptable to the ups and downs of life both in terms of daily and long-term challenges.

DISCUSSION

The data provided by the women supplied the foundation for the development of the Physical Activity Evolution behavioral framework describing the adoption and maintenance of physical activity among African American women. The construction of a framework that identifies both

Appendix D

Figure 2 Taxonomy of planning methods

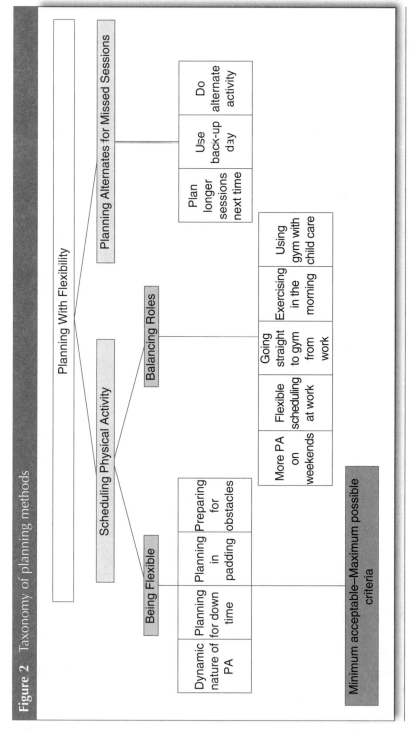

Note: PA = physical activity.

Table 2	Illustrative Quotes for Selected Conditions
Condition	Quotation
Planning Methods	" . . . missing one or two workouts during the week isn't going to cause me to gain all that weight back. You have to be disciplined and again, a little flexibility. I mean I am not going to get depressed and then go eat a bag of Oreo's—okay I missed this and just go ahead. Perhaps there is something I can do, take a walk around the block or something like that in place of it or take the stairs . . . I try to do at least something."
	(from focus group) "Well a lot of the things I liked that you said that you viewed exercise as being dynamic and I think that is important and I think that people who have integrated physical activity into their lifestyle also find the time to have flexibility even though they are being active, they have managed to add some type of flexibility because life situations change. That was good."

psychological and behavioral steps in the process of developing a long-term, physically active lifestyle fills a gap in the literature and serves to forward the science behind the development and implementation of effective physical activity interventions.

Although the call for investigating physical activity as a process has been made (Dishman, 1987), it is difficult to make overall comparisons of the Physical Activity Evolution framework to other behavioral process frameworks because they are largely unavailable. The TTM (Prochaska & DiClemente, 1983) is one of few process models applied to exercise behavior, and the only one widely implemented. In the absence of a selection of process models through which to study exercise behavior, substantive models or frameworks specific to physical activity have been developed but gone largely unnoticed (Laverie, 1998; Medina, 1996). As such, there is no empirical evidence beyond the founding studies to provide support for the utility of these frameworks.

The most pertinent of these studies was a dissertation that undertook a grounded theory study of the journey from nonexerciser to exerciser (Medina, 1996). The resulting framework identified three phases of identity development with some parallels to the Physical Activity Evolution phases. Medina's framework provides support for four important elements of the Physical Activity Evolution model: personal fit of the physical activity regimen, the dynamic nature of the process itself, physical activity as a reinforcing behavior, and integration of physical activity into the lifestyle. These commonalities arising from two separate studies exemplify the potential for understanding physical activity behavior when considered as a process and studied using a contextual method. Although different populations were investigated and the resulting models reflected these differing viewpoints, several important features of the underlying process emerged from both studies.

When considering conceptualizing participation in physical activity as evolving through separate, dynamic phases, as was elucidated in this study, the TTM provides an obvious comparison. The Physical Activity Evolution framework posits a clear Initiation Phase where women are contemplating and subsequently acting on a need or desire to start a physical activity program. In this phase, women are experimenting with the behavior, building skills, and learning what features work for them related to their goals and lifestyles. Support for this finding can be found in a meta-analysis conducted with 80 study samples measuring one or more of the constructs of the TTM (Marshall & Biddle, 2001). The largest effect size was for the movement from Preparation to Action (Cohen's $d = 0.85$), as would be expected. An unexpected finding was evidence of small to moderate increases in physical activity from Precontemplation to Contemplation (Cohen's $d = 0.34$). This finding may provide support for the behavioral experimentation seen in the present study. Even when people have not fully committed to trying to adopt an active lifestyle, they might be testing various aspects of the behavior in preparation for that change in commitment. Without the knowledge and skills gleaned from this phase of the adoption process, the ability to adjust and recommit based on the fit of the regimen would not be possible.

Another key finding of this study was the distinct difference between behavioral acquisition or action and behavioral integration or maintenance. Furthermore, in this study, behavioral integration was elucidated as a dynamic state, one that needed to be periodically evaluated and adjusted via the Modification Loop. Two studies using the TTM provided support for the concept of a dynamic maintenance phase with its own unique characteristics requiring continued use of skills and techniques to maintain the behavior change (Bock, Marcus, Pinto, & Forsyth, 2001; Buckworth & Wallace, 2002). Because long-term behavior change is the primary mechanism by which the health benefits of physical activity can be realized, this aspect of the behavioral framework is an important contribution to the limited work available in the area of understanding of how to maintain this behavior.

The Cessation Loop is another crucial element of the Physical Activity Evolution process. The experience of relapse was universal among the women and not separate from the process of integrating physical activity into daily life. A relapse did not mean she was no longer a physically active woman. More accurately, it meant that she was in a distinct phase of lifestyle integration, which when handled positively, as was the experience of each of the women in this study, would result in further behavioral participation and development of skills in relapse prevention. Women did not revert to the beginning of the process once they overcame relapse because they were different at that point than when they had started; rather, they reentered the process through their renewed commitment (in the Transition Phase). This concept of potentially cycling back through phases while remaining different from when the process began also is reflected in Medina's (1996) finding. The spiral conceptualization of the TTM (Prochaska, DiClemente, & Norcross, 1992) also allows for relapse and recycling through the stages. There is limited evidence available on the application of the TTM in the physical activity domain using a relapse conceptualization. However, one study was found (Bock et al., 2001) that provided support for this phase of the behavioral process. Further support for conceptualizing relapse as a natural phase of physical activity adoption and maintenance whose successful navigation is crucial to progression through the process can be found from application of the Relapse Prevention Model (RPM; Marlatt & Gordon, 1985) in the physical activity domain (Belisle, Roskies, & Levesque, 1987; King & Frederiksen, 1984).

In general, studies investigating the full process of physical activity adoption through maintenance provide the best comparison to the current theory. It is clear that work is limited in this area. The actual process of behavioral integration in the physical activity domain has remained largely untapped. Medina's (1996) study and some of the work using the TTM and RPM provide support for the present study's conceptualization of this process. There is still much work to be done. Once the full process of behavioral integration is better understood, constructs can be operationalized and pathways postulated and quantified. Until then, further attention is needed to refining, and in some cases integrating, the process models available at this time.

PRACTICAL IMPLICATIONS

Although the process model proposed in this study is a new framework for understanding physical activity evolution among African American women, the following important lessons can be garnered for future efforts at program design: (a) attention should be paid to learning how to navigate life changes and potential obstacles after the Integration Phase by including techniques for modifying a regimen to fit into daily life, plans for dealing with future challenges, and learning a variety of activity options for different goals and preferences; (b) during the Initiation Phase, programs should focus on the fit of the prescribed regimen to the desired goals of the woman, ensuring that the selected activities fit both her lifestyle and the results important to her; and (c) programs should guide women in the planning of their physical activity regimens to include flexibility and dynamic qualities, perhaps using the minimum acceptable-maximum possible criteria.

STUDY LIMITATIONS

Limitations of this study stem from two main areas: the chosen methodology and the study population. Grounded theory requires data collection in an environment constructed by the researcher and the participant. Although measures were put in place to maximize credibility and dependability, it is possible that different investigators with different groups of participants would have had different findings. Another factor to consider is selection bias. It is possible that women who desired to participate were somehow different than those who elected not to call or those that decided not to participate after screening.

Although each of these limitations should be considered, many elements of the study design were included to ensure that the study was not weakened by these issues. For example, peer debriefing and member checking were both used to ensure that the conclusions of the researcher were indeed grounded in the data. Transcripts were reviewed by the principal investigator and her coinvestigators to check for appropriate interview style and rich data quality. Careful documentation of each data collection and analysis phase was employed. These methods exemplify only a few of the techniques used to ensure that the data collected were of high quality and that the conclusions inferred from those data were grounded in the women's experiences.

Appendix D

CONCLUSION

This study has made an important contribution to the knowledge base on the development of physical activity among African American women. Future studies can use the knowledge gained to further theory development in this area and expand theory development to women of other backgrounds and situations. These findings also can be used to inform intervention development and spur further investigation into some of the important practical implications. Furthermore, the concept of investigating health behaviors among people who have successfully incorporated those behaviors into their daily lives should be further used in research studies. By studying women who have successfully adopted a behavior, strategies to overcome known barriers can be elucidated and applied to intervention planning for other women.

REFERENCES

Ainsworth, B. E., Irwin, M., Addy, C., Whitt, M., & Stolarcyzk, L. (1999). Moderate physical activity patterns of minority women: The cross-cultural activity participation study. *Journal of Women's Health and Gender-Based Medicine, 8(6)*, 805–813.

Banks-Wallace, J., & Conn, V. (2002). Intervention to promote physical activity among African American women. *Public Health Nursing, 19(5)*, 321–335.

Belisle, M., Roskies, E., & Levesque, J. M. (1987). Improving adherence to physical activity. *Health Psychology, 6(2)*, 159–172.

Bock, B. C., Marcus, B. H., Pinto, B. M., & Forsyth, L. H. (2001). Maintenance of physical activity following an individualized motivationally tailored intervention. *Annals of Behavioral Medicine, 23(2)*, 79–87.

Brownson, R., Eyler, A., King, A. C., Brown, D., Shyu, Y. -L., & Sallis, J. (2000). Patterns and correlates of physical activity among U.S. women 40 years and older. *American Journal of Public Health, 90(2)*, 264–270.

Buckworth, J., & Wallace, L. S. (2002). Application of the Transtheoretical Model to physically active adults. *Journal of Sports Medicine and Physical Fitness, 42(3)*, 360–367.

Carter-Nolan, P. L., Adams-Campbell, L. L., & Williams, J. (1996, September). Recruitment strategies for Black women at risk for non-insulin-dependent diabetes mellitus into exercise protocols: A qualitative assessment. *Journal of the National Medical Association, 88*, 558–562.

Centers for Disease Control and Prevention. (2001). Physical activity trends: United States, 1990–1998. *MMWR Weekly, 50(9)*, 166–169.

Centers for Disease Control and Prevention. (2002). *Chronic disease overview: U.S. Department of Health and Human Services.* Washington, DC: Author.

Centers for Disease Control and Prevention. (2003). *Behavioral risk factor surveillance system survey data.* Atlanta, GA: Author.

Corbin, C., Nielsen, A., Bordsdorf, L., & Laurie, D. (1987). Commitment to physical activity. *International Journal of Sport Psychology, 18,* 215–222.

Dishman, R. (1987). Exercise adherence and habitual physical activity. In W. P. Morgan & S. G. Goldstein (Eds.), *Exercise and mental health* (pp. 57–83) Washington, DC: Hemisphere.

Fleury, J., & Lee, S. M. (2006). The Social Ecological Model and physical activity in African American women. *American Journal of Community Psychology, 37,* 129–140.

Friedenreich, C., & Orenstein, M. (2002). Physical activity and cancer prevention: Etiologic evidence and biological mechanisms. *Journal of Nutrition, 132,* 3456S–3465S.

Godin, G., & Shephard, R. (1985). A simple method to assess exercise behavior in the community. *Canadian Journal of Applied Sports Science, 10,* 141–146.

Henderson, K., & Ainsworth, B. (2000). Sociocultural perspectives on physical activity in the lives of older African American and American Indian women: A cross-cultural activity participation study. *Women and Health, 31(1),* 1–20.

King, A. C., Castro, C., Wilcox, S., Eyler, A., Sallis, J., & Brownson, R. (2000). Personal and environmental factors associated with physical inactivity among different racial-ethnic groups of U.S. middle-aged and older-aged women. *Health Psychology, 19(4),* 354–364.

King, A. C., & Frederiksen, L. W. (1984). Low-cost strategies for increasing exercise behavior: Relapse preparation training and social support. *Behavior Modification, 8(1),* 3–21.

King, A. C., Stokols, D., Talen, E., Brassington, G. S., & Killingsworth, R. (2002). Theoretical approaches to the promotion of physical activity: Forging a transdisciplinary paradigm. *American Journal of Preventive Medicine, 23(2S),* 15–25.

Laverie, D. A. (1998). Motivations for ongoing participation in a fitness activity. *Leisure Sciences, 20(4),* 277–302.

Lincoln, Y. S., & Guba, E. G. (1985). *Naturalistic inquiry.* Beverly Hills, CA: Sage.

Malarcher, A., Casper, M., Matson-Koffman, D., Brownstein, J., Croft, J., & Mensah, G. (2001). Women and cardiovascular disease: Addressing disparities through prevention research and a national comprehensive state-based program. *Journal of Women's Health and Gender-Based Medicine, 10(8),* 717–724.

Marlatt, G. A., & Gordon, J. R. (1985). *Relapse prevention: Maintenance strategies in the treatment of addictive behaviors.* New York: Guilford.

Marshall, S., & Biddle, S. (2001). The transtheoretical model of behavior change: A metaanalysis of applications to physical activity and exercise. *Annals of Behavioral Medicine, 23(4),* 229–246.

Medina, K. (1996). *The journey from nonexerciser to exerciser: A grounded theory study.* San Diego, CA: University of San Diego Press.

Muhr, T. (1994). Atlas.TI (Version 4.2) [Computer software]. Thousand Oaks, CA: Sage.

National Center for Health Statistics. (2004). *Health United States 2004 with chartbook on trends in the health of Americans with special feature on drugs.* Hyattsville, MD: U.S. Department of Health and Human Services, Centers for Disease Control and Prevention.

Pate, R. R., Pratt, M., Blair, S. N., Haskell, W. L., Macera, C. A., Bouchard, C, et al. (1995). Physical activity and public health: A recommendation from the Centers for Disease Control and Prevention and the American College of Sports Medicine. *JAMA, 273(5),* 402–407.

Patton, M. (1990). *Qualitative evaluation and research methods* (2nd ed.). Newbury Park, CA: Sage.

Prochaska, J., & DiClemente, C. C. (1983). Stages and processes of self-change of smoking: Toward an integrative model of change. *Journal of Consulting and Clinical Psychology, 51,* 390–395.

Prochaska, J., DiClemente, C., & Norcross, J. (1992). In search of how people change: Applications to addictive behaviors. *American Psychologist, 47(9),* 1102–1114.

Spradley, J. P. (1979). *The ethnographic interview.* Orlando, FL: Harcourt Brace.

Sternfeld, B., Ainsworth, B. E., & Quesenberry, C. (1999). Physical activity patterns in a diverse population of women. *Preventive Medicine, 28,* 313–323.

Strauss, A., & Corbin, J. (1998). *Basics of qualitative research: Techniques and procedures for developing grounded theory.* Thousand Oaks, CA: Sage.

U.S. Department of Health and Human Services. (1996). *Physical activity and health: A report of the Surgeon General.* Atlanta, GA: Author.

U.S. Department of Health and Human Services. (2000). *Healthy People 2010: Volume II* (2nd ed.). Washington, DC: Government Printing Office.

U.S. Department of Health and Human Services. (2001). *The Surgeon General's call to action to prevent and decrease overweight and obesity.* Rockville, MD: Author.

Wilbur, J., Miller, A. M., Chandler, P., & McDevitt, J. (2003). Determinants of physical activity and adherence to a 24-week home-based walking program in African American and Caucasian women. *Research in Nursing and Health, 26(3),* 213–224.

Appendix E

An Ethnography—"Rethinking Subcultural Resistance: Core Values of the Straight Edge Movement"

Ross Haenfler

"By focusing their message at their families, subcultural peers, mainstream youth, and the larger society, sXe created a multilayered resistance that individuals could customize to their own interests."

ABSTRACT. This article reconceptualizes subcultural resistance based on an ethnographic examination of the straight edge movement. Using the core values of straight edge, the author's analysis builds on new subcultural theories and suggests a framework for how members construct and understand their subjective experiences of being a part of a subculture. He suggests that adherents hold both individual and collective meanings of resistance and express their resistance via personal and political methods. Furthermore, they consciously enact resistance at the

(Continued)

Author's Note: I would like to thank Patti Adler for her support and guidance. I would also like to thank the reviewers for their helpful comments.

Source: This article originally appeared in the *Journal of Contemporary Ethnography, 33*(4), 406–436. Copyright 2004, Sage Publications, Inc.

Appendix E

(Continued)

micro, meso, and macro levels, not solely against an ambiguous "adult" culture. Resistance can no longer be conceptualized in neo-Marxist terms of changing the political or economic structure, as a rejection only of mainstream culture, or as symbolic stylistic expression. Resistance is contextual and many layered rather than static and uniform.

KEYWORDS: resistance; straight edge; subculture; youth; punk

Resistance has been a core theme among both subcultural participants and the scholars who study them. Early subcultural theorists associated with Birmingham University's Centre for Contemporary Cultural Studies (CCCS) concentrated on the ways youth symbolically resisted mainstream or "hegemonic" society through style, including clothing, demeanor, and vernacular (Hebdige 1979). Subcultures emerged in resistance to dominant culture, reacting against blocked economic opportunities, lack of social mobility, alienation, adult authority, and the "banality of suburban life" (Wooden and Blazak 2001, 20). Theorists found that young working-class white men joined deviant groups to resist conforming to what they saw as an oppressive society (Hebdige 1979; Hall and Jefferson 1976). Scholars have given a great deal of attention to whether these youth subcultures resist or reinforce dominant values and social structure (Hebdige 1979; Willis 1977; Brake 1985; Clarke, Hall, Jefferson, and Roberts 1975). The CCCS emphasized that while subcultural style was a form of resistance to subordination, ultimately resistance merely reinforced class relations (Cohen 1980; Willis 1977). Therefore, any such resistance was illusory; it gave subculture members a feeling of resistance while not significantly changing social or political relations (Clarke et al. 1975). In fact, according to this view, subcultures often inadvertently reinforce rather than subvert mainstream values, recasting dominant relationships in a subversive style (see Young and Craig 1997).

The CCCS has drawn substantial criticism for ignoring participants' subjectivity, failing to empirically study the groups they sought to explain, focusing too much on Marxist/class–based explanations and grand theories, reifying the concept of subculture, and overemphasizing style

(Muggleton 2000; Clarke [1981] 1997; Blackman 1995; Widdicombe and Wooffitt 1995). Based on solid ethnographic work, contemporary theorists have acknowledged the fluidity of subcultures and retooled the notion of resistance to include the subjective understandings of participants. Leblanc (1999), studying female punks, found that resistance included both a subjective and objective component. Leblanc redefined resistance broadly as political behavior, including discursive and symbolic acts. Postmodern theorists have further questioned CCCS ideas of resistance, suggesting that many narratives can simultaneously be true, contingent on one's perspective. They encourage us to examine subcultural quests for authenticity from the participants' points of view, paying particular attention to the individualistic, fragmented, and heterogeneous natures of subcultures (Muggleton 2000; Rose 1994; Grossberg 1992). Viewed in this way, subcultural involvement is more a personal quest for individuality, an expression of a "true self," rather than a collective challenge. In fact, most members have an "anti-structural subcultural sensibility" (Muggleton 2000, 151), view organized movements with suspicion, and instead criticize "mainstream society" in individualized ways (Gottschalk 1993, 369).

Each of these critiques demands a broader understanding of resistance that accounts for members' individualistic orientations. Resistance may be "political behavior" broadly defined, but how individuals express and understand their involvement needs further attention. My analysis builds on new subcultural theories and suggests a framework for how members construct and understand their subjective subcultural experiences. I suggest that adherents hold both individual and collective meanings of resistance and express their resistance via personal and political methods. Furthermore, they consciously enact resistance at the micro, meso, and macro levels, emerging at least partly in reaction to other subcultures instead of solely against an ambiguous "adult" culture. Resistance can no longer be conceptualized in neo-Marxist terms of changing the political or economic structure, as a rejection only of mainstream culture, or as symbolic stylistic expression. A conceptualization of resistance must account for individual opposition to domination, "the politicization of the self and daily life" (Taylor and Whittier 1992, 117) in which social actors practice the future they envision (Scott 1985; Melucci 1989, 1996). Resistance is contextual and many layered rather than static and uniform.

As a relatively unstudied movement, straight edge (sXe) provides an opportunity to rethink and expand notions of resistance. The straight edge[1] movement emerged on the East Coast of the United States from the punk subculture of the early 1980s. The movement arose primarily as a response to the punk scene's nihilistic tendencies, including drug and alcohol abuse, casual sex, violence, and self-destructive "live-for-the-moment" attitudes. Its founding members adopted a "clean-living" ideology, abstaining from alcohol, tobacco, illegal drugs, and promiscuous sex. Early sXe youth viewed punk's self-indulgent rebellion as no rebellion at all, suggesting that in many ways punks reinforced mainstream culture's intoxicated lifestyle in a mohawked, leather-jacketed guise.

Straight edge remains inseparable from the hardcore[2] (a punk genre) music scene. Straight edge bands serve as the primary shapers of the group's ideology and collective identity. Hardcore "shows"[3] (small concerts) are an important place for sXers[4] to congregate, share ideas, and build solidarity. Since its beginnings, the movement has expanded around the globe, counting tens of thousands of young people among its members. In the United States, the typical sXer is a white, middle-class male, aged fifteen to twenty-five. Straight edgers clearly distinguish themselves from their peers by marking a large X, the movement's symbol, on each hand before attending punk concerts. While scholars have thoroughly researched other postwar youth subcultures such as hippies, punks, mods, skinheads, and rockers (e.g., Hall and Jefferson 1976; Hebdige 1979; Brake 1985), we know little about sXe, despite its twenty-year history.

The basic tenets of sXe are quite simple: members abstain, completely, from drug, alcohol, and tobacco use and usually reserve sexual activity for caring relationships, rejecting casual sex. These sXe "rules" are absolute; there are no exceptions, and a single lapse means an adherent loses any claim to the sXe identity. Members commit to a lifetime of clean living. They interpret their abstention in a variety of ways centered on resistance, self-realization, and social transformation. Clean living is symbolic of a deeper resistance to mainstream values, and abstinence fosters a broader ideology that shapes sXers' gender relationships, sense of self, involvement in social change, and sense of community.

This article fills a gap in the literature by giving an empirical account of the sXe movement centered on a description of the group's core values. I begin by providing a very brief overview of several previous subcultures, to place sXe in a historical context. I then discuss my involvement in the sXe scene and the methods I employed throughout my research. Next, I examine the group's core values, focusing on how members understand their involvement.[5] Finally, I provide a new framework for analyzing members' experiences that encompasses the multitude of meanings, sites, and methods of resistance.

PREVIOUS YOUTH SUBCULTURES

Studies of hippies, skinheads, and punks demonstrate both similarities and profound differences between these groups and the sXe movement. Hippies evolved in the mid-1960s from the old beatnik and folknik subcultures (Irwin 1977; Miller 1999). Their lifestyle was a reaction to the stifling homogeneity of the 1950s, emphasizing communalism over conformity and deliberate hedonism over reserve (Miller 1991). "If it feels good, then do it so long as it doesn't hurt anyone else" was the scene's credo. Hippie core values included peace, racial harmony, equality, liberated sexuality, love, and communal living (Miller 1991). They rejected compulsive consumerism, delayed gratification, and material success (Davis 1967). "Dope," however, was one of the group's most visible characteristics (Miller 1991; Irwin 1977). Dope differed from drugs; dope, such as LSD and marijuana, was good, while drugs, such as speed and downers, were bad. For hippies, dope expanded the mind, released inhibitions, boosted creativity, and was part of the revolution. It was the means to discovering a new ethic, heightening awareness, and "understanding and coping with the evils of American culture" (Miller 1991, 34). LSD "gave the mind more power to choose, to evaluate, even, perhaps, to reason" (Earisman 1968, 31). Like dope, sex, in its own way, was revolutionary. "Free love" rejected the responsibilities normally associated with sexual relationships: marriage, commitment, and children (Earisman 1968). By practicing what most at the time would call promiscuous sex, the hippies deliberately threw their irreverence for middle-class values in the face of dominant society (Irwin 1977).

Skinheads received a great deal of attention during the 1990s, as reports of their growing membership in neo-Nazi groups infiltrated both popular media and scholarly work (Bjorgo and Wilte 1993; Moore 1994; Young and Craig 1997). Skinheads emerged in late-1960s Britain as an offshoot of the mod subculture (Cohen 1972; Hebdige 1979). While most of the fashion-conscious mods listened to soul music, frequented discotheques, and dressed in impeccably pressed trousers and jackets, the "hard mods," who eventually became the skinheads, favored ska and reggae, local pubs, and a working-class "uniform" of heavy boots, close-cropped hair, Levi jeans, plain shirts, and braces (suspenders) (Brake

1985). While the mods attempted to emulate the middle-class, hip 1960s style, the skins were ardently working class. Nearly everything about skinheads revolved around their working-class roots. Hard work and independence were among their core values; they abhorred people, such as some hippies, who they believed "live off the system." Skinheads were extremely nationalistic and patriotic, adorning themselves with tattoos, T-shirts, and patches of their country's flag. After a long day at work, they enjoyed drinking beer with their friends at the local pub. Although there were some women skins, males dominated the subculture and often reinforced traditional patriarchal ideals of masculinity.

The original skinheads borrowed heavily from the West Indian culture, adopting their music, mannerisms, and style, including among their number a variety of races. While they were not violently racist at the level of the current neo-Nazi groups, these skins, both black and white, engaged in violence against Pakistani immigrants ("Pakibashing") (Hebdige 1979, 56). Eventually, with reggae's turn to Rastafarianism and black pride, many white skinheads became increasingly racist. At the turn of the century, three main types of skinheads prevailed: neo-Nazis (racist), skinheads against racism (e.g., Skinheads Against Racial Prejudice), and nonpolitical skinheads, who took neither a racist nor an antiracist stand (Young and Craig 1997). Skinheads were quite visible at punk, ska, and Oi! music shows, though the nonpolitical and antiracist skins were more prevalent. Very rarely, a skinhead was also sXe.[6]

In many ways, punk was a reaction to "hippie romanticism" and middle-class culture; punk celebrated decline and chaos (Brake 1985, 78; Fox 1987; O'Hara 1999). In mid-1970s Britain, youth faced a lack of job opportunities or, at best, the prospect of entering a mainstream world they found abhorrent (Henry 1989). They attempted to repulse dominant society by valuing anarchy, hedonism, and life in the moment. Early punks borrowed heavily from the styles of Lou Reed, David Bowie ("Ziggy Stardust"), and other glam-rock and new-wave artists. Adorned with safety pins, bondage gear, heavy bright makeup, torn clothing, flamboyant hairstyles, and spiked leather jackets, punks lived by their motto "No Future," celebrating rather than lamenting the world's decline. They embraced alienation, and their "nihilist aesthetic" included "polymorphous, often willfully perverse sexuality, obsessive individualism, a fragmented sense of self" (Hebdige 1979, 28).

Like the skinheads, punks disdained hippies; the preeminent punk band the Sex Pistols titled one of their live recordings "Kill the Hippies" (Heylin 1998, 117). Unlike the skins, and like the hippies, however, punks chose to reject society, conventional work, and patriotism. Many used dangerous drugs to symbolize "life in the moment" and their self-destructive, nihilistic attitude (Fox 1987). Straight edge emerged relatively early in the punk scene and has shared certain values and styles with punks, hippies, and skins ever since. While some punks today are sXe, the two scenes have become relatively distinct, and the sXe movement has replaced many of the original antisocial punk values with prosocial ideals.

METHOD

My first encounter with sXe occurred in 1989 at the age of fifteen through my involvement in a Midwest punk rock scene. As I attended punk shows and socialized with the members, I noticed that many kids scrawled large Xs on their hands with magic marker before they went to a concert. I eventually learned that the X symbolized the clean-living sXe lifestyle and that many punks in our scene had taken on a totally drug- and alcohol-free way of life. Having tried the alcohol-laden life of most of my peers, I quickly discovered it was not for me. I despised feeling I had to "prove" myself (and my manhood) again and again by drinking excessively. I could not understand why the "coolest," the most highly regarded men were often the ones who most degraded women. Furthermore, given my family's history of alcoholism, I wanted to avoid my relatives' destructive patterns. Finally, the local sXers' involvement in progressive politics and activist organizations connected with my interest in social justice and environmentalism. My association with sXers led me to adopt the sXe ideology as what I viewed, at the time, to be an alternative to peer pressure and a proactive avenue to social change. After a period of careful consideration (like many punks, I was suspicious of "rules"), I made known my commitment to avoid consuming alcohol, drugs, and tobacco, and the group accepted me as one of their own. Since then, I have attended more than 250 hardcore shows, maintained the lifestyle, and associated with many sXers on a fairly regular basis. The data I present result from more than fourteen years of observing the sXe movement in a variety of settings and roles and interviewing members of the scene.

During college, my involvement with sXe waned, and for several years I had little contact with the group. After completing my undergraduate career, I moved to "Clearweather," a metropolitan area in the western United States, to begin graduate training. I lived in a predominantly white university town of approximately ninety thousand people, attending a large research university with twenty-five thousand students. Soon after arriving, I sought out the local hardcore scene and began attending shows. The setting's richness and my interests led me to take advantage of this opportunistic research situation (Riemer 1977). My four-year absence from the scene allowed me to approach the setting with a relatively fresh perspective, while my personal involvement and knowledge of the sXe ideology enabled me to gain entrée into the local scene very quickly. Since fall 1996, I have participated in the sXe scene as a complete member (Adler and Adler 1987).

I gathered data primarily through longitudinal participant observation (Agar 1996) with sXers from 1996 to 2001. The sXers I studied were mostly area high school or university students from middle-class backgrounds. My contacts grew to include approximately sixty sXers in the local area and another thirty sXe and non-sXe acquaintances associated with the larger metropolitan hardcore scene. My interaction with the group occurred primarily at hardcore shows and simply socializing at sXers' houses.

To supplement my participant observation, I conducted unstructured, in-depth interviews with seventeen sXe men and eleven women between the ages of seventeen and thirty. To learn from a variety of individuals, I selected sXers with differing levels of involvement in the scene, including new and old adherents, and individuals who had made the movement central or peripheral to their lives. I conducted in-depth interviews at sXers' homes or at public places free from disturbances, recording and later transcribing each session. Though I organized the sessions around particular themes, I left the interviews unstructured enough that individuals could share exactly what sXe meant to them. I sometimes asked for referrals in a snowball fashion (Biernacki and Waldorf 1981), though I knew most participants well enough to approach them on my own. The variety of participants allowed me continually to cross-check reports and seek out evidence disconfirming my findings (Campbell 1975; Stewart 1998; see also Douglas 1976). Through participant observation, I was able to examine how participants' behaviors differed from their stated intentions. I consciously distanced myself from the setting to maintain a critical outlook by continually questioning my observations and consulting with colleagues to gain an outsider perspective. I was especially attentive to variations on the patterns I discovered.

In an effort to expand my knowledge of sXe beyond my primary circle of contacts, I sought interviews with adherents from outside of the local scene, including individuals from other cities and members of touring out-of-state bands who played in Clearweather. I sometimes contacted other individuals around the country via e-mail with specific questions. I also spent several days in New York City, Los Angeles, and Connecticut to experience the scenes there, taking field notes and conducting informal interviews. In addition to participant observation, casual conversation, and interviews, I examined a variety of other sources including newspaper stories, music lyrics, World Wide Web pages, and sXe 'zines,[7] coding relevant snippets of information into my field notes.

To record and organize my data, I took brief notes at shows and other events that I immediately afterward expanded into more full field notes on computer. Using headings and subheadings, I coded data according to particular topics of interest, beginning the process of organizing data into useful and interesting categories (Charmaz 1983). Throughout my research, I sought patterns and emerging typologies of data (Lofland and Lofland 1995). Reexamining the coded field notes and transcribed interviews led me to analyze several themes, including the subculture's core values. I continually refined these themes as I gathered more data through emergent, inductive analysis (Becker and Geer 1960).

Straight Edge Core Values

A core set of sXe values and ideals guided and gave meaning to members' behavior: positivity/clean living, reserving sex for caring relationships, self-realization, spreading the message, and involvement in progressive causes. Adherents maintained that sXe meant something different to each person assuming the identity, and as with any group, individual members' dedication to these ideals varied. However, while individuals were free to follow the philosophy in various ways, often adding their own interpretations, these fundamental values underlay the entire movement.

T-shirt slogans, song lyrics, tattoos, and other symbols constantly reminded sXers of their mission and dedication: "It's OK Not to Drink," "True till Death," and "One Life Drug Free" were among the more popular messages. The "X," sXe's universal symbol, emerged in the early 1980s, when music club owners marked the hands of underage concertgoers with an X to ensure that bartenders would not serve them alcohol (see Lahickey 1997, 99). Soon, the kids intentionally marked their own hands both to signal club workers of their intention not to drink and, more importantly, to make a statement of pride and defiance to other kids at the shows. The movement appropriated the X, a symbol meant to be negative, transforming its meaning into discipline and commitment to a drug-free lifestyle.[8] Youth wore Xs on their backpacks, shirts, and necklaces; they tattooed them on their bodies and drew them on their school folders, skateboards, cars, and other possessions. The X united youth around the world, communicating a common set of values and experiences. Straight edgers found strength, camaraderie, loyalty, and encouragement in their sXe friends, valuing them above all else.[9] For many, sXe became a "family," a "brotherhood," a supportive space to be different together. A powerful sense of community, based in large part on the hardcore music scene, was the glue that held sXe and its values together for twenty years.

Like the other youth movements, sXe was a product of the times and culture that it resisted; oppositional subcultures do not emerge in a vacuum (Kaplan and Lööw 2002). The lifestyle reflects the group's emergence during a time of increasing conservatism and religious fundamentalism, an escalating drug war, and Nancy Reagan's "Just Say No" campaign. The rise of the New Christian Right in the late 1970s and early 1980s contributed to a more conservative national climate that influenced youth values (Liebman and Wuthnow 1983). Fundamentalism gained appeal among populations who felt they were losing control of their way of life (Hunter 1987). The unyielding, black-and-white strictures on behavior of sXe were similar to fundamentalist religion's rigid, clear-cut beliefs (Marty and Appleby 1993). In particular, sXe's emphasis on clean living, sexual purity, lifetime commitment, and meaningful community was reminiscent of youth evangelical movements, while the focus on self-control suggested Puritanical roots. In addition to these conservative influences, sXe was, in many ways, a continuation of New Left middle-class radicalism oriented toward "issues of a moral or humanitarian nature," a radicalism whose payoff is "in the emotional satisfaction derived from expressing personal values in action" (Parkin 1968, 41). The movement's core values reflect this curious blend of conservative and progressive influences.

Positive, Clean Living

The foundation underlying the sXe identity was positive, clean living. It was, as Darrell Irwin (1999) suggested, fundamentally about subverting the drug scene and creating an alternative, drug-free environment. Clean living was the key precursor to a positive life. Many sXers shunned caffeine and medicinal drugs, and most members were committed vegetarians or vegans.[10] Positive living had broad meaning, including questioning and resisting society's norms, having a positive attitude, being an individual, treating people with respect and dignity, and taking action to make the world a better place. Straight edgers claimed that one could not fully question dominant society while under the influence of drugs, and once one questioned social convention, substance use, eating meat, and promiscuous sex were no longer appealing. Therefore, clean living and positivity were inseparable; they reinforced one another and constituted the foundation for all other sXe values. "Joe,"[11] an eighteen-year-old high school senior, explained how the "positivity" he gained from sXe shaped his life:

> To me, I guess what I've gotten from [sXe] is living a more positive lifestyle. Striving to be more positive in the way you live. Because where I was at when I found it was really (laughs) I was really negative myself. I was negative around people and influenced them to be negative. I was surrounded by negativity. Then I found this and it was like something really positive to be a part of. Also, like the ethics, drug free, alcohol free, no promiscuous sex. It's just saying no to things that are such a challenge for people my age, growing up at that time. It's a big thing for some people to say "No."

Refusing drugs and alcohol had a variety of meanings for individual sXers, including purification, control, and breaking abusive family patterns. Purification literally meant being free from toxins that threatened one's health and potentially ruined lives. Popular T-shirt slogans proclaimed "Purification—vegan straight edge" and "Straight edge—my commitment against society's poisons." Straight edgers believed that drugs and alcohol influenced people to do things they would normally not do, such as have casual sex, fight, and harm themselves. By labeling themselves as more "authentic" than their peers who used alcohol and drugs, sXers created an easy way to distinguish themselves. They experienced a feeling of uniqueness, self-confidence, and sometimes superiority by rejecting the typical teenage life. Refusing alcohol and drugs symbolized refusing the "popular" clique altogether as well as the perceived nihilism of punks, hippies, and skinheads.

The movement provided young people a way to feel more in control of their lives. Many youth felt peer pressure to drink alcohol, smoke cigarettes, or try illegal drugs. For some, this pressure created feelings of helplessness and lack of control; acceptance often hinged on substance use. Straight edgers reported that the group gave them a way to feel accepted without using and helped them maintain control over their personal situations. Many sXers celebrated the fact that they would never wake up after a night of binge drinking wondering what had happened the previous evening. Adherents reported that sXe allowed them to have a "clear" mind and be free to make choices without artificial influence. Walter, a reserved twenty-one-year-old university student, explained,

> I don't make any stupid decisions. . . . I like to have complete control of my mind, my body, my soul. I like to be the driver of my body, not some foreign substance that has a tendency to control other people. I get a sense of pride from telling other people, "I don't need that stuff. It might be for you but I don't need that stuff." And people are like, "Whoa! I respect that. That's cool."

In addition to the personalized meanings the identity held for adherents, sXers viewed their abstinence as a collective challenge. The group offered a visible means of separating oneself from most youth and taking a collective stand against youth culture and previous youth subcultures, including punks, skinheads, and hippies. Furthermore, for many positivity and refusing drugs and alcohol were symbolic of a larger resistance to other societal problems including racism, sexism, and greed.

Straight edgers made a lifetime commitment to positive, clean living. They treated their abstinence and adoption of the sXe identity as a sacred vow, calling it an "oath," "pledge," or "promise." Members made no exceptions to this rule. Patrick, an easy-going twenty-year-old musician and ex-football player, said, "If you just sip a beer, or take a drag off of a cigarette, you can never call yourself straight edge again. There's no slipping up in straight edge." Ray, raised in an alcoholic family and already heavily tattooed at age nineteen, compared the sXe vow to vows of matrimony: "It's true till death. Once you put the X on your hand, it's not like a wedding ring. You can always take a wedding ring off, but you can't wash the ink from your hands." Ray proceeded to show me a tattoo on his chest depicting a heart with "True till Death" written across it. Many sXe youth had similar tattoos, signifying the permanence of their commitment.

Some sXers took their commitment so seriously they labeled people who broke their vows of abstinence as traitors or "sellouts." Despite their vehement insistence they would "stay true" forever, relatively few sXers maintained the identity beyond their early to midtwenties. Many maintained the values and rarely used alcohol or drugs, but "adult" responsibilities and relationships infringed on their involvement in the scene. When formerly sXe individuals began drinking, smoking, or using drugs, adherents claimed they had "sold out" or "lost the edge." While at times losing the edge caused great conflict, I observed that more often the youth's bonds of friendship superseded resentment and disappointment, and they remained friends. However, a former sXer's sXe friends often expressed deep regret and refused to allow the transgressor to claim the identity ever again. Brent, a serious and outspoken twenty-two-year-old vegan, said, "It's frustrating to see people who you think are your friends make such heavy decisions without consulting you. . . . It's not a betrayal like turning around. It's just that you feel abandoned. . . . It's demoralizing." Kate, a twenty-two-year-old activist, explained her frustration with sellouts:

> It was hard for me at first because I think when people do that it takes away the power of sXe. When people are like, "I'm sXe" and then the next day they're not. It—not delegitimizes completely—in a way it takes away some of the legitimacy of the movement. . . . It definitely upset me a little bit. How can you go from claiming sXe one day and the next day just forget about it completely? That was the main thing, I just didn't understand it.

When particularly outspoken or well-known members of the scene sold out, sXers spoke as if another hero had fallen. A very small minority of individuals did base their friendships on adherence to the movement and almost practiced "shunning," the religious equivalent of casting someone out. It was this type of action, despite its rarity, that contributed to outsiders' conceptions of sXe as a judgmental, dogmatic group. Straight edge youth were less likely to socialize regularly with people who used simply because of the incompatibility of the lifestyles. Straight edgers rarely openly criticized friends who had sold out, but during interviews participants expressed to me a deeper frustration and sense of betrayal than they would ever publicly show.

Reserving Sex for Caring Relationships

Reserving sex for caring relationships was an extension of the positive, clean lifestyle. Straight edgers viewed casual sex as yet another downfall of dominant society, their counterparts in other youth subcultures, and their more mainstream peers. It carried the possibility of sexually transmitted diseases and feelings of degradation and shame. Whereas hippies viewed liberated sex as revolutionary, punks saw it as just another pleasure, and skinheads valued sex as a supreme expression of masculinity, sXers saw abstinence from "promiscuous" sex as a powerful form of resistance. Rejecting the casualness of many youth sexual encounters, they believed that sexual relationships entailed much more than physical pleasure. They were particularly critical of their image of the "predatory," insatiable male, searching for sex wherever he could get it. Kent, a twenty-one-year-old university student with several colorful tattoos, said, "My personal views have to do with self-respect, with knowing that I'm going to make love with someone I'm really into, not a piece of meat." Kyle, a twenty-three-year-old senior architecture major at Clearweather University, said, "For me personally, I won't sleep around with a bunch of people just for health's sake. A good positive influence. [Sex] doesn't mean anything if you don't care about a person." Walter, the university student, said,

> For me it's just choosing how I want to treat my body. It's not something I'm just going to throw around. I'm not going to smoke or use drugs. My body is something that I honor. It's something we should respect. I think sex, if you're gonna do it you should do it, but you shouldn't throw your body around and do it with as many people as you want. If you love your body so much as to not do those things to your body you should have enough respect to treat women and sex how they deserve to be treated.

Though sXe values regarding sexuality appeared conservative when compared to many other youth subcultures, sXers were neither antisex nor homophobic as a group. Premarital sex was not wrong or "dirty" in the sense of some traditional religious views, and numerous sXers and sXe bands took a strong stance against homophobia.[12] Sex could be a positive element of a caring relationship. Believing that sex entailed power and emotional vulnerability, sXers strove to minimize potentially negative experiences by rejecting casual sex. Kevin, a twenty-seven-year-old martial artist who had dropped out of high school, said,

> To this day I'm by no means celibate; however . . . in the last eight years I've had sex with three girls. I'm not celibate by any means but I also don't believe in fuckin' bullshit meaningless sex. So those tenets kind of took place in my life even though I didn't take it to the actual celibacy extreme. . . . It should be on an emotional level. It's an addiction like everything else. My first understanding of sXe was to not be addicted.

There was no direct religious basis for sXe views on sex. In fact, many of the sXers I associated with grew up with no formal religious involvement, and almost none of them were presently involved in formal religion. While a few sXers connected their sXe and Christian identities, the group advocated no form of religion, and most adherents were deeply suspicious or critical of organized faiths.

Most sXers also believed that objectifying women was pervasive and wrong, rejecting the stereotypical image of high school males. A local sXe band (five male members) decried sexual abuse and rape: "This song is the most important song we play. It's about the millions of women who have suffered rape. One out of four women will be the victim of a sexual assault in her lifetime. We've got to make it stop." The movement's "rule" against promiscuous sex was more difficult for members to enforce, and thus there was greater variation in belief regarding sex than substance use. Several of my participants, both males and females aged twenty-one to twenty-three, had consciously decided to postpone sex because they had not found someone with whom they felt an intimate emotional attachment. Most of the young women believed not drinking reduced their risk of being sexually assaulted or otherwise put in a compromising situation. Jenny, an eighteen-year-old college freshman and activist, said,

> Like I said, it's all about control over your own body, over your own life. It's about reclaiming, claiming your dignity and self-respect. Saying I'm not going to put this stuff into my body. I'm not going to have you inside of my body if I don't want you in there. It all just very much ties together. I like sXe because it allows me to make very rational, intelligent decisions. That's one of the decisions I think it's really important to think through very carefully. I'm not against premarital sex at all. But personally, I've got to be in love.

Some adherents insisted that sex should be reserved for married couples, while a few believed sXe placed no strictures on sexual activity. Only one young man with relatively little connection to the Clearweather scene had a reputation as a "player." A minority of sXe men were little different than the hypermasculine stereotype they sought to reject. Most insisted that sex between strangers or near strangers was potentially destructive, emotionally and possibly physically, and that positivity demanded that sex should be part of an emotional relationship based on trust.

Self-Realization

Like members of other subcultures, sXers sought to create and express a "true" or "authentic" identity amid a world that they felt encouraged conformity and mediocrity. Straight edgers claimed that resisting social standards and expectations allowed them to follow their own, more meaningful path in life toward greater self-realization. Like punks, they abhorred conformity and insisted on being "true to themselves." Similar to hippies, sXers believed that as children we have incredible potential that is "slowly crushed and destroyed by a standardized society and mechanical teaching" (Berger 1967, 19). Subcultures, like social movements, engage in conflict over cultural reproduction, social integration, and socialization; they are often especially concerned with quality of life, self-realization, and identity formation (Habermas 1984–87; Buechler 1995). Straight edgers believed toxins such as drugs and alcohol inhibited people from reaching their full potential. This view sharply contrasted with the hip version of self-realization through dope (Davis 1968). For sXers, drugs of any kind inhibited rather than enabled self-discovery; they believed people were less genuine and true to themselves while high. A clear, focused mind helped sXers achieve their highest goals. Kate, the activist, said, "If you have a clear mind you're more likely to be aware of who you are and what things around you really are rather than what somebody might want you to think they are. A little bit more of an honest life, being true to yourself." Elizabeth, a twenty-six-year-old with an advanced degree who had been sXe and vegetarian for many years, said,

> You're not screwed up on drugs and alcohol and you can make conscientious decisions about things. You're not letting some drug or alcohol subdue your emotions and thoughts. You're not desensitizing yourself to your life. And if you're not desensitizing your life, then yeah, you're gonna feel more things. The more you feel, the more you move, the more that you grow. . . . I truly believe [sXers] are living and feeling and growing, and it's all natural growth. It's not put off. That's a unique characteristic.

Like adherents of previous subcultures, sXers constructed a view of the world as mediocre and unfulfilling, believing society encouraged people to medicate themselves with crutches such as drugs, alcohol, and sex to forget their unhappiness. Straight edgers felt the punks', skinheads', and hippies' associations with these things blunted their opportunities to offer meaningful resistance. Substances and social pressures clouded clear thought and individual expression. Claiming that many people used substances as a means to escape their problems, the movement encouraged members to avoid escapism, confront problems with a clear mind, and create their own positive, fulfilling lives. Brent emphatically insisted that self-realization did not require drugs:

> There are ways to open your mind without drinking and smoking. . . . You definitely don't have to take mushrooms and sit out in the desert to have a spiritual awakening or a catharsis of any sort. People don't accept that. People think you're uptight. . . . There is a spiritual absence in the world I know right now, in America. To be money driven is the goal. It's one of the emptiest, least fulfilling ways to live your life. . . . The way people relieve themselves of the burdens of their spiritual emptiness is through drugs and alcohol. The way people see escape is sometimes even through a shorter lifespan, through smoking. To be sXe and to understand and believe that means you have opened the door for yourself to find out why we're really on this earth, or what I want to get out of a relationship with a person, or what I want my kids to think of me down the line.

Straight edgers rarely spoke openly about self-realization, and they would likely scoff at anything that suggested mysticism or enlightenment (which they would connect to hippies and therefore drugs). Nevertheless, for many, underlying the ideology was an almost spiritual quest for a genuine self, a "truth." Some connected sXe to other identities: "queer edge," feminism, and activism, for example. For others, sXe offered a means of overcoming abusive family experiences. Mark, a quiet sixteen-year-old new to the scene, claimed sXe as a protest: "Straight edge to me, yeah, it's a commitment to myself, but to me it's also a protest. I don't want to give my kids the same life I had from my father."

Spreading the Message

Straight edge efforts at resistance transcended members' simple abstention. Straight edgers often actively encouraged other young people to become drug and alcohol free. Some hippies believed their "ultimate social mission is to 'turn the world on'—i.e. Make everyone aware of the potential virtues of LSD for ushering in an era of universal peace, freedom, brotherhood and love" (Davis 1968, 157). Likewise, many sXers undertook a mission to convince their peers that resisting drugs, rather than using them, would help create a better world. A minority of sXers, labeled "militant" or "hardline" by other sXers, were very outspoken, donning Xs and sXe messages at nearly all times and confronting their peers who used.

While sXe promoted individuality and clear, free thought, for some adherents the rigid lifestyle requirements created conformity, close-mindedness, and intolerance, a far cry from the "positivity" the movement promulgated. There was an ongoing tension within the movement over how much members should promote their lifestyle. At one extreme was the "live and let live" faction—individuals should make their own choices, and sXers have no right to infringe on that choice. At the other end was the more militant branch, often composed of new adherents, who believed sXers' duty lay in showing users the possibilities of a drug-free lifestyle. Most sXers maintained that their example was enough. Jenny, the student-activist, said,

> I wanna show people there's a community out there that it doesn't make you a fucking dork to be sXe. There are other people out there who are really, really into it. There's a whole group of people you can belong to. You don't have to belong to just them obviously. I just think it can be a really positive thing for people. I go to a dorm where you walk down every fucking hall and the smell of pot knocks you upside the head. I just think that in that case it's really important to get your message out there. . . . I think the best political, social, personal statement you can make is to live by example. That's definitely what I try to do.

Cory, an artist and veteran of the scene at age twenty-one, explained why sXers should set an example for others:

> It's all about calling yourself straight edge. You could be drug free and you can not drink and not smoke and go to parties and do whatever, but you're not helping out. There's a pendulum in society and it's tilted one way so far, and sitting in the middle of the pendulum isn't going to help it swing back. There needs to be more straight edgers on the other side to help even it out, at the least.

Thus, while adherents maintained that sXe was a personal lifestyle choice rather than a movement directed toward others, many members "wore their politics on their sleeves" in a not-so-subtle attempt to encourage others to follow their path. Wearing a shirt with an sXe message may be a personal stylistic decision, but when an entire group of people wears such shirts that so clearly defy the norm, style has the potential to become collective challenge.

Straight edge resistance also targeted the corporate interests of alcohol and tobacco, which adherents claimed profit from people's addictions and suffering. Kate, who clearly connected sXe with her activism, said, "By rejecting Miller Lite and Coors, they have less control over me and my life because I'm not giving them my money; I'm not supporting them." Brent, the outspoken vegan, said,

> Each individual in society is connected to one another. When you hurt yourself, you're hurting your society. You're leading by example; your kids will see what you're doing and they'll pick it up. . . . Resisting temptation, resisting what's thrown at you day after day, by your peers, by your parents, by their generation, by businesspeople, by what's hip and cool on MTV. Resistance is huge. That's why sXe is a movement. . . . It's all connected: resisting drugs, resisting rampant consumerism, resisting voting Democrat when you can vote third party.

By focusing their message at their families, subcultural peers, mainstream youth, and the larger society, sXe created a multilayered resistance that individuals could customize to their own interests.

Involvement in Social Change

Like members of the other subcultures, sXers often became involved in a variety of social causes. The sXe youth with whom I associated insisted that working for social change was not a prerequisite of sXe. Indeed, only a few belonged to the substantial activist community in our city. However, many viewed involvement in social change as a logical progression from clean living that led them to embrace progressive concerns and become directly involved at some level. Clean living and positivity led to clear thinking, which in turn created a desire to resist and self-realize. This entire process opened them up to the world's problems, and their concerns grew.[13] Tim, twenty-seven, the singer of a very popular sXe band, explained,

> The reasoning behind [sXe] is to have a clear mind and to use that clear mind to reach out to other people and do what you can to start thinking about fairness, thinking about how to make things more just in society and the world as a whole. . . . It's about freedom. It's about using that freedom that clarity of mind that we have as a vehicle for progression, to make ourselves more peaceful people. And by making ourselves more peaceful people we make the world a more just place. (Sersen 1999)

Jenny considered sXe central to her activism:

I think every element of my life philosophy is very much interconnected. They all sort of fit together like a puzzle piece. The connection I make between sXe and political activism is sort of that whole attitude like you see something wrong, fix it. I don't like the things that drugs and drinking bring about in society so I fix it by fixing myself. When I see other problems in society as well, I have the same drive to fix it by doing everything that I can do. It's all about claiming power, saying, "All right, I'm in charge of my life. I can do as much good as I want to do."

Kevin, the martial artist, believed that sXe was fundamentally about becoming a strong person in every aspect of life. Strength included rejecting stereotypes and prejudices:

Technically, according to the "rules," you can be homophobic and racist and fuckin' sexist and shit like that and still technically be sXe. You're not drinking; you're not smoking; you're not doing drugs. But I don't personally, on a personal level, I wouldn't consider that person sXe. Because they're weak. I don't think you can be sXe and weak.

Again contrasting against the hippies, punks, and skinheads, for sXers, a clear, drug-free mind was pivotal to developing a consciousness of resistance. The movement provided a general opening up or expansion of social awareness. Kent, the rather quiet young man with many tattoos, said, "I would never have even considered being vegetarian or vegan if it wasn't for sXe. Once you go sXe, I don't really think you're supposed to stop there. It's supposed to open you up to more possibilities. . . . It just makes me think differently. It makes you not so complacent."

In the mid-1980s to late 1980s, sXe became increasingly concerned with animal rights and environmental causes. Influential leaders in bands called for an end to cruelty against animals and a general awareness of eco-destruction. At least three out of four sXers were vegetarian, and many adopted completely cruelty-free, or vegan, lifestyles. Among the approximately sixty sXers I associated with regularly, only fifteen ate meat. Several individuals had "vegan" tattooed on their bodies. Others led or actively participated in a campus animal defense organization. Essentially, the movement framed (see Snow, Rochford, Worden, and Benford 1986) animal rights as a logical extension of the positivity frame underpinning the entire lifestyle, much like reserving sex for caring relationships and self-realization. Brian, an extremely positive and fun-loving twenty-one-year-old, explained vegetarianism's connection to sXe: "sXe kids open their minds a lot more. They're more conscious of what's around them. . . . Some people think it's healthier and other people like me are more on the animal liberation thing." Elizabeth, the older veteran, said,

> If you are conscientious and care about the environment or the world, which perhaps more sXe people are than your average population, then [animal rights is] just going to be a factor. You're going to consider "How can I make the world a better place?" Well, being vegetarian is another place you can start. . . . I'm glad it's usually a part of the sXe scene because it just goes along with awareness and choices. What kind of things are you doing to yourself and how is that impacting the world and the environment? The big corporate-owned beef lots and cutting down the rainforests . . . the most impactful thing you can do for the environment is to stop eating meat.

Some sXe youth involved themselves in social justice causes such as homelessness, human rights, and women's rights. They organized benefit concerts to raise money for local homeless shelters, and often the price of admission to shows included a canned good for the local food pantry or a donation to a women's shelter. I observed several sXers participating in local protests against the World Bank and International Monetary Fund in conjunction with the large 1999–2000 protests in Seattle and Washington, D.C., and others took part in a campus antisweatshop campaign. Similar to progressive punks, some sXe youth printed 'zines on prisoners' rights, fighting neo-Nazism, challenging police brutality, and various human rights and environmental issues.

Many sXe women disdained more traditional female roles and appreciated the scene as a space in which they felt less pressure to live up to gender expectations, and the movement encouraged men to reject certain hypermasculine traits and challenge sexism on a personal level. A majority of bands wrote songs against sexism, and many young sXe men demonstrated an exceptional understanding of gender oppression given their ages and experiences. However, despite the movement's claims of community and inclusivity, some sXe women felt isolated and unwelcome in the scene. Men significantly outnumbered women, often creating a "boys club" mentality exemplified by the masculine call for "brotherhood." The almost complete lack of female musicians in bands, the hypermasculine dancing at shows, and the male cliques reinforced the movement's own unspoken gender assumptions that women were not as important to the scene as men and ensured that many women would never feel completely at home.

While some sXers joined animal rights, women's rights, environmental, and other groups, most strove to live out their values in everyday life rather than engage in more conventional "political" protest (e.g., picketing, civil disobedience, petitioning). Instead of challenging tobacco, beer, or beef companies directly, for example, a sXer refuses their products and might boycott Kraft (parent company of cigarette manufacturer Phillip Morris), adopt a vegetarian lifestyle, or wear a shirt to school reading "It's OK not to drink. Straight Edge" or "Go Vegan!" In sXe and other youth movements, the personal was political. Subcultures are themselves politically meaningful, and they often serve as a bridge to further political involvement.

CONCLUSION

Straight edgers' understandings of the group's core values show that resistance is much more complex than a stylistic reaction to mainstream culture. I conclude by discussing an analytical framework for understanding the individual and collective meanings, multiple sites, and personal and political methods of resistance of any subculture.

Members of youth subcultures construct both individualized and collective meanings for their participation. Participants may hold individualized meanings that are not central to the group's ideology while simultaneously maintaining collective understandings of the subculture's significance. Widdicombe and Wooffitt (1995), for example, found that "punk may be constituted both through shared goals, values and so on, and through individual members" (p. 204). Subcultures help define "who I am" during the uncertainty of coming of age (p. 25). They offer a space for experimentation and a place to wrestle with questions about the world, creating a "home" for identity in a modern era when personal identity suffers a homelessness brought about by the forces of modernity (Melucci 1989; Giddens 1991). Thus, at the individual level, resistance entails staking out an individual identity and asserting subjectivity in an adversarial context. In addition, for most participants, individualized resistance is symbolic of a larger collective oppositional consciousness. The collective meanings central to the sXe identity included defying the stereotypical "jock" image, setting a collective example for other youth, supporting a drug-free social setting, and avoiding society's "poisons" that dull the mind. Youth claimed the sXe label rather than simply remaining "drug free" specifically because they believed their individual choices would add up to a collective challenge. Here, resistance involves collectively showing disapproval for some aspect of culture, questioning dominant goals, making an invisible ideology visible, and creating an alternative.

Members of youth subcultures understand their resistance at the macro, meso, and micro levels.[14] Past theorizing on resistance has privileged mainstream hegemonic adult culture, the class structure, or the state as the macro-level target of subcultural resistance (Hall 1972). Indeed, sXers rejected aspects of a culture they believed marketed alcohol and tobacco products to youth, established alcohol use as the norm, promoted conformity, and glorified casual sexual encounters. In addition to challenging culture at the macro level, youth movements offer resistance at the meso level. Straight edgers focused much, if not most, of their message toward their fellow youth, reacting against mainstream youth and perceived contradictions in other subcultures. Overall, sXe illustrates that subcultures form in reaction to other subcultures as well as the larger social structure. Members resisted what they saw as youth culture's fixation on substance use and sex; punks' "no future" and nihilistic tendencies; skinheads' patriotism, sexism, and working-class ideology, as well as some members' racism; and hippies' drug use, passivity, and escapism—believing that these undermine the resistance potential each of these groups share. However, despite its insistence on countering counterculture, sXe co-opted many values of the previous youth movements, clearly owing its "question everything" mentality and aggressive music to punk, its intimation of self-realization and cultural challenge to hippies, and its clean-cut image, personal accountability, and sense of pride to skinheads. Analyzing youth movements at the meso level in terms of their relationship to other youth cultures is vital to an accurate understanding of these groups, as is recognizing the identity battles within the group. Youth reflexively examine their own groups and often attempt to resolve intragroup contradictions. Leblanc (1999, 160) noted, for example, that female punks "subvert the punks' subversion" just as some sXers resisted militant "tough guys" within their scene. All youth movements share disdain for the mainstream; how they express their contempt and challenge existing structures depends in large part on current and previous youth subcultures that often become meso-level targets for change. No doubt the contradictions in sXe will provoke new innovations both within sXe and from other subcultures seeking to transcend sXe's limitations.

Finally, sXers also reported resistance at the micro level as they rejected the substance abuse within their families and made changes in their individual lives. Many sXers claimed that they abstained from drugs and alcohol at least in part in defiance of family members' substance abuse or their own addictive tendencies. Clearly, meanings of subcultural involvement extend beyond contradictions in adult culture and the class structure.

Furthermore, sXe demonstrated that subcultures use many methods of resistance, both personal and political. Distrustful of political challenges and organized social activism, subcultures often embody a more individualistic opposition. Many sXers did seek to change youth culture, but their primary methods were very personal: leading by example, personally living the changes they sought, expressing a personal style, and creating a space to be "free" from their perceived constraints of peer pressure and conformity to mainstream culture.[15] As Widdicombe and Wooffitt (1995) noted in their study of punk identity, "We observed in particular that these oppositional narratives do not invoke radical activities or public displays of resistance; rather, they are fashioned around the routine, the personal and the everyday" (p. 204). Everyday resistance has political consequences (Scott 1985), and (collective) resistance and (individual) authenticity/ realization are not mutually exclusive (Muggleton 2000). Buechler (1999, 151) wrote, "In the case of life politics, the politicized self and the self-actualizing self become one and the same. The microphysics of power also points to identity as the battleground in contemporary forms of resistance" (see also Giddens 1991).

Though focused on personal methods of resistance, sXers understood their involvement in political terms as well.[16] Their abstinence from drugs, alcohol, and casual sex was an essential component of a broader resistance to dominant society and mainstream youth culture. As Buechler (1999) pointed out, "Although this form of politics originates on the microlevel of personal identity, its effects are not likely to remain confined to this level" (p. 150). The movement engages in what Giddens (1991, 214–15) called "life politics"—a "politics of choice," a "politics of lifestyle," a "politics of self-actualization," and a "politics of life decisions." Through their individual actions, sXers seek a "remoralizing of social life" (Buechler 1999, 150). For example, becoming a vegetarian or vegan may be an individualistic dietary choice, but when a subculture does so and advocates their choice, it opens up possibilities for other youth. As Leblanc (1999) noted, the intent to influence others is an important component of resistance: "Accounts of resistance must detail not only resistant acts, but the subjective intent motivating these as well. . . . Such resistance includes not only behaviors, but discursive and symbolic acts" (p. 18).

Looking at resistance through the lens of meanings, sites, and methods forces us to reexamine the "success" of subcultural resistance. Analyzing sXe's core values shows that members' understandings of resistance are many layered and contextual. The issue of resistance goes beyond whether a subculture resists dominant culture to how members construct resistance in particular situations and contexts. Certainly, sXe, like other subcultures, has illusory tendencies; the movement's contradictions include its antisexist yet male-centered ideology. However, examining sXe with the framework I suggest shows that involvement has real consequences for the lives of its members, other peer groups, and possibly mainstream society. Personal realization and social transformation are not mutually exclusive (Calhoun 1994). Although sXe has not created a revolution in either youth or mainstream culture, it has for more than twenty years, however, provided a haven for youth to contest these cultures and create alternatives.

NOTES

1. Straight edgers abbreviate straight edge as sXe. The *s* and the *e* stand for straight edge, and the *X* is the straight edge symbol.

2. Hardcore is a more aggressive, faster style of punk. Though punk and hardcore overlap, in the 1990s the two scenes increasingly became distinct. While present in both scenes, sXe is considerably more prevalent in the hardcore scene. The hardcore style is more clean-cut than punk.

3. Punks and sXers draw a sharp distinction between "shows" and "concerts." Shows attract a much smaller crowd, are less expensive, feature underground bands, often showcase local bands, and are set up by local kids in the scene at little or no profit. Concerts are large, commercialized, for-profit ventures typically featuring more mainstream bands.

4. Straight edge individuals never refer to themselves as *straight edgers* and find the term quite funny. It likely comes from media portrayals of the group. Adherents call themselves sXe "kids," no matter their ages. I use *straight edger* in this article simply for ease of communication.

5. See Muggleton (2000) for a discussion on the importance of grounding any subcultural analysis in members' subjective experiences.

6. I encountered one antiracist skinhead who also claimed to be sXe. He eventually dropped out of both groups, however. An older Latino sXer I knew, a veteran of the scene, claimed he was a skinhead many years ago.

7. Individuals or small groups produce 'zines filled with artwork, stories, record and concert reviews, band interviews, and columns on everything from police brutality and animal rights to homelessness and freeing journalist and former Black Panther Mumia Abu-Jamal from prison. 'Zines, like concerts, are generally DIY; that is, kids create them at home, distribute them, and rarely make any money off of them (in fact, 'zines often cost the producers a great deal of money).

8. Movements often appropriate and modify their oppressors' symbols. The gay and lesbian liberation movement changed the pink triangle from a Nazi death camp label for homosexuals into a symbol for unity and pride. The American Indian movement turned the American flag upside down to demonstrate its disgust with the U.S. government.

9. The community in Clearweather was very tight knit. In addition to shows, frequent potlucks, movie nights, parties, hanging out at popular campus locations, involvement in local animal rights activism, and even the occasional sleepover kept members in regular contact. Many sXe youth lived together. With the advent of e-mail and the Internet, sXe kids communicated via a virtual community around the country and sometimes the globe.

10. Veganism had become such a significant part of sXe by the late 1990s that many sXers gave it equal importance to living drug and alcohol free. Thus, many sXe vegans would self-identify as "vegan straight edge," and some bands identify as "vegan straight edge" rather than simply "straight edge." Veganism, while still widely practiced, had a declining presence after 2000.

11. All names are pseudonyms.

12. The popular bands Earth Crisis, Outspoken, and Good Clean Fun encouraged listeners to challenge homophobia. At one time, there was even a Web site dedicated to "Queer Edge."

13. Earth Crisis, one of the most popular sXe bands, sings, "An effective revolutionary, with the clarity of mind that I've attained."

14. Leblanc's (1999) work with punk girls illustrates multiple sites of resistance to hegemonic gender constructions. At the macro level, these young women resist society's dominant constructions of femininity; at the meso level, they resist gender roles in punk; and at the micro level, they challenge gender constructions in their families and focus on personal empowerment and self-esteem.

15. Leblanc (1999, 17) wrote, "Whereas subculture theorists conceptualize resistance as stylistic, and feminist theorists consider discursive accounts, recent critics of resistance theorizing have begun to examine the behavioral forms of resistance constructed by oppressed individuals in their everyday lives."

16. "To an increasing degree, problems of individual identity and collective action become meshed together: the solidarity of the group is inseparable from the personal quest" (Melucci 1996, 115).

REFERENCES

Adler, P. A., and P. Adler. 1987. *Membership roles in field research.* Newbury Park, CA: Sage.

Agar, M. H. 1996. *The professional stranger: An informal introduction to ethnography.* 2nd ed. San Diego, CA: Academic Press.

Becker, H. S., and B. Geer. 1960. Participant observation: The analysis of qualitative field data. In *Human organization research: Field relations and techniques,* edited by Richard N. Adams and Jack J. Preiss, 267–89. Homewood, IL: Dorsey.

Berger, B. M. 1967. Hippie morality—More old than new. *Trans-Action* 5(2): 19–26.

Biernacki, P., and D. Waldorf. 1981. Snowball sampling. *Sociological Research and Methods* 10:141–63.

Bjorgo, T., and R. Wilte, eds. 1993. *Racist violence in Europe.* New York: St. Martin's.

Blackman, S. J. 1995. *Youth: Positions and oppositions—Style, sexuality and schooling.* Aldershot, UK: Avebury.

Brake, M. 1985. *Comparative youth culture: The sociology of youth culture and youth subcultures in America, Britain, and Canada.* London: Routledge Kegan Paul.

Buechler, S. M. 1995. New social movement theories. *Sociological Quarterly* 36:441–64.

———. 1999. *Social movements in advanced capitalism: The political economy and cultural construction of social activism.* New York: Oxford University Press.

Calhoun, C. 1994. *Social theory and the politics of identity.* Oxford, UK: Blackwell.

Campbell, D. T. 1975. Degrees of freedom and the case study. *Comparative Political Studies* 8:178–93.

Charmaz, K. 1983. The grounded theory method: An explication and interpretation. In *Contemporary field research: A collection of readings,* edited by R. M. Emerson, 109–26. Boston: Little, Brown.

Clarke, G. [1981] 1997. Defending ski-jumpers: A critique of theories of youth subcultures. In *The subcultures reader,* edited by K. Gelder and S. Thornton. London: Routledge.

Clarke, J., S. Hall, T. Jefferson, and B. Roberts. 1975. Subcultures, cultures, and class: A theoretical overview. In *Resistance through rituals: Youth subcultures in post-war Britain,* edited by S. Hall and T. Jefferson. London: Hutchinson.

Cohen, S. 1972. *Folk devils and moral panics: The creation of the mods and the rockers.* Oxford, UK: Martin Robertson.

———. 1980. Symbols of trouble. In *Folk devils and moral panics: The creation of the mods and the rockers.* Oxford, UK: Martin Robertson.

Davis, F. 1967. Focus on the flower children. Why all of us may be hippies someday. *Trans-Action* 5(2):10–18.

———. 1968. Heads and freaks: Patterns and meanings of drug use among hippies. *Journal of Health and Social Behavior* 9(2):156–64.

Douglas, J. D. 1976. *Investigative social research.* Beverly Hills, CA: Sage.

Earisman, D. L. 1968. *Hippies in our midst.* Philadelphia: Fortress.

Earth Crisis. 1995. The discipline. On *Destroy the machines.* Compact disc. Chicago: Victory Records.

Fox, K. J. 1987. Real punks and pretenders: The social organization of a counterculture. *Journal of Contemporary Ethnography* 16(3):344–70.

Giddens, A. 1991. *Modernity and self-identity: Self and society in the late modern age.* Stanford, CA: Stanford University Press.

Good Clean Fun. 2001. Today the scene, tomorrow the world. On *Straight outta hardcore.* Compact disc. Washington, DC: Phyte Records.

Gottschalk, S. 1993. Uncomfortably numb: Countercultural impulses in the postmodern era. *Symbolic Interaction* 16(4):351–78.

Grossberg, L. 1992. *We gotta get out of this place: Popular conservatism and postmodern culture.* New York: Routledge.

Habermas, J. 1984–87. *The theory of communicative action.* Translated by T. McCarthy. Boston: Beacon.

Hall, S. 1972. Culture and the state. In *The state and popular culture,* edited by Milton Keynes. Berkshire, UK: Open University Press.

Hall, S., and T. Jefferson, eds. 1976. *Resistance through rituals: Youth subcultures in post-war Britain.* London: Hutchinson.

Hebdige, D. 1979. *Subcultures: The meaning of style.* London: Methuen.

Henry, T. 1989. *Break all rules! Punk rock and the making of a style.* Ann Arbor: University of Michigan Research Press.

Heylin, C. 1998. *Never mind the bollocks, here's the Sex Pistols: The Sex Pistols.* New York: Schirmer Books.

Hunter, J. D. 1987. *Evangelism: The coming generation.* Chicago: University of Chicago Press.

Irwin, D. 1999. The straight edge subculture: Examining the youths' drug-free way. *Journal of Drug Issues* 29(2):365–80.

Irwin, J. 1977. *Scenes.* Beverly Hills, CA: Sage.

Kaplan, J., and H. Lööw, eds. 2002. *The cultic milieu: Oppositional subcultures in an age of globalization.* Walnut Creek, CA: AltaMira Press.

Lahickey, B. 1997. *All ages: Reflections on straight edge.* Huntington Beach, CA: Revelation Books.

Leblanc, L. 1999. *Pretty in punk: Girls' gender resistance in a boys' subculture.* New Brunswick, NJ: Rutgers University Press.

Liebman, R. C., and R. Wuthnow, eds. 1983. *The new Christian Right: Mobilization and legitimation.* Hawthorne, NY: Aldine.

Lofland, J., and L. Lofland. 1995. *Analyzing social settings: A guide to qualitative observation and analysis.* 3rd ed. Belmont, CA: Wadsworth.

Marty, M. E., and R. S. Appleby, eds. 1993. *Fundamentalism and the state.* Chicago: University of Chicago Press.

Melucci, A. 1989. *Nomads of the present: Social movements and individual needs in contemporary society.* Philadelphia: Temple University Press.

———. 1996. *Challenging codes: Collective action in the information age.* New York: Cambridge University Press.

Miller, T. 1991. *The hippies and American values.* Knoxville: University of Tennessee Press.

———. 1999. *The 60s communes: Hippies and beyond.* Syracuse, NY: Syracuse University Press.

Moore, D. 1994. *The lads in action: Social process in an urban youth subculture.* Aldershot, UK: Arena.

Muggleton, D. 2000. *Inside subculture: The postmodern meaning of style.* Oxford, UK: Berg.

O'Hara, C. 1999. *The philosophy of punk: More than noise.* London: AK Press.

Parkin, F. 1968. *Middle class radicalism: The social bases of the British campaign for nuclear disarmament.* New York: Praeger.

Riemer, J. 1977. Varieties of opportunistic research. *Urban Life* 5(4):467–77.

Rose, T. 1994. *Black noise: Rap music and black culture in contemporary America.* New York: Routledge.

Scott, J. 1985. *Weapons of the weak: Everyday forms of peasant resistance.* New Haven, CT: Yale University Press.

Sersen, B., producer and director. 1999. *Release.* Film. Chicago: Victory Records.

Snow, D. A., E. B. Rochford Jr., S. K. Worden, and R. D. Benford. 1986. Frame alignment processes, micromobilization, and movement participation. *American Sociological Review* 51:464–81.

Stewart, A. 1998. *The ethnographer's method.* Thousand Oaks, CA: Sage.

Strife. 1997. To an end. On *In this defiance.* Compact disc. Chicago: Victory Records.

Taylor, V., and N. E. Whittier. 1992. Collective identity in social movement communities: Lesbian feminist mobilization. In *Frontiers in social movement theory,* edited by A. D. Morris and C. M. Mueller, 104–29. New Haven, CT: Yale University Press.

Widdicombe, S., and R. Wooffitt. 1995. *The language of youth subcultures: Social identity in action.* London: Harvester Wheatsheaf.

Willis, P. 1977. *Learning to labor: How working class kids get working class jobs.* New York: Columbia University Press.

Wooden, W. S., and R. Blazak. 2001. *Renegade kids, suburban outlaws: From youth culture to delinquency.* 2nd ed. Belmont, CA: Wadsworth.

Young, K., and L. Craig. 1997. Beyond white pride: Identity, meaning and contradiction in the Canadian skinhead subculture. *Canadian Review of Sociology and Anthropology* 34(2):175–206.

Youth of Today. 1986. Youth crew. On *Can't close my eyes.* LP record. Huntington Beach, CA: Revelation Records.

Appendix F

A Case Study—"Campus Response to a Student Gunman"

Kelly J. Asmussen

John W. Creswell

With increasingly frequent incidents of campus violence, a small, growing scholarly literature about the subject is emerging. For instance, authors have reported on racial [12], courtship and sexually coercive [3, 7, 8], and hazing violence [24]. For the American College Personnel Association, Roark [24] and Roark and Roark [25] reviewed the forms of physical, sexual, and psychological violence on college campuses and suggested guidelines for prevention strategies. Roark [23] has also suggested criteria that high-school students might use to assess the level of violence on college campuses they seek to attend. At the national level, President Bush, in November 1989, signed into law the "Student Right-to-Know and Campus Security Act" (P.L. 101-542), which requires colleges and universities to make available to students, employees, and applicants an annual report on security policies and campus crime statistics [13].

One form of escalating campus violence that has received little attention is student gun violence. Recent campus reports indicate that violent crimes from thefts and burglaries to assaults and homicides are on the rise at colleges and universities [13]. College campuses have been shocked by killings such as those at The University of Iowa [16], The University of Florida [13], Concordia University in Montreal, and the University of Montreal-Ecole Polytechnique [22]. Incidents such as these raise critical concerns, such as psychological trauma, campus safety, and disruption of

Source: The material in this appendix is reprinted from the Journal of Higher Education, 66, 575–591. Copyright 1995, the Ohio State University Press. Used by permission.

campus life. Aside from an occasional newspaper report, the postsecondary literature is silent on campus reactions to these tragedies; to understand them one must turn to studies about gun violence in the public school literature. This literature addresses strategies for school intervention [21, 23], provides case studies of incidents in individual schools [6, 14, 15], and discusses the problem of students who carry weapons to school [1] and the psychological trauma that results from homicides [32].

A need exists to study campus reactions to violence in order to build conceptual models for future study as well as to identify campus strategies and protocols for reaction. We need to understand better the psychological dimensions and organizational issues of constituents involved in and affected by these incidents. An in-depth qualitative case study exploring the context of an incident can illuminate such conceptual and pragmatic understandings. The study presented in this article is a qualitative case analysis [31] that describes and interprets a campus response to a gun incident. We asked the following exploratory research questions: What happened? Who was involved in response to the incident? What themes of response emerged during the eight-month period that followed this incident? What theoretical constructs helped us understand the campus response, and what constructs were unique to this case?

THE INCIDENT AND RESPONSE

The incident occurred on the campus of a large public university in a Midwestern city. A decade ago, this city had been designated an "all-American city," but more recently, its normally tranquil environment has been disturbed by an increasing number of assaults and homicides. Some of these violent incidents have involved students at the university.

The incident that provoked this study occurred on a Monday in October. A forty-three-year-old graduate student, enrolled in a senior-level actuarial science class, arrived a few minutes before class, armed with a vintage Korean War military semiautomatic rifle loaded with a thirty-round clip of thirty caliber ammunition. He carried another thirty-round clip in his pocket. Twenty of the thirty-four students in the class had already gathered for class, and most of them were quietly reading the student newspaper. The instructor was en route to class.

The gunman pointed the rifle at the students, swept it across the room, and pulled the trigger. The gun jammed. Trying to unlock the rifle, he hit the butt of it on the instructor's desk and quickly tried firing it again.

Again it did not fire. By this time, most students realized what was happening and dropped to the floor, overturned their desks, and tried to hide behind them. After about twenty seconds, one of the students shoved a desk into the gunman, and students ran past him out into the hall and out of the building. The gunman hastily departed the room and went out of the building to his parked car, which he had left running. He was captured by police within the hour in a nearby small town, where he lived. Although he remains incarcerated at this time, awaiting trial, the motivations for his actions are unknown.

Campus police and campus administrators were the first to react to the incident. Campus police arrived within three minutes after they had received a telephone call for help. They spent several anxious minutes outside the building interviewing students to obtain an accurate description of the gunman. Campus administrators responded by calling a news conference for 4:00 P.M. the same day, approximately four hours after the incident. The police chief as well as the vice-chancellor of Student Affairs and two students described the incident at the news conference. That same afternoon, the Student Affairs office contacted Student Health and Employee Assistance Program (EAP) counselors and instructed them to be available for any students or staff requesting assistance. The Student Affairs office also arranged for a new location, where this class could meet for the rest of the semester. The Office of Judicial Affairs suspended the gunman from the university. The next day, the incident was discussed by campus administrators at a regularly scheduled campuswide cabinet meeting. Throughout the week, Student Affairs received several calls from students and from a faculty member about "disturbed" students or unsettling student relations. A counselor of the Employee Assistance Program consulted a psychologist with a specialty in dealing with trauma and responding to educational crises. Only one student immediately set up an appointment with the student health counselors. The campus and local newspapers continued to carry stories about the incident.

When the actuarial science class met for regularly scheduled classes two and four days later, the students and the instructor were visited by two county attorneys, the police chief, and two student mental health counselors who conducted "debriefing" sessions. These sessions focused on keeping students fully informed about the judicial process and having the students and the instructor, one by one, talk about their experiences and explore their feelings about the incident. By one week after the incident, the students in the class had returned to their standard class format. During this time, a few students, women who were concerned about violence in general, saw Student Health Center counselors. These counselors also fielded questions from several dozen parents who inquired about the counseling services and the level of safety on campus. Some parents also called the campus administration to ask about safety procedures.

In the weeks following the incident, the faculty and staff campus newsletter carried articles about post-trauma fears and psychological trauma. The campus administration wrote a letter that provided facts about the incident to the board of the university. The administration also mailed campus staff and students information about crime prevention. At least one college dean sent out a memo to staff about "aberrant student behavior," and one academic department chair requested and held an educational group session with counselors and staff on identifying and dealing with "aberrant behavior" of students.

Three distinctly different staff groups sought counseling services at the Employee Assistance Program, a program for faculty and staff, during the next several weeks. The first group had had some direct involvement with the assailant, either by seeing him the day of the gun incident or because they had known him personally. This group was concerned about securing professional help, either for the students or for those in the group who were personally experiencing effects of the trauma. The second group consisted of the "silent connection," individuals who were indirectly involved and yet emotionally traumatized. This group recognized that their fears were a result of the gunman incident, and they wanted to deal with these fears before they escalated. The third group consisted of staff who had previously experienced a trauma, and this incident had retriggered their fears. Several employees were seen by the EAP throughout the next month, but no new groups or delayed stress cases were reported. The EAP counselors stated that each group's reactions were normal responses. Within a month, although public discussion of the incident had subsided, the EAP and Student Health counselors began expressing the need for a coordinated campus plan to deal with the current as well as any future violent incidents.

THE RESEARCH STUDY

We began our study two days after the incident. Our first step was to draft a research protocol for approval by the university administration and the Institutional Review Board. We made explicit that we would not become involved in the investigation of the gunman or in the therapy to students or staff who had sought assistance from counselors. We also limited our study to the reactions of groups on campus rather than expand it to include off-campus groups (for example, television and newspaper coverage). This bounding of the study was consistent with an exploratory qualitative case study design [31], which was chosen because models and variables were not available for assessing a campus reaction to a gun incident in higher education. In the constructionist tradition, this study incorporated the paradigm assumptions of an emerging design, a context-dependent inquiry, and an inductive data analysis [10]. We also bounded the study by time (eight months) and by a single case (the campus community). Consistent with case study design [17, 31], we identified campus administrators and student newspaper reporters as multiple sources of information for initial interviews. Later we expanded interviews to include a wide array of campus informants, using a semi-structured interview protocol that consisted of five questions: What has been your role in the incident? What has happened since the event that you have been involved in? What has been the impact of this incident on the university community? What larger ramifications, if any, exist from the incident? To whom should we talk to find out more about the campus reaction to the incident? We also gathered observational data, documents, and visual materials (see table 1 for types of information and sources).

The narrative structure was a "realist" tale [28], describing details, incorporating edited quotes from informants, and stating our interpretations of events, especially an interpretation within the framework of organizational and psychological issues. We verified the description and interpretation by taking a preliminary draft of the case to select informants for feedback and later incorporating their comments into the final study [17, 18]. We gathered this feedback in a group interview where we asked: Is our description of the incident and the reaction accurate? Are the themes and constructs we have identified consistent with your experiences? Are there some themes and constructs we have missed? Is a campus plan needed? If so, what form should it take?

THEMES

Denial

Several weeks later we returned to the classroom where the incident occurred. Instead of finding the desks overturned, we found them to be

Table 1 Data Collection Matrix: Type of Information by Source

Information/Information Source	Interviews	Observations	Documents	Audio-Visual Materials
Students involved	Yes		Yes	
Students at large	Yes			
Central administration	Yes		Yes	
Campus police	Yes	Yes		
Faculty	Yes	Yes	Yes	
Staff	Yes			
Physical plant		Yes	Yes	
News reporters/papers/television	Yes		Yes	Yes
Student health counselors	Yes			
Employee Assistance Program counselors	Yes			
Trauma expert	Yes		Yes	Yes
Campus businesses			Yes	
Board members			Yes	

neatly in order; the room was ready for a lecture or discussion class. The hallway outside the room was narrow, and we visualized how students, on that Monday in October, had quickly left the building, unaware that the gunman, too, was exiting through this same passageway. Many of the students in the hallway during the incident had seemed unaware of what was going on until they saw or heard that there was a gunman in the building. Ironically though, the students had seemed to ignore or deny their dangerous situation. After exiting the building, instead of seeking a hiding place that would be safe, they had huddled together just outside the building. None of the students had barricaded themselves in classrooms or offices or had exited at a safe distance from the scene in anticipation that the gunman might return. "People wanted to stand their ground and stick around," claimed a campus police officer. Failing to respond to the potential danger, the class members had huddled together outside the building, talking nervously. A few had been openly emotional and crying. When asked about their mood, one of the students had said, "Most of us were kidding about it." Their conversations had led one to believe that they were dismissing the incident as though it were trivial and as though no one had actually been in danger. An investigating campus police officer was not surprised by the students' behavior:

It is not unusual to see people standing around after one of these types of incidents. The American people want to see excitement and have a morbid curiosity. That is why you see spectators hanging around bad accidents. They do not seem to understand the potential danger they are in and do not want to leave until they are injured.

This description corroborates the response reported by mental health counselors: an initial surrealistic first reaction. In the debriefing by counselors, one female student had commented, "I thought the gunman would shoot out a little flag that would say 'bang.'" For her, the event had been like a dream. In this atmosphere no one from the targeted class had called the campus mental health center in the first twenty-four hours following the incident, although they knew that services were available. Instead, students described how they had visited with friends or had gone to bars; the severity of the situation had dawned on them later. One student commented that he had felt fearful and angry only after he had seen the television newscast with pictures of the classroom the evening of the incident.

Though some parents had expressed concern by phoning counselors, the students' denial may have been reinforced by parent comments. One student reported that his parents had made comments like, "I am not surprised you were involved in this. You are always getting yourself into things like this!" or "You did not get hurt. What is the big deal? Just let it drop!" One student expressed how much more traumatized he had been as a result of his mother's dismissal of the event. He had wanted to have someone whom he trusted willing to sit down and listen to him.

Fear

Our visit to the classroom suggested a second theme: the response of fear. Still posted on the door several weeks after the incident, we saw the sign announcing that the class was being moved to another undisclosed building and that students were to check with a secretary in an adjoining room about the new location. It was in this undisclosed classroom, two days after the incident, that two student mental health counselors, the campus police chief, and two county attorneys had met with students in the class to discuss fears, reactions, and thoughts. Reactions of fear had begun to surface in this first "debriefing" session and continued to emerge in a second session.

The immediate fear for most students centered around the thought that the alleged assailant would be able to make bail. Students felt that the assailant might have harbored resentment toward certain students and that he would seek retribution if he made bail. "I think I am going to be afraid when I go back to class. They can change the rooms, but there is nothing stopping him from finding out where we are!" said one student. At the first debriefing session the campus police chief was able to dispel some of this fear by announcing that during the initial hearing the judge had denied bail. This announcement helped to reassure some students about their safety. The campus police chief thought it necessary to keep the students informed of the gunman's status, because several students had called his office to say that they feared for their safety if the gunman were released.

During the second debriefing session, another fear surfaced: the possibility that a different assailant could attack the class. One student reacted so severely to this potential threat that, according to one counselor, since the October incident, "he had caught himself walking into class and sitting at a desk with a clear shot to the door. He was beginning to see each classroom as a 'battlefield.'" In this second session students had sounded angry, they expressed feeling violated, and finally [they] began to admit that they felt unsafe. Yet only one female student immediately accessed the available mental health services, even though an announcement had been made that any student could obtain free counseling.

The fear students expressed during the "debriefing" sessions mirrored a more general concern on campus about increasingly frequent violent acts in the metropolitan area. Prior to this gun incident, three young females and a male had been kidnapped and had later been found dead in a nearby city. A university football player who experienced a psychotic episode had severely beaten a woman. He had later suffered a relapse and was shot by police in a scuffle. Just three weeks prior to the October gun incident, a female university student had been abducted and brutally murdered, and several other homicides had occurred in the city. As a student news reporter commented, "This whole semester has been a violent one."

SAFETY

The violence in the city that involved university students and the subsequent gun incident that occurred in a campus classroom shocked the typically tranquil campus. A counselor aptly summed up the feelings of many: "When the students walked out of that classroom, their world had become very chaotic; it had become very random, something had happened that robbed them of their sense of safety." Concern for safety became a central reaction for many informants.

When the chief student affairs officer described the administration's reaction to the incident, he listed the safety of students in the classroom as his primary goal, followed by the needs of the news media for details about the case, helping all students with psychological stress, and providing public information on safety. As he talked about the safety issue and the presence of guns on campus, he mentioned that a policy was under consideration for the storage of guns used by students for hunting. Within four hours after the incident, a press conference was called during which the press was briefed not only on the details of the incident, but also on the need to ensure the safety of the campus. Soon thereafter the university administration initiated an informational campaign on campus safety. A letter, describing the incident, was sent to the university board members. (One board member asked, "How could such an incident happen at this university?") The Student Affairs Office sent a letter to all students in which it advised them of the various dimensions of the campus security office and of the types of services it provided. The Counseling and Psychological Services of the Student Health Center promoted their services in a colorful brochure, which was mailed to students in the following week. It emphasized that services were "confidential, accessible, and professional." The Student Judiciary Office advised academic departments on various methods of dealing with students who exhibited abnormal behavior in class. The weekly faculty newsletter stressed that staff needed to respond quickly to any post-trauma fears associated with this incident. The campus newspaper quoted a professor as saying, "I'm totally shocked that in this environment, something like this would happen." Responding to the concerns about disruptive students or employees, the campus police department sent plainclothes officers to sit outside offices whenever faculty and staff indicated concerns.

An emergency phone system, Code Blue, was installed on campus only ten days after the incident. These thirty-six ten-foot-tall emergency phones, with bright blue flashing lights, had previously been approved, and specific spots had already been identified from an earlier study. "The phones will be quite an attention getter," the director of the Telecommunications Center commented. "We hope they will also be a big detractor [to crime]." Soon afterwards, in response to calls from concerned students, trees and shrubbery in poorly lit areas of campus were trimmed.

Appendix F

Students and parents also responded to these safety concerns. At least twenty-five parents called the Student Health Center, the university police, and the Student Affairs Office during the first week after the incident to inquire what kind of services were available for their students. Many parents had been traumatized by the news of the event and immediately demanded answers from the university. They wanted assurances that this type of incident would not happen again and that their child[ren were] safe on the campus. Undoubtedly, many parents also called their children during the weeks immediately following the incident. The students on campus responded to these safety concerns by forming groups of volunteers who would escort anyone on campus, male or female, during the evening hours.

Local businesses profited by exploiting the commercial aspects of the safety needs created by this incident. Various advertisements for self-defense classes and protection devices inundated the newspapers for several weeks. Campus and local clubs [that] offered self-defense classes filled quickly, and new classes were formed in response to numerous additional requests. The campus bookstore's supply of pocket mace and whistles was quickly depleted. The campus police received several inquiries by students who wanted to purchase handguns to carry for protection. None [was] approved, but one wonders whether some guns were not purchased by students anyway. The purchase of cellular telephones from local vendors increased sharply. Most of these purchases were made by females; however, some males also sought out these items for their safety and protection. Not unexpectedly, the price of some products was raised as much as 40 percent to capitalize on the newly created demand. Student conversations centered around the purchase of these safety products: how much they cost, how to use them correctly, how accessible they would be if students should need to use them, and whether they were really necessary.

RETRIGGERING

In our original protocol, which we designed to seek approval from the campus administration and the Institutional Review Board, we had outlined a study that would last only three months—a reasonable time, we thought, for this incident to run its course. But during early interviews with counselors, we were referred to a psychologist who specialized in dealing with "trauma" in educational settings. It was this psychologist who mentioned the theme of "retriggering." Now, eight months later, we begin to understand how, through "retriggering," that October incident could have a long-term effect on this campus.

This psychologist explained retriggering as a process by which new incidents of violence would cause individuals to relive the feelings of fear, denial, and threats to personal safety that they had experienced in connection with the original event. The counseling staffs and violence expert also stated that one should expect to see such feelings retriggered at a later point in time, for example, on the anniversary date of the attack or whenever newspapers or television broadcasts mentioned the incident again. They added that a drawn-out judicial process, during which a case were "kept alive" through legal maneuvering, could cause a long period of retriggering and thereby greatly thwart the healing process. The fairness of the judgment of the court as seen by each victim, we were told, would also influence the amount of healing and resolution of feelings that could occur.

As of this writing, it is difficult to detect specific evidence of retriggering from the October incident, but we discovered the potential consequences of this process firsthand by observing the effects of a nearly identical violent gun incident that had happened some eighteen years earlier. A graduate student carrying a rifle had entered a campus building with the intention of shooting the department chairman. The student was seeking revenge, because several years earlier he had flunked a course taught by this professor. This attempted attack followed several years of legal maneuvers to arrest, prosecute, and incarcerate this student, who, on more than one occasion, had tried to carry out his plan but each time had been thwarted by quick-thinking staff members who would not reveal the professor's whereabouts. Fortunately, no shots were ever fired, and the student was finally apprehended and arrested.

The professor who was the target of these threats on his life was seriously traumatized not only during the period of these repeated incidents, but his trauma continued even after the attacker's arrest. The complex processes of the criminal justice system, which, he believed, did not work as it should have, resulted in his feeling further victimized. To this day, the feelings aroused by the original trauma are retriggered each time a gun incident is reported in the news. He was not offered professional help from the university at any time; the counseling services he did receive were secured through his own initiative. Eighteen years later his entire department is still affected in that unwritten rules for dealing with disgruntled students and for protecting this particular professor's schedule have been established.

CAMPUS PLANNING

The question of campus preparedness surfaced during discussions with the psychologist about the process of "debriefing" individuals who had been involved in the October incident [19]. Considering how many diverse groups and individuals had been affected by this incident, a final theme that emerged from our data was the need for a campuswide plan. A counselor remarked, "We would have been inundated had there been twenty-five to thirty deaths. We need a mobilized plan of communication. It would be a wonderful addition to the campus considering the nature of today's violent world." It became apparent during our interviews that better communication could have occurred among the constituents who responded to this incident. Of course, one campus police officer noted, "We can't have an officer in every building all day long!" But the theme of being prepared across the whole campus was mentioned by several individuals.

The lack of a formal plan to deal with such gun incidents was surprising, given the existence of formal written plans on campus that addressed various other emergencies: bomb threats, chemical spills, fires, earthquakes, explosions, electrical storms, radiation accidents, tornadoes, hazardous material spills, snowstorms, and numerous medical emergencies. Moreover, we found that specific campus units had their own protocols that had actually been used during the October gun incident. For example, the police had a procedure and used that procedure for dealing with the gunman and the students at the scene; the EAP counselors debriefed staff and faculty; the Student Health counselors used a "debriefing" process when they visited the students twice in the classroom following the incident. The question that concerned us was, what would a campuswide plan consist of, and how would it be developed and evaluated?

As shown in table 2, using evidence gathered in our case, we assembled the basic questions to be addressed in a plan and cross-referenced these questions to the literature about post-trauma stress, campus violence, and the disaster literature (for a similar list drawn from the public school literature, see Poland and Pitcher [21]). Basic elements of a campus plan to enhance communication across units should include determining what the rationale for the plan is; who should be involved in its development; how it should be coordinated; how it should be staffed; and what specific procedures should be followed. These procedures might include responding to an immediate crisis, making the campus safe, dealing with external groups, and providing for the psychological welfare of victims.

Table 2 Evidence From the Case, Questions for a Campus Plan, and References

Evidence From the Case	Question for the Plan	Useful References
Need expressed by counselors	Why should a plan be developed?	Walker (1990); Bird et al. (1991)
Multiple constitutes reacting to incident	Who should be involved in developing the plan?	Roark & Roark (1987); Walker (1990)
Leadership found in units with their own protocols	Should the leadership for coordinating be identified within one office?	Roark & Roark (1987)
Several unit protocols being used in incident	Should campus units be allowed their own protocols?	Roark & Roark (1987)
Questions raised by students reacting to case	What types of violence should be covered in the plan?	Roark (1987); Jones (1990)
Groups/individuals surfaced during our interviews	How are those likely to be affected by the incident to be identified?	Walker (1990); Bromet (1990)
Comments from campus police, central administration	What provisions are made for the immediate safety of those in the incident?	
Campus environment changed after incident	How should the physical environment be made safer?	Roark & Roark (1987)
Comments from central administration	How will the external publics (e.g., press, businesses) be apprised of the incident?	Poland & Pitcher (1990)
Issue raised by counselors and trauma specialist	What are the likely sequelae of psychological events for victims?	Bromet (1990); Mitchell (1983)
Issue raised by trauma specialist	What long-term impact will the incident have on victims?	Zelikoff (1987)
Procedure used by Student Health Center counselors	How will the victims be debriefed?	Mitchell (1983); Walker (1990)

DISCUSSION

The themes of denial, fear, safety, retriggering, and developing a campus-wide plan might further be grouped into two categories, an organizational and a psychological or social-psychological response of the campus community to the gunman incident. Organizationally, the campus units responding to the crisis exhibited both a loose coupling [30] and an inter-dependent communication. Issues such as leadership, communication, and authority emerged during the case analysis. Also, an environmental response developed, because the campus was transformed into a safer place for students and staff. The need for centralized planning, while allowing for autonomous operation of units in response to a crisis, called for organizational change that would require cooperation and coordination among units.

Sherrill [27] provides models of response to campus violence that reinforce as well as depart from the evidence in our case. As mentioned by Sherrill, the disciplinary action taken against a perpetrator, the group counseling of victims, and the use of safety education for the campus community were all factors apparent in our case. However, Sherrill raises issues about responses that were not discussed by our informants, such as developing procedures for individuals who are first to arrive on the scene, dealing with non-students who might be perpetrators or victims, keeping records and documents about incidents, varying responses based on the size and nature of the institution, and relating incidents to substance abuse such as drugs and alcohol.

Also, some of the issues that we had expected after reading the literature about organizational response did not emerge. Aside from occasional newspaper reports (focused mainly on the gunman), there was little campus administrative response to the incident, which was contrary to what we had expected from Roark and Roark [25], for example. No mention was made of establishing a campus unit to manage future incidents—for example, a campus violence resource center—reporting of violent incidents [25], or conducting annual safety audits [20]. Aside from the campus police mentioning that the State Health Department would have been prepared to send a team of trained trauma experts to help emergency personnel cope with the tragedy, no discussion was reported about formal linkages with community agencies that might assist in the event of a tragedy [3]. We also did not hear directly about establishing a "command center" [14] or a crisis coordinator [21], two actions recommended by specialists on crisis situations.

On a psychological and social-psychological level, the campus response was to react to the psychological needs of the students who had been directly involved in the incident as well as to students and staff who had been indirectly affected by the incident. Not only did signs of psychological issues, such as denial, fear, and retriggering, emerge, as expected [15], gender and cultural group issues were also mentioned, though they were not discussed enough to be considered basic themes in our analysis. Contrary to assertions in the literature that violent behavior is often accepted in our culture, we found informants in our study to voice concern and fear about escalating violence on campus and in the community.

Faculty on campus were conspicuously silent on the incident, including the faculty senate, though we had expected this governing body to take up the issue of aberrant student or faculty behavior in their classrooms [25]. Some informants speculated that the faculty might have been passive about this issue because they were unconcerned, but another explanation might be that they were passive because they were unsure of what to do or whom to ask for assistance. From the students we failed to hear that they responded to their posttraumatic stress with "coping" strategies, such as relaxation, physical activity, and the establishment of normal routines [29]. Although the issues of gender and race surfaced in early conversations with informants, we did not find a direct discussion of these issues. As Bromet [5] comments, the sociocultural needs of populations with different mores must be considered when individuals assess reactions to trauma. In regard to the issue of gender, we did hear that females were the first students to seek out counseling at the Student Health Center. Perhaps our "near-miss" case was unique. We do not know what the reaction of the campus might have been had a death (or multiple deaths) occurred, although, according to the trauma psychologist, "the trauma of no deaths is as great as if deaths had occurred." Moreover, as with any exploratory case analysis, this case has limited generalizability [17], although thematic generalizability is certainly a possibility. The fact that our information was self-reported and that we were unable to interview all students who had been directly affected by the incident so as to not intervene in student therapy or the investigation also poses a problem.

Despite these limitations, our research provides a detailed account of a campus reaction to a violent incident with the potential for making a contribution to the literature. Events emerged during the process of reaction that could be "critical incidents" in future studies, such as the victim response, media reporting, the debriefing process, campus changes, and the evolution of a campus plan. With the scarcity of literature on campus violence related to gun incidents, this study breaks new ground by identifying themes and conceptual frameworks that could be examined in future cases. On a practical level, it can benefit campus administrators who are looking for a plan to respond to campus violence, and it focuses attention on questions that need to be addressed in such a plan. The large number of different groups of people who were affected by this particular gunman incident shows the complexity of responding to a campus crisis and should alert college personnel to the need for preparedness.

EPILOGUE

As we conducted this study, we asked ourselves whether we would have had access to informants if someone had been killed. This "near-miss" incident provided a unique research opportunity, which could, however, only approximate an event in which a fatality had actually occurred. Our involvement in this study was serendipitous, for one of us had been employed by a correctional facility and therefore had direct experience with gunmen such as the individual in our case; the other was a University of Iowa graduate and thus familiar with the setting and circumstances surrounding another violent incident there in 1992. These experiences obviously affected our assessment of this case by drawing our attention to the campus response in the first plan and to psychological reactions like fear and denial. At the time of this writing, campus discussions have been held about adapting the in-place campus emergency preparedness plan to a critical incident management team concept. Counselors have met to discuss coordinating the activities of different units in the event of another incident, and the police are working with faculty members and department staff to help identify potentially violence-prone students. We have the impression that, as a result of this case study, campus personnel see the interrelatedness and the large number of units that may be involved in a single incident. The anniversary date passed without incident or acknowledgment in the campus newspaper. As for the gunman, he is still incarcerated awaiting trial, and we wonder, as do some of the students he threatened, if he will seek retribution against us for writing up this case if he is released. The campus response to the October incident continues.

REFERENCES

1. Asmussen, K. J. "Weapon Possession in Public High Schools." *School Safety* (Fall 1992), 28–30.

Appendix F

2. Bird, G. W., S. M. Stith, and J. Schladale. "Psychological Resources, Coping Strategies, and Negotiation Styles as Discriminators of Violence in Dating Relationships." *Family Relations,* 40 (1991), 45–50.

3. Bogal-Allbritten, R., and W. Allbritten. "Courtship Violence on Campus: A Nationwide Survey of Student Affairs Professionals." *NASPA Journal,* 28 (1991), 312–18.

4. Boothe, J. W., T. M. Flick, S. P. Kirk, L. H. Bradley, and K. E. Keough. "The Violence at Your Door." *Executive Educator* (February 1993), 16–22.

5. Bromet, E. J. "Methodological Issues in the Assessment of Traumatic Events." *Journal of Applied Psychology,* 20 (1990), 1719–24.

6. Bushweller, K. "Guards with Guns." *American School Board Journal* (January 1993), 34–36.

7. Copenhaver, S., and E. Grauerholz. "Sexual Victimization among Sorority Women." *Sex Roles: A Journal of Research,* 24 (1991), 31–41.

8. Follingstad, D., S. Wright, S. Lloyd, and J. Sebastian. "Sex Differences in Motivations and Effects in Dating Violence." *Family Relations,* 40 (1991), 51–57.

9. Gordon, M. T., and S. Riger. *The Female Fear.* Urbana: University of Illinois Press, 1991.

10. Guba, E., and Y. Lincoln. "Do Inquiry Paradigms Imply Inquiry Methodologies?" In *Qualitative Approaches to Evaluation in Education,* edited by D. M. Fetterman. New York: Praeger, 1988.

11. Johnson, K. "The Tip of the Iceberg." *School Safety* (Fall 1992), 24–26.

12. Jones, D. J. "The College Campus as a Microcosm of U.S. Society: The Issue of Racially Motivated Violence." *Urban League Review,* 13 (1990), 129–39.

13. Legislative Update. "Campuses Must Tell Crime Rates." *School Safety* (Winter 1991), 31.

14. Long, N. J. "Managing a Shooting Incident." *Journal of Emotional and Behavioral Problems,* 1 (1992), 23–26.

15. Lowe, J. A. "What We Learned: Some Generalizations in Dealing with a Traumatic Event at Cokeville." Paper presented at the Annual Meeting of the National School Boards Association, San Francisco, 4–7 April 1987.

16. Mann, J. *Los Angeles Times Magazine,* 2 June 1992, pp. 26–27, 32, 46–47.

17. Merriam, S. B. *Case Study Research in Education: A Qualitative Approach.* San Francisco: Jossey-Bass, 1988.

18. Miles, M. B., and A. M. Huberman. *Qualitative Data Analysis: A Sourcebook of New Methods.* Beverly Hills, Calif.: Sage, 1984.

19. Mitchell, J. "When Disaster Strikes." *Journal of Emergency Medical Services* (January 1983), 36–39.

20. NSSC Report on School Safety. "Preparing Schools for Terroristic Attacks." *School Safety* (Winter 1991), 18–19.

21. Poland, S., and G. Pitcher. *Crisis Intervention in the Schools.* New York: Guilford, 1992.

22. Quimet, M. "The Polytechnique Incident and Imitative Violence against Women." *SSR,* 76 (1992), 45–47.

23. Roark, M. L. "Helping High School Students Assess Campus Safety." *The School Counselor,* 39 (1992), 251–56.

24. ——. "Preventing Violence on College Campuses." *Journal of Counseling and Development,* 65 (1987), 367–70.

25. Roark, M. L., and E. W. Roark. "Administrative Responses to Campus Violence." Paper presented at the annual meeting of the American College Personnel Association/National Association of Student Personnel Administrators, Chicago, 15–18 March 1987.

26. "School Crisis: Under Control," 1991 [video]. National School Safety Center, a partnership of Pepperdine University and the United States Departments of Justice and Education.

27. Sherill, J. M., and D. G. Seigel (eds.). *Responding to Violence on Campus.* New Directions for Student Services, No. 47. San Francisco: Jossey-Bass, 1989.

28. Van Maanen, J. *Tales of the Field.* Chicago: University of Chicago Press, 1988.

29. Walker, G. "Crisis-Care in Critical Incident Debriefing." *Death Studies,* 14 (1990), 121–33.

30. Weick, K. E. "Educational Organizations as Loosely Coupled Systems." *Administrative Science Quarterly,* 21 (1976), 1–19.

31. Yin, R. K. *Case Study Research, Design and Methods.* Newbury Park, Calif.: Sage, 1989.

32. Zelikoff, W. I., and I. A. Hyman. "Psychological Trauma in the Schools: A Retrospective Study." Paper presented at the annual meeting of the National Association of School Psychologists, New Orleans, La., 4–8 March 1987.

References

Aanstoos, C. M. (1985). The structure of thinking in chess. In A. Giorgi (Ed.), *Phenomenology and psychological research* (pp. 86–117). Pittsburgh, PA: Duquesne University Press.

Agar, M. H. (1980). *The professional stranger: An informal introduction to ethnography.* San Diego, CA: Academic Press.

Agar, M. H. (1986). *Speaking of ethnography.* Beverly Hills, CA: Sage.

Agger, B. (1991). Critical theory, poststructuralism, postmodernism: Their sociological relevance. In W. R. Scott & J. Blake (Eds.), *Annual Review of Sociology* (Vol. 17, pp. 105–131). Palo Alto, CA: Annual Reviews.

American Anthropological Association. (1967). *Statement on problems of anthropological research and ethics.* Adopted by the Council of the American Anthropological Association. Arlington, VA: Author.

American Psychological Association. (2010). *Publication manual of the American Psychological Association* (6th ed.). Washington, DC: Author.

Anderson, E. H., & Spencer, M. H. (2002). Cognitive representations of AIDS: A phenomenological study. *Qualitative Health Research, 12,* 1338–1352.

Angen, M. J. (2000, May). Evaluating interpretive inquiry: Reviewing the validity debate and opening the dialogue. *Qualitative Health Research, 10,* 378–395.

Angrosino, M. V. (1989a). *Documents of interaction: Biography, autobiography, and life history in social science perspective.* Gainesville: University of Florida Press.

Angrosino, M. V. (1989b). Freddie: The personal narrative of a recovering alcoholic—Autobiography as case history. In M. V. Angrosino (Ed.), *Documents of interaction: Biography, autobiography, and life history in social science perspective* (pp. 29–41). Gainesville: University of Florida Press.

Angrosino, M. V. (1994). On the bus with Vonnie Lee. *Journal of Contemporary Ethnography, 23,* 14–28.

Angrosino, M. V. (2007). *Doing ethnographic and observational research.* Thousand Oaks, CA: Sage.

Armstrong, D., Gosling, A., Weinman, J., & Marteau, T. (1997). The place of interrater reliability in qualitative research: An empirical study. *Sociology, 31,* 597–606.

Asmussen, K. J., & Creswell, J. W. (1995). Campus response to a student gunman. *Journal of Higher Education, 66,* 575–591.

Atkinson, P., Coffey, A., & Delamont, S. (2003). *Key themes in qualitative research: Continuities and changes.* Walnut Creek, CA: AltaMira.

Atkinson, P., & Hammersley, M. (1994). Ethnography and participant observation. In N. K. Denzin & Y. S. Lincoln (Eds.), *Handbook of qualitative research* (pp. 248–261). Thousand Oaks, CA: Sage.

Babchuk, W. A. (2011). Grounded theory as a "family of methods": A genealogical analysis to guide research. *US-China Education Review, 8*(2), 1548–1566.

Barbour, R. S. (2000). The role of qualitative research in broadening the "evidence base" for clinical practice. *Journal of Evaluation in Clinical Practice, 6*(2), 155 163.

Barritt, L. (1986). Human sciences and the human image. *Phenomenology and Pedagogy, 4*(3), 14–22.

Bazeley, P. (2002). The evolution of a project involving an integrated analysis of structured qualitative and quantitative data: From N3 to NVivo. *International Journal of Social Research Methodology, 5,* 229–243.

Bernard, H. R. (1994). *Research methods in anthropology: Qualitative and quantitative approaches* (2nd ed.). Thousand Oaks, CA: Sage.

Beverly, J. (2005). *Testimonio,* subalternity, and narrative authority. In N. K. Denzin & Y. S. Lincoln (Eds.), *The Sage handbook of qualitative research* (3rd ed., pp. 547–558). Thousand Oaks, CA: Sage.

Birks, M., & Mills, J. (2011). *Grounded theory: A practical guide.* London: Sage.

Bloland, H. G. (1995). Postmodernism and higher education. *Journal of Higher Education, 66,* 521–559.

Bogdan, R. C., & Biklen, S. K. (1992). *Qualitative research for education: An introduction to theory and methods.* Boston: Allyn & Bacon.

Bogdan, R., & Taylor, S. (1975). *Introduction to qualitative research methods.* New York: John Wiley.

Bogdewic, S. P. (1992). Participant observation. In B. F. Crabtree & W. L. Miller (Eds.), *Doing qualitative research* (pp. 45–69). Newbury Park, CA: Sage.

Borgatta, E. F., & Borgatta, M. L. (Eds.). (1992). *Encyclopedia of sociology* (Vol. 4). New York: Macmillan.

Brickhous, N., & Bodner, G. M. (1992). The beginning science teacher: Classroom narratives of convictions and constraints. *Journal of Research in Science Teaching, 29,* 471–485.

Brimhall, A. C., & Engblom-Deglmann, M. L. (2011). Starting over: A tentative theory exploring the effects of past relationships on postbereavement remarried couples. *Family Process, 50*(1), 47–62.

Brown, J., Sorrell, J. H., McClaren, J., & Creswell, J. W. (2006). Waiting for a liver transplant. *Qualitative Health Research, 16*(1), 119–136.

Burrell, G., & Morgan, G. (1979). *Sociological paradigms and organizational analysis.* London: Heinemann.

Carspecken, P. F., & Apple, M. (1992). Critical qualitative research: Theory, methodology, and practice. In M. L. LeCompte, W. L. Millroy, & J. Preissle (Eds.), *The handbook of qualitative research in education* (pp. 507–553). San Diego, CA: Academic Press.

Carter, K. (1993). The place of a story in the study of teaching and teacher education. *Educational Researcher, 22,* 5–12, 18.

Casey, K. (1995/1996). The new narrative research in education. *Review of Research in Education, 21,* 211–253.

Chan, E. (2010). Living in the space between participant and researcher as a narrative inquirer: Examining ethnic identity of Chinese Canadian students as conflicting stories to live by. *The Journal of Educational Research, 103,* 113–122.

Charmaz, K. (1983). The grounded theory method: An explication and interpretation. In R. Emerson (Ed.), *Contemporary field research* (pp. 109–126). Boston: Little, Brown.

Charmaz, K. (2005). Grounded theory in the 21st century: Applications for advancing social justice studies. In N. K. Denzin & Y. S. Lincoln (Eds.), *The Sage handbook of qualitative research* (3rd ed., pp. 507–536). Thousand Oaks, CA: Sage.

Charmaz, K. (2006). *Constructing grounded theory.* London: Sage.

Chase, S. (2005). Narrative inquiry: Multiple lenses, approaches, voices. In N. K. Denzin & Y. S. Lincoln (Eds.), *The Sage handbook of qualitative research* (3rd ed., pp. 651–680). Thousand Oaks, CA: Sage.

Cheek, J. (2004). At the margins? Discourse analysis and qualitative research. *Qualitative Health Research, 14,* 1140–1150.

Chenitz, W. C., & Swanson, J. M. (1986). *From practice to grounded theory: Qualitative research in nursing.* Menlo Park, CA: Addison-Wesley.

Cherryholmes, C. H. (1992). Notes on pragmatism and scientific realism. *Educational Researcher, 14,* 13–17.

Churchill, S. L., Plano Clark, V. L., Prochaska-Cue, M. K., Creswell, J. W., & Onta-Grzebik, L. (2007). How rural low-income families have fun: A grounded theory study. *Journal of Leisure Research, 39*(2), 271–294.

Clandinin, D. J. (Ed.). (2006). *Handbook of narrative inquiry: Mapping a methodology.* Thousand Oaks, CA: Sage.

Clandinin, D. J., & Connelly, F. M. (2000). *Narrative inquiry: Experience and story in qualitative research.* San Francisco: Jossey-Bass.

Clarke, A. E. (2005). *Situational analysis: Grounded theory after the postmodern turn.* Thousand Oaks, CA: Sage.

Clifford, J., & Marcus, G. E. (Eds.). (1986). *Writing culture: The poetics and politics of ethnography.* Berkeley: University of California Press.

Colaizzi, P. F. (1978). Psychological research as the phenomenologist views it. In R. Vaile & M. King (Eds.), *Existential phenomenological alternatives for psychology* (pp. 48–71). New York: Oxford University Press.

Connelly, F. M., & Clandinin, D. J. (1990). Stories of experience and narrative inquiry. *Educational Researcher, 19*(5), 2–14.

Conrad, C. F. (1978). A grounded theory of academic change. *Sociology of Education, 51,* 101–112.

Corbin, J., & Morse, J. M. (2003). The unstructured interactive interview: Issues of reciprocity and risks when dealing with sensitive topics. *Qualitative Inquiry, 9*, 335–354.

Corbin, J., & Strauss, A. (1990). Grounded theory research: Procedures, canons, and evaluative criteria. *Qualitative Sociology, 13*(1), 3–21.

Corbin, J., & Strauss, A. (2007). *Basics of qualitative research: Techniques and procedures for developing grounded theory* (3rd ed.). Thousand Oaks, CA: Sage.

Cortazzi, M. (1993). *Narrative analysis.* London: Falmer Press.

Crabtree, B. F., & Miller, W. L. (1992). *Doing qualitative research.* Newbury Park, CA: Sage.

Creswell, J. W. (1994). *Research design: Qualitative and quantitative approaches.* Thousand Oaks, CA: Sage.

Creswell, J. W. (2009). *Research design: Qualitative, quantitative, and mixed methods approaches* (3rd ed.). Thousand Oaks, CA: Sage.

Creswell, J. W. (2012). *Educational research: Planning, conducting, and evaluating quantitative and qualitative research* (4th ed.). Upper Saddle River, NJ: Pearson Education.

Creswell, J. W., & Brown, M. L. (1992). How chairpersons enhance faculty research: A grounded theory study. *Review of Higher Education, 16*(1), 41–62.

Creswell, J. W., & Maietta, R. C. (2002). Qualitative research. In D. C. Miller & N. J. Salkind (Eds.), *Handbook of social research* (pp. 143–184). Thousand Oaks, CA: Sage.

Creswell, J. W., & Miller, D. L. (2000). Determining validity in qualitative inquiry. *Theory Into Practice, 39,* 124–130.

Creswell, J. W., & Plano Clark, V. L. (2011). *Designing and conducting mixed methods research* (2nd ed.). Thousand Oaks, CA: Sage.

Crotty, M. (1998). *The foundations of social research: Meaning and perspective in the research process.* London: Sage.

Czarniawska, B. (2004). *Narratives in social science research.* Thousand Oaks, CA: Sage.

Daiute, C., & Lightfoot, C. (Eds.). (2004). *Narrative analysis: Studying the development of individuals in society.* Thousand Oaks, CA: Sage.

Davidson, F. (1996). *Principles of statistical data handling.* Thousand Oaks, CA: Sage.

Deem, R. (2002). Talking to manager-academics: Methodological dilemmas and feminist research strategies. *Sociology, 36*(4), 835–855.

Denzin, N. K. (1989a). *Interpretive biography.* Newbury Park, CA: Sage.

Denzin, N. K. (1989b). *Interpretive interactionism.* Newbury Park, CA: Sage.

Denzin, N. K., & Lincoln, Y. S. (1994). *The Sage handbook of qualitative research.* Thousand Oaks, CA: Sage.

Denzin, N. K., & Lincoln, Y. S. (2000). *The Sage handbook of qualitative research* (2nd ed.). Thousand Oaks, CA: Sage.

Denzin, N. K., & Lincoln, Y. S. (2005). *The Sage handbook of qualitative research* (3rd ed.). Thousand Oaks, CA: Sage.

Denzin, N. K., & Lincoln, Y. S. (2011). Introduction: The discipline and practice of qualitative research. *The Sage handbook of qualitative research* (4th ed., pp. 1–19). Thousand Oaks, CA: Sage.

Dey, I. (1993). *Qualitative data analysis: A user-friendly guide for social scientists.* London: Routledge.

Dey, I. (1995). Reducing fragmentation in qualitative research. In U. Keele (Ed.), *Computer-aided qualitative data analysis* (pp. 69–79). Thousand Oaks, CA: Sage.

Daiute, C., & Lightfoot, C. (Eds.). (2004). *Narrative analysis: Studying the development of individuals in society.* Thousand Oaks, CA: Sage.

Dukes, S. (1984). Phenomenological methodology in the human sciences. *Journal of Religion and Health, 23*(3), 197–203.

Edel, L. (1984). *Writing lives: Principia biographica.* New York: Norton.

Edwards, L. V. (2006). Perceived social support and HIV/AIDS medication adherence among African American women. *Qualitative Health Research, 16,* 679–691.

Eisner, E. W. (1991). *The enlightened eye: Qualitative inquiry and the enhancement of educational practice.* New York: Macmillan.

Elliott, J. (2005). *Using narrative in social research: Qualitative and quantitative approaches.* London: Sage.

Ellis, C. (1993). "There are survivors": Telling a story of sudden death. *The Sociological Quarterly, 34,* 711–738.

Ellis, C. (2004). *The ethnographic it: A methodological novel about autoethnography.* Walnut Creek, CA: AltaMira.

Ely, M. (2007). In-forming re-presentations. In D. J. Clandinin (Ed.), *Handbook of narrative inquiry: Mapping a methodology.* Thousand Oaks, CA: Sage.

Ely, M., Anzul, M., Friedman, T., Garner, D., & Steinmetz, A. C. (1991). *Doing qualitative research: Circles within circles.* New York: Falmer Press.

Emerson, R. M., Fretz, R. I., & Shaw, L. L. (1995). *Writing ethnographic fieldnotes.* Chicago: University of Chicago Press.

Erlandson, D. A., Harris, E. L., Skipper, B. L., & Allen, S. D. (1993). *Doing naturalistic inquiry: A guide to methods.* Newbury Park, CA: Sage.

Ezeh, P. J. (2003). Integration and its challenges in participant observation. *Qualitative Research, 3,* 191–205.

Fay, B. (1987). *Critical social science.* Ithaca, NY: Cornell University Press.

Ferguson, M., & Wicke, J. (1994). *Feminism and postmodernism.* Durham, NC: Duke University Press.

Fetterman, D. M. (2010). *Ethnography: Step by step* (3rd ed.). Thousand Oaks, CA: Sage.

Finders, M. J. (1996). Queens and teen zines: Early adolescent females reading their way toward adulthood. *Anthropology & Education Quarterly, 27,* 71–89.

Fischer, C. T., & Wertz, F. J. (1979). An empirical phenomenology study of being criminally victimized. In A. Giorgi, R. Knowles, & D. Smith (Eds.), *Duquesne studies in phenomenological psychology* (Vol. 3, pp. 135–158). Pittsburgh, PA: Duquesne University Press.

Flinders, D. J., & Mills, G. E. (1993). *Theory and concepts in qualitative research.* New York: Teachers College Press.

Foucault, M. (1972). *The archeology of knowledge and the discourse on language* (A. M. Sheridan Smith, Trans.). New York: Harper.

Fox-Keller, E. (1985). *Reflections on gender and science.* New Haven, CT: Yale University Press.

Friese, S. (2012). *Qualitative data analysis with ATLAS.ti.* Thousand Oaks, CA: Sage.

Gamson, J. (2000). Sexualities, queer theory and qualitative research. In N. K. Denzin & Y. S. Lincoln (Eds.), *Handbook of qualitative research* (2nd ed., pp. 347–365). London: Sage.

Garcia, A. C., Standlee, A. I., Bechkoff, J., & Cui, Y. (2009). Ethnographic approaches to the Internet and computer-mediated communication. *Journal of Contemporary Ethnography, 38*(1), 52–84.

Gee, J. P. (1991). A linguistic approach to narrative. *Journal of Narrative and Life History/Narrative Inquiry, 1,* 15–39.

Geertz, C. (1973). Deep play: Notes on the Balinese cockfight. In C. Geertz (Ed.), *The interpretation of cultures: Selected essays* (pp. 412–435). New York: Basic Books.

Geiger, S. N. G. (1986). Women's life histories: Method and content. *Signs: Journal of Women in Culture and Society, 11,* 334–351.

Gergen, K. (1994). *Realities and relationships: Soundings in social construction.* Cambridge, MA: Harvard University Press.

Gilchrist, V. J. (1992). Key informant interviews. In B. F. Crabtree & W. L. Miller (Eds.), *Doing qualitative research* (pp. 70–89). Newbury Park, CA: Sage.

Gilgun, J. F. (2005). "Grab" and good science: Writing up the results of qualitative research. *Qualitative Health Research, 15,* 256–262.

Giorgi, A. (Ed.). (1985). *Phenomenology and psychological research.* Pittsburgh, PA: Duquesne University Press.

Giorgi, A. (1994). A phenomenological perspective on certain qualitative research methods. *Journal of Phenomenological Psychology, 25,* 190–220.

Giorgi, A. (2009). *The descriptive phenomenological method in psychology: A modified Husserlian approach.* Pittsburgh, PA: Duquesne University Press.

Glaser, B. G. (1978). *Theoretical sensitivity.* Mill Valley, CA: Sociology Press.

Glaser, B. G. (1992). *Basics of grounded theory analysis.* Mill Valley, CA: Sociology Press.

Glaser, B., & Strauss, A. (1965). *Awareness of dying.* Chicago: Aldine.

Glaser, B., & Strauss, A. (1967). *The discovery of grounded theory.* Chicago: Aldine.

Glaser, B., & Strauss, A. (1968). *Time for dying.* Chicago: Aldine.

Glesne, C., & Peshkin, A. (1992). *Becoming qualitative researchers: An introduction.* White Plains, NY: Longman.

Goffman. E. (1989). On fieldwork. *Journal of Contemporary Ethnography, 18,* 123–132.

Grigsby, K. A., & Megel, M. E. (1995). Caring experiences of nurse educators. *Journal of Nursing Research, 34,* 411–418.

Gritz, J. I. (1995). *Voices from the classroom: Understanding teacher professionalism.* Unpublished manuscript, Administration, Curriculum, and Instruction, University of Nebraska–Lincoln.

Guba, E. G. (1990). The alternative paradigm dialog. In E. G. Guba (Ed.), *The paradigm dialog* (pp. 17–30). Newbury Park, CA: Sage.

Guba, E. G., & Lincoln, Y. S. (1988). Do inquiry paradigms imply inquiry methodologies? In D. M. Fetterman (Ed.), *Qualitative approaches to evaluation in education* (pp. 89–115). New York: Praeger.

Guba, E. G., & Lincoln, Y. S. (1989). *Fourth generation evaluation.* Newbury Park, CA: Sage.

Gubrium, J. F., & Holstein, J. A. (2003). *Postmodern interviewing.* Thousand Oaks, CA: Sage.

Haenfler, R. (2004). Rethinking subcultural resistance: Core values of the straight edge movement. *Journal of Contemporary Ethnography, 33,* 406–436.

Hamel, J., Dufour, S., & Fortin, D. (1993). *Case study methods.* Newbury Park, CA: Sage.

Hammersley, M., & Atkinson, P. (1995). *Ethnography: Principles in practice* (2nd ed.). New York: Routledge.

Harding, P. (2009). *Tinkers.* New York: Bellevue Literary Press.

Harding, S. (1987). *Feminism and methodology.* Bloomington: Indiana University Press.

Harper, W. (1981). The experience of leisure. *Leisure Sciences, 4,* 113–126.

Harris, C. (1993). Whiteness as property. *Harvard Law Review, 106,* 1701–1791.

Harris, M. (1968). *The rise of anthropological theory: A history of theories of culture.* New York: T. Y. Crowell.

Harley, A. E., Buckworth, J., Katz, M. L., Willis, S. K., Odoms-Young, A., & Heaney, C. A. (2009). Developing long-term physical activity participation: A grounded theory study with African American women. *Health Education & Behavior, 36*(1), 97–112.

Hatch, J. A. (2002). *Doing qualitative research in education settings.* Albany: State University of New York Press.

Heilbrun, C. G. (1988). *Writing a woman's life.* New York: Ballantine.

Heron, J., & Reason, P. (1997). A participatory inquiry paradigm. *Qualitative Inquiry, 3,* 274–294.

Hill, B., Vaughn, C., & Harrison, S. B. (1995, September/October). Living and working in two worlds: Case studies of five American Indian women teachers. *The Clearinghouse, 69*(1), 42–48.

Howe, K., & Eisenhardt, M. (1990). Standards for qualitative (and quantitative) research: A prolegomenon. *Educational Researcher, 19*(4), 2–9.

Huber, J., & Whelan, K. (1999). A marginal story as a place of possibility: Negotiating self on the professional knowledge landscape. *Teaching and Teacher Education, 15,* 381–396.

Huberman, A. M., & Miles, M. B. (1994). Data management and analysis methods. In N. K. Denzin & Y. S. Lincoln (Eds.), *Handbook of qualitative research* (pp. 420–444). Thousand Oaks, CA: Sage.

Huff, A. S. (2009). *Designing research for publication.* Los Angeles, CA: Sage.

Husserl, E. (1931). *Ideas: General introduction to pure phenomenology* (D. Carr, Trans.). Evanston, IL: Northwestern University Press.

Husserl, E. (1970). *The crisis of European sciences and transcendental phenomenology* (D. Carr, Trans.). Evanston, IL: Northwestern University Press.

Jacob, E. (1987). Qualitative research traditions: A review. *Review of Educational Research, 57,* 1–50.

James, N., & Busher, H. (2007). Ethical issues in online educational research: protecting privacy, establishing authenticity in email interviewing. *International Journal of Research & Method in Education, 30*(1), 101–113.

Jorgensen, D. L. (1989). *Participant observation: A methodology for human studies.* Newbury Park, CA: Sage.

Josselson, R., & Lieblich, A. (Eds.). (1993). *The narrative study of lives* (Vol. 1). Newbury Park, CA: Sage.

Karen, C. S. (1990, April). *Personal development and the pursuit of higher education: An exploration of interrelationships in the growth of self-identity in returning women students—summary of research in progress.* Paper presented at the annual meeting of the American Educational Research Association, Boston.

Kearney, M. H., Murphy, S., & Rosenbaum, M. (1994). Mothering on crack cocaine: A grounded theory analysis. *Social Science Medicine, 38*(2), 351–361.

Kelle, E. (Ed.). (1995). *Computer-aided qualitative data analysis.* Thousand Oaks, CA: Sage.

Kemmis, S., & Wilkinson, M. (1998). Participatory action research and the study of practice. In B. Atweh, S. Kemmis, & P. Weeks (Eds.), *Action research in practice: Partnerships for social justice in education* (pp. 21–36). New York: Routledge.

Kerlinger, F. N. (1979). *Behavioral research: A conceptual approach.* New York: Holt, Rinehart & Winston.

Kidder, L. (1982). Face validity from multiple perspectives. In D. Brinberg & L. Kidder (Eds.), *New directions for methodology of social and behavioral science: Forms of validity in research* (pp. 41–57). San Francisco: Jossey-Bass.

Kincheloe, J. L. (1991). *Teachers as researchers: Qualitative inquiry as a path of empowerment.* London: Falmer Press.

Komives, S. R., Owen, J. E., Longerbeam, S. D., Mainella, F. C., & Osteen, L. (2005). Developing a leadership identity: A grounded theory. *Journal of College Student Development, 46*(6), 593–611.

Koro-Ljungberg, M., & Greckhamer, T. (2005). Strategic turns labeled "ethnography": From description to openly ideological production of cultures. *Qualitative Research, 5*(3), 285–306.

Krueger, R. A., & Casey, M. A. (2009). *Focus groups: A practical guide for applied research* (4th ed.). Thousand Oaks, CA: Sage.

Kus, R. J. (1986). From grounded theory to clinical practice: Cases from gay studies research. In W. C. Chenitz & J. M. Swanson (Eds.), *From practice to grounded theory* (pp. 227–240). Menlo Park, CA: Addison-Wesley.

Kvale, S. (2006). Dominance through interviews and dialogues. *Qualitative Inquiry, 12,* 480–500.

Kvale, S., & Brinkmann, S. (2009). *InterViews: Learning the craft of qualitative research interviewing.* Los Angeles, CA: Sage.

Labaree, R. V. (2002). The risk of "going observationalist": Negotiating the hidden dilemmas of being an insider participant observer. *Qualitative Research, 2,* 97–122.

Ladson-Billings, G., & Donnor, J. (2005). The moral activist role in critical race theory scholarship. In N. K. Denzin & Y. S. Lincoln (Eds.), *The Sage handbook of qualitative research* (3rd ed., pp. 279–201). Thousand Oaks, CA: Sage.

LaFrance, J., & Crazy Bull, C. (2009). Researching ourselves back to life: Taking control of the research agenda in Indian Country. In D. M. Mertens & P. E. Ginsburg (Eds.), *The handbook of social research ethics* (pp. 135–149). Los Angeles, CA: Sage.

Lancy, D. F. (1993). *Qualitative research in education: An introduction to the major traditions.* New York: Longman.

Landis, M. M. (1993). *A theory of interaction in the satellite learning classroom.* Unpublished doctoral dissertation, University of Nebraska–Lincoln.

Lather, P. (1991). *Getting smart: Feminist research and pedagogy with/in the postmodern.* New York: Routledge.

Lather, P. (1993). Fertile obsession: Validity after poststructuralism. *Sociological Quarterly, 34,* 673–693.

Lauterbach, S. S. (1993). In another world: A phenomenological perspective and discovery of meaning in mothers' experience with death of a wished-for baby: Doing phenomenology. In P. L. Munhall & C. O. Boyd (Eds.), *Nursing research: A qualitative perspective* (pp. 133–179). New York: National League for Nursing Press.

LeCompte, M. D., & Goetz, J. P. (1982). Problems of reliability and validity in ethnographic research. *Review of Educational Research, 51,* 31–60.

LeCompte, M. D., Millroy, W. L., & Preissle, J. (1992). *The handbook of qualitative research in education.* San Diego, CA: Academic Press.

LeCompte, M. D., & Schensul, J. J. (1999). *Designing and conducting ethnographic research* (Ethnographer's toolkit, Vol. 1). Walnut Creek, CA: AltaMira.

Leipert, B. D., & Reutter, L. (2005). Developing resilience: How women maintain their health in northern geographically isolated settings. *Qualitative Health Research, 15,* 49–65.

Lemay, C. A., Cashman, S. B., Elfenbein, D. S., & Felice, M. E. (2010). A qualitative study of the meaning of fatherhood among young Urban fathers. *Public Health Nursing, 27*(3), 221–231.

LeVasseur, J. J. (2003). The problem of bracketing in phenomenology. *Qualitative Health Research, 13*(3), 408–420.

Lieblich, A., Tuval-Mashiach, R., & Zilber, T. (1998). *Narrative research: Reading, analysis, and interpretation.* Thousand Oaks, CA: Sage.

Lightfoot Lawrence, S., & Davis, J. H. (1997). *The art and science of portraiture.* San Francisco: Jossey-Bass.

Lincoln, Y. S. (1995). Emerging criteria for quality in qualitative and interpretive research. *Qualitative Inquiry, 1,* 275–289.

Lincoln, Y. S. (2009). Ethical practices in qualitative research. In D. M. Mertens & P. E. Ginsberg (Ed.), *The handbook of social research ethics* (pp. 150–169). Los Angeles, CA: Sage.

Lincoln, Y. S., & Guba, E. G. (1985). *Naturalistic inquiry.* Beverly Hills, CA: Sage.

Lincoln, Y. S., & Guba, E. G. (2000). Paradigmatic controversies, contradictions, and emerging confluences. In N. K. Denzin & Y. S. Lincoln (Eds.), *Handbook of qualitative research* (2nd ed., pp. 163–188). Thousand Oaks, CA: Sage.

Lincoln, Y. S., Lynham, S. A., & Guba, E. G. (2011). Paradigmatic controversies, contradictions, and emerging confluences. In N. K. Denzin & Y. S. Lincoln (Eds.), *The Sage handbook of qualitative research* (4th ed., pp. 97–128). Thousand Oaks, CA: Sage.

Lipson, J. G. (1994). Ethical issues in ethnography. In J. M. Morse (Eds.), *Critical issues in qualitative research methods* (pp. 333–355). Thousand Oaks, CA: Sage.

Lofland, J. (1974). Styles of reporting qualitative field research. *American Sociologist, 9,* 101–111.

Lofland, J., & Lofland, L. H. (1995). *Analyzing social settings: A guide to qualitative observation and analysis* (3rd ed.). Belmont, CA: Wadsworth.

Lomask, M. (1986). *The biographer's craft.* New York: Harper & Row.

Lopez, K. A., & Willis, D. G. (2004). Descriptive versus interpretive phenomenology: Their contributions to nursing knowledge. *Qualitative Health Research, 14*(5), 726–735.

Luck, L., Jackson, D., & Usher, K. (2006). Case study: A bridge across the paradigms. *Nursing Inquiry, 13,* 103–109.

Madison, D. S. (2005). *Critical ethnography: Methods, ethics, and performance.* Thousand Oaks, CA: Sage.

Marshall, C., & Rossman, G. B. (2010). *Designing qualitative research* (5th ed.). Thousand Oaks, CA: Sage.

Martin, J. (1990). Deconstructing organizational taboos: The suppression of gender conflict in organizations. *Organization Science, 1,* 339–359.

Mastera, G. (1995). *The process of revising general education curricula in three private baccalaureate colleges.* Unpublished manuscript, Administration, Curriculum, and Instruction, University of Nebraska–Lincoln.

Maxwell, J. (2005). *Qualitative research design: An interactive approach* (2nd ed.). Thousand Oaks, CA: Sage.

Maxwell, J. A. (2012). *A realist approach for qualitative research*. Los Angeles, CA: Sage.

May, K. A. (1986). Writing and evaluating the grounded theory research report. In W. C. Chenitz & J. M. Swanson (Eds.), *From practice to grounded theory* (pp. 146–154). Menlo Park, CA: Addison-Wesley.

McCracken, G. (1988). *The long interview*. Newbury Park, CA: Sage.

McVea, K., Harter, L., McEntarffer, R., & Creswell, J. W. (1999). Phenomenological study of student experiences with tobacco use at City High School. *High School Journal, 82*(4), 209–222.

Merleau-Ponty, M. (1962). *Phenomenology of perception* (C. Smith, Trans.). London: Routledge & Kegan Paul.

Merriam, S. (1988). *Case study research in education: A qualitative approach*. San Francisco: Jossey-Bass.

Merriam, S. B. (1998). *Qualitative research and case study applications in education*. San Francisco: Jossey-Bass.

Mertens, D. M. (2003). Mixed methods and the politics of human research: The transformative-emancipatory perspective. In A. Tashakkori & C. Teddlie (Eds.), *Handbook of mixed methods in social & behavioral research* (pp. 135–164). Thousand Oaks, CA: Sage.

Mertens, D. M. (2009). *Transformative research and evaluation*. New York: Guilford Press.

Mertens, D. M. (2010). *Research and evaluation in education and psychology: Integrating diversity with quantitative, qualitative, and mixed methods* (3rd ed.). Thousand Oaks, CA: Sage.

Mertens, D. M., & Ginsberg, P. E. (2009). *The handbook of social research ethics*. Los Angeles, CA: Sage.

Miles, M. B., & Huberman, A. M. (1994). *Qualitative data analysis: A sourcebook of new methods* (2nd ed.). Thousand Oaks, CA: Sage.

Miller, D. W., Creswell, J. W., & Olander, L. S. (1998). Writing and retelling multiple ethnographic tales of a soup kitchen for the homeless. *Qualitative Inquiry, 4*(4), 469–491.

Miller, W. L., & Crabtree, B. F. (1992). Primary care research: A multimethod typology and qualitative road map. In B. F. Crabtree & W. L. Miller (Eds.), *Doing qualitative research* (pp. 3–28). Newbury Park, CA: Sage.

Millhauser, S. (2008). *Dangerous laughter*. New York: Knopf.

Morgan, D. L. (1988). *Focus groups as qualitative research*. Newbury Park, CA: Sage.

Morrow, R. A., & Brown, D. D. (1994). *Critical theory and methodology*. Thousand Oaks, CA: Sage.

Morrow, S. L., & Smith, M. L. (1995). Constructions of survival and coping by women who have survived childhood sexual abuse. *Journal of Counseling Psychology, 42*, 24–33.

Morse, J. M. (1994). Designing funded qualitative research. In N. K. Denzin & Y. S. Lincoln (Eds.), *Handbook of qualitative research* (pp. 220–235). Thousand Oaks, CA: Sage.

Morse, J. M., & Field, P. A. (1995). *Qualitative research methods for health professionals* (2nd ed.). Thousand Oaks, CA: Sage.

Morse, J. M., & Richards, L. (2002). *README FIRST for a user's guide to qualitative methods.* Thousand Oaks, CA: Sage.

Moss, P. (2007). Emergent methods in feminist research. In S. N. Hesse-Biber (Ed.), *Handbook of feminist research methods* (pp. 371–389). Thousand Oaks, CA: Sage.

Moustakas, C. (1994). *Phenomenological research methods.* Thousand Oaks, CA: Sage.

Munhall, P. L., & Oiler, C. J. (Eds.). (1986). *Nursing research: A qualitative perspective.* Norwalk, CT: Appleton-Century-Crofts.

Muncey, T. (2010). *Creating autoethnographies.* Los Angeles, CA: Sage.

Murphy, J. P. (with Rorty, R.). (1990). *Pragmatism: From Peirce to Davidson.* Boulder, CO: Westview Press.

Natanson, M. (Ed.). (1973). *Phenomenology and the social sciences.* Evanston, IL: Northwestern University Press.

National Academy of Sciences. (2000). *Scientific research in education.* Washington, DC: National Research Council.

Nelson, L. W. (1990). Code-switching in the oral life narratives of African-American women: Challenges to linguistic hegemony. *Journal of Education, 172,* 142–155.

Neuman, W. L. (2000). *Social research methods: Qualitative and quantitative approaches* (4th ed.). Boston: Allyn & Bacon.

Neyman, V. L. (2011). *Give my heart a voice: Reflections on self and others through the looking glass of pedagogy: An auto-ethnography.* Doctoral dissertation, National-Louis University. Retrieved from http://vufind.carli.illinois .edu/vf-nlu/Search/Home?lookfor=Vera+Neyman&type=all&start_over=1 &submit=Find

Nicholas, D. B., Lach, L., King, G., Scott, M., Boydell, K., Sawatzky, B., Reisman, J., Schippel, E., & Young, N. L. (2010). Contrasting internet and face-to-face focus groups for children with chronic health conditions: Outcomes and participant experiences. *International Journal of Qualitative Methods, 9*(1), 105–121.

Nielsen, J. M. (Ed.). (1990). *Feminist research methods: Exemplary readings in the social sciences.* Boulder, CO: Westview Press.

Nieswiadomy, R. M. (1993). *Foundations of nursing research* (2nd ed.). Norwalk, CT: Appleton & Lange.

Nunkoosing, K. (2005). The problems with interviews. *Qualitative Health Research, 15,* 698–706.

Oiler, C. J. (1986). Phenomenology: The method. In P. L. Munhall & C. J. Oiler (Eds.), *Nursing research: A qualitative perspective* (pp. 69–82). Norwalk, CT: Appleton-Century-Crofts.

Olesen, V. (2011). Feminist qualitative research in the Millennium's first decade: Developments, challenges, prospects. In N. K. Denzin & Y. S. Lincoln (Eds.), *The Sage handbook of qualitative research* (4th ed., pp. 129–146). Thousand Oaks, CA: Sage.

Ollerenshaw, J. A., & Creswell, J. W. (2002). Narrative research: A comparison of two restorying data analysis approaches. *Qualitative Inquiry, 8,* 329–347.

Olson, L. N. (2004). The role of voice in the (re)construction of a battered woman's identity: An autoethnography of one woman's experiences of abuse. *Women's Studies in Communication, 27,* 1–33.

Padilla, R. (2003). Clara: A phenomenology of disability. *The American Journal of Occupational Therapy, 57*(4), 413–423.

Padula, M. A., & Miller, D. L. (1999). Understanding graduate women's reentry experiences: Case studies of four psychology doctoral students in a Midwestern university. *Psychology of Women Quarterly, 23,* 327–343.

Parker, L., & Lynn, M. (2002). What race got to do with it? Critical race theory's conflicts with and connections to qualitative research methodology and epistemology. *Qualitative Inquiry, 8*(1), 7–22.

Patton, M. Q. (1980). *Qualitative evaluation methods.* Beverly Hills, CA: Sage.

Patton, M. Q. (1990). *Qualitative evaluation and research methods.* Newbury Park, CA: Sage.

Personal Narratives Group. (1989). *Interpreting women's lives.* Bloomington: Indiana University Press.

Phillips, D. C., & Burbules, N. C. (2000). *Postpositivism and educational research.* Lanham, MD: Rowman & Littlefield.

Pink, S. (2001). *Doing visual ethnography.* London: Sage.

Pinnegar, S., & Daynes, J. G. (2007). Locating narrative inquiry historically: Thematics in the turn to narrative. In D. J. Clandinin (Ed.), *Handbook of narrative inquiry: Mapping a methodology* (pp. 3–34). Thousand Oaks, CA: Sage.

Plummer, K. (1983). *Documents of life: An introduction to the problems and literature of a humanistic method.* London: George Allen & Unwin.

Plummer, K. (2011a). Critical humanism and queer theory: Living with the tensions. In N. K. Denzin & Y. S. Lincoln (Eds.), *The Sage handbook of qualitative research* (4th ed., pp. 195–207). Thousand Oaks, CA: Sage.

Plummer, K. (2011b). Postscript 2011 to living with the contradictions: Moving on: Generations, cultures and methodological cosmopolitanism. In N. K. Denzin & Y. S. Lincoln (Eds.), *The Sage handbook of qualitative research* (4th ed., pp. 208–211). Thousand Oaks, CA: Sage.

Polkinghorne, D. E. (1989). Phenomenological research methods. In R. S. Valle & S. Halling (Eds.), *Existential-phenomenological perspectives in psychology* (pp. 41–60). New York: Plenum Press.

Polkinghorne, D. E. (1995). Narrative configuration in qualitative analysis. *Qualitative Studies in Education, 8,* 5–23.

Prior, L. (2003). *Using documents in social research.* London: Sage.

Ravitch, S. M., & Riggan, M. (2012). *Reason & rigor: How conceptual frameworks guide research.* Los Angeles, CA: Sage.

Reinharz, S. (1992). *Feminist methods in social research.* New York: Oxford University Press.

Rex, L. A. (2000). Judy constructs a genuine question: A case for interactional inclusion. *Teaching and Teacher Education, 16,* 315–333.

Rhoads, R. A. (1995). Whales tales, dog piles, and beer goggles: An ethnographic case study of fraternity life. *Anthropology and Education Quarterly, 26,* 306–323.

Richards, L., & Morse, J. M. (2007). *README FIRST for a users guide to qualitative methods* (2nd ed.). Thousand Oaks, CA: Sage.

Richardson, L. (1990). *Writing strategies: Reaching diverse audiences.* Newbury Park, CA: Sage.

Richardson, L. (1994). Writing: A method of inquiry. In N. K. Denzin & Y. S. Lincoln (Eds.), *Handbook of qualitative research* (pp. 516–529). Thousand Oaks, CA: Sage.

Richardson, L., & St. Pierre, E. A. (2005). Writing: A method of inquiry. In N. K. Denzin & Y. S. Lincoln (Eds.), *The Sage handbook of qualitative research* (3rd ed., pp. 959–978). Thousand Oaks, CA: Sage.

Riemen, D. J. (1986). The essential structure of a caring interaction: Doing phenomenology. In P. M. Munhall & C. J. Oiler (Eds.), *Nursing research: A qualitative perspective* (pp. 85–105). Norwalk, CT: Appleton-Century-Crofts.

Riessman, C. K. (1993). *Narrative analysis.* Newbury Park, CA: Sage.

Riessman, C. K. (2008). *Narrative methods for the human sciences.* Los Angeles, CA: Sage.

Rorty, R. (1983). *Consequences of pragmatism.* Minneapolis: University of Minnesota Press.

Rorty, R. (1990). Pragmatism as anti-representationalism. In J. P. Murphy (Ed.), *Pragmatism: From Peirce to Davidson* (pp. 1–6). Boulder, CO: Westview Press.

Rosenau, P. M. (1992). *Post-modernism and the social sciences: Insights, inroads, and intrusions.* Princeton, NJ: Princeton University Press.

Rossman, G. B., & Wilson, B. L. (1985). Numbers and words: Combining quantitative and qualitative methods in a single large-scale evaluation study. *Evaluation Review, 9*(5), 627–643.

Roulston, K., deMarrais, K., & Lewis, J. B. (2003). Learning to interview in the social sciences. *Qualitative Inquiry, 9,* 643–668.

Rubin, H. J., & Rubin, K. S. (2012). *Qualitative interviewing* (3rd ed.). Los Angeles, CA: Sage.

Saldaña, J. (2011). *Fundamentals of qualitative research.* Oxford: Oxford University Press.

Sampson, H. (2004). Navigating the waves: The usefulness of a pilot in qualitative research. *Qualitative Research, 4,* 383–402.

Sanjek, R. (1990). *Fieldnotes: The makings of anthropology.* Ithaca, NY: Cornell University Press.

Schwandt, T. A. (2007). *The Sage dictionary of qualitative inquiry* (3rd ed.). Thousand Oaks, CA: Sage.

Silverman, D. (2005). *Doing qualitative research: A practical handbook* (2nd ed.). London: Sage.

Slife, B. D., & Williams, R. N. (1995). *What's behind the research? Discovering hidden assumptions in the behavioral sciences.* Thousand Oaks, CA: Sage.

Smith, L. M. (1987). The voyage of the Beagle: Field work lessons from Charles Darwin. *Educational Administration Quarterly, 23*(3), 5–30.

Smith, L. M. (1994). Biographical method. In N. K. Denzin & Y. S. Lincoln (Eds.), *Handbook of qualitative research* (pp. 286–305). Thousand Oaks, CA: Sage.

Solorzano, D. G., & Yosso, T. J. (2002). Critical race methodology: Counterstorytelling as an analytical framework for education research. *Qualitative Inquiry, 8*(1), 23–44.

Sparkes, A. C. (1992). The paradigms debate: An extended review and celebration of differences. In A. C. Sparkes (Ed.), *Research in physical education and sport: Exploring alternative visions* (pp. 9–60). London: Falmer Press.

Spiegelberg, H. (1982). *The phenomenological movement* (3rd ed.). The Hague, Netherlands: Martinus Nijhoff.

Spindler, G., & Spindler, L. (1987). Teaching and learning how to do the ethnography of education. In G. Spindler & L. Spindler (Eds.), *Interpretive ethnography of education: At home and abroad* (pp. 17–33). Hillsdale, NJ: Lawrence Erlbaum.

Spradley, J. P. (1979). *The ethnographic interview.* New York: Holt, Rinehart & Winston.

Spradley, J. P. (1980). *Participant observation.* New York: Holt, Rinehart & Winston.

Staples, A., Pugach, M. C., & Himes, D. J. (2005). Rethinking the technology integration challenge: Cases from three urban elementary schools. *Journal of Research on Technology in Education, 37*(3), 285–311.

Stake, R. (1995). *The art of case study research.* Thousand Oaks, CA: Sage.

Stake, R. E. (2005). Qualitative case studies. In N. K. Denzin & Y. S. Lincoln (Eds.), *The Sage handbook of qualitative research* (3rd ed., pp. 443–466). Thousand Oaks, CA: Sage.

Stake, R. E. (2006). *Multiple case study analysis.* New York: Guilford Press.

Stake, R. E. (2010). *Qualitative research: Studying how things work.* New York: Guilford Press.

Stewart, A. J. (1994). Toward a feminist strategy for studying women's lives. In C. E. Franz & A. J. Stewart (Eds.), *Women creating lives: Identities, resilience and resistance* (pp. 11–35). Boulder, CO: Westview Press.

Stewart, D., & Mickunas, A. (1990). *Exploring phenomenology: A guide to the field and its literature* (2nd ed.). Athens: Ohio University Press.

Stewart, D. W., & Shamdasani, P. N. (1990). *Focus groups: Theory and practice.* Newbury Park, CA: Sage.

Stewart, K., & Williams, M. (2005). Researching online populations: The use of online focus groups for social research. *Qualitative Research, 5,* 395–416.

Strauss, A. (1987). *Qualitative analysis for social scientists.* New York: Cambridge University Press.

Strauss, A., & Corbin, J. (1990). *Basics of qualitative research: Grounded theory procedures and techniques.* Newbury Park, CA: Sage.

Strauss, A., & Corbin, J. (1998). *Basics of qualitative research: Techniques and procedures for developing grounded theory* (2nd ed.). Thousand Oaks, CA: Sage.

Stringer, E. T. (1993). Socially responsive educational research: Linking theory and practice. In D. J. Flinders & G. E. Mills (Eds.), *Theory and concept in qualitative research: Perspectives from the field* (pp. 141–162). New York: Teachers College Press.

Sudnow, D. (1978). *Ways of the hand.* New York: Knopf.

Suoninen, E., & Jokinen, A. (2005). Persuasion in social work interviewing. *Qualitative Social Work, 4,* 469–487.

Swingewood, A. (1991). *A short history of sociological thought.* New York: St. Martin's Press.

Tashakkori, A., & Teddlie, C. (Eds.). (2003). *Handbook of mixed methods in the social and behavioral sciences.* Thousand Oaks, CA: Sage.

Taylor, S. J., & Bogdan, R. (1998). *Introduction to qualitative research methods: A guidebook and resource* (3rd ed.). New York: John Wiley.

Tesch, R. (1988). *The contribution of a qualitative method: Phenomenological research.* Unpublished manuscript, Qualitative Research Management, Santa Barbara, CA.

Tesch, R. (1990). *Qualitative research: Analysis types and software tools.* Bristol, PA: Falmer Press.

Therberge, N. (1997). "It's part of the game": Physicality and the production of gender in women's hockey. *Gender & Society, 11*(1), 69–87.

Thomas, J. (1993). *Doing critical ethnography.* Newbury Park, CA: Sage.

Thomas, W. I., & Znaniecki, F. (1958). *The Polish peasant in Europe and America.* New York: Dover. (Originally published 1918–1920)

Tierney, W. G. (1995). (Re)presentation and voice. *Qualitative Inquiry, 1,* 379–390.

Tierney, W. G. (1997). *Academic outlaws: Queer theory and cultural studies in the academy.* London: Sage.

Trujillo, N. (1992). Interpreting (the work and the talk of) baseball. *Western Journal of Communication, 56,* 350–371.

Turner, W. (2000). *A genealogy of queer theory.* Philadelphia: Temple University Press.

Van Kaam, A. (1966). *Existential foundations of psychology.* Pittsburgh, PA: Duquesne University Press.

Van Maanen, J. (1988). *Tales of the field: On writing ethnography*. Chicago: University of Chicago Press.

van Manen, M. (1990). *Researching lived experience*. New York: State University of New York Press.

van Manen, M. (2006). Writing qualitatively, or the demands of writing. *Qualitative Health Research, 16,* 713–722.

Wallace, A. F. C. (1970). *Culture and personality* (2nd ed.). New York: Random House.

Wang, C., & Burris, M. A. (1994). Empowerment through photo novella: Portraits of participation. *Health Education & Behavior, 21*(2), 171–186.

Watson, K. (2005). Queer theory. *Group Analysis, 38*(1), 67–81.

Weis, L., & Fine, M. (2000). *Speed bumps: A student-friendly guide to qualitative research*. New York: Teachers College Press.

Weitzman, E. A., & Miles, M. B. (1995). *Computer programs for qualitative data analysis*. Thousand Oaks, CA: Sage.

Wheeldon, J., & Ahlberg, M. K. (2011). *Visualizing social science research: Maps, methods, & meaning*. Los Angeles, CA: Sage.

Whittemore, R., Chase, S. K., & Mandle, C. L. (2001). Validity in qualitative research. *Qualitative Health Research, 11,* 522–537.

Willis, P. (1977). *Learning to labour: How working class kids get working class jobs*. Westmead, UK: Saxon House.

Winthrop, R. H. (1991). *Dictionary of concepts in cultural anthropology*. Westport, CT: Greenwood Press.

Wolcott, H. F. (1983). Adequate schools and inadequate education: The life history of a sneaky kid. *Anthropology and Education Quarterly, 14*(1), 2–32.

Wolcott, H. F. (1987). On ethnographic intent. In G. Spindler & L. Spindler (Eds.), *Interpretive ethnography of education: At home and abroad* (pp. 37–57). Hillsdale, NJ: Lawrence Erlbaum.

Wolcott, H. F. (1990a). On seeking—and rejecting—validity in qualitative research. In E. W. Eisner & A. Peshkin (Eds.), *Qualitative inquiry in education: The continuing debate* (pp. 121–152). New York: Teachers College Press.

Wolcott, H. F. (1990b). *Writing up qualitative research*. Newbury Park, CA: Sage.

Wolcott, H. F. (1992). Posturing in qualitative research. In M. D. LeCompte, W. L. Millroy, & J. Preissle (Eds.), *The handbook of qualitative research in education* (pp. 3–52). San Diego, CA: Academic Press.

Wolcott, H. F. (1994a). The elementary school principal: Notes from a field study. In H. F. Wolcott (Ed.), *Transforming qualitative data: Description, analysis, and interpretation* (pp. 115–148). Thousand Oaks, CA: Sage.

Wolcott, H. F. (1994b). *Transforming qualitative data: Description, analysis, and interpretation*. Thousand Oaks, CA: Sage.

Wolcott, H. F. (2008a). *Ethnography: A way of seeing* (2nd ed.). Walnut Creek, CA: AltaMira.

Wolcott, H. F. (2008b). *Writing up qualitative research* (3rd ed.). Thousand Oaks, CA: Sage.

Wolcott, H. F. (2010). *Ethnography lessons: A primer.* Walnut Creek, CA: Left Coast Press.

Yin, R. K. (2009). *Case study research: Design and method* (4th ed.). Thousand Oaks, CA: Sage.

Yussen, S. R., & Ozcan, N. M. (1997). The development of knowledge about narratives. *Issues in Educational Psychology: Contributions From Educational Psychology, 2,* 1–68.

Ziller, R. C. (1990). *Photographing the self: Methods for observing personal orientation.* Newbury Park, CA: Sage.

Author Index

Aanstoos, C. M., 136
Ada, A. F., 305
Adams-Campbell, L. L., 349
Addy, C., 349
Adler, P., 377
Adler, P. A., 377
Agar, M. H., 90, 150, 183, 377
Agger, B., 7, 31, 214
Ainsworth, B., 349
Ainsworth, B. E., 349
Allen, S. D., 251, 252
Anderson, E. H., 111, 114–115, 122,
        133, 139, 194, 216, 219, 228–229
Angen, M. J., 248, 250, 255
Angrosino, M. V., 137, 155, 163,
        166–167, 282, 290
Anzul, M., 6, 246, 251–252
Apple, M., 93–94
Appleby, R. S., 379
Armstrong, D., 253
Asmussen, K. J., 3, 14, 52, 112, 119,
        123, 140, 142, 156, 163, 168,
        184–185, 188, 199–200, 217–219,
        238–239, 252, 270–271, 295
Atkinson, P., 91, 95, 156, 162, 167,
        174, 176, 188, 216, 233–234,
        292–293, 298
Ayers, W., 322

Banks, J. A., 305
Banks-Wallace, J., 349
Barbour, R. S., 24, 51
Barbules, N. C., 24
Barritt, L., 133
Bartlett, J. G., 328
Bazeley, P., 204
Bechkoff, J., 159, 161
Becker, H. S., 378
Belisle, M., 365

Benford, R. D., 389
Berger, B. M., 385
Beverly, J., 73
Biddle, S., 364
Biernacki, P., 377
Biklen, S. K., 91, 154, 167
Bismilla, V., 305
Bjorgo, T., 374
Blackman, S. J., 372
Blair, S. N., 348
Blazak, R., 371
Bloland, H. G., 27, 299
Bock, B. C., 364–365
Bode, P., 305
Bogdan, R., 5, 24, 300
Bogdan, R. C., 91, 154, 167
Borgatta, E. F., 27, 77
Borgatta, M. L., 27, 77
Bouchard, C., 348
Boydell, K., 159, 161
Brake, M., 371, 373, 375
Brassington, G. S., 349
Brauhn, N. E. H., 330, 343
Breitbart, W., 329
Brinkmann, S., 163–164, 173
Bromet, E. J., 412
Brown, D., 348
Brown, D. D., 30–31, 297
Brown, M. L., 85, 87, 150,
        162, 197, 231, 289
Brownson, R., 348–349
Brownstein, J., 349
Buckworth, J., 3, 111, 116, 123,
        139, 197, 232, 287, 364
Buechler, S. M., 385, 393
Bullough, R. V., 306
Burris, M. A., 161
Busher, H., 159, 161
Butler, L. D., 330

Calhoun, C., 394
Cameron, L., 328–329, 343
Campbell, D. T., 377
Carger, C., 307
Carpenter, D. R., 329, 331
Carspecken, P. F., 93–94
Carter, K., 74
Carter-Nolan, P. L., 349
Casey, K., 72
Casey, M. A., 159, 164
Cashman, S. B., 137
Casper, M., 349
Castro, C., 349
Chan, E,, 111–113, 133, 139, 155,
    192, 219, 225, 305–307, 310
Chandler, P., 349
Charmaz, K., 25, 84–88, 90, 157,
    196–197, 230, 232, 261–262,
    287, 378
Chase, S., 70–73
Chase, S. K., 248, 250
Check, J., 5
Chen, X., 330
Chenitz, W. C., 231
Cherryholmes, C. H., 28
Chow, P., 305
Chun, M. B. J., 307
Clandinin, D. J., 27, 70–71, 73–75,
    161, 189, 217, 220, 223–225, 272,
    278, 282, 284, 304, 307–309, 320
Clarke, A. E., 27, 84
Clarke, G., 372
Clarke, J., 371
Clifford, J., 214
Cochrane, M., 310
Cochran-Smith, M., 305, 322
Coffey, A., 91
Cohen, S., 305, 371, 374
Colaizzi, P. F., 80, 115, 194, 228,
    279, 327, 331, 332
Conle, C., 306
Conn, V., 349
Connelly, F. M., 27, 71, 73–75, 161,
    189, 217, 220, 223–225, 272, 278,
    282, 284, 304, 307–310, 320
Connolly, F. M., 70
Conrad, C. F., 231, 287
Cook-Sather, A., 306

Corbin, J., 24, 51, 83–90, 117, 152,
    155, 172, 195–197, 201, 213,
    230, 250, 260–262, 274,
    286–290, 351–352
Cortazzi, M., 71, 74
Crabtree, B. F., 7, 185
Craig, L., 371, 374–375
Crazy Bull, C., 57
Creswell, J. W., 3, 5–6, 14, 20, 24, 52,
    57, 61–62, 73–75, 85, 87, 89, 100,
    112, 119, 123, 130–131, 133, 135,
    138, 140, 142, 150, 156–157,
    162–163, 168, 184–185, 188–189,
    194, 197, 199–200, 203, 209, 213,
    217–219, 231, 238–239, 250, 252,
    255, 270–271, 276, 283, 289,
    295–296, 298, 300
Croft, J., 349
Crotty, M., 19, 25
Cui, Y., 159, 161
Cummins, J., 305, 311
Czarniawska, B., 70, 73, 75, 161, 186,
    215, 218, 220, 224, 284

Daiute, C., 27, 70–71
Davidson, F., 175
Davis, F., 374, 385–386
Daynes, J. G., 70, 75–76, 157, 283
Deem, R., 30
Delamont, S., 91
deMarrais, K., 172
Demme, J., 335
Denzin, N. K., 3–5, 7, 16, 19–20,
    22–24, 27, 43–44, 51, 72–73, 93,
    97, 189, 214, 224, 235, 258, 273,
    279, 282–284, 296, 299
Dewey, J., 307
Dey, I., 182
DiClemente, C., 365
DiClemente, C. C., 349, 363
Diefenbach, M. A., 343
Dishman, R., 363
Dominguez, L. M., 330
Donner, J., 23
Douaihy, A., 328
Douglas, J. D., 377
Dufour, S., 97
Dukes, S., 80, 157, 273, 279

Echeverría, P. S., 329
Edel, L., 76, 258
Eisenhardt, M., 53, 255
Eisner, E. W., 246
Elfenbein, D. S., 137
Elliott, J., 71, 150, 176
Ellis, C., 73, 151, 282
Ely, M., 6, 220, 246, 251 252
Emerson, R. M., 171, 234–235
Erlandson, D. A., 251–252
Eyler, A., 348–349
Ezeh, P. J., 172

Farber, E. W., 330
Fay, B., 26, 30, 297
Felice, M. E., 137
Fetterman, D. M., 12, 91–93,
    95–96, 155, 162, 198–199,
    234–235, 251, 291–293
Feuerverger, G., 306
Field, N., 330
Field, P. A., 11
Fine, M., 43, 50, 56, 171–173, 215
Fischer, C. T., 217
Fleury, J., 349
Flinders, D. J., 301
Forsyth, L. H., 364–365
Fortin, D., 97
Fothergill-Bourbonnais, F., 330
Foucault, M., 84
Fox, K. J., 375–376
Fox-Keller, E., 29
Frankel, R. M., 333
Frederiksen, L. W., 365
Fretz, R. I., 171, 234–235
Friedenreich, C., 348
Friedman, T., 6, 246, 251–252
Friese, S., 201
Fryback, P. B., 330, 343

Gallant, J. E., 328
Gamson, J., 33
Garcia, A. C., 159, 161
Garner, D., 6, 246, 251–252
Gay, G., 305
Gee, J. P., 75, 192
Geer, B., 378
Geiger, S. N. G., 283

Gergen, K., 150
Giampapa, F., 305
Giddens, A., 391, 393
Gilchrist, V. J., 293
Gilgun, J. F., 215, 218
Gill, M., 330
Ginsberg, P. E., 57
Giorgi, A., 77, 79–80, 194, 217, 259, 285
Glaser, B., 84
Glaser, B. G, 84
Glaser, B. G., 197
Glesne, C., 102, 151,
    174, 214, 251–252
Goetz, J. P., 245
Goffman, E., 235
Gordon, J. R., 365
Gore, F. C., 330
Gosling, A., 253
Gottschalk, S., 372
Gramling, L. F., 330, 342
Grigsby, K. A., 228
Gritz, J. I., 141
Grossberg, L., 372
Guba, E. G., 18–20, 25, 35,
    120, 187, 237, 246, 249–252,
    256, 271, 296, 299, 352

Habermas, J., 385
Haenfler, R., 31, 112, 118,
    123, 139, 199, 219, 236
Hall, S., 371, 373, 392
Hamel, J., 97
Hammersley, M., 91, 95, 156, 162,
    167, 174, 176, 188, 216,
    233–234, 292–293, 298
Harding, P., 242
Harley, A. E., 3, 111, 116, 123,
    139, 197, 232, 287
Harper, W., 228
Harris, C., 31
Harris, E. L., 251–252
Harris, M., 90
Harter, L., 24, 194
Haskell, W. L., 348
Hatch, J. A., 50, 55–56
He, M. F., 305–306, 310, 322
Heaney, C. A., 3, 111, 116, 123,
    139, 197, 232, 287

Hebdige, D., 371, 373–375
Heilbrun, C. G., 284
Henderson, K., 349
Henry, S. B., 329
Henry, T., 375
Heron, J., 26
Heylin, C., 375
Himes, D. J., 138
Holzemer, W. L., 329
Hopkins, B. L., 329
Howe, K., 53, 255
Huber, J., 75, 157, 304, 309
Huber, M., 304, 309
Huberman, A. M., 155, 164, 180,
    182, 185, 187, 251–254, 296
Huff, A. S., 18
Hunter, J. D., 379

Idler, E. L., 328–329
Igoa, C., 305
Irwin, D., 379
Irwin, J., 374
Irwin, M., 349
Israelski, D., 330

Jackson, D., 29
Jackson, P., 320, 322
James, N., 159, 161
Jefferson, T., 371, 373
Jokinen, A., 172
Jonnalagadda, S. S., 329
Jorgensen, D. L., 162, 293
Josselson, R., 71

Kao, G., 307
Kaplan, J., 379
Katz, M. L., 3, 111, 116, 123,
    139, 197, 232, 287
Kearney, M. H., 333
Kelle, E., 202
Kemmis, S., 5, 26
Kerlinger, F. N., 301
Kidder, L., 247
Killingsworth, R., 349
Kim, U., 307
Kincheloe, J. L., 31
King, A. C., 348–349, 365
King, G., 159, 161

Komives, S. R., 137
Koopman, C., 330
Kouritzin, S. G., 305, 311
Krueger, R. A., 159, 164
Kus, R. J., 231
Kvale, S., 163–164, 173

Labarre, R. V., 172
Lach, L., 159, 161
Ladson-Billings, G., 23, 305–306
LaFrance, J., 57
Lahickey, B., 378
Lancy, D. F., 7
Landis, M. M., 262
Laschinger, S. J., 330
Lather, P., 29, 247
Lauterbach, S. S., 162
Laverie, D. A., 363
Leblanc, L., 372, 392, 394
LeCompte, M. D., 29, 51,
    91, 93, 95, 162, 245
Lee, S. J., 306–307
Lee, S. M., 349
Lemay, C. A., 137
Leoni, L., 305
LeVasseur, J. J., 83
Leventhal, E. A., 328–329, 343
Leventhal, H., 328–329, 343
Levesque, J. M., 365
Lewis, J. B., 172
Li, G., 307
Lieblich, A., 71
Liebman, R. C., 379
Lightfoot, C., 27, 70–71
Lincoln, Y. S., 3–5, 7, 16, 19–20, 22–25,
    27, 35, 43–44, 51, 53, 56–57, 97,
    120, 187, 237, 246, 249–252,
    256–257, 271, 296, 299, 352
Lipson, J. G., 174
Lofland, J., 170, 263, 378
Lofland, L., 378
Lofland, L. H., 170
Lomask, M., 225
Longerbeam, S. D., 137
Lööw, H., 379
Luck, L., 29
Lynham, S. A., 19, 35, 249
Lynn, M., 31–32, 297

Macera, C. A., 348
Madison, D. S., 30–31, 91, 93, 180, 291, 297
Maietta, R. C., 203, 209
Mainella, F. C., 137
Malarcher, A., 349
Mandle, C. L., 248, 250
Marcus, B. H., 364–365
Marcus, G. E., 214
Marlatt, G. A., 365
Marouf, F., 330
Marshall, C., 53, 63, 82, 131, 133, 138, 156
Marshall, S., 364
Marteau, T., 253
Martin, J., 186
Marty, M. E., 379
Mastera, G., 142
Matson-Koffman, D., 349
Maxwell, J., 64
Maxwell, J. A., 23
May, K. A., 229
McCain, N. L., 330, 342
McCaleb, S. P., 305
McCracken, G., 161
McDaniel, J. S., 330
McDevitt, J., 349
McDonald, M., 329
McEntarffer, R., 24, 194
McVea, K., 24, 194
Meadows, L. M., 333
Medina, K., 363, 365
Megel, M. E., 228
Melucci, A., 372, 391
Mensah, G., 349
Merleau-Ponty, M., 77, 331
Merriam, S., 251–252
Merriam, S. B., 97, 100, 236, 238
Mertens, D. M., 19, 26, 33–34, 56, 302
Mickunas, A., 77, 285
Miles, M. B., 155, 164, 180, 182, 185, 187, 201, 251–254, 296
Miller, A. M., 349
Miller, D. L., 75, 250
Miller, D. W., 6, 24, 276
Miller, T., 374
Miller, W. L., 7, 185
Millroy, W. L., 93, 95

Mills, G. E., 301
Moodley, K. A., 305
Moonen, D. J., 330
Moore, D., 374
Morgan, D. L., 164
Morrow, M. L., 162
Morrow, R. A., 30–31, 297
Morrow, S. L., 87, 231
Morse, J. M., 5, 11, 43, 50, 129, 139, 152, 172, 332–333
Moss, P., 30
Moustakas, C., 20, 24–25, 76–82, 115–116, 193–194, 225–226, 228, 259–260, 273, 279, 284–286
Muggleton, D., 372, 393
Muhr, T., 351
Muncey, T., 73, 151, 282
Murphey, M. S., 304, 309
Murphy, J. P., 28
Murray Orr, A., 304, 309

Natanson, M., 77
Nelson, L. W., 235
Neuman, W. L., 20
Neyman, V. L., 73
Nicholas, D. B., 159, 161
Nieswiadomy, R. M., 77
Nieto, S., 305
Norcross, J., 365
Nunkoosing, K., 173

Odoms-Young, A., 3, 111, 116, 123, 139, 197, 232, 287
O'Hara, C., 375
Oiler, C. J., 77
Olander, L. S., 6, 24, 276
Olesen, V., 29–30, 297
Ollerenshaw, J. A., 73–74, 189, 283
Orenstein, M., 348
Osteen, L., 137
Owen, J. E., 137
Ozcan, N. M., 189

Parker, L., 31–32, 297
Parkin, F., 379
Passik, S., 329
Pate, R. R., 348
Patton, M., 350

Patton, M. Q., 28, 182, 251
Pearce, M., 304, 309
Peshkin, A., 151, 174, 214, 251–252
Phillion, J., 305–306, 310, 322
Phillips, D. C., 24
Pink, S., 93
Pinnegar, S., 70, 75–76, 157, 283
Pinto, B. M., 364, 365
Pitcher, G., 410
Plano Clark, V. L., 5, 89
Plummer, K., 32–33, 73, 155,
    175, 258, 283
Poland, S., 410
Polkinghorne, D. E., 72, 75, 77, 80, 82,
    157, 162, 227, 259, 285
Pratt, M., 348
Preissle, J., 93, 95
Prochaska, J., 349, 363, 365
Pugach, M. C., 138

Quesenberry, C., 349

Ravitch, S. M., 131
Reason, P., 26
Reilly, C. A., 329
Reinert, B. R., 330, 343
Reisman, J., 159, 161
Richards, L., 5, 43, 50, 129
Richardson, L., 54, 214–215, 217–219,
    235–236, 249, 257, 297, 302
Riemen, D. J., 157, 194
Riemer, J., 377
Riessman, C. K., 71–75, 114, 189,
    192–193, 220, 223–225, 250, 284
Riggan, M., 131
Roark, E. W., 399, 412
Roark, M. L., 399, 412
Roberts, B., 371
Rochford, E. B., 389
Rodriguez, R., 305
Rolon-Dow, R., 306
Rorty, R., 28
Rose, T., 372
Rosenbloom, C. A., 329
Rosenfeld, B., 329
Roskies, E., 365
Ross, V., 305, 307, 310
Rossman, G. B., 28, 53, 63, 82, 131,
    133, 138, 156

Roulston, K., 172
Rubin, H. J., 163
Rubin, K. S., 163
Russell, J. M., 330

Saldaña, J., 5
Sallis, J., 348–349
Sampson, H., 165, 171
Sanjek, R., 171, 292
Sarroub, L. K., 306
Sawatzky, B., 159, 161
Saxon, E., 335
Schaper, P. E., 330
Schensul, J. J., 29, 51, 91, 95, 162
Schippel, E., 159, 161
Schubert, W., 322
Schwandt, T. A., 25
Schwartz, J. A., 330
Scott, J., 372, 393
Scott, M., 159, 161
Sersen, B., 388
Shamdasani, P. N., 164
Shaw, L. L., 171, 234–235
Sherill, J. M., 412
Shyu, Y. -L., 348
Silverman, D., 253
Singh, N., 328
Skipper, B. L., 251–252
Slife, B. D., 27, 299, 301
Smith, K. V., 330
Smith, L. M., 283
Smith, M. L., 87, 162, 231
Smith-Hefner, N., 306
Snow, D. A., 389
Solorzano, D. G., 32
Spencer, M. H., 111, 114, 115, 122,
    133, 139, 194, 216, 219, 228–229
Spiegel, D., 330
Spiegelberg, H., 77
Spindler, G., 262–263
Spindler, L., 262–263
Spradley, J. P., 138, 162–163, 187, 198,
    276, 278, 290–291, 293, 351
Stake, R., 52, 98–101, 123, 136, 150,
    199, 214, 217, 236, 243, 250, 252,
    264, 271, 279, 293–295
Stake, R. E., 97–98
Standlee, A. I., 159, 161
Staples, A., 138

Steinmetz, A. C., 6, 246, 251–252
Sternfeld, B., 349
Stewart, A., 377
Stewart, A. J., 29, 297
Stewart, D, 77, 285
Stewart, D. W., 164
Stewart, K., 159
Stokols, D., 349
Stolarcyzk, L., 349
St. Pierre, E. A., 214, 249, 257
Strauss, A., 24, 51, 83–90, 117, 155,
    195–197, 201, 213, 230, 250,
    260–262, 274, 286–290, 351–352
Streubert, H. J., 329, 331
Stringer, E. T., 27, 299
Sudnow, D., 235
Suoninen, E., 172
Swanson, J. M., 231
Swingewood, A., 77

Talen, E., 349
Tashakkori, A., 28
Taylor, S., 5, 300
Taylor, S. J., 24
Taylor, V., 372
Teddlie, C., 28
Tesch, R., 5, 7, 77, 80, 296
Thaler, H., 329
Thomas, J., 27, 31, 93, 243, 291–292
Thomas, W. I., 97
Tierney, W. G., 33, 217
Trujillo, N., 137
Turner, J. A., 330, 343
Turner, W., 32
Tuval-Mashiach, R., 71

Usher, K., 29

Valdes, G., 307
Van Kaam, A., 80
Van Maanen, J., 91, 93, 233, 236, 293
van Manen, M., 76–81, 83, 194–195,
    215, 227, 260, 284
Villegas, A. M., 305
Vogl, D., 329

Waldorf, D., 377
Wallace, A. F. C., 276

Wallace, L. S., 364
Wang, C., 161
Watson, K., 32–33, 300
Weinman, J., 253
Weis, L., 43, 50, 56, 171–173, 215
Weitzman, E. A., 201
Wertz, F. J., 217
Whelan, K., 75, 157
Whitt, M., 349
Whittemore, R., 248, 250
Whittier, N. E., 372
Widdicombe, S., 372, 391, 393
Wilbur, J., 349
Wilcox, S., 349
Wilkinson, M., 5, 26
Williams, J., 349
Williams, M., 159
Williams, R. N., 27, 299, 301
Willis, P., 31, 371
Willis, S. K., 3, 111, 116, 123,
    139, 197, 232, 287
Wilson, B. L., 28
Wilte, R., 374
Winthrop, R. H., 95
Wolcott, H. F., 7, 20, 47, 91–92,
    94–95, 140, 157, 162, 180, 182,
    184, 197–198, 233, 236, 247,
    276, 290–292
Wong-Fillmore, L., 305, 312
Wooden, W. S., 371
Wooffitt, R., 372, 391, 393
Worden, S. K., 389
Wuthnow, R., 379

Xu, S., 305–306, 310

Yin, R. K., 5, 24, 29, 97–101,
    162, 165, 199, 237–239,
    279, 294–295
Yosso, T. J., 32
Young, K., 371, 374–375
Young, N. L., 159, 161
Yussen, S. R., 189

Zilber, T., 71
Ziller, R. C., 161
Zine, J., 306
Znaniecki, F., 97

Subject Index

Access and rapport, 151–154
  institutional review boards, 152
  within the five approaches, 153–154
Aesthetic merit, of qualitative
  research, 257
Ai Mei Zhang, 111, 192
Analysis of themes, 101
Anderson, Elizabeth H., 114–116,
  327–346
Approaches to inquiry. *See* Qualitative
  approaches to inquiry
Artifacts, 95
Asmussen, Kelly J., 119–121, 399–416
Assertions, 101
Audiences, for writings, 217
Authenticity, 250
Autobiography, 54
Autoethnography, 73
Awareness of Dying (Glaser and
  Strauss), 84
Axial coding, 85–86
Axiological assumption, 20–22

Behaviors, 90
Biographical study, 72
Bounded system, 97
Bowie, David, 375
Bracketing, 83
Buckworth, Janet, 116–117, 347–369

"Campus Response to a Student
  Gunman" (Asmussen and
  Creswell), 119–121, 399–416
  discussion, 412–414
  epilogue, 414
  incident and response, 400–402
  research study, 402–403
  themes, 403–406
Case description, 97

Case study, 12, 97–102, 263–265
  analysis and representation,
    199–200
  challenges, 101–102
  defining features of, 98–99
  definition and
    background, 97–98
  discussion of, 119–121
  evaluation standards, 263–265
  example, 119–121, 399–416
  procedures for conducting,
    100–101
  template for coding,
    209 (figure)
  "turning the story," 271–272
  types of, 99–100
  writing structure, 236–239
Case themes, 97
Categories, 86, 184
Causal conditions, 86, 89
Central phenomenon, 89
Central question, 138–141
Chan, Elaine, 112–114, 303–326
Chronology, 192
Clusters of meaning, 82
Codes, 184
Coding, 184
Coding paradigm, 89
"Cognitive Representations
    of AIDS" (Anderson and
    Spencer), 114–116, 327–346
  discussion, 342–345
  literature review, 329–330
  method, 331
  procedure, 331–333
  results, 333–342
Collective case study, 99
Complete observer, 167
Complete participant, 166

Complex reasoning, in
    qualitative research, 45
Computer programs, sampling
    of, 203–204
    ATLAS.ti, 203
    HyperRESEARCH, 204
    MAXQDA, 203
    QSRNVivo, 204
Computer use, in qualitative data
    analysis, 201–210
    advantages and disadvantages, 201–202
    choosing among computer
        programs, 209–210
    research approaches and, 204–209
    sampling of computer
        programs, 203–204
Conditional matrix, 87
Consent form, 153 (figure), 166
Consequences, 86, 89
Constant comparative method, 86
Constructivist, 42
Constructivist grounded theory, 84, 86–88
Constructivist/interpretivist research
    format, 61 (example)
Context, 89
Context of the case, 101
Creswell, John W., 119–121, 399–416
Critical ethnography, 93
Critical race theory (CRT), 31–32
Critical theory, 30–31
Cross-case analysis, 101
Cultural interpretation, 92
Cultural portrait, 96
Culture-sharing group, 90, 92
    analysis of, 95
    description of, 96
    interpretation of, 197

Data, forms of, 157–168
    interviewing, 163–166
    observation, 166–170
Data analysis and representation,
    179–212
    analysis strategies, 180–182
    comparing research approaches,
        200–201
    computer use in, 201–210

within approaches to
    inquiry, 189–200
Data analysis spiral, 182–188
    data interpretation, 187
    data organization, 182–183
    describing, classifying, and
        interpreting data into codes
        and themes, 184–187
    reading and memoing, 183–184
    representing and visualizing the
        data, 187–188
Data collection, 145–178
    access and rapport, 151–154
    data collection circle, 146–175
    data forms, 157–168
    data storage, 175
    field issues, 171–175
    purposeful sampling, 154–157
    recording procedures, 168–171
    research approaches
        compared, 176–177
    site or individual, 147–151
    storage, 175
Deception, 167
Deductive logic, in qualitative
    research, 45
"Developing Long-Term Physical
    Activity Participation: A
    Grounded Theory Study with
    African American Women"
    (Harley, Buckworth, Katz, Willis,
    Odoms-Young, and Heaney),
    116–117, 347–369
    conclusion, 367
    data collection, 351–352
    discussion, 361–365
    method, 350–351
    practical implications, 366
    results, 352–361
    study limitations, 366
Dimensionalized properties, 195
Direct interpretation, 199
Disability interpretive lens, 34
Disability theories, 33–34
Discriminant sampling, 90
*Duquesne Studies in
    Phenomenological Psychology*, 80

Embedded analysis, 100
Embedded writing strategies, 220–239
Emergent design, in qualitative research, 47
Emic, 92, 96
Encoding writings, 217–219
Epiphany, 224
Epistemological assumption, 20–22
Epoche, 80, 83
Essence, 80, 82
Essential, invariant structure, 82
Ethical issues
   in data collection, 174–175
   in qualitative research, 58–59 (table)
   in the research process, 56–60
Ethnography, 12, 90–96, 197–199, 262–263
   analysis and representation, 197–199
   challenges, 96
   defining features of, 91–93
   definition and background, 90–91
   discussion of, 118–119
   evaluation standards, 262–263
   example, 118–119, 370–398
   procedures for conducting, 94–96
   template for coding, 208 (figure)
   "turning the story," 274–276
   types of, 93–94
   writing structure, 232–236
Etic, 96
Evaluation standards, 243–268
   comparison of five approaches, 265
   criteria, 255–265

Feminist, 42
Feminist research approaches, 29
Feminist theories, 29–30
Field issues, in data collection, 171–175
   documents and audiovisual materials, 174
   ethical issues, 174–175
   interviews, 172–173
   observations, 172
   organization, access to, 171–172

Fieldwork, 92, 95
Foreshadowing, 225
Function, 95

Gatekeeper, 94
Gay theory, 32
Generalizability, 101
Glaser, Barney, 83, 84
Goodchild, Les, 1
Grounded theory, 12, 83–90, 260–262
   analysis and representation, 195–197
   challenges, 89–90
   defining features of, 85
   definition and background, 83–84
   discussion of, 116–117
   evaluation standards, 260–262
   example, 116–117, 347–369
   procedures for conducting, 88–89
   template for coding, 208 (figure)
   "turning the story," 273–274
   types of, 86–88
   writing structure, 229–232

Haenfler, Ross, 118–119, 370–398
Harley, Amy E., 116–117, 347–369
Hanks, Tom, 335
Heaney, Catherine A., 116–117, 347–369
Hermeneutical phenomenology, 79
Historical contexts, 74
Holistic account, in qualitative research, 47
Holistic analysis, 100
Holistic perspective, 95
Homosexual theory, 32
Horizontalization, 82
Husserl, Edmund, 77

Imaginative variation, 82
Immersion, 90Impact, of qualitative research, 257
Inductive logic, in qualitative research, 45
Information, 97
Inquiry, approaches to. See Qualitative approaches to inquiry
Institutional review boards, 152
Instrumental case study, 99

Intentionality of consciousness, 77
Intercoder agreement, 253
Interpretation, 187
Interpretive frameworks, 15–41
  critical race theory (CRT), 31–32
  critical theory, 30–31
  disability theories, 33–34
  feminist theories, 29–30
  linked to philosophical
    assumptions, 35–38
  postmodern perspectives, 27
  postpositivism, 23–24
  pragmatism, 28–29
  queer theory, 32–33
  social constructivism, 24–25
  transformative frameworks, 25–27
Interpretivist, 42
Intervening conditions, 86, 89
Interviewing, 163–166
Interview procedures, 166
Interview protocol, 164, 165 (figure)
Interviews, 172–173
Intrinsic case, 98
Intrinsic case study, 99
In vivo codes, 185
Ironic validation, 247
Irwin, Darrell, 379

Katz, Mira L., 116–117, 347–369
Key informants, 94
King, Edith, 1

Language, 90
Layers of analysis, 188 (figure)
Lesbian theory, 32
Life course stages, 70
Life history, 73
Lived experiences, 76
"Living in the Space between
  Participant and Researcher as a
  Narrative Inquirer: Examining
  Ethnic Identity of Chinese
  Canadian Students as Conflicting
  Stories to Live By" (Chan),
  112–114, 303–326
  conclusion, 322
  discussion, 320–322

  method, 308–309
  results, 309–320
  theoretical framework, 307–308
Logic diagram, 89

Maximum variation
  sampling, 156
Maxwell's nine arguments
  for a qualitative proposal,
  64 (example)
Memoing, 89
Methodological assumption, 21–22
Methodological congruence, 50
Methodology, of qualitative
  research, 22
Multiple methods, in qualitative
  research, 45
Multisite study, 97

Narrative Inquiry, 71
Narrative research, 11, 70–76, 258–259
  analysis and representation,
    189–193
  challenges, 76
  defining features of, 71–73
  definition and background, 70–71
  discussion of, 112–114
  evaluation standards, 258–259
  example, 112–114, 303–326
  procedures for
    conducting, 73–76
  template for coding, 207 (figure)
  "turning the story," 272–273
  types of, 72–73
  writing structure, 220–225
Narrative structures, comparison of,
  239–240
Narrative Study of Lives, 71
Naturalistic generalizations, 200
Natural setting, in qualitative
  research, 45
Nonparticipant/observer as
  participant, 167

Observation, 166–170
Observational protocol, 169
Observations (field), 172

Odoms-Young, Angela,
    116–117, 347–369
Ontological assumption, 20–22
Open coding, 86
Oral history, 73
Overall writing strategies, 220–239

Paradigms, 18
Paralogic validation, 247
Participant(s), 94
    as observer, 166–167
    meaning, in qualitative research, 47
    observation, 90
Patterns, 199
Perspectives
    qualitative, 255–257
    reliability, 253–255
    validation, 244–249
Phenomenological data analysis, 82
Phenomenology, 12, 76–83, 259–260
    analysis and representation,
        193–195
    challenges, 82–83
    defining features of, 78–79
    definition and background, 76–77
    discussion of, 114–116
    evaluation standards, 259–260
    example of, 114–116, 327–346
    philosophical perspectives
        in, 77–78
    procedures for conducting, 80–82
    template for coding, 207 (figure)
    "turning the story," 273
    types of, 79–80
    writing structure, 225–229
Phenomenon, 78
Philosophical assumptions, 15–41
    axiological assumption, 20–22
    importance of, 19–22
    epistemological assumption, 20–22
    framework for
        understanding, 16–18
    linked to interpretive
        frameworks, 35–38
    methodological assumption, 21–22
    ontological assumption, 20–22
    writing into qualitative studies, 22

Philosophical beliefs, and interpretive
    frameworks, 36–37 (table)
Philosophical perspectives, in
    phenomenology, 77–78
Philosophy, 16
    importance of, in research, 18–19
    interpretive frameworks,
        linking to, 35–38
Photo elicitation, 161
Physical activity evolution model,
    352–354, 355 (figure)
    cessation loop, 359–360
    context and conditions, 360
    initiation phase, 354–356
    integration phase, 357–358
    modification loop, 358–359
    planning methods, 360–361
    transition phase, 356–357
Pilot testing, 165
Positivism, 23
Postmodernism, 27
Postmodernist, 42
Postmodern perspectives, 27
Postpositivism, 23–24
Pragmatism, 28–29
Progressive-regressive method, 224
Properties, 89
Propositions, 86
Psychological approach, 71
Purposeful sampling, 100, 154–157
Purpose statement, 134–138
    case study example, 138 (example)
    encoding, words to use in,
        136 (table)
    ethnographic example,
        137 (example)
    grounded theory example,
        137 (example)
    narrative example, 137 (example)
    phenomenological example,
        137 (example)

Qualitative approaches to inquiry,
    2, 69–110
    by authors and their disciplines/
        fields, 8–10 (table)
    central features of, 121–123

comparison of, 102–106
data analysis within, 179–212
differences among, 121–124
examples, 111–128, 303–416
selecting, 7–12, 123–124
See also Case study; Ethnography;
    Grounded theory; Narrative
    research; Phenomenology;
    Qualitative research;
    Qualitative studies
Qualitative constructivist/interpretivist
    format, 61 (example)
Qualitative inquiry, typology of
    sampling strategies in, 158 (table)
Qualitative perspectives, 255–257
Qualitative proposal, nine arguments
    for (Maxwell), 64 (example)
Qualitative research, 44
    characteristics of, 43–47
    components of, 270 (figure)
    data collection approaches in,
        158 (table)
    evaluation criteria in, 255–265
    interpretive standards of, 257
    plan or proposal structure, 61–64
    reliability in, 244–255
    social justice interpretive
        frameworks in, 34–35
    validation in, 244–255
    when to use, 47–48
    See also Qualitative approaches to
        inquiry; Qualitative studies
Qualitative studies, designing, 42–68
    characteristics of good, 53–55
    elements in all research
        phases, 55–56
    ethical issues in all research
        phases, 56–60
    preliminary considerations, 50–51
    process steps, 51–55
    researcher requirements, 49
Qualitative studies, introducing and
    focusing, 129–144
    purpose statement, 134–138
    research problem statement,
        130–134
    research questions, 138–142

Qualitative studies, writing, 213–242
    audiences for, 217
    encoding, 217–219
    narrative structures,
        comparison of, 239–240
    overall and embedded writing
        strategies, 220–239
    quotes in, 219
    reflexivity and representations
        in, 214–217
Qualitative transformative research
    format, 62 (example)
Qualitative validation, perspectives
    and terms used in,
    244–245 (table)
Queer theory, 32–33
Quotes, in writings, 219

Race, as social construct, 32
Reagan, Nancy, 379
Realist ethnography, 93
Reciprocity, 55, 95
Recording procedures, 168–171
Reed, Lou, 375
Reflexivity, 47, 214–217, 257
Regan-Smith, Martha G., 64
Reliability
    in qualitative research,
        244–255
    perspectives, 253–255
Research design, 49. *See also*
        Qualitative research;
        Qualitative studies
Researcher, as key instrument in
        qualitative research, 45
Research plan or proposal, general
        structure of, 61–64
Research problem, 130
    sample section, 132 (figure)
    statement, 130–134
Research process, 17–18
Research questions, 138–142
    central question, 138–140
    central question, example, 141
    subquestions, 140–141
    subquestions, examples, 141–142
Restorying, 74

"Rethinking Subcultural Resistance:
   Core Values of the Straight
   Edge Movement" (Haenfler),
   118–119, 370–398
   conclusion, 391–394
   method, 376–391
Retriggering, 408–409
Rhetorical structure, 223
Rhizomatic validation, 247
Richardson, Laurel, 214

Sample size, 157
Sampling strategies, in qualitative
   inquiry, 158 (table)
Saturate (fully develop) a model, 89
Selective coding, 85–86
Self-Regulation Model of Illness
   Representation, 328
Single individual, 74
Social constructivism, 24–25
Social justice interpretive
   frameworks, 23, 34–35
Social science theories, 23
Spencer, Margaret Hull, 114–116,
   327–346
Stories, 71
Strategies, 86
Strauss, Anselm, 83, 84
Structural description, 80, 82, 273
Structure, 82
Subquestions, 140–142
Substantive contribution, of
   qualitative research, 257
Substantive-level theory, 89
Systematic procedures grounded
   theory, 86–87

Testimonios, 73
Textural description, 80, 82, 273
Themes, 101, 186, 335 (table)
Theoretical/interpretivist lens
   research format, 63 (example)
Theoretical sampling, 86
Theory, generate or discover, 83
Time for Dying (Glaser and Strauss), 84
Transcendental phenomenology, 80
Transformative research format,
   62 (example)
Transformative frameworks, 25–27
Triangulation, 251

Trustworthiness, 63, 250
Turning points, 72
"Turning the story," 269–280
   case study, 271–272
   ethnography, 274–276
   grounded theory, 273–274
   narrative research, 272–273
   phenomenology, 273

Validation, 63, 243–268
   in qualitative research, 244–255
   perspectives on, 244–249
   strategies, 53, 250–253
   voluptuous, 247
Verification, 250
Verisimilitude, 54, 218
Violence study, major dimensions of,
   271–277
   case study, 271–272
   ethnography, 274–277
   grounded theory study, 273–274
   narrative study, 272–273
   phenomenology, 273
Voluptuous validation, 247

Willis, Sharla K., 116–117, 347–369
Within-case analysis, 101
Within-site study, 97
Wolcott, Harry, 1, 169
Writing Culture, 214
Writing strategies, 214–219
   audiences for, 217
   encoding, 217–219
   quotes in, 219
   reflexivity and representations in,
      214–217
Writing strategies, overall and
   embedded, 220–239,
   221–222 (table)
   case study writing structure, 236–239
   ethnographic writing
      structure, 232–236
   grounded theory writing
      structure, 229–232
   narrative writing
      structure, 220, 223–225
   phenomenological writing
      structure, 225–229

Zhang, Ai Mei, 111, 192

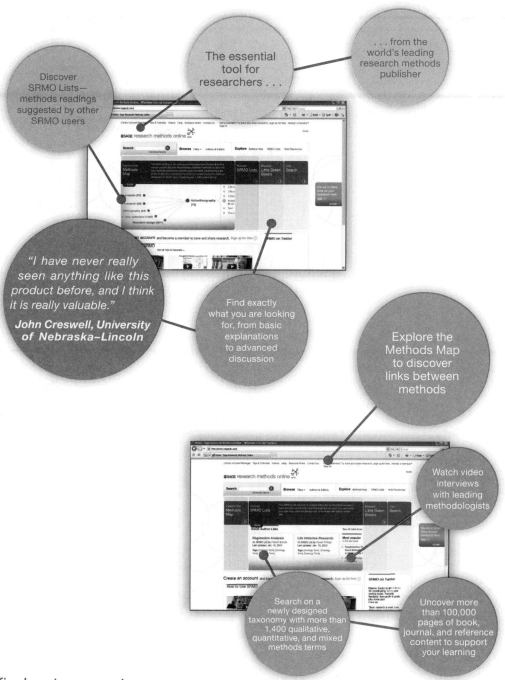

$SAGE research**methods**
The Essential Online Tool for Researchers

The essential tool for researchers . . .

. . . from the world's leading research methods publisher

Discover SRMO Lists— methods readings suggested by other SRMO users

"*I have never really seen anything like this product before, and I think it is really valuable.*"
John Creswell, University of Nebraska–Lincoln

Find exactly what you are looking for, from basic explanations to advanced discussion

Explore the Methods Map to discover links between methods

Watch video interviews with leading methodologists

Search on a newly designed taxonomy with more than 1,400 qualitative, quantitative, and mixed methods terms

Uncover more than 100,000 pages of book, journal, and reference content to support your learning

find out more at
srmo.sagepub.com